Blood Brothers

THE ANZAC GENESIS

Jeff Hopkins-Weise is a professional historian with a strong interest and background in Australian, New Zealand and Pacific history. Australian born, Jeff grew up in Brisbane, and studied at the University of Queensland where he has attained three degrees and specialised in history.

Jeff has a background in cultural heritage research and management while engaged in various capacities for the Queensland Parks and Wildlife Service and the Environmental Protection Agency, and most recently with curatorial and collection management roles with the Queensland Museum, and the Main Roads Heritage Centre in Toowoomba for the Queensland Department of Main Roads. In early 2008, he received a three year appointment as an Honorary Research Fellow for the Queensland Museum.

Jeff holds membership with various historical organisations and professional bodies, and is currently President of the Professional Historians Association (Queensland).

He has a teenage son Kurt, who is about to start his own university studies, and a loving archaeologist partner, Elspeth.

Blood Brothers

THE ANZAC GENESIS

JEFF HOPKINS-WEISE

Wakefield Press
1 The Parade West
Kent Town
South Australia 5067
www.wakefieldpress.com.au

First published in Australia 2009 by arrangement with Penguin Group (NZ)

All images from author's research collection
Maps by Outline Draughting and Graphics Ltd

Designed and typeset by Pindar NZ
Printed in Australia by McPherson's Printing Group

National Library of Australia Cataloguing-in-Publication entry

Author: Hopkins-Weise, Jeffrey Ellis.
Title: Blood brothers: the ANZAC genesis/Jeff Hopkins-Weise.
ISBN: 978 1 86254 838 1 (pbk.).

Notes:
Includes index.
Bibliography.

Subjects:
New Zealand Wars, 1843–1847.
New Zealand Wars, 1843–1847 — Participation, Australian.
New Zealand Wars, 1860–1872.
New Zealand Wars, 1860–1872 — Participation, Australian.
New Zealand — History — Maori Wars, 1845–1847 — Participation, Australian.
New Zealand — History — Taranaki War, 1860–1861 — Participation, Australian.
New Zealand — History — New Zealand Wars, 1860–1872 — Participation, Australian.

Dewey Number: 993.021

CONTENTS

ABBREVIATIONS

Repositories:

AOT: Archives Office of Tasmania
AONSW: Archives Office of New South Wales
AWM: Australian War Memorial
NANZ: National Archives of New Zealand
QSA: Queensland State Archives
SRSA: State Records of South Australia

Government publications and papers:

AJHRNZ: Appendix to the Journals of the House of Representatives of New Zealand
JHRNZ: Journals of the House of Representatives of New Zealand
NSWGG: New South Wales Government Gazette
NZAL 1863: The New Zealand Army List [1863]
NZAL 1864: The New Zealand Army List: 30 November 1864
NZAL 1872: The New Zealand Army List: Corrected to 29 February 1872
NZG: New Zealand Gazette
NZPD: New Zealand Parliamentary Debates
QGG: Queensland Government Gazette
VGG: Victoria Government Gazette

Journals, periodicals, and series:

ADB: Australian Dictionary of Biography
HRA: Historical Records of Australia
Sabretache: Sabretache: The Journal and Proceedings of the Military Historical Society of Australia
The Volunteers: The Volunteers: The Journal of the New Zealand Military Historical Society

Countries, colonies (or states/territories):

ACT: Australian Capital Territory
NSW: New South Wales
NZ: New Zealand

ACKNOWLEDGEMENTS

This book is based on the original research undertaken for my Master of Philosophy thesis ('Australian Involvement in the New Zealand Wars of the 1840s and 1860s') submitted to the School of History, Philosophy, Religion, and Classics at the University of Queensland in 2003. During my research I received valuable assistance from the staff of various Australian and New Zealand libraries and repositories and the University of Queensland. These include my supervisors Associate Professors Clive Moore and Raymond Evans; Queensland State Archives; the Fryer & Social Sciences & Humanities Libraries at the University of Queensland; Archives Office of New South Wales; Archives Office of Tasmania; Australian Archives (Canberra); Australian War Memorial; Catholic Church Archives (Brisbane); Mitchell Library; National Archives of New Zealand; National Library of Australia; National Museum of Australia; and State Records of South Australia.

Other individuals also gladly provided me access to their own research or family history for which I am greatly appreciative, such as Rod Pratt, Michael Murrie-Jones, R.D. Williams, Dorothea Cheshire, Ben Henri, Stan Hannaford, and the late George Livingston Baker. Along the way I was fortunate to have the valuable friendship and support of friends, fellow postgraduates, and family who made this journey that little bit easier. These include Peter Backen, Chris Whiting, Dr Bryan Jamison, Dr Dave Cameron and Bernie Logan, Rod Pratt, Michael and Kath Murrie-Jones, Phil and Amanda Lock (and the 'Lock Flock'), my Mum and Dad (Alice and Graham Hopkins), and my late Aunt, Marie Ellis, OAM. One other individual must be singled out for particular praise here — Dr Frank Glen. Many years back I wrote to Frank to discuss tentative steps in seeking information on Australians in the New Zealand wars after reading his *For Glory and a Farm*. This initial letter has led to a special ongoing friendship. Frank, this work is a testament to our friendship and the solid foundations established by your earlier efforts in this area of shared Australian and New Zealand history.

I must not forget to also mention my son Kurt, who witnessed the long and difficult path this research took through to thesis, many articles, and now this publication. I would also like to extend special thanks for the interest and faith that Jeff Atkinson at Penguin Books has had in my work, and his belief that it deserved a wider audience and recognition. Thanks too to the other hard working staff at Penguin Books such as Emma Beckett and editor Mike Wagg who all helped make this happen. And finally to my partner Elspeth Mackenzie, who not only always encourages me in my research and interests, but supported me financially and emotionally through my later efforts to resurrect my original thesis and rework it into this publication — my sincere thanks.

Introduction

A FRIEND INDEED – PRELUDE, 1834–1845

THIS IS A HISTORY of the New Zealand wars of the 1840s and 1860s. But the story does not concentrate merely on the day-to-day events in New Zealand itself. Instead, it explores the largely forgotten or ignored support which New Zealand derived from its sister colonies across the Tasman. For the first time, the depth and involvement of Australia – both in respect to colonial and imperial resources and implications – is explored and the contention made that it is in these wars that the true genesis of an Australian–New Zealand military tradition is to be found. The involvement and interaction of the Australian colonies in the wars that plagued New Zealand during the 1840s and 1860s shows just how strong the ties uniting Australia and New Zealand from the late eighteenth well into the nineteenth centuries actually were. At the same time, New Zealand's wars are drawn into the broader context of British Empire history, for this is a complex and detailed shared history in which the wars were a defining moment in reaffirming a bond of kinship between all the colonies of British Australasia.[1]

The advancing tide of European settlement, commerce and trade, with its inevitable frontier tensions, conflicts and wars over land, cultural clashes and misunderstandings is a common theme on either side of the Tasman. While the ways in which Aboriginal and Maori peoples reacted or resisted, plus the colonial or imperial responses, were somewhat different between the countries it is in the New Zealand wars during the 1840s, but especially in the 1860s, that the true

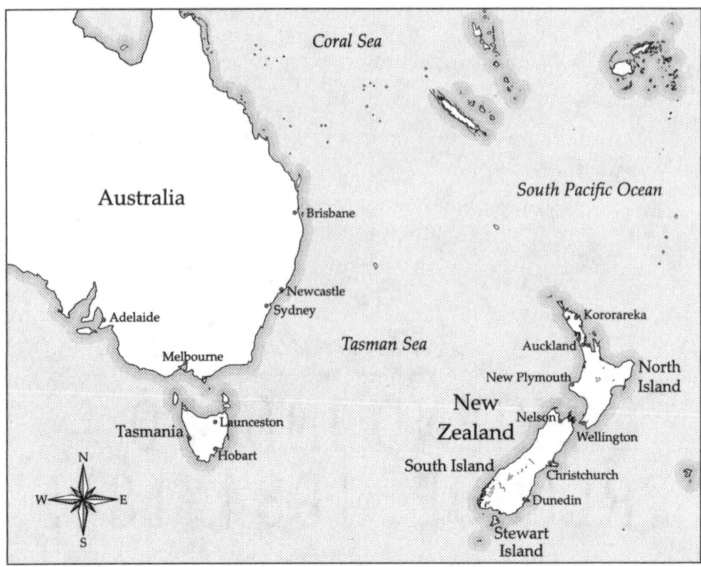

Australia and New Zealand.

foundation of the Australian and New Zealand military culture and traditions was laid. For it is a British Empire-derived military culture, tempered with the implications of settler society conflicts, that is still the basis for so much of the military traditions of the defence forces of the countries we know today as the separate nation-states of New Zealand and Australia.

Although not claiming in any way that the many participants were Anzacs as defined by the 1915 Gallipoli experience, it is nonetheless true that many New Zealand soldiers had fathers, grandfathers or other ancestors who had fought as Maori, colonial or imperial military personnel during the wars of the 1840s and 1860s. The common inter-colonial movements of individuals or families between the various colonies of British Australasia would also lead to numbers of later Australian soldiers having similar family heritage associations with the New Zealand wars. As later generations, the military personnel of these two nations fought and died together and forged what has become known as the 'Anzac legend'. But it should not be forgotten that the genesis of this bond as 'blood brothers' derived from these earlier conflicts, when colonists and imperial representatives on both sides of the Tasman united in a resolve to settle New Zealand's wars.

In a nascent form of 'unity in crisis' – more fully documented in later Empire conflicts and involvement – the Australian colonies united to play a crucial role in New Zealand's wars.[2] The enormous amount of logistical and commissariat materials procured from the Australian colonies was crucial in the unfolding of the various New Zealand campaigns, as were the many thousands of men who departed Australia to serve across the Tasman. This history details these aspects of Australia's contributions, as well as providing insights into the responses by Australian colonial society to the unfolding events and issues of the wars in New Zealand. The crucial role played by this 'Australian home front' is yet another layer to the complexities of the New Zealand wars not previously considered.

Any assessment of colonial Australasia must also take into account Australia's protracted history of frontier warfare with indigenous peoples on the continent, Tasmania, New Guinea and adjacent Pacific Islands. Despite the various literature produced since the 1970s, Australians still do not appreciate the importance of the internal colonial wars fought for domination of the land. Nor has Australia's frontier conflict been properly examined in relation to those occurring in other British settler societies such as New Zealand, Canada or South Africa. In a re-examination of the Tasmanian Wars (1824–31), Henry Reynolds emphasises that Tasmanian Aboriginal people 'fought a war against the colonists', but that 'their achievements in both war and peace have been overlooked'. He then comes to the crux of the matter when he asserts: 'In the forging of the Anzac legend there was no desire to link the new tradition, based on overseas engagements, with the much older story of conflict with the indigenous people within Australia. Conceptually, the two traditions were kept continents apart. This separation has influenced attitudes to both Aborigines and to warfare.'[3] Just as the 'Black wars' were largely expunged from the colonial experience, so has Australia's involvement in the New Zealand wars been a generally neglected aspect of Australian (and New Zealand) military history.

In fact, one of the principal reasons for the sparseness of the available history dealing with involvement in the New Zealand wars is the impact of this Anzac legend upon virtually all Australian military history since 1915. It is not difficult to find disregard of the colonial experience of war in Australasia prior to the Anglo-Boer War (1899–1902). John Laffin in *Anzacs at War*, for instance, made the sweeping claim that 'Australian and New Zealand military heritage has existed only since the Boer War', and that precious little took place prior to that time.[4] Not only does such a statement demonstrate considerable ignorance of Australasian colonial history, including the diverse nature of Australia's involvement in New Zealand's wars — an ignorance that has virtually been enshrined as canonical by Australian historians — but it serves to underline how, even today, most Australians have little or no real understanding of the lengthy experience of frontier warfare that continued in their country into the early twentieth century. Nor do Australians know much about the frontier conflict which occurred in the Torres Strait, New Guinea and other Pacific destinations impacted upon by Australian-derived traders, missionaries and government officials.[5] The legend of

Anzac so strongly espoused by C.E.W. Bean, and taken up by numerous historians since, has dictated an almost total excision of not only Australia's frontier history, but its involvement in New Zealand's wars.

A further factor contributing to a lack of appreciation of a shared Australasian history has been the long-held assumption that Australia's and New Zealand's histories end at their respective coastlines and could not possibly extend across the Tasman. The creation of rigid Australian and New Zealand territorial boundaries in 1901 has become the dominant feature of the region, overlooking the shared history of the British Australasian colonies. Although the Anzac legend interweaves the two nations during the twentieth century, prior Australian involvement in their neighbour's affairs has been ignored or downplayed to such a degree that it is viewed as irrelevant to both Australian and New Zealand history.[6]

Contributing also to the discounting of Australia's involvement in the New Zealand wars is the misconception that the military settlers recruited in the Australian colonies in 1863 and 1864 were mercenaries. Similarly, it has often been argued that as a body of troops recruited by the New Zealand government they do not constitute an Australian force. Yet the recruitment of military settlers in Australia in 1863 was not only condoned by Australian colonial governments and imperial representatives, but also supported as part of a greater overall effort to assist New Zealand. The commencement of recruiting in Sydney in August even led the *Sydney Morning Herald* to identify the raising 'in the Australias [of] a corps to assist' as precisely that — an *Australian* corps — and quite possibly the first articulation of this notion.[7] In New Zealand many enlistees served in military settler units with quite distinctive Australian identities. These included the 'Victorian Contingent' and the 'New South Wales Contingent' within the Waikato Military Settlers during 1863, followed by the 'Melbourne Contingent', the major component of the Taranaki Military Settlers, in 1864. As such, these troops had a direct Australian identification, though of course cloaked as 'citizens of an Empire'.[8] Another observation, perhaps more attributable to Australian soldiers in later conflicts, saw the Melbourne *Argus's* own correspondent report that these military settler volunteers complained that beer was unobtainable: 'They have had to march without beer, to fight without beer, and to stand the rain, cold, and heat with a gill of fiery rum as their only stimulant.'[9]

Firstly, when taking into account the shared Australian–New Zealand composition of all that has become the notional spirit of Anzac, it 'is ironic but nevertheless true that the first military force of Australians to leave . . . [for] service overseas was recruited and despatched not by an Australian colonial government but by the New Zealand government'.[10] Secondly, the military settlers were not mercenaries at all, but a properly enrolled military force sworn to comply and serve under British military law and order. They were attested on the Bible and

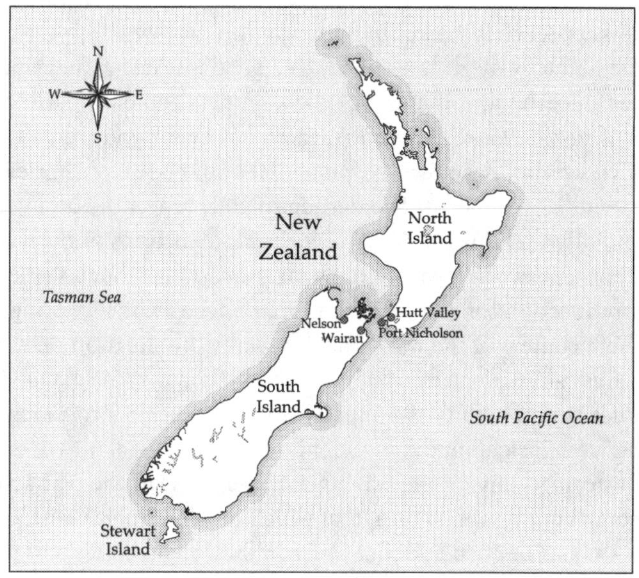

The North and South Islands of New Zealand.

took the oath of allegiance to Queen Victoria, and were bound by the British Mutiny Acts and Articles of War (and associated New Zealand government Acts).[11] Thirdly, the use of military settlers or military pensioners has a long history in the British Empire (and indeed from Roman times). Such military forces were viewed as a legitimate method of providing troops capable of both policing and then settling frontier areas. They were utilised with varying degrees of success in Canada, Africa and Australia (in colonies such as Tasmania, New South Wales and Western Australia) as well as New Zealand. In fact, a form of military settlement had already been established with the arrival in 1847 of the first elements of the New Zealand Fencibles, a force of military pensioners sent from Britain to assist with the colonisation of Auckland Province.[12]

The seminal work on Australian involvement in New Zealand's wars is by a New Zealander, Frank Glen, in *For Glory and a Farm*.[13] To a lesser extent, the contributions by Norman Bartlett have aided the available, though limited, understandings in this area.[14] Glen's efforts were the first to conclude that the wars of the 1860s had a significant Australian involvement, but generally both Australian and New Zealand historians have largely overlooked his ground-breaking efforts. The other sources available are narrowly focused studies such as those concentrating on the Waikato Military Settler Regiments, which almost totally ignore the role and place of the equally important Taranaki Military

Settlers. This approach is evident in Barton's effort that, while appearing to say so much, in fact seductively glides over the true depth of Australian involvement.[15]

However, since the contributions of Glen, Bartlett, and Barton, almost nothing in the way of new or more detailed research has been produced advancing an Australian viewpoint, despite a growing number of popular histories. Many of the works written over the last two decades merely repeat old and very general information, often relying on early New Zealand histories of the wars such as the useful but time-worn texts of Gudgeon and Cowan.[16] Such work continues to have a predilection for recounting the grand deeds while ignoring the social and economic context of the wars, and especially the situation on what can be termed an Australian home front during the 1840s and 1860s.[17] One important exception has been Dalton's 1966 reassessment of the 1860s campaigns. This contributed fresh insights and drew attention to the colonial bias of much of the accepted historiography on the subject at the expense of the true scope of the imperial contribution, and in turn, that which derived from Australia.[18] Dalton pointed to various important deficiencies in the accepted views of these wars, and tellingly noted that a 'thorough scholarly history of the wars' had not yet been undertaken.[19]

Another crucial and more recent exception has been the body of work by James Belich, and in particular his ground-breaking *The New Zealand Wars*, in which he offered thought-provoking reassessments of the wars and New Zealand history in general.[20] This work blew a welcome breath of fresh air across tired subject matter largely told through the eyes of the 'Pakeha' (or European) victors. Belich's contributions though certainly not designed to investigate in detail the involvement from across the Tasman nonetheless provide stepping stones to better explore this period of history for both Australia and New Zealand.

In looking at manpower contributions to the wars in New Zealand it must always be remembered that many thousands of men present at the conflict were either Australian born, enlisted from Australia, or else their port of departure was in one of the Australian colonies. Of the estimated 2500 men who comprised the 1863 and 1864 Australian military settler recruiting missions, many did not serve solely with the military settlers. Hundreds went on to join various other colonial units such as the Colonial Defence Force (cavalry), Patea Rangers, Bay of Plenty Cavalry Volunteers and, from 1867, the Armed Constabulary. Similarly, the 205 men from the 1868–69 Victorian recruiting mission for New Zealand's Armed Constabulary are totally unrecognised. A number also travelled across the Tasman to enrol in the New Zealand colonial forces on their own initiative, either before or after other formal recruiting missions for the military settlers or the Armed Constabulary.

Likewise, it should be noted that such events occurred during a time of high

Empire, where precedence was given in Australasian colonial communities to imperial or British identification – the 'crimson thread of kinship'.[21] Although all the colonies of the region concerned were separate entities in one sense, they were also very much part of that group in the Asia-Pacific region known as the 'Australasian colonies' or 'British Australasia'.[22]

Attention must also be directed to modern notions of 'Australian' or 'New Zealander' as inappropriate concepts. Colonists were always primarily British, despite whether one was actually born in the Australasian colonies or simply one of the many migrants who sought out these colonies as a new home. For example, men in the Australian colonies were also enlisted in the line regiments of the British Army in garrison, such as the 40th and 12th Regiments. Men were also recruited for Royal Navy vessels (especially out of the port of Sydney) – which then served in New Zealand waters. A significant number of men (and their families) also went to New Zealand because of the opportunities of land offered by way of military settler service, while others individually followed their own 'call of Empire'. Such people were sometimes inspired by earlier military service or impelled by hardship during periods of economic decline. Others involved in the volunteer movements, which had expanded in the early 1860s due to war scares and imperial defence reductions, enlisted to 'do their bit' and see 'real action'. New Zealand's wars provided a stimulus to Australia's volunteer movement in 1860 and 1863, too, although these effects were sometimes short-lived.

In this same vein, the imperial military resources extracted for use in New Zealand left the Australian colonies feeling vulnerable to the effects of outside powers such as France, Russia and the United States. New Zealand's wars therefore can be viewed as creating an atmosphere whereby Australian colonial governments were forced to consider their own defence needs more closely. Total reliance on England was simply not feasible due to the level of imperial involvement required across the Tasman.

Manpower and material contributions

The diverse group of men that departed Australian colonies for New Zealand – in hundreds of cases followed by loved ones – had a direct impact on the favourable outcome of these wars. Many families accompanied the troops, or followed on the heels of their military settler fathers and husbands. Military service was in fact a form of assisted immigration.[23] Military families such as the Fencibles from 1847, followed by the military settlers from 1863, would play significant roles in the establishment of settlements in the Waikato, Taranaki, and other North Island locations. Such families were able to contribute to New Zealand society beyond the short-term military service of their menfolk; and despite the failure of the

1860s military settler scheme, men and their families also moved into other areas of employment and enterprise.

An awareness of the diversity of men, women and children who arrived in New Zealand from Australia as a result of the wars allows for a new appraisal of Australia's importance in these conflicts. These many thousands played a considerable role in the overall outcome of the wars and in the tensions that continued for decades thereafter. At the same time, it should not be forgotten that there was a similar impact, albeit on a smaller scale, during the 1840s. The significance of Australian involvement in the 1840s conflicts, in relation to the initial development and population sizes of New Zealand, New South Wales and Van Diemen's Land, is as vital to overall outcomes as that which occurred in subsequent decades.

Australia was also crucial to the overall operation of the wars for many other reasons. These are as diverse as moral support and fundraising for settler refugees from the Bay of Islands (1845) or Taranaki (1860), or for troop casualties and assistance to their families, and restrictions upon the sale or trade of warlike stores to the Maori. Also included here is the willingness to provide (and in some cases manufacture) considerable quantities of arms, munitions, heavy weapons, transport equipment, riverboats and gunboats, and the provision of foodstuffs, horses, cattle and other associated logistical material. Australia in the mid-nineteenth century played a role not unlike its function in the Pacific War of 1941–45: a logistical and commissariat staging post for all manner of troops, supplies and war material required for the successful conduct of external military campaigns. It also provided a convenient locale from which recruits or regular troops could be obtained in times of imagined or real crisis.

Geographical proximity was particularly important when taking into account the enormous distances and times involved for communications between Australasia and Britain, and for reinforcements and supplies in turn to then arrive. It could take almost eight months to obtain a reply to a query sent from New Zealand before the extension of the telegraph into this region in the 1870s, and when reinforcements were needed in that country in 1860, it took eighty-two days to rush out the 2/14th Regiment from Ireland.[24] This experience is particularly evident throughout the period 1842–1847, and then again during 1860, 1863 and again in 1868.

The place of the British Army and Royal Navy

The units of the British Army and Royal Navy which served in the Australasian colonies during the early to mid nineteenth century represented the moral and physical manifestation of Empire in the distant south-west Pacific region. The presence of 'redcoats' and 'Jack Tars' as the day-to-day imperial representatives provided a sense of security and strength often beyond their actual numbers on station or in garrison – 'a form of imperial bluff that masked considerable weaknesses and vulnerability'.[25] Through this imperial presence, Australasians were constantly reminded of their inclusion within a greater coalition of colonies and territories that made up the powerful British Empire.

Writers of Australian military history have consistently neglected the role of British soldiers and sailors in colonial Australia. Often this has occurred because of the blinkered approach of seeing such military personnel as British only, and not Australian. As a result, the recruitment of colonials into the British line regiments in garrison – some Australian born, others immigrants to these colonies – has received little or no recognition. These largely unrecognised 'Australian' colonials went on to serve in New Zealand during the 1860s. The 40th Regiment garrisoned in Melbourne especially, but also the 12th Regiment in Sydney, enlisted or recruited men to bring regimental numbers up to strength from the late 1850s into the 1860s.[26] Expanding Russian and French interests in the Asia-Pacific region during 1858–59 led to considerable defence concerns. One move to bolster available forces saw Victorian military and governmental authorities taking steps to recruit 300 additional men for the 40th Regiment during late 1859.[27] Evidence of the hundreds of men who joined such line regiments is revealed in studies of military deserters, or those who took their discharge in New Zealand in the 1860s.[28]

The discharge of soldiers in a location such as New Zealand does not of course mean that they stayed in that colony as settlers. Numbers of the soldiers of the 12th and 40th Regiments who took their discharge in New Zealand quickly departed to return to the Australian colonies. The *Argus* in June 1866 reported one such example where approximately seventy men of the 40th who had just discharged in New Zealand had left that colony for Victoria for the purpose of settlement, while acknowledging that numbers of other discharged soldiers were remaining in Auckland.[29] Such former soldiers did this because of better opportunities in Australia, to return to family or friends, or to take up job offers made while part of the garrison forces before their departure for New Zealand service. These return cross-Tasman travellers are further examples of the inter-colonial fluidity that existed throughout the nineteenth century, and are indicative of a greater willingness to travel from colony to colony in search of better economic or social conditions. Such discharged personnel maintained long-term social and economic connections in Australia, as did the many who remained in New Zealand, long after their war service had terminated.

Too few detailed studies of the role and experience of these regiments in Australasia exist, and historical writing has largely failed to rescue evidence of the importance of the social and economic interactions between the British Army and colonial Australasians. Again, the impact of the Anzac legend, compounded by the myth of the peaceful settlement of Australia, has inflicted a deathly silence on discussion of the service of the British Army in Australia during the colonial years.

John Bach's seminal work on the history of the Royal Navy on the Australia Station set out to establish the role and significance of the naval presence in Australasia and the south-west Pacific.[30] He also drew attention to how the 1840s conflict in New Zealand provided the Royal Navy with not only an opportunity to distinguish itself but also encouraged the development of the Sydney naval station.[31] The necessities of naval support and intervention in the New Zealand campaigns of 1845–47 provided the Admiralty with the opportunity to separate the Australia area from the East Indies Station, which in turn led to the eventual establishment of the Australia Station in 1859. With the outbreak of warfare in the 1860s, 'the ships from Australia were part of the new Australia Station, under its own commodore and theoretically in a much better position to give effective assistance to the colonists'.[32] Indications of colonial enlistment into the Royal Navy can be gleaned from lists of naval deserters for the period.[33] In this respect, the Royal Navy of the Australia Station, as well as its Sydney base, divulges another aspect to Australia's pivotal role in the New Zealand wars.

The Australian humanitarian and home-front experience

A further aspect of involvement in the New Zealand wars not previously acknowledged is the organisation of and contributions to relief funds.[34] Australian support in the 1860s for the Taranaki settler relief fund and British soldier family relief is in fact indicative of earlier relief efforts and its impact on settlers, civilians or families caught up in such conflicts as the Crimean War and the 'Indian Mutiny'. The New Zealand wars would generate activism for three such funds – one created for the Bay of Islands settlers in 1845, and the other two for the Taranaki settler relief fund and British soldier family relief in the 1860s.

In relation to the families of British soldiers or sailors killed or incapacitated in New Zealand especially, the contributions from Australian relief funds were of immense value and should not be underestimated, as the Army 'made no provision for widows and orphans of regular soldiers' during this period.[35] Short-term relief was also provided for abandoned families of military settlers during 1863–64, as well as for those military settler families who experienced difficulties during the following years in subsisting and obtaining sufficient funds to finally allow them to travel to New Zealand to join their spouses.

Another element requiring elaboration is the depth of Australian awareness of the events transpiring in New Zealand. These were disseminated beyond simply the standard or illustrative press. Australians became aware of other information, discussion and debate by way of public lectures held in Schools of Art or Mechanics' Institutes. Throughout the nineteenth century, 'the public lecture served as a major vehicle for enlightenment and for entertainment', and in Australia such lectures offered a 'bewildering range of subjects' in even the remotest Institute or School of Arts.[36] Particularly during the 1860s, Australians were not only keen but were able to involve themselves from afar in New Zealand, its wars, aspects of Maori culture and warfare, and even the history of units of the British Army now serving across the Tasman.

Analysis of anti-war or peace movements is one more sadly neglected area. In revealing information both about the tentative beginnings of opposition to war in general, and directed opposition to, or concerns about, the campaigns being carried out against the Maori, the New Zealand wars are a unique source for the origins of Australian anti-war activities. Many colonials during the 1860s would no doubt have had some understanding of the terrible cost of war, as was revealed by news of the earlier Crimean War, but the press reportage of the enormous carnage under way in the American Civil War (1861–65) no doubt left many people more sensitive to war's human cost and suffering.[37]

At the same time there were those seeking to eradicate the 'native' problem once and for all, who countered Christian or philanthropic motivations with their own versions of what was necessary to fulfil the predictions of a 'dying race' and the will of British colonisation. The bane of such colonial elements in the mid-1860s was the Aborigines' Protection Society centred at Exeter Hall in London. Analysis of the colonial press in 1864 reveals that the Society commenced a campaign to address the welfare of the Maori of New Zealand, particularly in relation to the proposed enormity of land confiscations to follow on from the successful termination of the campaigns of 1863–64. The position of the Society drew howls of condemnation and ridicule from many quarters, but nonetheless offered a different viewpoint to the more common consensus. Of course it attracted only minority support or sympathies in Australasia – generally based on Christian values and interpretations or associated philanthropic attitudes.[38] The wars that occurred in New Zealand inspired a great diversity of commentary and criticism, and opposition to them and the treatment of the Maori is in evidence, although such beliefs and opinions should be weighed up more broadly with experiences and events taking place across the British Empire and with other indigenous peoples.

The Australian–New Zealand prelude

To fully grasp the importance of Australian involvement in New Zealand's wars first requires an exploration of the precedents of the 1830s and earlier 1840s. It is through an appreciation of these early military expeditions, defence fears, or calls for military assistance which occurred from 1834, variously during the early 1840s, and leading right up to the outbreak of conflict in the Bay of Islands during 1845, that we can gauge Australia's more significant long-term military involvement in New Zealand.

Most histories of the New Zealand wars are flawed because they lack any true depth in their understandings of the cross-Tasman connections. They either fail to acknowledge, or pass over, the crucial maritime bridge and all that it brought with it to give the wars a very real Australian colonial context. It was the development of an ever-increasing military role of the Australian colonies in New Zealand affairs during this early period that laid the foundation for the better-known and dramatic events of the wars of the 1860s.

Australia's Pacific frontier, trade, and its impact

Australia's cross-Tasman connections were an integral part of the eastern expansion of the Australian colonial frontier — a maritime frontier that extended into the Pacific from the 1790s.[39] But this ever-expanding maritime frontier was detrimental to many indigenous peoples caught up in its spread and development. William Barrett Marshall, assistant surgeon aboard HMS *Alligator*, left a personal record of his impressions of the Bay of Islands in 1834, where he witnessed first-hand the adverse impact the trade in weapons, gunpowder, tobacco and alcohol was having on the Maori people.[40] Much of this trade emanated from Sydney and Hobart Town, though American and other nations' whaling or trading vessels also contributed. By the 1810s, Maori demand for European firearms was rapidly increasing, their use diffusing from the initial contact regions in the north, to southern regions through the 1820s and 1830s. This non-traditional weaponry transformed Maori society in a bloody internecine period that became known as the 'Musket Wars'. Commencing in the early 1800s, intensified by the gun trade, this period of extended inter-tribal warfare was the largest conflict ever to take place in New Zealand, killing upwards of 20,000 people.[41]

Australia became one of the main arsenals from which Maori obtained guns and gunpowder. Between 1829 and 1831 the number of firearms in New Zealand is estimated to have doubled. In 1831 alone, merchants from Sydney traded some 6000 muskets for flax.[42] McKillop, a Royal Navy officer, recalled in his reminiscences how important the trade in flax had become by the 1840s,

Sydney, the capital of New South Wales, from the *Illustrated London News*, 10 January 1846.

The town of Auckland, New Zealand, from the *Illustrated London News*, 4 October 1851.

especially in relation to its usefulness to the burgeoning maritime and whaling industries.[43] Assessment of shipping export records out of Sydney between 14 April and 23 May 1831 helps to give an appreciation of the scale of the arms trade. During these weeks ten vessels departed for New Zealand, and amongst their total cargoes were sixty-five cases of muskets, seventy-one casks of gunpowder, six barrels and eleven kegs of gunpowder, fifteen hundredweight (cwt) of lead, and three casks of musket balls.[44] The return to Sydney of the *Currency Lass* from

New Zealand in July 1831 with a cargo of spars and twenty tons of flax is indicative of the reciprocal nature of the gun trade.[45]

A more gruesome by-product of the enormous human toll of the Musket Wars was a cross-Tasman trade in preserved Maori heads. Europeans first became acquainted with 'mokomokai' during Cook's first voyage of exploration, with one specimen being acquired at Queen Charlotte Sound in January 1770. Later contact with whalers and sealers brought about the trade in heads, 'which increased markedly once a desire for muskets became general' amongst the Maori.[46] The governor of New South Wales was so appalled by the extent of this trade that he issued a government notice on 16 April 1831 to eradicate it, ordering customs officers to report any future attempts to import preserved heads.[47] Governor Darling subsequently imposed a fine of £40 on any individual found trying to sell such items, which appears to have had the desired effect by the early 1830s.[48]

The ease and familiarity with European weaponry perpetuated by the thriving Australian musket trade, combined with Maori sophistication in warfare, generated a people quite capable of confronting – and as it turned out on occasions, defeating – the forces of imperial and colonial intrusion in New Zealand. The Maori shipboard experience throughout the early decades of contact with European whalers and traders also provided access to the wonders of new goods and technology. 'Maori "learnt the ropes" quickly and served on the ships of all nationalities in New Zealand waters. Many travelled to Australia, Asia, North America, England and Europe . . . In Sydney and Hobart Maori sailors were a common sight in the 1820s and 1830s.'[49]

Even the art of artillery was acquired and incorporated into traditional Maori warfare and fortifications. Here it should be remembered that trading and whaling vessels were often armed with such weaponry, especially necessary for protection while carrying out their activities in regions such as the Pacific and Asia. Cowan, an early historian of the New Zealand wars, noted this experience, concluding that the 'merchant sailor of 1845 had to be a gunner too; and it is aboard these traders and whalers that some of our young Ngapuhi . . . have learned to load, lay, and fire artillery'.[50] Maori fortifications assaulted by imperial troops in the Bay of Islands in 1845–46 were found to contain an array of variously acquired artillery pieces. At Ohaeawai, the pa possessed two iron 9-pounders, one 4-pounder, and a swivel 2-pounder cannon, and at Ruapekapeka, one small piece and one 18-pounder. Similar surprises were in store for imperial and colonial forces at Meremere in 1863 and again at Paterangi in 1864.[51] The growth of the musket trade, and the ability of the Maori to obtain modern weaponry by the time of the 1840s conflict, soon saw such arms used to great effect against imperial troops.[52]

What is obvious, then, for the decades leading up to the 1840s, is the extreme importance of the port of Sydney for so much of New Zealand's contact and trade experience. It was from Sydney that most personnel and finances were obtained for the maintenance of missions, and the whaling, trading and timber industries being carried out across the Tasman. 'Sydney had long been one of New Zealand's most important cities, and for a century New Zealand was one of Sydney's most important hinterlands.'[53] Therefore, throughout the nineteenth century the 'Tasman Sea was more bridge than barrier' — a regularly plied maritime causeway from which New Zealand derived considerable and repeated military support from Australia.[54] Australia's geographical proximity ensured this growth in cross-Tasman trade and communications, which in turn easily lent itself to adaptation to supply New Zealand's war needs into the 1860s.

HMS *Alligator* rescue expedition, 1834

The 1834 rescue mission undertaken by HMS *Alligator*, the government schooner *Isabella*, and a detachment of the 50th Regiment is highly significant in the context of later involvements in New Zealand. This expedition was the first true military operation undertaken from the Australian colonies to any external destination. Although the plea for assistance on this occasion did not arrive in Sydney from a New Zealand official, but rather a ship's master, the event marks the beginnings of direct military participation in the affairs of New Zealand. Here was the precursor for Australia becoming that convenient locale where, in time of real or perceived crisis, army and naval forces or other assistance could be obtained to deal with the Maori.

During August 1834 the *Sydney Herald* documented a growing number of 'hostile dispositions' displayed by the Maori as reported by vessels returning from New Zealand. The *Lucy Ann* found itself in difficulties with Maori near Otago, while the *Amity*'s crew complained 'the natives committed some depredations' against the cutter *Alexander M'Leay* while it was collecting a cargo on the coast near Hokianga. The *Herald* relayed that nearly 'all the masters of vessels trading to New Zealand complain of the want of a man-of-war, or some protection from the natives'.[55] Among these vessels was the schooner *Joseph Weller* that arrived on the evening of 17 August, bringing news of the wreck of the whaler *Harriet*, and the 'assassination' of Captain Hall and twelve seamen by the Maori. Captain Guard, who had left Sydney in the *Harriet*, also arrived aboard the *Joseph Weller* and was reported as 'the only person that could escape from the natives,—the rest of the ship's company being kept prisoners'.[56]

Four days later the *Herald* decried 'the committal of fresh atrocities by the Natives . . . upon the defenceless Settlers and Traders' in New Zealand. But it was the 'last and most revolting act of these savages', 'the murder of twelve shipwrecked British seamen, attached to the *Harriet*', that rankled the most. The 'outrages of these cannibals' was described as having become so 'daring and insolent in their conduct' that one ship's captain, Anglim, with ten years' experience in the New Zealand trade, declared his intention 'of giving up his post, and not again visiting the island, unless some protection be afforded by the Government'. Various ships' captains (including Guard) demanded action and a meeting with the governor. To add weight to this issue, the press carried a lengthy narrative by Captain Guard of the wreck of the *Harriet* and the 'misfortunes experienced by himself and crew'.[57]

In a despatch to England, Governor Bourke recorded details of the meeting he had with Guard and the Executive Council, which had been called together to consider measures that could be undertaken. But 'the Council was not unanimous in the advice proffered', with the dissenting voice in this matter being the colonial treasurer.[58] But on the advice of the Executive Council, Bourke now determined on a military rescue expedition as the only course of action open, utilising HMS *Alligator* commanded by Captain Lambert and the government schooner *Isabella* to carry the necessary troops. The *Herald* complimented the government for its prompt decision to act 'with spirit in thus taking up the cause of the Ship Masters and others'.[59] While the governor's orders may well have been to ensure the release of the hostages held by the Maori in Taranaki, the public saw this expedition as a timely punitive expedition to teach the Maori the superiority of British arms.

The two vessels departed Sydney for New Zealand on 31 August 1834. On board HMS *Alligator* was a detachment of twenty-five 50th Regiment troops commanded by Lieutenant Gunton, and aboard the *Isabella* were forty soldiers of the same regiment under the command of Captain Johnston and Ensign W.H. Wright.[60] Johnston actually appears to hold the distinction of being the first person to volunteer his services in Australia for military service in New Zealand, with this officer's volunteer spirit acknowledged as such in the press.[61]

Bourke's letter of instruction to Captain Lambert outlined the purpose and parameters for action of the military on this expedition to Taranaki: 'it will be advisable to abstain from any act of immediate retaliation . . . lest it should excite a spirit of revenge or hostility', but if 'the restoration of the prisoners should not be accomplished by amicable means, the Council recommend that force should be employed to effect it'.[62] This recommendation, to use force if circumstances dictated, allowed the 50th Regiment soldiers and Royal Marines and seamen involved to pursue a number of aggressive actions that cost the local Maori dearly. The *Alligator* bombarded several pa, and forces sent ashore burned and destroyed villages, canoes and gardens.

At Waimate pa on 8 October, despite a British flag of truce, the troops involved lost control and opened fire. Assistant Surgeon Marshall's personal account of this assault described the desperate efforts of Ensign Wright, who tried to get the troops to stop firing but 'was entirely disregarded . . . until . . . bodies were seen stretched upon the sands'.[63] Marshall's account also indicates serious problems associated with the discipline of this detachment, pointing out that most had only recently arrived from England in various small detachments, 'and only a few had been any time in the army, fewer still with their regiment . . . The whole company had hardly been completed at Sydney, when ordered on the expedition.'[64] These totally unprepared and inexperienced soldiers had been given opportunities to show their mettle against a 'savage' foe, which they discharged with great relish.

The *Isabella* arrived back in Sydney on 11 November 1834, bringing the first reports of the actions and success of the expedition in obtaining the release of the hostages.[65] Two days later HMS *Alligator* arrived, carrying Mrs Guard and her children. In an editorial on 17 November, the *Herald* provided its readership with a detailed account of the events associated with the 'successful termination of the enterprise'.[66] Van Diemen's Land press reportage of the expedition was similarly detailed, but by contrast openly acknowledged the cost in human life: 'We little imagined, when we had the pain to record the recent sanguinary conflict with the Aborigines at Swan river [Western Australia], that we should so soon have to narrate another extensive sacrifice of human life in New Zealand.'[67] Whatever the causes for the hostage-taking by the Taranaki Maori, the end result was that it created a situation whereby the authorities in New South Wales felt compelled to deploy a significant military force in a planned expedition, leading to considerable bloodshed and destruction of Maori settlements and food reserves.[68]

In December, Governor Bourke detailed his final thoughts on the matter in a despatch to England, in which he considered 'it essential to the success, perhaps to the existence of the trading establishments formed on that Island, and to the maintenance of good order' that one Royal Navy warship be made available for station in New Zealand waters.[69] As economic activity increased in New Zealand, it became obvious to Australian authorities that a greater military presence would be required. However, the initial presence being sought of a vessel of the Royal Navy was not immediately forthcoming due to the reluctance of the imperial government to sanction any additional expenditure or make forces available. The call for military assistance in New Zealand, though, was to resurrect itself throughout the 1840s.

Establishment of the colony of New Zealand in 1840

In 1840 New Zealand became a separate colony, with Captain William Hobson, Royal Navy, appointed lieutenant-governor. Despite its independent status, the colony of New Zealand still relied heavily on New South Wales for much of its civil, police and military requirements.[70] New Zealand in fact remained for military purposes a part of the Australian command until early 1861, when a separate command was established. The first British troops ordered to be stationed there during 1840 were a detachment of the 80th Regiment made available from the garrison in New South Wales, commanded by Major Thomas Bunbury.[71] Apart from Bunbury, this detachment comprised three officers, eighty-four other ranks, one commissariat officer and one storekeeper. They embarked aboard the government storeship *Buffalo*, sailing on 5 April for the Bay of Islands to assist Governor Hobson in the administration of the new colony. In September the same year a small additional contingent of the 80th arrived under Captain Foster, increasing Bunbury's total available force to 106 troops. These 80th troops were to be allocated to the Bay of Islands and Auckland, as well as Port Nicholson (Wellington) where the first influx of Wakefield free settlers in 1840 created an atmosphere of simmering tensions over questions of the validity of land purchases with local Maori. These New Zealand Company settlers also agitated for separate government, a situation Hobson was not going to tolerate. He ensured this 'independence' was squashed by prompt despatch of New South Wales Mounted Police and a contingent of the 80th Regiment to restore the supremacy of the Crown.[72]

The settlement at Wellington (Port Nicholson), from the *Illustrated London News*, 25 March 1843.

Tauranga tensions, and calls for military assistance, 1842–43

Hobson died on 10 September 1842, and until a replacement could be sent the New Zealand Colonial Secretary, Willoughby Shortland, administered the fledgling colony. On 29 November, Shortland left Auckland to visit Wellington, on the way calling at Tauranga to continue negotiations for the peaceful transfer to the Crown of land in dispute between the Tauranga and Thames Maori. Upon arrival, he discovered the region was in the midst of escalating tribal tensions that appeared on the brink of exploding into major tribal conflict. So concerned was Shortland with this situation that he sent his aide-de-camp, Captain Best of the 80th, back to Auckland to bring Major Bunbury and as many troops as possible. In the meantime, convinced that outside help was going to be required, Shortland wrote to Major-General O'Connell in Sydney for troop reinforcements, and penned a similar letter to the senior naval officer in Sydney seeking an 'efficient naval force'.

In early 1843 O'Connell determined that reinforcements would be made available to Shortland. This additional military detachment consisted of one company of the 96th Regiment commanded by Captain Eyton, ordered from Van Diemen's Land and sent direct to Auckland, arriving in February. Despite the high tensions on all sides, this Tauranga affair dissipated without further tribal conflict. Bunbury's 80th detachment remained on hand until early March of that year, with Shortland successfully convincing the tribes that the troops stationed there were only to ensure the maintenance of peace between all parties.[73]

The 'Wairau Affray' and calls for military assistance, 1843

During the 1840s, settler pressure in the Hutt Valley, the Wairau, Taranaki and the Waikato to acquire the most desirable land was met by growing Maori resistance. Clashes occurred, leading rapidly to political and military confrontation. As was the common pattern, opportunities for trade (and what was perceived initially as wealth) offered by the initial incoming European settlers were welcomed. Maori also sold land, sometimes with the aim of resolving long-standing tribal rivalries; only when it was too late did they realise that the consequence of seeking an ally against their Maori enemies was simply to replace these with a new Pakeha enemy. This situation degenerated into Maori disillusionment and dissatisfaction as they began to comprehend all that European colonisation brought in its wake.[74] There was also the realisation that a marked difference existed between the few Europeans who had come prior to 1840 as traders, whalers, sealers and missionaries, and the many that now flooded in. These post-1840 settlers came 'to settle, to claim, occupy, and cultivate the land. They displayed an insatiable appetite, gave the land itself a commercial value'; colonisation 'became a tide that flowed but never ebbed'.[75]

Settlers and capital from New South Wales and Van Diemen's Land contributed to this process of European colonisation in New Zealand. The *Cornwall Chronicle* in 1840 acknowledged the role of certain 'Launcestonians', but also drew attention to dangers associated with contact between Europeans and Maori, including concerns over land and the dealings of the New Zealand Land Company. 'The natives ... are a manly, determined and brave, yet suspicious and cunning set of men, who are not be gulled quite so easily as the aborigines of the Australian Colonies, they have learnt *to trade* from the Europeans, and are competent to judge of the values of their lands.'[76]

The Maori people were perceived as a superior 'native' race, one not easily overwhelmed by the might of European material and spiritual culture or technology. An 1841 editorial by 'an old colonist of Van Diemen's Land' returning from New Zealand reported on the progress of colonisation. Stating his belief that small farms between fifty and 100 acres 'will succeed well', he warned that the Maori are 'lords of the soil, who begin to look with disdain and jealousy upon the fresh arrivals of English intruders'.[77] Similar views continued even after the outbreak of warfare in the Bay of Islands and the disturbances in the Wellington-Hutt Valley region. The *Britannia and Trades' Advocate* in 1846 expressed concern that the Maori simply did not understand the true nature of their land dealings – neither with the New Zealand Land Company, nor when they ceded sovereignty to the British Crown via the 1840 Treaty of Waitangi. 'What has occurred in South America, in North America, in Australia, will be acted over again in New Zealand. A predatory warfare between the pioneers of cultivation and the aboriginal owners of the soil will deepen by degrees in intensity, and become at last a war of extermination.'[78] Disputes very rapidly arose around the New Zealand Land Company settlements of Port Nicholson and at Nelson in the South Island where land sales 'presented an opportunity for subtle utu [revenge or satisfaction], and Wakefield's New Zealand Company went to little trouble to ascertain the rightful owners'.[79] The subsequent 'Wairau Affray' near Nelson on 17 June 1843 was to become the first bloody test of Maori independence against the imposition of British sovereignty.[80]

In early July 1843 the *Sydney Morning Herald* was reporting on the growing unrest at Port Nicholson: 'The natives were imposing upon the settlers at the outstations in every direction, by demanding payment for the land which, in many instances, had been purchased from the New Zealand Company', but the Company in turn had declared it would not compensate any settlers so pressured.[81] This paper was soon to receive news of events at Wairau and reported with regret 'that a very serious affray, only the first, we fear, of a series, has taken place between some natives and some Europeans'. With this first shedding of blood, 'a general rising of the unchristianised natives throughout the island' was feared. To combat such eventualities the *Herald* urged the necessity of sending at least 200 soldiers to protect the residents at Port Nicholson as soon as possible.[82] At a public meeting in Wellington on 19 June, local citizens also expressed their concerns about their undefended situation and called for military aid. This resulted in a memorial forwarded to the imperial government via the governor at Auckland, as well as to the governor of New South Wales for action on his part.[83]

Following news of the Wairau 'massacre' being received in Auckland, Acting-Governor Shortland promptly despatched a force of fifty soldiers to Wellington as well as making an application to New South Wales Governor Gipps for reinforcements. Despite the *Sydney Morning Herald*'s disquiet, Gipps did ensure that HMS *North Star* was ordered to New Zealand bearing additional troops. In a despatch to Lord Stanley on 3 August, he outlined the action taken after consultations with Captain Sir J. Everard Home (who was now the senior naval officer on the station) and General O'Connell. Home would sail after taking on board a detachment of troops, but with the clear understanding not to land these soldiers unless he considered it 'absolutely necessary for the protection of the lives and property of Her Majesty's subjects'; if not required, they were to return to Sydney.[84]

On 1 August, HMS *North Star* departed Sydney for Port Nicholson carrying fifty-two officers and men of the 80th Regiment.[85] Arriving at Wellington on 31 August, after first calling at Auckland, Captain Home assessed that the situation in the south of the North Island did not require the troops to be disembarked. Nor was there the necessity to take any action whatsoever, and as set out in his orders from Gipps, he returned to Sydney.[86]

On 27 September 1843 the citizens of Nelson wrote another memorial to the governor of Van Diemen's Land. This informed him of the serious state of affairs and indicated the threat felt by the settlers in this South Island area. Because of concerns about an expected attack on Nelson, this communication was a direct call for military aid.[87] To add weight to such urgency, the vessel *Sisters*, which bore this appeal for assistance to Hobart, also carried nearly fifty people 'who had fled hither for protection'. Concurrently, advice was received that a number of persons had also reached Launceston for the same purpose.[88] Panic was also rife in Wellington, where other settlers similarly sought escape to Sydney after the events at Wairau.[89]

The governor of Van Diemen's Land in the meantime determined to render 'sufficient & speedy' assistance and requested the Chief Secretary's Office to inform the senior army officer in the colony to forward by the convict vessel *Emerald Isle* such aid as was deemed necessary.[90] A detachment of 100 men of the

99th Regiment commanded by Captain Nicholson departed aboard this vessel on 15 October. Upon arrival at Port Nelson, Nicholson determined the force was not required ashore, and in accordance with instructions carried on to Sydney without disembarking these troops.[91] Although not required, it was the willingness of authorities in Hobart and Sydney to despatch forces promptly which would become a common point of reaction from the Australian side of the Tasman – and one that would take on grander proportions in the ensuing years.

In late 1843, Captain FitzRoy, Royal Navy, arrived in Sydney on his way to take up the governorship of New Zealand. Before his departure, a meeting of influential Sydney citizens produced an address for presentation to New Zealand's new governor, which acknowledged the presence of a considerable number of Sydney residents who had great interest in the 'progress' of British colonisation in New Zealand.[92] This exemplifies the major role Sydney-based economic interests had in the continued European expansion and settlement of New Zealand, and for whom Maori submission or defeat was desirable to ensure their continued profits and expanding markets.

Escalating tensions and military redistributions, 1844

The 80th Regiment received orders to depart for service in India in early 1844, and all its outlying detachments, including those serving in New Zealand, were recalled to Sydney. To replace the diminished number of troops available in New Zealand, additional elements of the 96th Regiment departed from Hobart Town in March 1844. The vessels *Marian Watson* and *Waterlily* originally brought 150 soldiers of the 96th who had been serving on Norfolk Island to Van Diemen's Land. On route to New Zealand, fifty of these soldiers were disembarked for duty at Launceston, while the remaining 100 continued in these vessels on 29 March. Brevet Lieutenant-Colonel William Hulme, who succeeded Bunbury in the local command in New Zealand, commanded these fresh 96th troops.[93]

Prior to Bunbury's departure, there continued to be simmering unrest throughout the European settler areas of the North Island. In Auckland, Bunbury had been deputising for FitzRoy, but 'was so disturbed over reports of a Maori rising that he advised the chief government officers that an attack on the soldiers could be expected', though this came to nothing. Earlier grave reports detailing Maori interference with settlers at New Plymouth had already led to Bunbury writing to Sydney asking General O'Connell to augment his available military force at Auckland by another 100 soldiers.[94] But with the departure of Bunbury and the 80th in April 1844, the only British regiment with troops now available in New Zealand was the 96th.[95]

Bay of Islands tensions and renewed requests for military reinforcements, 1844 and 1845

In the Bay of Islands during 1844–45, three acts of defiance executed by elements of the Nga Puhi tribe under Hone Heke and Kawiti led to the outbreak of the Northern War of 1845–46. These consisted of repeatedly cutting down the flagstaff carrying the Union Jack above the far northern settlement of Kororareka (Russell). Although such acts might at first sight seem insufficient to fuel a war, in actual fact the 'amputation of the flagstaff had substantive implications as well as symbolic significance. If the British could not protect the flagstaff of their largest settlement north of Auckland, what could they protect? And how much credibility could their claims to substantive sovereignty retain?'[96] One of the chief reasons for growing tensions amongst the Maori was the removal of the capital from the Bay of Islands to Auckland, and the imposition of customs dues – both of which aided in an exodus of Pakeha from the region. These factors in turn produced an economic downturn that impacted heavily upon certain hapu (sub-tribes) of the Nga Puhi and fuelled the actions of Heke and Kawiti during 1844–45.[97] The context for direct Australian concerns and support arose from the various calls for military reinforcements following these individual flagstaff incidents.

The town of Kororareka (Russell) in the Bay of Islands, from the *Illustrated London News*, 26 July 1845.

The first such instance occurred at Kororareka on 8 July 1844. Governor FitzRoy received the news two days later and took immediate action; as the 'Crown, represented by the flag, had been submitted to insult; the insult must be punished and the flag replaced'. He promptly sent an officer and thirty men of the 96th Regiment to Kororareka in the *Sydney* on the 13th.[98] This vessel then took news of events at the Bay of Islands and FitzRoy's request for military assistance to Sydney, arriving on 2 August. As a result of the 'Perilous State of Affairs in New Zealand', Governor Gipps wasted no time in bringing the matter before the New South Wales Executive Council, whereupon it was determined to despatch a force of troops to comply with FitzRoy's request.[99] On 5 August the *Sydney* departed for the Bay of Islands with 205 officers and men of the 99th Regiment.[100] It also carried two 6-pounder guns, apart from a large quantity of arms, ammunition, and other equipment and stores. By the time the detachment arrived at the Bay of Islands on 14 August, there were no longer any serious signs of disturbances. FitzRoy himself arrived at Kororareka on 25 August, accompanied by Lieutenant-Colonel Hulme, Captain Bennett and an additional small detachment of fifteen soldiers of the 96th from Auckland. Following meetings with various Nga Puhi chiefs on 2 September the situation appeared to be diffused, allowing troops to be returned to Auckland, and the 99th detachment to Sydney, by 14 September.[101]

On 10 January 1845 the flagstaff at Kororareka was again cut down. The news reached Sydney aboard the *Tryphena* a month later. The *Sydney Morning Herald* reported the news was 'anything but satisfactory . . . Governor Fitzroy has again found it necessary to send to the authorities of this colony for troops'.[102] The *Herald* added, 'it appears that from the vascillating [*sic*] course hitherto taken by the Governor, the natives entertain the impression that the British are weak, that they may do as they please. It will now probably be found out — if not too late indeed — that strong measures must be resorted to.'[103] FitzRoy's urgent application for military assistance to counter the Bay of Islands crisis, compounded with continuing tensions at Port Nicholson, necessitated Gipps to again confer with the Executive Council of New South Wales. To be of assistance to New Zealand in this instance it was determined to prepare two companies of the 58th Regiment for despatch on vessels to be hired for this task.[104]

Despite these intentions, delays occurred with the procurement of vessels to transport these troops, and only the *Velocity* tendered with success for this service.[105] The arrival in Sydney of HMS *North Star* on 3 March alleviated some of these difficulties as this vessel was now utilised for carrying a portion of the two companies of the 58th that were being held in readiness.[106] This delay at first seemed to be of no concern as FitzRoy's despatch for military assistance which arrived on 11 February 'indicated that troops were needed not in connection with any particular situation but as a result of general unrest'.[107] At the same time as troops of the 58th were preparing for departure, it was also reported that 'several gunners of the 99th Regiment have been practising daily . . . and will be sent . . . to accompany the troops'.[108]

To compound matters, news of strife in the southern districts of the North Island was also being received. Throughout February and March 1845 the press reported disturbances breaking out across the North Island. This escalating situation appeared likely to shortly develop into open conflict. On 31 March the *Sydney Morning Herald* detailed: 'The natives in the southern district are, like their brethren in the north, committing sad ravages, and . . . set the authority of the Government at defiance. . . . There can be no doubt that . . . a well-concerted attack upon the English will very shortly take place.'[109] In a letter to the editor, Robert D'Oyly of Sydney drew attention to the delays in providing New Zealand with military assistance. D'Oyly, who had only recently returned from New Zealand, made a prophetic plea to Gipps not to delay any further upon merely parsimonious grounds in sending troops: 'Should such a state of circumstances occur, after the time when troops *might* have got down to New Zealand, had your Excellency used despatch, the whole blame will be thrown on you; and you will find it difficult to exonerate yourself.'[110]

On 8 March the *Velocity* commenced loading ordnance stores, and two days later took on board fifty-two officers and men of the 58th. HMS *North Star* was also readied for sea, and 154 officers and men of the 58th embarked. The *North Star* departed for Auckland on 11 March and the *Velocity* followed suit the next day.[111] But the delays in departure of these troops meant that by the time of their arrival at Auckland — the *North Star* on 20 March and the *Velocity* on 23 March —events in New Zealand had already taken a considerable turn for the worse. The date of the troops' departure from Sydney actually coincided with the flagstaff being cut down for the third and final time and the settlement at Kororareka being sacked by the forces of Heke and Kawiti. Full-scale war had broken out in the Bay of Islands. The Australian colonies during 1845–47 were now to become the focal point from which the campaigns in New Zealand were effectively supplied with all available men, arms and other war material.

Chapter One
A HELPING HAND

ON 3 APRIL 1845, Sydney residents first became aware of the alarming news from New Zealand of the sacking of Kororareka in the Bay of Islands. The vessel *Slains Castle*, which bore this intelligence, left Auckland on 24 March carrying eighty-three refugees, which reinforced the drama for Sydney citizens.[1] Sydney's *Morning Chronicle* provided an account of the events which took place at Kororareka and the resultant panic that had set in: 'The inhabitants . . . were conveyed to Auckland, as soon as they could be after the affray . . . Many of the European settlers were determined to leave the colony as soon as they could.'[2]

Following Kororareka's fall many Auckland residents were similarly gripped with panic and fears of the Maori also descending upon their township. 'Many, believing that nothing but flight stood between them and annihilation, sold their lands and houses, their goods and chattels, for whatever their speculative neighbours would offer, and then sat down on the beach to wait for a ship to take them to Sydney.'[3] Some of these fearful citizens were among those who arrived aboard the *Slains Castle*, as well as later vessels to Australian ports such as Sydney and Hobart Town.[4] And it was the plight of these refugees which animated fellow Australian colonists to institute a settler relief fund to care for their immediate needs – the first such relief fund associated with the New Zealand wars.

The dramatic news from across the Tasman caused sentiments to run high in Sydney and led to calls for a public meeting, which on 5 April advertised for 'all parties friendly to the preservation of the Lives of the White Inhabitants in New Zealand' to take place that same day.[5] This meeting, despite its short notice, still attracted an audience of some 300, including various influential persons such as Francis Fisher, New Zealand attorney-general, John Smith, manager of the Union Bank at Wellington, the Reverend J.D. Lang, and other businessmen and traders from both Sydney and New Zealand. After some discussion it was resolved that 'a large number of troops and two steamers should be immediately forwarded to New Zealand, for the protection of the white inhabitants'.[6] The *Sydney Morning Herald* felt that the resolutions had not gone far enough, declaring: 'in consideration of the severe hardships to which many of our fellow-Britons in New Zealand had been driven by the sudden destruction of their property, it was expedient . . . a public subscription should be entered into for their relief'.[7]

Governor Gipps, however, declined to receive a deputation appointed at this meeting because of the 'dictatorial tone' of its resolution, though was reported as prepared to see any 'gentlemen interested in New Zealand'. This resulted in two individuals, Taylor and Wright, having an audience with the governor on 7 April. They discussed the delay in forwarding troops in February, and here Gipps defended his position and confirmed that FitzRoy's despatch at that time was not written so 'imperatively as has been generally supposed'. It was also made known that the governor had already commenced steps to send 250 troops within days.[8]

Letters to the editor at this juncture reveal some voices of dissent against the intended military action. J.W. Graves pointed out, 'that on my putting an amendment, substituting placable measures instead of armed force, I was clamorously cried down, in the usual Sydney manner, without being heard out: though, while Dr. Lang was pleased to pay some eulogium on my motive he thought it expedient to [c]ensure my measure'.[9] Graves also indicated the main proponents for a decisive military response were men of business and trade, who had considerable interests in New Zealand, which no doubt would be threatened by any hostile Maori actions.[10] Other voices evinced sympathy towards the Maori cause, and even praise for the actions of 'John Heki'. 'Philo Tangata Maori' on 22 April said that 'John Heke, the great leader, is a bold but not by any means a bloodthirsty man; his object has always been to prevent a foreign flag from flying in New Zealand, but not to destroy European life or property. Had he wished to annihilate Kororarika, he might have done so months ago.'[11] (Analogous allusions to the struggle of Hone Heke would even be used in Hobart in July 1845 to adorn placards during protests against taxation.)[12] Even in June 1846, impressions of Heke and his supporters could elicit such sentiments as those of J.J. Merrett: 'It will be clearly seen on referring to the sentiments of Heki and his relations, that notwithstanding their spirit of independence, and the language of bravado which characterises them, that there is a disposition to a peaceable arrangement.'[13]

The arrival of *Slains Castle* on 3 April also brought New Zealand Governor FitzRoy's plea for immediate military assistance. His despatch of 20 March 1845 pointed 'out in "the strongest terms . . . the absolute – the imperative necessity of immediately sending both Naval and Military Force, to save this Colony from ruin". He feared that unless prompt and effective measures were taken immediately other settlements might be destroyed.'[14] FitzRoy also took the liberty to send a similarly worded plea to Van Diemen's Land governor Sir Eardley Wilmot,[15] asserting that he expected Wilmot could be confidently relied upon to send at least one company direct to Wellington – no doubt an expectation of military support from Van Diemen's Land based on its willingness to send troops upon appeal during 1843.

Initial Australian reinforcements and other support

New South Wales's immediate contribution was the charter and preparation in Sydney of the vessels *Bee* and *Slains Castle* to convey detachments of the 58th Regiment to Auckland and Port Nicholson. The *Bee* departed for Wellington on 9 April carrying fifty-five officers and men of the 58th. On 10 April *Slains Castle* embarked troops and military stores before departing for Auckland the following day with 208 officers and men of the 58th Regiment. Also with the detachment were Lieutenant Elliott and Ensign O'Reilly of the 99th Regiment who were permitted to volunteer their services to the 58th to bolster officer numbers. Apart from these two officers, Lieutenant-General Sir Maurice O'Connell, commanding the forces in Australasia (1834–47), also permitted his own son, Lieutenant C.P. O'Connell, 51st Regiment, who had been acting as his aide-de-camp, to volunteer for New Zealand service as a staff officer.[16]

One of the problems faced in the Australian colonies at this time was the lack of any officers and men of the Royal Artillery. Artillery, and personnel to man such weapons, were wanted as an integral component of the field force being assembled in the Bay of Islands, as well as for defences at Auckland and in the south of the North Island. To alleviate this situation General O'Connell formed a temporary corps of artillery from soldiers from regiments such as the 99th. In February it had already been reported that several gunners of the 99th had for some time been practising in the use of artillery. The son of the Van Diemen's Land lieutenant-governor, Lieutenant Henry Eardley Wilmot, Royal Artillery, who had been serving his father as aide-de-camp, volunteered as commander of this stopgap artillery corps.[17] To complement the services of Lieutenant Wilmot, two retired Royal Artillery sergeants who had settled in Van Diemen's Land also came forward and offered their services.

Governor Wilmot in a despatch to Lord Stanley on 24 April detailed initial

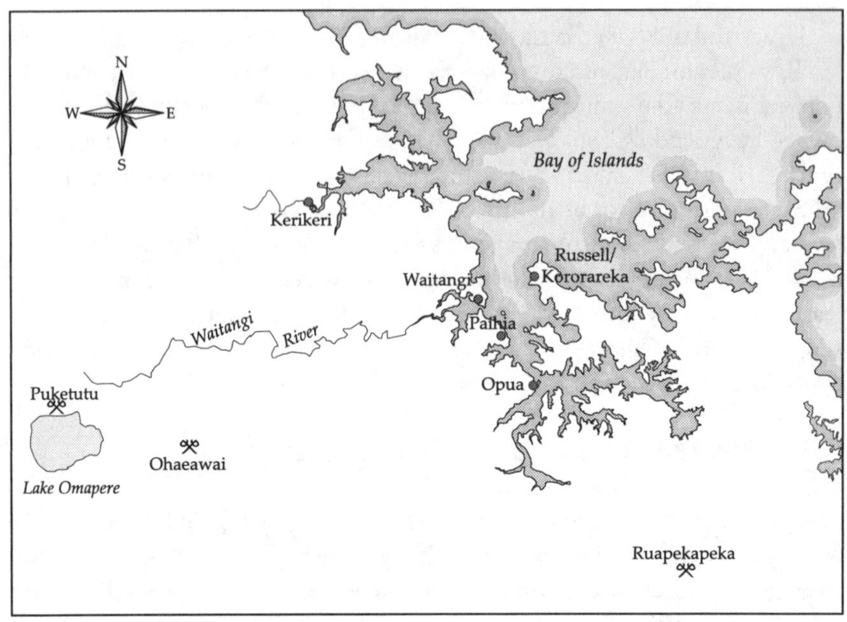

The Bay of Islands region of the North Island of New Zealand.

efforts undertaken in Van Diemen's Land following FitzRoy's request for 'immediate aid' being received in Hobart Town on 19 April. Wilmot this same day held consultation with the officer commanding the troops on the need for sending a company of soldiers, but this officer pointed out that he had received orders from General O'Connell 'not to send Troops out of this Island, under any circumstances'. Instead, Wilmot despatched the brig *Victoria* on 24 April back to Auckland 'with a large assortment of Ordnance Stores' and bullion from the Commissariat, as well as his Royal Artillery son to take command of guns sent from Sydney, accompanied by the two retired artillery sergeants who were 'Overseers over Convict Gangs, in the Convict Department'.[18]

Lieutenant Wilmot and former Sergeants Boyd and Kerr were to serve in the Bay of Islands at the expedition to assault Ohaeawai pa in June 1845. Here, Wilmot commanded twenty-five artillery militiamen manning two 6-pounder ship's guns and two 12-pounder carronades sent by Governor Gipps aboard the *British Sovereign* in May 1845. Lieutenant Wilmot also served in the expedition to take Ruapekapeka pa during December 1845 and January 1846. The ordnance used to bombard this fortification, in what was the biggest artillery barrage of the 1840s wars, included four Sydney-manufactured Coehorn mortars.[19]

One of the militia artillerymen who benefited from the experience and training offered by Lieutenant Wilmot and the former artillery sergeants was Mark Dent.

Dent served not just in the 1840s, but again in 1864 as a Melbourne-enlisted Waikato Military Settler. In 1871 he made application for the war medal for services he undertook as a non-commissioned officer in the 'Volunteer Artillery Company' in the Bay of Islands from 1845–46. He had volunteered for the artillery and was present at Ohaeawai where he was 'shot through the left thigh', as well as being present at the later expedition to assault Ruapekapeka. In Melbourne on 18 January 1864 he enlisted in the 4th Waikato Regiment (Regt. No. 112), stating his trade as veterinary surgeon, and attained the rank of sergeant.[20]

Another aspect of the support given by Van Diemen's Land was the possible use of military convicts to make up for the shortfall in troop numbers. The *Weekly Register*, on the topic of these rumours, outlined why Governor Wilmot had sought a 'return of the convicts serving in the colony who have been soldiers'. Taking into account current New Zealand affairs, Wilmot sought to ascertain what was 'the disposable military force' available in the colony, as 'soldiers transported for military offences are not felons in the proper acceptation of that word'. By establishing the 'number of that class of prisoners in the island', they 'might be employed in such a manner, as by their former habits and qualifications they may be found fitted, should it be necessary'.[21] Although the idea was not in the end taken up, it exhibits proactive contingency planning by an Australian governor to ensure his colony's internal and external defences.

Further reinforcements and other support, May 1845

In New South Wales, Gipps decided upon sending the remainder of the 58th Regiment, apart from small detachments located at Norfolk Island and Moreton Bay which could not be recalled in time. As part of the necessary military redistributions, all of the 58th troops stationed at Parramatta were recalled to Sydney, with elements of the 99th Regiment utilised to take over duties performed by the 58th.[22] In a despatch to Lord Stanley on 9 April, Gipps reported that following the departure of the reinforcements aboard the *Bee* and *Slains Castle* the available military force in New Zealand would exceed 650 men. He also indicated that there were currently only two warships, HMS *Hazard* and *North Star*, available on station in New Zealand.[23] This force enabled the first expedition to the Bay of Islands to take place, comprising some 400 imperial troops of the 58th and 96th Regiments, with a small party of forty volunteers. Commanded by Lieutenant-Colonel Hulme of the 96th, this expedition ended with the unsuccessful attack on Hone Heke's Puketutu pa near Lake Omapere in May 1845, resulting in some fifty British casualties.

In Sydney on 27 April 1845 Gipps received another despatch from FitzRoy 'pressing for all Military assistance that can be rendered', including a supply of arms and ammunition for the New Zealand Militia. Gipps authorised the military supplies, and following correspondence with General O'Connell preparations were also commenced to prepare a strong detachment of the 99th and various ordnance stores for departure.[24] On 3 May the Commissariat Office in Sydney issued a tender notice for the conveyance of 150 enlisted men, the requisite number of officers, and government stores to New Zealand. This additional force would comprise the headquarters elements of the 99th Regiment under the command of Lieutenant-Colonel Henry Despard. The vessel secured, the *British Sovereign*, took on board supplies and ordnance stores on 13 May. This included camp equipment for 150 troops and 30,000 rounds of musket ball cartridges. The large contingent of 99th Regiment troops, including a small contingent of the 96th Regiment, departed for Auckland on 18 May.[25]

The troops departing in April and May 1845 were the first from Australia for actual war service in New Zealand. Whereas all previous contingents were precautionary reinforcements, many of whom either did not disembark or else remained only a brief time, the soldiers of the 99th and 96th Regiments aboard the *British Sovereign* departed knowing the opening shots of war with the Maori had now taken place at Kororareka. The *Sydney Morning Herald* provided an account of this unique occasion, the first of many troop departures from Australia for the wars across the Tasman:

> . . . the troops . . . were drawn up in open column in the Barrack-square, when His Excellency the Commander of the Forces, accompanied by his staff, inspected them; they then marched off the ground in companies for the place of embarkation, headed by the band, playing the "British Grenadiers;" soon after . . . they proceeded on board . . . Total, 12 officers; 189 non-commissioned officers and privates: in all 201.[26]

In the field in New Zealand, Lieutenant-Colonel Despard was to hold the rank of colonel on the staff and would command all troops in the colony.

With the departure of the *British Sovereign* Gipps was able to inform Lord Stanley on 19 May that the available New Zealand force, excluding militia and the Royal Navy warships *North Star* and *Hazard*, would now comprise a total of 851 soldiers from the 96th, 58th and 99th Regiments.[27] These troop reinforcements in May made it possible to undertake a second and much larger expedition to the Bay of Islands in June 1845, but this foray ended in bloody defeat against Kawiti's fortified masterpiece of Ohaeawai, where some 114 were killed or wounded. Once the Maori inflicted this British reverse the pa was abandoned, though FitzRoy and Despard claimed a rather hollow victory in storming a now empty fortification. In late 1846 when rumours began that the 99th Regiment would be sent to India, the *Sydney Chronicle* sarcastically reminded readers of Despard's 'great fame ... by the capture of an empty pah in New Zealand'.[28]

Despite the obvious Maori skill at transforming their traditional mode of defence to the needs and impact of modern firearms and artillery, it should not be forgotten that imperial troops confronted similar obstacles in their campaigns against other enemies of the Empire. One such people were the Burmese, with whom Britain fought two wars in the 1820s and the 1850s: 'The Burmese natives are brave soldiers, and like the New Zealanders entrench themselves in stockades which it is extremely difficult to destroy.'[29]

Australian martial spirit and defence concerns

One early example of martial spirit stimulated by the New Zealand wars is evident in an offer of service by Patrick Reardon, military pensioner and Peninsula War veteran late of the 11th Regiment. Reardon wrote to the New South Wales governor on 7 April tendering his services, after hearing news of the 'attack by the natives' in New Zealand. He stated that although in his fifty-second year, he would again make his services available 'in the cause of humanity, should His Excellency be pleased to accept'.[30] Though Reardon's offer was not taken up, it was reported as well received by the governor who applauded 'his zeal in wishing to [again] serve his country'.[31]

The Bay of Islands conflict also led to calls for a 'permanent militia' in New Zealand, and later Sydney. 'Kororarika', in a letter in early April, hoped the 'recent events' would convince New Zealand's governor of the necessity of forming such a force to contribute to the colony's defences.[32] One former militia officer submitted that such sentiments ignored the legal requirements, training, arming and clothing, and other difficulties in establishing legitimate volunteer or militia forces, which in turn was responded to by 'An ex-West Indian Militia-Man'.[33] Later, during September, the possibility of an outbreak of war with the United States drew correspondence on the issue of Sydney's defences from 'Foresight'. Again this issue was of especial concern as so much of the colony's garrison was now either in, or planned for, despatch to New Zealand. '*Forewarned should be forearmed*' – with one remedy suggested here being the formation of volunteer corps.[34]

In South Australia, 'Fiat Justitia', during July, pointed out that this colony 'depends alone for her safety on a handful of British soldiers, and a few police; while even for the effective distribution of these, there is not a fortified spot in the whole of the Province'.[35] South Australia had already experienced rumours in April that all the troops would be withdrawn, no doubt the result of growing demands for more and more reinforcements for New Zealand.[36] In May 'Chevron' had reminisced on the true merits of the abortive 'Royal South Australian Volunteer Militia' in 1840, and no more so than its 'utility . . . in case of national danger'.[37] Added to such factors was the French threat in the Pacific. 'It is a disgrace that no effective local corps exist for the protection of our homes, our families, and our property' stated 'Chevron'. 'We want . . . an efficient local militia, in which every man . . . should be trained to bear arms.'[38] Such experiences during 1845 were precursors to similar concerns that arose in the various Australian colonies with the outbreak of the Crimean War in 1854 and again with later New Zealand conflicts in 1860 and 1863.

Australian settler relief efforts

The arrival of settler refugees in Sydney quickly set in train exertions for the welfare of these displaced New Zealand colonists. On the same day as the public meeting the *Sydney Morning Herald* commented that the Bishop of Australia, concerned about the great destitution amongst these refugees, had commenced efforts to 'alleviate their misfortunes'. This involved directing the clergy of several Sydney parishes to announce to their congregations that collections on the following Sunday would be for the immediate relief of the refugees.[39] On the suggestion of the Bishop, the Church of England clergy of Sydney met on 8 April to discuss a relief effort resulting in £100 being advanced to meet initial needs, which was soon despatched to New Zealand as half cash and half foodstuffs. On 12 April the *Herald* reminded its readers that all offerings and collections for the next day's services at St James', St Andrew's, St Philip's, and Trinity Churches in Sydney, as well as St Peter's, Cook's River, and St John's at Parramatta, would be devoted to settler relief.[40]

In Van Diemen's Land that same month, public efforts for settler relief appear to have been similarly taken up. The *Hobart Town Courier* acknowledged that the 'sufferings of their distressed fellow-brethren in New Zealand have scarcely become known through the colony when we find a subscription commenced on their behalf', lists for which were available at the different banks. Governor Wilmot was reported as heading the subscription list with £50, and Kerr, Bogle and Co. and Kennard, Chapman and Co., £10 each, with this latter firm remembered for its £200 in losses with the fall of Kororareka.[41] A relief committee was formed in Hobart, which in August asked the *Observer* to publish information received from the New Zealand colonial secretary on the colony's relief subscriptions, noting a draft for £80 had been presented.[42]

The turmoil in New Zealand indicated that many more settlers would soon depart for safer destinations in the Australian colonies. The *Herald* believed that increasing numbers would arrive in Sydney over the ensuing months. This publication also confirmed that in South Australia subscriptions were being raised to send for German settlers near Nelson in the South Island, who were likewise 'anxious to get away.'[43] Pastor Kavel, who administered to the German Lutherans at Klemzig and Hahndorf in South Australia, received correspondence from various German settler families numbering 100 persons in the vicinity of Nelson who were in fear of life and property, and proposed to raise a subscription to pay the passage of these people to the colony.[44] Subsequent press reports in June and September 1845 confirm the successful arrival of these German settlers from New Zealand.[45]

Restricting the trade in weapons and warlike stores

The trade in warlike stores was restricted to try and prevent the Maori accessing further arms and munitions. For many decades the cross-Tasman maritime trade had fuelled the increasing Maori desire for European weaponry. 'Justice and Mercy' wrote to Governor Gipps on 9 April 1845 via the medium of the *Sydney Morning Herald*, asserting that the New Zealand governor needed a law of equal power as that passed in Ireland 'relative to fire-arms, that the whole of the natives be disarmed; ... those who resisted, the arms and ammunition should be forcibly taken without compensation. Moreover, a heavy penalty should be laid on the whites who either sell or give arms or ammunition, and vessels liable to seizure that should take such things there.'[46]

The Maori ability to maintain such armouries, apart from the stockpiles of munitions and weapons already on hand, required supplies from European trading sources, some of which derived from Australian ports or via American whalers or other traders to New Zealand's coasts. The *Herald* reported that 'British subjects are supplying Heki with ammunition, by which they are rendered liable to punishment'.[47] Of course the fall of Kororareka in itself offered the Maori victors access to various stores and materials found throughout the settlement, including 1000 rounds of ball cartridge when the blockhouse near the flagstaff was captured. One of the speakers at the public meeting in Sydney on 5 April, Captain George Clayton, who himself had had to evacuate from Kororareka, estimated that some of the Maori had between three and four tons of ammunition at their disposal.[48]

On 9 May 1845 the American brig *Falco* left Adelaide for New Zealand carrying the United States Consul for New Zealand, Mr Williams. Apart from its important consular passenger, this vessel also carried 400 kegs of gunpowder amongst its cargo of commercial goods.[49] George Grey, then lieutenant-governor of South Australia, but soon to take up the governorship of New Zealand, was concerned by the *Falco*'s American passenger and cargo and drew attention to this ongoing arms trade.[50] American traders and officials at the Bay of Islands played a role in events, and American political intrigue was certainly a factor in the ferment associated with the outbreak of conflict.[51] Evidence of this American contribution was visible in the United States flag that fluttered at the bow of Hone Heke's war canoe, the supply of superior American percussion long rifles which outclassed the Brown Bess musket issued to the British soldier, and 'inflammatory propaganda that, in the minds of the disaffected Maoris, justified their actions'.[52]

From a personal inspection of the situation in the Bay of Islands in November, New Zealand's new governor returned to Auckland in early December 1845. There Grey attended to increasing the war effort and raising more volunteers, obtaining the necessary logistical and commissariat requirements for the field force at the Bay and implementing restrictions on the sales of arms and munitions. This arms trade had proven to be highly lucrative. Some Auckland merchants pursued these commercial ventures 'indiscriminately with few questions asked', as had merchants from Australia and elsewhere.[53] The Arms Importation Ordinance was passed on 13 December 1845, empowering the New Zealand governor to regulate by proclamation the prohibition, either throughout the colony, or within any particular district, the importation and sale of arms, gunpowder and associated warlike stores.[54] As would occur again during the 1860s, the governors and colonial authorities of the Australian colonies attempted to ensure such exports were limited according to New Zealand's standing restrictions, and these efforts remained in place into the 1850s.[55]

Upon receiving copies of this Arms Importation Ordinance in January 1846, the New South Wales authorities republished these for general public information in the colony's *Government Gazette*, repeating this action in February.[56] Gipps also ensured that New South Wales enacted its own restrictions, informing the Legislative Council on 9 October 1845 of his plans to further restrict the trade in gunpowder and warlike stores.[57] Thereafter, on 13 October the *Sydney Morning Herald* detailed the efforts that were to be undertaken:

> [N]o vessel having gunpowder or warlike stores . . . in greater quantity than may, in the opinion of the Collector or Chief Officer of Customs at the port of clearance, be required for the ordinary use and service of such vessel, shall be cleared at any port in the said colony, without license under the hand of the Governor, or the Colonial Secretary, or if in the district of Port Phillip, under the hand of the Superintendent of that district.[58]

On 16 October the Legislative Council assented to an Act to regulate for a limited time the exportation of gunpowder and warlike stores.[59]

Later in 1847 when the New South Wales's Gunpowder Exportation Act was due to expire, the governor submitted a message to the Legislative Council on the necessity of extending the provisions in order to maintain 'the tranquillity' of New Zealand. The colonial secretary also reminded members of the Legislative Council the purpose of this extension was the prevention of any exports of gunpowder or firearms which might fall 'into the hands of tribes hostile to the British Government'. After due process the Legislative Council passed the Gunpowder Exportation Act Continuation Bill on 2 June 1847, thus extending the colony's contributions to stemming this illicit cross-Tasman trade.[60]

George Grey's appointment to New Zealand

In May 1845 the British government decided to relieve Governor FitzRoy of his post. His replacement, George Grey, the lieutenant-governor in South Australia, was an individual already experienced in the Australian colonies. FitzRoy received the despatch from England on 1 October 1845 revoking his position and informing him of his replacement's arrival within weeks.[61]

On 14 October the East India Company warship *Elphinstone* arrived in South Australia bearing Grey's successor, Major Frederick Holt Robe, 87th Regiment, with the additional task of then conveying Grey to New Zealand.[62] The *Register* acknowledged the difficulty awaiting Grey, where the 'high *prestige* of the British name for martial achievements' was severely shaken by the loss of Kororareka, but 'still more so by the ill-judged, worse-conducted attacks on Heki's fastnesses, which have in every case been attended with severe and bloody defeat'.[63]

Grey also ensured the embarkation of a quantity of cash to help pay for further military expeditions, as well as munitions and other military equipment, including '350 stand of arms'.[64] He departed for Auckland on 26 October.[65] Thus New Zealand not only received a new governor, but one bearing welcome war material and funds to keep the imperial war machine operating. After initially arriving in Auckland, Grey then departed for the Bay of Islands on 22 November where he witnessed preparations being undertaken for a large military expedition to besiege Ruapekapeka pa in December 1845.

Exhibition of Maori images in Adelaide and Sydney

During June 1845, South Australians were able to glimpse impressions of the Maori people through an exhibition of watercolour paintings by artist George French Angas, entitled 'New Zealand Chiefs and South Australian Sketches'.[66] After a short viewing in Adelaide, this exhibition then departed for Sydney.[67] The portion of Angas's work on display devoted to the Maori no doubt was eagerly viewed out of the curiosity aroused by the events unfolding at the Bay of

Islands. In a lengthy assessment of Angas's artistry, the *South Australian Register* remarked that the exhibition 'excited an unusual degree of interest among the residents of Adelaide'.[68] This paper reported that Angas was not only the first artist to 'illustrate South Australia, but also the first professional artist, who has ever visited New Zealand, and wandered among the savages of those islands with this object'.[69] After arrival in Sydney on 20 July, this exhibition was again well received. Attendances exceeded 1200 visitors during July–August, including Governor and Lady Gipps, General Sir Maurice O'Connell and family, and Bishop Boulding.[70]

Continuing reinforcements and other support, 1845–46

Following the reinforcements despatched in April and May 1845, the remaining troops in New South Wales and other Australian stations were to undergo considerable redistribution. This took place to accommodate not only the troop departures already undertaken, but also in preparation for the remainder of the 58th Regiment being made available for service in New Zealand. The phased arrival of various detachments of the incoming 11th Regiment as convict ship guards was accelerated, and by December 1845 this allowed for all of the 96th Regiment detachment in Van Diemen's Land to be relieved. The arrival of the 11th also permitted a large detachment to be ordered to Norfolk Island where they relieved the 58th detachment for despatch to New Zealand. In addition, imperial authorities ordered the main body of another planned incoming regiment, the 65th, to be moved forward in March 1846.[71]

Apart from the Army preparations, the Sydney-based Royal Navy also organised itself for further service in New Zealand following the arrival from Auckland and the Bay of Islands of HMS *North Star* on 12 June 1845. This vessel carried with it Captain Robertson of HMS *Hazard*, who had been badly wounded during the defence of Kororareka on 11 March.[72] The arrival of the *North Star* provided an important opportunity for obtaining news on the current state of New Zealand affairs: 'we learn that an attempt to storm Heki's [Puketutu] pah . . . failed, adding to the reputation of Heki as a warrior . . . As soon as the forces retreated, Heki fell back further into the interior to another pah . . . said to be stronger than the one he had left.'[73] At Puketutu the *North Star* had lost one marine and one seaman killed, and one officer, three marines, and three seamen wounded from amongst its personnel who were serving ashore with the troops of the 58th and 96th Regiments and a contingent of seamen and marines from HMS *Hazard*.[74] As part of HMS *North Star*'s preparations for returning to New Zealand, additional crew were recruited while in harbour at Farm Cove, before departing on 17 July.[75]

As part of the concentration of the remaining elements of the 58th Regiment, the vessel *Ann* arrived in Sydney from Hobart Town on 13 June. On board were Lieutenant-Colonel Wynyard, four other officers, 196 rank and file and families of the 58th Regiment, as well as fifty-eight men of the 99th Regiment.[76] In late July a small detachment consisting of one subaltern and twenty-one soldiers of the 99th Regiment was ordered to march for Bathurst to relieve the 58th stationed there. At the same time, another detachment of the 99th, comprising one officer and fifty-two soldiers, was ordered to relieve the detachment of the 58th stationed at Moreton Bay.[77]

At the departure of the 58th Regiment from Bathurst, local residents held a public meeting on 8 August to farewell its commanding officer, Lieutenant G.H. Page, during which he was presented with an address signed by many residents.[78] Elements of the 58th at Port Macquarie were also recalled to Sydney, with Lieutenant Hay and twenty-five soldiers (and families) arriving aboard the *Maitland* on 12 August. Shortly after, on 14 August, the *Sovereign* arrived from Moreton Bay bringing Lieutenant Cooper and thirty-five soldiers (and families) of the 58th.[79] One final small contingent of the 58th made up of twelve soldiers and families arrived from Moreton Bay aboard the *Sovereign* on 31 August. This marked the final arrangements for gathering together the outlying detachments of the 58th in preparation for New Zealand.[80]

On 4 August Gipps informed Lord Stanley of the latest intelligence and despatches received from New Zealand: 'the "Pah," [of Ohaeawai] . . . had at . . . last, fallen into possession of the British Force under Colonel Despard, though not until ten days after the Troops had suffered a severe repulse, in which 39 men were killed, and between 60 and 70 wounded'. Governor FitzRoy took this opportunity again to request military assistance urgently, and once more Gipps and General O'Connell confirmed that under the circumstances more troops were warranted. As a result, an additional reinforcement of 200 soldiers of the 58th Regiment commanded by Lieutenant-Colonel Wynyard would be sent.[81]

Manufacture of Coehorn mortars in Sydney

A valuable addition to the limited artillery available in New Zealand in 1845–46 was the Sydney manufacture of a small quantity of Coehorn mortars – the beginnings of an Australian arms industry. These variant mortars were designed by Sydney resident Captain Gother Kerr Mann, and then cast at the foundry and engineering works of P.N. Russell & Company. One history of the Royal Artillery noted how the 'artillery matérial used in New Zealand was the most extraordinary mixture that was probably ever taken into the field'.[82] This included the 5½-inch Sydney-manufactured mortars which were only half the length of the standard service pattern.[83] The mortar itself was cast in brass and fitted to a separate cast-iron bed fixed to a wooden plank base. Because these particular types were much lighter than official designs and could be easily disassembled, this made them much more portable – a considerable benefit for the troops who had to manhandle such heavy weapons and stores through the difficult terrain around the Bay of Islands.

Captain Mann was born in England in 1809, his father a general in the Royal Engineers. He saw military service in the Bombay Horse Artillery of the East India Company, from which he arrived in Sydney on sick leave in 1836. While residing in Sydney he was allowed to retire from the Company's army in 1838.[84] In Sydney he became a civil engineer and was employed by the commanding Royal Engineer as a draughtsman in 1844. In this capacity he designed the proposed dry dock at Cockatoo Island, which was subsequently constructed under his supervision, and where he became engineer-in-charge.[85]

Because of his position, Mann had access to the government stores, where in May 1845 he noticed a quantity of 5½-inch shells: 'He at once adopted the idea of constructing a mortar for the purpose of throwing these shells into the enemy's camp.'[86] The first finished mortar was test-fired in the Sydney Domain on 8 September 1845, where Mann, having trained a party of soldiers from the 99th Regiment for the purpose, oversaw the trials. The *Sydney Morning Herald* reported that the 'practice was very good, . . . The mortar . . . is only about a foot long, was manufactured by Mr. Russell . . . It only weighs ninety pounds.'[87] Believed to be six in number, these mortars were made ready and presumed consigned aboard the *British Sovereign* departing on 22 September. They were first utilised in action in the attack on Ruapekapeka in both December 1845 and

British troops watching a Maori 'war dance' in the Bay of Islands. Note the kneeling soldier next to a Coehorn mortar, from the *Illustrated London News*, 16 January 1847.

January 1846, where the Maori referred to them as 'pot-guns' because of their shape and the shortness of the barrel.[88]

Departure of remaining elements of the 58th Regiment

In August 1845 the *British Sovereign* was chosen to convey the remaining 58th Regiment troops as soon as it arrived back in Sydney from the Bay of Islands. As part of the preparations, large quantities of military stores were also organised by the Commissariat Office for immediate shipment.[89] The *British Sovereign* arrived back on 27 August and immediately underwent some necessary repairs. After completion the vessel was loaded with a large quantity of ordnance stores, 'including howitzers, field pieces, and ammunition', on 10 September.[90] On 19 September 220 officers and men of the 58th Regiment embarked, and departed on 22 September. These reinforcements, supplies and artillery were a valuable addition to the force being assembled for the third and final expedition to the Bay of Islands.[91]

Military casualties in Sydney

During 1845–46 the arrival of military casualties in Sydney brought home the human cost of the conflict across the Tasman. Such convalescing soldiers imparted a very public face to the press accounts of the fighting and losses sustained at Puketutu and Ohaeawai. One of these individuals, Joseph G. Sims, a 58th Regiment colour sergeant, was invalided on 1 July 1845 after suffering a severe bullet wound to the knee at Ohaeawai. Sims thereafter became a settler in South Australia, before moving to Queensland in 1869 where he continued pastoral and other business pursuits until his death at Warwick in May 1897.[92]

One group of wounded troops arrived aboard the *Louisa Campbell* on 27 September 1845. This vessel returned to Sydney with Major Robertson of the 99th Regiment, Dr Stewart, 18th Regiment, and 'eight invalids' of the 99th Regiment.[93] Similarly, HMS *Castor* returned to Sydney from the Bay of Islands on 10 June 1846, and apart from a detachment of returning officers and men of the 58th Regiment, conveyed thirty invalid soldiers and twenty invalid seamen.[94] A military reminiscence in 1903 recalled that during the 1840s many of the wounded soldiers from New Zealand were brought back to the military barracks in George Street, Sydney, where their plight was no doubt in the public spotlight.[95]

It should also be remembered that some soldiers, although they did not depart for service across the Tasman, nonetheless played important support roles from within the Australian colonies. One such soldier was Sergeant William Millington of the 99th Regiment, who served as a hospital attendant in the Sydney military hospital during 1844–46. Here he would have assisted in the care of wounded or sick comrades transported back from New Zealand for treatment and recovery. Millington would later settle in Sydney after taking his discharge as an out-pensioner in March 1847.[96]

Continuing troop redistributions and other support, 1845–46

Apart from the main contingents of troops sent in April, May and September 1845, other small bodies of troops continued to be funnelled to New Zealand. In October a small detachment of the 99th Regiment, comprising twenty-four officers and men, embarked for the Bay of Islands aboard the *Regia*. After taking on these troops the vessel was also loaded with a cargo of gunpowder, and carried a consignment of bullocks and horses desperately needed to provide transport to assist in the movement of stores and artillery at the Bay of Islands. All arrived in time to take part in the major expedition that besieged Ruapekapeka, though Colonel Despard was to lament that only three horses and two of the bullocks survived the voyage from Sydney.[97]

The Commissariat in Van Diemen's Land advertised in October 1845 for vessels to convey a large detachment of the incoming 11th Regiment from Launceston to Norfolk Island. In turn such transports would then carry 220 officers and men of the 58th Regiment from Norfolk Island to New Zealand. This military transport service also involved redistributing detachments of the 99th Regiment in New Zealand back to Sydney, and elements of the 96th Regiment to Launceston. The *Louisa* and the *Waterlily* were selected for this task. General O'Connell wrote in early October that once the 58th detachment from Norfolk Island arrived, the whole of this regiment would now be available in New Zealand. The entire 58th Regiment, plus the flank companies of the 99th Regiment and the detachment of the 96th Regiment, would then give a total available force of some 1100 men.[98]

Orders from England had been received in Sydney in November 1845 to detach to New Zealand six companies belonging to the 58th, 96th and 99th Regiments. Six companies of the 11th Regiment, shortly expected to arrive in New South Wales, were also ordered across the Tasman. But the receipt of such orders did not take into account the ensuing events in New Zealand, nor the departure of troops already carried out during September 1845.[99] Though companies of the 11th never actually departed for New Zealand service, small numbers of this regiment's personnel or officers did in fact journey to the colony.

The first arrival of a Royal Artillery unit in Australia en route for New Zealand took place in December 1845 when a detachment commanded by Captain W. Henderson arrived at Hobart Town.[100] This detachment was later forwarded to

New Zealand from Sydney aboard HMS *Driver* on 12 January 1846. The *Driver* arrived unexpectedly in Sydney from Hong Kong on 7 January 'to obtain a supply of fuel and provisions, preparatory to proceeding to New Zealand'. Apart from this vessel's initial resupply needs, tenders were also advertised for conveying 500 tons of coal to Auckland for use while serving in New Zealand waters. This Royal Artillery detachment also took with them two travelling gun carriages for 24-pounders which were manufactured in Sydney.[101]

During January another detachment of the 99th Regiment was also preparing for departure from Sydney. As part of this process, Major Edward Last, who commanded this regiment's detachment and the stockades at Newcastle, was recalled to Sydney.[102] Last's departure from Newcastle in turn created considerable local reaction, even before the public turnout to see him depart. The Manchester Unity presented him with an address, and a deputation from the Newcastle Mechanics' Institute waited upon him in the military barracks, where another address was read.[103] The *Lloyds* was used to carry these troops as well as twenty-four cattle for use by the Commissariat. The troops, totalling four officers and 105 soldiers of the 99th Regiment, plus 'six government men' charged with caring for the consignment of cattle, departed on 13 January.[104]

His strength bolstered by all the soldiers and sailors that had now been despatched to New Zealand, Governor Grey was able to field a force of some 1700 troops, commanded by Colonel Despard, for the third and largest expeditionary force to the Bay of Islands.[105] This expedition ended with the massive artillery assault on Ruapekapeka during January 1846 and the pa's capture when it was virtually empty of Maori defenders, in circumstances that are still unclear and debated. Nonetheless, after Ruapekapeka, peace was established in the Bay of Islands, albeit largely a peace on Maori terms with no penalties and no loss of land inflicted by the government. However, what this northern peace did allow Grey to do in February 1846 was redeploy 800 troops to Wellington to combat the mounting tensions being experienced in this southern region.

Wellington–Hutt Valley conflict, and further calls for reinforcements, 1846–47

The end of the war in the north in early 1846 now afforded Governor Grey the opportunity to utilise a large portion of the Australian-derived military force and war material to finally deal with the situation in the south. Fighting in the Wellington–Hutt Valley region of the North Island broke out in March 1846 and continued sporadically until August. While these outbreaks were complicated conflicts, the actual fighting involved was very small-scale.

The tension over disputed land purchases had been running high in Wellington

Images of Te Rangihaeata (left) and Te Rauparaha (right), from the *Illustrated London News*, 29 June 1844.

since 1842. The Ngati Rangitahi, with tribal connections in Wanganui, were particularly reluctant to part with their cultivations on disputed land in the Hutt Valley which the settlers believed they had purchased. Ngati Rangitahi were backed by their Wanganui relatives led by Topine Te Mamaku and a section of the Ngati Toa led by Te Rangihaeata. While both these men had displayed great ability and mana over the preceding years, their respective forces probably never exceeded 200 warriors, despite the colonial press ominously warning that the number involved could be as high as 900.[106]

Grey implemented a rapid increase in the military presence in the region, exploiting in the process tenuous tribal interrelations in order to weaken the hold of the Ngati Toa. At the same time, Te Rangihaeata and his Wanganui ally, Te Mamaku, were able to carry out some successful, though limited, raiding in the disputed Hutt Valley area. Although Grey and the British forces were never wholly successful militarily in this region, they were able to enjoy the nominal support or neutrality of many fellow tribesmen and allies of the insurgents. These included Te Rauparaha, as well as those who resented Te Mamaku and Te Rangihaeata and were willing to take up arms against the 'rebels'.

A surprise Maori attack at Boulcott's Farm on 16 May 1846 appeared to herald the commencement of a fresh military threat. As a result, Grey shortly after requested from General O'Connell in Sydney as many troops as could be spared to be sent directly to Wellington.[107] After receiving news of the events unfolding in the Hutt Valley, Governor Gipps commented to Lord Stanley that the 'intelligence from New Zealand . . . is distressing'.[108] Once again the situation seemed to warrant more military resources and Australian authorities acceded to New Zealand's request. Accordingly, in Sydney 183 officers and men of the 65th and 58th Regiments embarked on board the *Levant*, departing for Port Nicholson on 9 July, and arriving thirteen days later.[109]

In respect to the Royal Navy, HMS *Castor* had recently returned to Sydney from Auckland and the Bay of Islands on 10 June to 'victual and refit'. While at harbour at Farm Cove, the *Castor* recruited additional personnel before departing for Auckland again on 17 July.[110] Nearby Newcastle was also the main locale from which the Royal Navy obtained the quantities of coal necessary to keep the modern steam-driven warship HMS *Driver* operating in New Zealand waters.[111] In January 1846 this vessel was reported as requiring 500 tons of coal for its use, with the Sydney Commissariat Office accordingly advertising tenders for the supply of coal to be delivered to Auckland.[112] And although New Zealand was obtaining large quantities of 'warlike stores' direct from England to assist with the military operations, the Australian colonies nonetheless provided other much-needed and easily accessible logistical and commissariat material throughout 1845 and 1846.[113]

Despite the fact that Grey was unable to achieve a decisive military victory in the south, by August 1846 his European forces and Maori allies were able to force Te Rangihaeata north of Waikanae.[114] The British were also able to score one more coup in the region when they seized the neutral chief Te Rauparaha, and others, in an early-morning surprise raid on his pa on 23 July 1846. Although Grey argued that Te Rauparaha's seizure was necessary because he allegedly was secretly supporting Te Rangihaeata, historians have more recently suggested another possible motive. Te Rauparaha was accessible to capture, whereas Te Rangihaeata was still proving himself a master of elusiveness, and the 'arrest of so important a Maori leader was a bold assertion of government power'. But this move was also to give 'the British a reputation for duplicity which seriously hampered the resolution of subsequent disputes'.[115] Governor Grey compounded matters further with the mistreatment of other Maori prisoners captured in the Hutt Valley.[116]

Although Grey's policy of imposing British authority by military methods was highly popular with settlers, missionaries and officials, it was achieved at the cost of brushing aside 'moral and legal principles'. He had declared martial law, seized Te Rauparaha and held him without trial, transported five Maori to Van Diemen's Land after military court martial, and had a Wanganui chief executed as an example rather than for personal guilt of capital crimes.[117]

Maori political prisoners to Van Diemen's Land

On 1 August 1846, scouts of the allied Ngati Awa captured the minor Upper Wanganui chief Te Wareaitu. His brother, Te Rangiatea, was also taken, probably because he was too sick to take part in the flight following Te Wareaitu's capture.[118] On 13 August the Ngati Awa Maori allies captured further prisoners at Pari Pari, near Porirua – this time eight half-starved supporters of Rangihaeata who had come down from the hills in search of food.[119] Court-martial proceedings against these Maori captives were commenced at Paremata on 14 and 15 September 1846.[120]

On 14 September Te Rangiatea was tried and found guilty of being found in possession of a spear, and of helping, though not of having taking part in, a raid on Boulcott's Farm on 16 May. Because of apparent 'insanity' he avoided the death penalty and was instead sentenced to imprisonment for life, though died from heart disease in a Wellington hospital later in 1846.[121] On 15 September Te Wareaitu was also tried and found guilty of being taken in open rebellion, and also of aiding but not of having taken part in the skirmish on 16 May. He was sentenced to death by hanging, which was carried out two days later.[122] In later years, a contemporary of Governor Grey criticised the handling of this case, noting that Te Wareaitu 'was tried with all the forms of military law and with all the substance of injustice'.[123]

Major Last of the 99th, under whose authority the proceedings of the courts martial were being carried out, began to have reservations about the wisdom of the proceedings and whether further executions would serve any purpose as a display of the government's powers.[124] Deciding that the one execution would suffice, he sent the remaining eight prisoners to Wellington to be tried by civil authorities. In Wellington, civil jurisdiction was refused, and the recently arrived new senior military officer, Lieutenant-Colonel McCleverty, 99th Regiment, ordered Major Last to convene a fresh court to try the prisoners. One of the remaining prisoners, Te Korohunga, was pardoned on account of being only a boy, and was returned to Wanganui.[125]

On 12 October the court martial was finally reconvened and 'proceeded to its pre-ordained conclusion'.[126] That same day the seven remaining Maori were found guilty of 'having on or about the 14 August 1846 taken arms in open rebellion against the Queen's Sovereign Authority and Government of New Zealand'. The sentence of the court was that these seven were to be transported as felons for the term of their natural lives.[127] Two of the convicted, Matiu Tikiaki and Topi, never left New Zealand, as Grey took the extraordinary step of keeping them in Auckland, allegedly in order to provide testimony towards the case (which never eventuated) against Te Rauparaha.[128]

It was this case, the trial and subsequent execution of Te Wareaitu, which galvanised significant public concern and attention in Van Diemen's Land. The colonial press followed events cautiously but was extremely critical regarding the injustice of the actions. Radical circles in Hobart, no doubt similar to Sydney, fuelled these outspoken viewpoints. Yet, despite the considerable attention of the public and press to this affair, there was little that appears as an anti-war position, apart from voices of concern about Maori welfare. Perhaps a more radical stance existed in Van Diemen's Land society relating to the convict system and its role in the colony, and the broader impact of 'political' prisoners of many races and creeds. This in turn may have radicalised public and press attitudes. Van Diemen's Land society also had decades of experience with Maori as shipboard travellers prior to these 1846 events, as well as long-term trade links with New Zealand. The colony's press certainly exhibited clear and abiding concerns about Maori and New Zealand affairs throughout the 1830s and 1840s.

An initial lengthy report in the *Hobart Town Courier* was carried under the caption: 'Atrocious Murder!!! Execution of one of the Rebels'.[129] This report noted with concern that although all was quiet at present, 'it is possible that a succession of tragedies similar to that described have been enacted'.[130] Later, the same newspaper was to point out that even the press in New Zealand was finally speaking out against the execution of Te Wareaitu.[131] Other Van Diemen's Land papers such as the *Colonial Times* took up this case as well, issuing a detailed editorial commentary not only on the execution, but also Grey's conduct in the matter: 'It is impossible to characterise in terms sufficiently expressive of abhorrence the detestable crime of Governor Grey . . . in the murder of the gallant New Zealand chief Wareaitu.'[132] Weeks later, when the five Maori convicts arrived in Hobart Town, the *Colonial Times* maintained its incensed stance, seeing their presence simply as further evidence of Grey's despicable conduct.[133]

Van Diemen's Land convict records provide descriptions and information on these Maori prisoners, all of whom were recorded as tried and convicted for life for rebellion. They arrived in Hobart Town aboard HMS *Castor* on 16 November 1846: Prisoners No. 765 *Te Waretiti*; No. 766 *Hohepa Te Umuroa*; No. 767 *Te Kumete*; No. 768 *Matiuma*; and No. 769 *Te Rahui.*[134] The *Hobart Town Courier* took up the case of these five Maori arrivals, expressing the view that while 'we have nothing to say of the dead' (in reference to the execution of Te Wareaitu), 'we have much to plead for the living'.[135] This lengthy editorial went on to outline great concern over the treatment of the Maori convicts, and the original intention to send them to Port Arthur.[136] Public concerns in Van Diemen's Land relating to the accommodation of the Maori prisoners were finally allayed when it was decided to despatch them to Maria Island to better ensure their isolation from the 'worst influences' of the mainstream convict population, and where they were also placed under the charge of an overseer with New Zealand experience. In this manner these Maori prisoners served their time until early 1848 when pardons arrived from England, allowing Van Diemen's Land authorities to ensure their repatriation to New Zealand in March, thereby bringing to a close a unique episode in Australian convict history.[137]

British government decision to remove troops for New Zealand

The main body of the incoming 65th Regiment finally arrived in Sydney aboard the *Java* on 14 October 1846, having left London six months earlier. These troops did not disembark at Sydney but proceeded on to New Zealand, where this vessel would later return with elements of the 99th and 58th Regiments.[138] The *Sydney Morning Herald* reported shortly after on the 'Military Changes and Movements' that would now take place, with the 65th detachment, which had for some time been in Sydney, proceeding to New Zealand with the main body of the regiment just arrived. The Sydney detachment of the 65th comprised 126 officers and men, while the main body, which arrived aboard the *Java*, consisted of 620 officers and men.[139] The *Java* subsequently departed Sydney for New Zealand on 6 November where this substantial body of troops augmented that colony's available military force.[140]

Many of the 99th, 96th and 58th Regiment elements serving in New Zealand during 1845–46 were not sent from the Australian colonies with the intention of ending up as part of that colony's permanent force. They were regarded merely as reinforcements to undertake necessary short-term military operations or defences. Once such operations were complete or the immediate threat of further conflict appeared over, some of these troops returned to their former Australian garrisons. For instance, the headquarters and a large party of the 58th Regiment returned to Sydney aboard the *Java* in December 1846, though only to depart once more for New Zealand shores months later.[141]

In late March 1847 the British government directed a large proportion of the imperial garrison stationed in New South Wales to New Zealand. Interestingly, the *Sydney Morning Herald* here concluded: 'we think we shall be able to show that there ought always to be a considerable force within reach of Sydney; and that from Sydney, as a central depôt, a force could be sent to any part of the Australasian colonies or New Zealand at the shortest notice – as ships can at any time be obtained'.[142] This notion of New South Wales as the 'central depôt' had in fact been the situation since 1840, but became especially evident during the mounting tensions and subsequent outbreak of conflict over 1844–45.

Several days following this initial report on troop reductions it was rumoured the 58th Regiment was again to be sent to New Zealand.[143] The *Herald* in editorials during April decried the thought of troop reductions for the sake of New Zealand, and on 16 April boldly headlined: 'New South Wales Sacrificed To New Zealand'.[144] New South Wales's public enthusiasm for further bolstering of New Zealand defences was now in retreat. Despite this vocal opposition to such moves, orders from England were received in Sydney confirming the increase in the military force for New Zealand. In correspondence from Earl Grey, dated 24 November 1846, the situation regarding the expected distribution of troops in Australasia was clearly set out.[145]

Sir Charles FitzRoy (who replaced Gipps) confirmed to Earl Grey on 30 April 1847 that after consultation with Lieutenant-General O'Connell the whole of the 58th Regiment would be sent as soon as transport was procured.[146] On 20 May the Sydney Commissariat Office advertised for tenders to convey troops, families, stores and other military equipment to New Zealand.[147] During June the last of the outlying detachments of the 58th were all returned to Sydney in preparation, and on 1 July the *Pestonjee Bomanjee* departed with eight officers and 174 other ranks of the 58th.[148]

Diminished troop numbers in New South Wales had an immediate adverse effect on the staffing and efficiency of the colony's Mounted Police force. This colonial frontier force relied heavily for its personnel on regular officers or enlisted rank soldiers seconded from the imperial regiments in garrison. Reduction in funds made available for the force thereafter saw its numbers curtailed and then its discontinuance altogether by the end of 1850.[149] Similarly, the withdrawal of this portion of the colony's troops, compounded by the disbandment of the Border Police, necessitated the decision to raise a troop of Native Police for the colony's Middle District in 1848.[150] In other locations the departure of imperial troop detachments, which in certain locations became a permanent measure, necessitated the obvious need for a greater police presence.[151]

Despite these orders from England, the removal of the troops and the colony's available 'protective force' was still an issue of some debate in the New South Wales Legislative Council, apart from continuing to attract significant editorial comment during late May.[152] News received from New Zealand in June, though, acted to dispel opposition to troop departures, as a 'large portion of the natives in the southern districts appear to be up in arms . . . and the unfortunate settlers of Manawatu and Wanganui have been compelled to desert their homes and proceed to . . . Wellington. Previous arrivals had given us information of the murder of the family of a settler named Gilfallen.'[153] In support of the view that more troops should be sent, the *Sydney Morning Herald* republished the opinion expressed in the *Wellington Independent* (on 19 May), part of an in-depth account of developments taking place at Wanganui and Manawatu. Does this news not convince our 'Sydney contemporaries' that 'a powerful force must be maintained for years to come in these islands? British supremacy has yet to be asserted, and nothing can save the several settlements, except vigorous and decided measures.'[154] The next day the *Herald* conceded that the news now arriving from New Zealand 'should serve to allay the indignation of the people of this colony at the removal of our troops'.[155]

Wanganui conflict, and renewed calls for military assistance, 1847

During March–April 1847 the New Zealand government's military resources were concentrated mainly at Wellington (655 troops), while only 185 were stationed at Wanganui. However, tensions around Wanganui and surrounding districts were such that Governor Grey sent HMS *Racehorse* to Sydney with messages for General O'Connell not to delay the despatch of reinforcements earlier requested for use in the military occupation of the Manawatu.[156] The Wanganui garrison was also under orders by Grey not to undertake any offensive actions until the reinforcements from Sydney arrived.[157]

This situation deteriorated on 18 April 1847 following the attack on the Gilfallen settler family. As soon as news of these murders reached Auckland, Grey proceeded to Wanganui with a company of the 65th Regiment, before proceeding on to Wellington. He then returned to Wanganui with 100 further soldiers of this regiment.[158] By June it was reported that after the arrival of Grey at Wanganui, 'the rebel natives, after a few skirmishes, retired into the interior'.[159] Some of the final shots of New Zealand's 1840s conflict took place on 19 July in what became known as the Battle of St John's Wood – an indecisive engagement outside the township of Wanganui. The final Maori appearance in force outside

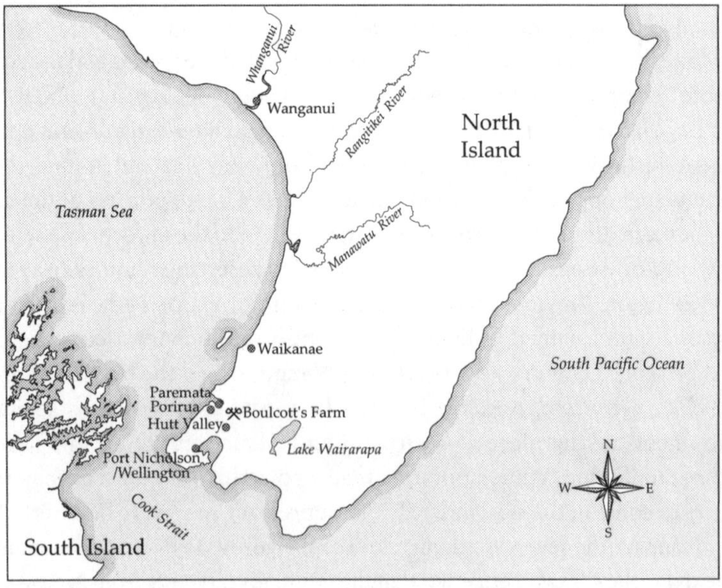

The southern region of the North Island of New Zealand, including the Hutt Valley, Wellington (Port Nicholson) and Cook Strait.

of Wanganui's defences occurred shortly after, on 23 July, when small parties attempted to skirmish forward and were met with a couple of rounds of artillery fire. After this the Maori retired, thus ending the blockade of Wanganui and any further offensive actions by either side.[160]

By early August 1847 the threats in the environs around Wanganui had dissipated to such a degree that the detachment of the 99th Regiment retained at Wellington by Grey could now be returned to Sydney.[161] Other elements of both the 99th and 96th Regiments similarly returned to Australia by late 1847.[162] By comparison, the 58th Regiment was to remain in lengthy garrison in New Zealand until 1858,[163] and the 65th Regiment served long enough to take part in conflicts during the 1860s, before departing for England in late 1865.[164]

Opposition and other attitudes to the war in New Zealand

Although one could not say that an anti-war movement as such developed in the 1840s, there were certainly sympathetic stirrings towards the Maori. During this time several people penned some remarkably romanticised accounts of the struggle of Maori leaders like Hone Heke. These literary offerings added to the already visible public discussions indicating concerns for what was occurring in New Zealand, or support for the Maori cause evident in letters to the editor, such as those printed during 1845. One such contributor was Henry Halloran, a poet and civil servant. In New South Wales he became a close friend and correspondent of Henry Parkes, was highly regarded and accepted in Sydney's literary circles, and from the 1840s had many of his verses published in magazines and newspapers.[165]

One study of Charles Harpur (the first native-born Australian poet) noted that he and Halloran each had strong feelings towards New Zealand's war.[166] Halloran expressed his idealised musings on the struggle under way in the Bay of Islands in *Three Sonnets About New Zealand Matters*, published in September 1845.[167] Here he compared Heke to 'Arminius and Cassivelaunus and Caractacus, who also fought against invaders'.[168] As Halloran was a civil servant his verses were published under a pseudonym. Harpur, though, no doubt knew who the author was and was spurred to create his own verse in praise of Heke in which he 'compared the Maori leader to William Tell and William Wallace ... and Sparta's three hundred', though this poem was not published until 1847.[169] Throughout his life Harpur wrote numerous verses and critiques, with political contributions on such diverse issues as republicanism, anti-transportation, self-government and adult franchise. He was also the author of the poem 'A Wail From The Bush', a reminder of the Myall Creek Massacre of Aborigines in New South Wales in 1838,[170] and associated with many of the figures comprising Sydney's literary circles.[171] A version of his 1847 verse appeared in a later compilation of work produced by his widow.[172] Harpur took a serious attitude to moral and political questions, believing that war had to be justifiable. He bitterly opposed the 1840s war in New Zealand, and that in the Crimea in the 1850s, but would later write in support of the Italians fighting for independence against the Austrians.[173]

Critiques of military imperialism were most often discernible amongst radical intellectual and literary circles in places such as Sydney. The struggles of the Maori, in turn, offered these radical or republican elements – especially those with sympathies towards the nationalistic struggles of the Irish or Scots – easy literary analogies praising like-minded struggles for liberation and freedom from imperial power or oppression. Although not strictly a peace movement, such radical elements within colonial society tendered alternative viewpoints to the more mainstream attitudes expressed as a result of the wars against the Maori during 1845–47.

Australian postscript to the 1840s conflict

Though these wars came to an end in 1847, the service and sacrifice of the imperial troops were on occasion remembered in the Australian colonies, such as in the biographical reminiscence series entitled 'War Service Records' in Tasmania's *Britannia and Trades' Advocate* during late 1848. Though dealing with broader military experience generally, such items nonetheless reminded readers of the warfare across the Tasman or the other campaigns and battles in which the Empire had been involved. These stories featured a variety of serving (or former) imperial officers from various line regiments as well as the Royal Engineers, Royal Marines and Royal Navy. Officers depicted with New Zealand service included Colonel Despard, 99th Regiment, and Lieutenant-Colonel Hulme, 96th Regiment – both regiments that served out their final Australian garrison years in Tasmania.[174]

New Zealand's wars were also to be quickly recalled on the occasions of so-called victories. The first instance of celebrations on the anniversary of the capture of Ruapekapeka took place in 1847 when Army and Navy officers stationed in Wellington, New Zealand, celebrated with a dinner at Barrett's Hotel.[175] A Tasmanian example took place in 1852 on the anniversary of the pa's capture. The *Tasmanian Colonist* reported that this commemorative dinner event was organised by the enlisted men of the 99th Regiment, and reminded its readership that twenty-two privates, two officers, and one sergeant of that regiment lost their lives during this recent conflict across the Tasman. It also described how the event included several of the men appearing 'in the New Zealand costume, paint, blankets, and all, and displayed a New Zealand corroboree in language which we did not understand'.[176]

Such occasions, though, appear to have been maintained only while such regiments remained in Australian garrisons. The departure of the 99th in 1856 took with it the traditions and anniversaries of the regiment to its next place of garrison. Although, of course, discharged or retired officers and men who remained in the Australian colonies no doubt took opportunities to occasionally gather and remember their service and fallen comrades. In the Tasmanian context this is very likely. H.B. Stoney, a captain in the 99th Regiment, discussed his intention of forming a military settlement in the colony to cater for 'some three or four hundred soldiers of the 99th Regiment quartered in Tasmania, who were entitled to their discharge' in his 1856 book, *A Residence in Tasmania*. Although this scheme did not eventuate, it does confirm that hundreds of former 99th personnel became settlers, amongst whom would have been proud veterans of the New Zealand wars.[177]

In its later years of Australian service, the 99th Regiment had moved from Sydney to Hobart in 1848, and it was here that its personnel also undertook to commemorate the losses amongst the officers and enlisted men of the regiment during 1845–46. As a result, a unique 12.2-metre freestone pillar memorial was completed in 1850 at the Anglesea Barracks in Hobart. The 99th Regiment Memorial is not only Australia's first ever war memorial, but is the only one of its kind ever contemporaneously erected in the Australian colonies to mark the New Zealand wars.[178] The departure of regiments such as the 99th for England in 1856, and the 96th for India in early 1849, allowed memories to fade, though not altogether to be forgotten. The ongoing legacy of the 99th Regiment's memorial at Hobart's Anglesea Barracks ensures that a glimmer of regimental memory is retained as part of this Australian city's heritage landscape.[179]

Chapter Two

CALLED UPON ONCE MORE

THE PERIOD 1848 TO 1860 is marked by significant economic co-operation between Maori and European settlers, although at the same time, growing friction over sovereignty and land was developing between the races in New Zealand. During the 1850s, Maori reluctance to sell land to quench the demand of ever-increasing settler arrivals intensified throughout the North Island. New Zealand's settler population (excluding military personnel) in 1847 was estimated to be almost 14,500; by 1851 this figure was almost 27,000. But by 1858 settler numbers had reached nearly 59,500, for the first time eclipsing the Maori, who were then estimated to be just over 56,000. By 1861 the colony's settler numbers almost totalled 98,000, whereas Maori numbers had declined to just over 55,000.[1]

Part of this resistance to land selling came about through the emergence of the Maori confederation that became known as the King Movement. Centred on the Waikato, though not restricted to that region in its support, in 1858 this movement elected the first Maori king. Strong Maori opposition to land selling also existed outside of the King Movement, but the stage was set for a showdown between settler and imperial interests versus Maori autonomy and resistance to further land sales. In 1860 the sale of the Waitara Block – 600 acres of prime Taranaki land – would be the spark to ignite this contest to determine European or Maori ascendancy.

The year 1860 also marked the resumption of significant Australian military involvement. Although much has been written on the wars, most has not only tended to overlook the scale of Australia's contribution but also its importance in determining a final outcome in favour of New Zealand's Pakeha settlers. This does not mean that Maori resistance, both aggressive and passive, did not continue beyond the 1860s, but that the European domination of much Maori territory was confirmed by the events of this decade. It was these events, supported by majority public sentiment in the Australian colonies, as well as by both the colonial and imperial authorities, which aided in the outcome. As the *Sydney Morning Herald* extolled in 1860:

> We are defending ourselves in consolidating the possession of New Zealand. The British power there is a bulwark to our own safety. . . . We are not only Colonists: we are more, we are Britons. Our interest is more than the defence of the city in which we live. We belong to a glorious empire . . . To defend its outposts is to protect its heart.[2]

In other words, the war in New Zealand was not a war in isolation – it was a war in which Australia would be a major player in events about to unfold.

The co-operation between Australia's imperial military and civil representatives, such as governors and colonial legislatures, should not be underestimated in this process either. The willingness of Australian colonial governments to interact with both the imperial authorities and the government of New Zealand during the 1860s, although sometimes grudging, and with an eye to self-interest, suggests that a nascent form of Australian foreign policy was emerging. These events occurred in a period of high imperial patriotism, not independent nationalism. Australasian support or involvement in the Sudan (1885), the Anglo-Boer War (1899–1902), China (1900–01), World War I and arguably even World War II (especially during 1939–40) was due to imperial interests and allegiance to Britain as the perceived motherland of Australasia. Australia's involvement in the New Zealand wars must be similarly incorporated into this pattern.

Restrictions on warlike stores

One of the initial ways in which the Australian colonies combined to aid New Zealand was once more with regulations prohibiting the export of warlike stores. During 1860–61 the Australian colonies ensured the continuation of restrictions on the export of arms or other potential warlike stores that might find their way into Maori hands.[3] With the outbreak of conflict in Taranaki, the issue of warlike stores was once again in the public spotlight.

In early April 1860 both houses of the New South Wales legislature discussed with interest the news of the recent 'Disturbances in New Zealand'.[4] This led to prohibition, but also measures by New South Wales to invite 'the passage of similar Acts by the Legislatures of the other Australian colonies'.[5] On 4 May 1860 'An Act to regulate for a limited time the Exportation of Gunpowder and Warlike Stores' received the governor's assent upon the advice and consent of the legislature.[6] Later in 1862, when this Act was about to expire, the government reassessed the situation and again considered it 'expedient' to extend such restrictions, resulting in the Gunpowder Export Restriction Act on 13 October, in force for a further two years.[7]

Tasmania also acted early, with Governor Sir Henry Young on 13 April 1860 issuing a proclamation restricting such trade.[8] Of note here is New Zealand correspondence dated 15 May, in which the colonial secretary drew attention to the state of Victoria's recent proclamation on warlike stores exports, requesting Tasmania to issue a similar provision. Tasmania had in fact taken the initiative on this problem and a proclamation pre-dated Victoria's by several days, though the time and irregularity of the cross-Tasman mail system obviously had yet to reveal Tasmania's prompt support of her sister colony.[9]

Victorians became aware of the New Zealand restrictions on the sale of arms and ammunitions on 16 April 1860.[10] Authorities there responded with immediate support for their sister colony with the proclamation of their own restrictions assented to by Governor Barkly on 17 April.[11] This Act was revoked shortly afterward and replaced with amended restrictions proclaimed on 17 July.[12] Within days, it was rumoured that a large quantity of ball cartridges had been

The settlement at New Plymouth, Taranaki, showing the military encampment on Mount Eliot, from the *Illustrated London News*, 23 August 1856.

seized by customs authorities in Melbourne in the process of being conveyed to the wharves for New Zealand, but after investigation this allegation was found to be false.[13]

South Australia was also made aware of New Zealand's restrictions in April following receipt of news of the outbreak of the 'Taranaki Rebellion'.[14] As a result, this colony shortly thereafter enacted its own legislation to prohibit the export of warlike stores. On 3 May Governor MacDonnell assented to South Australia's attempt to restrict this flow of weaponry.[15] Meanwhile, in Queensland, the *Moreton Bay Courier* had in April published Taranaki Province's proclamation prohibiting the sale of arms and ammunition for public information.[16]

Later in August the Queensland colonial secretary received from his New Zealand counterpart information that a vessel named *Camilla* was 'suspected of having illegally landed goods' upon the South Island of New Zealand.[17] New Zealand authorities requested that Australian colonial authorities maintain vigilance in policing ongoing cross-Tasman trade.[18] Queensland's Governor Bowen informed his New Zealand counterpart of his colony's support in this time of conflict. Queensland had not only enacted its own 'Act to regulate the exportation of Warlike Stores' but also passed on its sympathies to fellow countrymen in New Zealand. Bowen here also added an extract from a speech to parliament to outline clearly Queensland's willingness to assist not only with these warlike stores restrictions, but also by allowing British troops allotted for the new colony's defence to instead be offered to New Zealand.[19] The correspondence between Queensland and New Zealand during September–October 1860 is clear evidence of the degree of British patriotism in the Australasian colonies, which overrode sentiments of parochialism between individual colonies. Later in 1862, following an inquiry from the Secretary of State for the Colonies into efforts in force restricting exports of warlike stores, Bowen replied with satisfaction not only on the part he had played in Queensland's 1860 restrictions, but that they were still in force.[20]

Impact on New South Wales's volunteer movement and offers of service

The departure of large numbers of the British troop garrison from Sydney engendered an atmosphere of concern regarding the colony's defence. New South Wales lagged behind in the encouragement and development of a volunteer movement evident in other colonies such as Victoria, South Australia and Tasmania. The military exigencies of the New Zealand war now left New South Wales's defences lacking. Although the outbreak of the Crimean War had led to considerable military fervour and raising of volunteer forces, by the late

1850s these corps had all but vanished.[21] One of those former volunteers, 'Ready', asserted that all that was required was an immediate call-out of all previous serving personnel and a force would be ready for 'active service here, if needed; and even . . . for a brush in New Zealand . . . should a demand arise'.[22] Such blustering enthusiasm could not, however, compensate for an immediate injection of organisation and training, money, weapons and equipment – something that would take many months to be put in place.

Despite the hurdles facing a renewed volunteer movement, this did not stifle expressions of martial zeal among Sydney's populace, as evident in a letter by 'A Citizen' to the *Sydney Morning Herald*: 'I am sure our Volunteer Force, if there had been one ready, would have willingly and promptly offered their services to the Government, for the performance of all the military duties of this place, so as to have permitted every soldier of the 12th Regiment and of the Artillery to go . . . to aid the cause . . . [in New Zealand]. That this cannot be done is no fault of our citizens.'[23] Letters by 'A Volunteer', 'Civis', 'H.R.' and 'J.C.' continued to appear during July debating the colony's defences and the need for the mobilisation of volunteers. This commentary was evoked not merely in light of the war in New Zealand, but combined with the perception of a growing French threat in the Pacific – quite apart from the indignity of 'Victoria, South Australia, and even the young colony of Queensland, each [having] their corps of volunteer infantry, cavalry, and Artillery'.[24]

Community agitation to form volunteer units continued to ferment in August, with the New Zealand war reported as a major motivation.[25] Even in October, 'Observer' in the *Herald* noted the injury done 'through the obstinate refusal . . . of the Government to call out and revive the original corps some months ago. Had they been permitted to turn out, they would have taken upon themselves the military duties of the colony, as the Victorian corps have done . . . What a miserable demonstration of military ability for so great and wealthy a country as New South Wales, the parent colony of Australasia!'[26]

In November Governor Denison reviewed the development of New South Wales's volunteer movement, reaffirming the importance of the New Zealand war in stimulating its resurgence. He also pointed out that it was a direction urged more by public pressure than any governmental initiative, and argued that its eventual efficiency would be ensured by the active involvement of experienced regular officers such as Lieutenant-Colonel John Francis Kempt of the 12th Regiment.[27] As it was, New South Wales's volunteer forces did not achieve any semblance of sufficient numbers or efficiency until early 1861, by which time some 1700 men were enrolled.[28] On the first review of volunteers held in that year, the *Herald* reminded readers that New South Wales 'cannot boast of having been the foremost' in developing this movement. This paper offered reasons for the colony's complacency, highlighting the fact that the resurrection of the volunteer movement was in part due to the impact of the Taranaki conflict:

> We have been so accustomed to having our barracks sufficiently filled, and ... in our noble harbour two or three British men-of-war, that the necessity of providing for self-defence independently of Imperial aid, was not very strongly apparent to the public mind. But the almost total desertion of the city by both the military and naval force ... to ... New Zealand ... reminded us very forcibly that the exigencies of war might at any time denude us of our borrowed resources, and expose us to danger ...[29]

It should also be recognised that internal civil disturbances during 1860–61 added to concerns about defences and the need for an efficient body of volunteers. This was particularly the case regarding the diminished numbers of British soldiers and sailors on hand to assist the civil power if required. At the same time, such eventualities also dictated against total commitment of all available imperial troops in the colony for use in Taranaki.

In May 1860 a demonstration by 500 unemployed at the Legislative Assembly in Sydney developed into a riot. Following this incident, the press reported that 'the coincidence of its violent manifestation just at the moment when the troops usually stationed at Sydney had been removed to New Zealand will in all probability be made use of with undue force by persons who take a hasty view of the matter'.[30] During December, growing race tensions between European and Chinese miners erupted in riots at the Lambing Flats goldfields. This unrest continued to simmer into 1861, when the situation was believed serious enough to warrant a contingent of available Royal Artillery (with three artillery pieces) and the 12th Regiment to be despatched in February to quell the strife. These regular troops did not return to Sydney until June.[31] Shortly after their return the situation again flared and more troops were sent to these troubled goldfields in July, this time including Royal Navy personnel from HMS *Fawn*.[32]

The war in New Zealand therefore played a significant role in New South Wales's affairs beyond the short-term implications of the colony's military support. Patriotic support for a sister colony had to be weighed up against internal fears or pressures. Total commitment of imperial resources could not occur, and in turn, impetuses toward self-reliance for defence needs were revived.

Impact on Victorian volunteer movement and offers of service

The Crimean War was also a major stimulus to the formation and development of a volunteer movement in Victoria. Government support and public enthusiasm ensured the growth of the movement, which peaked in late 1860 with more than 4000 members. The Taranaki War now offered a unique situation whereby volunteers were able to take on active roles following the departure of the bulk of the colony's imperial garrison to New Zealand. Volunteers were utilised for mounting guard at vulnerable locations such as Government House, the Treasury, the powder magazines at Batman's Hill and Footscray, and at the Victoria Barracks.[33] With many of Melbourne's volunteers performing guard duties, the government in the Legislative Assembly asserted provisions would be made to pay them for such services. The government also discussed amending the Volunteer Corps Act so as to increase numbers to 10,000 if necessary, as the 'state of Europe and of affairs in New Zealand justified' such steps.[34] It was not until early November 1860 that the volunteers around Melbourne were relieved following the arrival of a fresh draft of 40th Regiment troops, who with the small numbers already in the city, made up sufficient numbers of imperial soldiers to now resume these duties themselves.[35]

Another impact of the war was its stimulus to growth of martial sentiment and participation in Victoria's volunteer movement during the latter half of 1860. In reporting a general parade of Melbourne volunteer units at the Prince's Bridge Reserve in July, the *Age* asserted that there 'seems to be a general desire among our citizen soldiers to have a brush with the Maories [*sic*], provided Government will find arms and opportunity'.[36] At Sandhurst in October the volunteer movement was pushed ahead with considerable success. Chairman of the meeting held at the Sandhurst Town Hall, attended by some 800 persons, was Police Magistrate Mr L. M'Lachlan. In support of the creation of a Sandhurst corps, M'Lachlan pointed out that despite being too old to join himself, in his youth he had been a volunteer who served in the 1840s conflict against Hone Heke in the Bay of Islands. Loud cheers were reported to have followed his patriotic remarks, no doubt aiding the establishment of this particular volunteer corps and influencing men to come forward.[37]

The war also drew a considerable spirit of volunteerism for actual service in New Zealand if called upon. In April 1860 'Rifleman' from St Kilda expressed the belief that the services of Victoria's volunteers should be offered to the government to garrison Melbourne so as to allow the authorities to despatch as large a force of troops to Taranaki as possible. In conclusion, 'Rifleman' remarked: 'I make this suggestion, feeling assured that the volunteers of Victoria are not altogether "feather-bed soldiers," but, as far as private duties permit, are ready, not alone for garrison, but even active service, if required.'[38] In July 'A Volunteer who will go to New Zealand' suggested that as all the 40th was likely to be sent and more troops would be required in this conflict, three or four hundred of Victoria's volunteers should be despatched as soon as possible to assist. He concluded by stating that he felt 'convinced that the Victorian Volunteer Rifles will uphold the character they have obtained in their own country, and will, by their deeds, prove themselves real "chips of the old block".'[39] Other volunteers willingly offering their services perceived the lack of available suitable weapons as a hindrance to their patriotic efforts.[40] These tentative moves towards voluntary enlistment for New Zealand saw such offers of service continue to appear in the *Argus* throughout July and August.[41] This spirit of martial fervour, though untapped in 1860–61, would find a ready market in 1863 and 1864 when New Zealand's military settler recruiting took place and was particularly successful in Victoria. Such letters to the editor are in fact indications of the extent to which the call of the Empire could be evoked from among the colony's citizenry.

Civil disturbances ending in riots also occurred in Victoria in 1860–61, adding to concerns about defence when so many of the colony's imperial force were serving across the Tasman. In August 1860 a serious riot took place at Parliament House, reported by the *Argus* as 'a vile attempt . . . to overawe and intimidate the House of Assembly on the land question'. With the military away in New Zealand, 'an opportunity too good to be resisted' took place.[42] Apart from the vigilance and actions of the constabulary, the volunteers were now deemed capable and at a high state of readiness to assist in quelling civil unrest.[43] A similar event occurred during July–August 1861 when the Kyneton Volunteers were called out to assist in quelling rioting railroad workers on the Malmesbury–Woodend line; even in June 1863 a threatened railway riot at Sandhurst saw the Eaglehawk and Sandhurst Volunteers mobilised to aid the civil authorities.[44] The self-reliance brought upon Victorian authorities as a result of the war across the Tasman no doubt aided the martial enthusiasm of the volunteers, as it did the willingness of police magistrates to call upon such services during times of perceived civil unrest.

Impact on Queensland and South Australia

In early 1860 Governor Bowen of Queensland sought to obtain an initial garrison detachment of fifty-two officers and men for the newly created colony's military protection. In these undertakings he also stated his desire to encourage 'Imperial feeling', that is, 'the existing feeling of pride and affection towards the Mother-Country' which was enhanced by the presence of imperial soldiers.[45] News of the outbreak of conflict in Taranaki, though, lowered Queensland's expectations to a smaller detachment of one officer and twenty-five men. But Major-General Pratt had to reply that he was currently unable to provide even this small detachment for Brisbane. Not only was New South Wales reluctant to allow any further drain on its diminished garrison to satisfy its new northern neighbour, the demand for reinforcements for New Zealand was the priority, although troops would be sent when possible.[46]

Orders were finally issued in July 1860 'to send with as little delay as possible' a detachment consisting of one officer and twenty-eight other ranks from Sydney.[47] Commissariat preparations saw that it would be another six months before such troops materialised, though Colour-Sergeant William Green of the 12th Regiment arrived to fulfil the role of drill instructor to Queensland's volunteers in August.[48] It was not until January 1861 that a detachment consisting of Lieutenant D.T. Seymour (later Queensland's first police commissioner in 1864) and twenty-seven soldiers and families of the 12th arrived in Brisbane.[49] Thus, the Taranaki War had a direct impact on the proper establishment of Queensland's allotment of imperial troops and defence during 1860–61, as it was to continue to do so into 1862–63 with the build-up and subsequent commencement of the Waikato campaign.

In South Australia, the news of developments in Taranaki led the colony's senior Army officer, Major Thomas Nelson of the 40th, to apply for active service.[50] Nelson also played an important role with the colony's volunteer forces as inspecting field officer.[51] He departed Adelaide for Taranaki on 24 April 1860, where he took command of the four companies of the 40th.[52] The *Register* was later to acknowledge Major Nelson's valuable contributions during the Taranaki conflict.[53] In his absence the duties of command of the troops in the colony fell to Captain F.S. Blyth. Blyth, too, would serve in New Zealand later, during 1863–64, where he distinguished himself, was promoted, and eventually rose to command the 40th Regiment.

While South Australia's garrison troops were not called upon to depart for service in 1860, its volunteer movement was stirred considerably by patriotic feelings. In a letter to the editor on 16 April, 'A Volunteer' offered suggestions of assistance, with New Zealand affairs 'looking so threatening', including using the volunteers to undertake the various guard duties around Adelaide in place of the regular troops. This would allow more imperial solders to be made available for New Zealand.[54] But a letter by 'A Marksman' was not supportive of such a proposal, though its author did agree with the notion of sending garrison troops to support their fellow New Zealand colonists, as retaining them would be viewed as a very selfish act 'while we are in safety and our brethren there are involved in a contest with savages'.[55]

By July 1860 the available war news in South Australia indicated matters were far from under control in Taranaki, and led to expectations that all available regular garrison troops throughout the Australian colonies would soon be ordered to New Zealand.[56] The *South Australian Register* acknowledged reaction in the parliament to the effects of the war on this and other Australian colonies in the

> cheers of the House of Assembly yesterday at the announcement that the defence of the colony must devolve on the volunteers whilst the troops were dispatched to New Zealand . . . But if the worst comes to the worst, we are sure that the very existence of the Adelaide Regiment will be regarded as a sufficient protection . . . in this great emergency.[57]

The *Register* shortly after reported that a company of the 40th Regiment numbering some seventy men would prepare to embark as soon as possible for Melbourne en route to New Zealand.

Within days, however, telegrams were received from Army Headquarters in Melbourne countermanding this directive and ordering the force: 'To stand fast for the present. Nothing decided.' This was reported as 'agreeable news' as far as South Australia was concerned, and it was suggested this reversal arose from correspondence between the governor and General Pratt in which he had apparently expressed 'his unwillingness' for these troops to be removed.[58]

During this time certain South Australian volunteers felt obliged to take matters into their own hands. Captain Biggs, the staff-adjutant of the Volunteer Military Force, offered his services to train and later command in the field any persons who might come forward to volunteer for New Zealand. The *South Australian Register* also added that many of South Australia's volunteers were 'anxious to abandon their services here, and to undertake military service against' the Maori.[59] Shortly thereafter, the press reported the government's rejection of Biggs' offer.[60]

Throughout these developments, events surrounding the volunteers in Victoria also attracted attention, though in Melbourne what was occurring was on a far greater scale, eliciting the sardonic observation: 'One would suppose, from the tone of the Melbourne papers received . . . that the Maories were in Hobson's Bay and about to make a descent upon the city. Military enthusiasm appeared to affect every one.'[61] The *Register* also voiced its opposition to any portion of the volunteer force being sent to New Zealand, arguing that the Australian colonies did not have the men to spare for 'foreign wars, however just; nor would troops raised in this manner' be the sort who should be sent into action against the Maori. Though this position was tempered by the acknowledgement that any individuals determined to go to the war could do so by enlisting in the regular forces about to depart.[62]

Because Queensland only became a separate colony in 1859, it had neither a volunteer movement nor a British garrison to help foster any significant military atmosphere. Nevertheless, the developing strife in New Zealand did assist in stimulating the formation of the colony's first volunteers – the Queensland Rifle Corps. The first meeting to establish this corps was held at the Police Office in Brisbane on 12 March, spurred by news from Taranaki, and especially of the

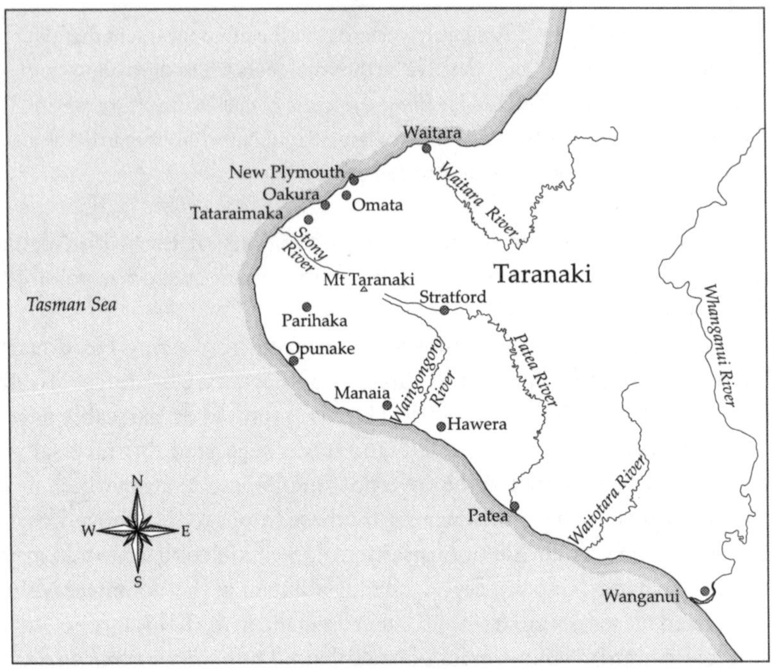

The west coast region of the North Island of New Zealand, showing Taranaki Province south to Wanganui.

efforts undertaken by that province's rifle volunteers,[63] who were identified as similar to the body now sought to be constituted in Brisbane.[64]

Opposition, or attitudes, to war

Though there appears to be little to indicate much direct opposition to the war effort in Taranaki, sympathies were indeed expressed by some that the Maori people had a right to wage their struggle. In looking for general opposition to war during the 1860s, evidence can be found on Christian scriptural grounds, especially that which was espoused by the Society of Friends, or Quakers.[65] The Quakers certainly contributed to a general opposition to war, and during 1860 Britain's ongoing war in China, together with the outbreak of war in New Zealand, no doubt fuelled such calls. Press in Australia provided detailed proceedings of an important meeting of London Quakers and their Christian message on the subject of war: 'Our country is dear to us; we honour our Sovereign, and prize our free institutions; and we desire that our national policy, and that of other professedly Christian countries, may accord with the spirit and precepts of our

Holy Redeemer, who came "not to destroy men's lives, but to save them".'[66]

Prominent intellectuals or radicals of influence in the Australian colonies such as Reverend J.D. Lang, Charles Harpur, or Daniel Deniehy, though, were not interested in making common cause with the Quakers, who were quietly working for peace.[67] Of course there were even those, such as J.H. Hewitt, who argued at this time that the 'War Spirit in the Colonies' was *defensible* on scriptural grounds. Taking to task the views of the Reverend Lang, Hewitt stated his intention to battle 'this Goliath of the Peace Society . . . taking nothing but a few plain truths from the Word of God, as David selected his stones . . . to fight with the champion of the Philistines'.[68]

The war in Taranaki also drew an array of commentaries, both critical and defensive, on the role and impact of the various missionaries and churches in New Zealand. Although there was little outright opposition to the war, there certainly was considerable criticism of the affairs in the colony, and the actions of the colonists or governor. 'C. Melbourne' (possibly the Bishop of Melbourne writing under this pseudonym), defended the Church of England against the position of the *Argus*:

> The present war . . . has occasioned the greatest pain in every one who is interested in the prosperity of the colony, or in the welfare of the Maories, and to none, I am sure, more than the missionaries. I believe that the Government is in the right; but much allowance is to be made for the Maories, who cannot understand our laws, and are jealous of their land passing into the hands of strangers. . . . And I would add, that it ill becomes us to condemn a people for particular acts of outrage towards English colonists, when we call to mind the barbarous acts of which English colonists have been guilty, towards the poor helpless original inhabitants of the countries of which they take possession.[69]

Clearly some colonists were concerned about the Maori people, and it is sentiments such as these which would echo throughout the 1860s.[70]

Australian logistical, commissariat and manpower support

During 1860–61 Britain became an arsenal from which New Zealand would receive all manner of military stores, weapons and equipment, as well as soldiers and sailors. This contribution was especially important, as the demands of the Taranaki campaign required a massive influx of imperial military might.[71] All the same, there existed the problem of distance and time involved in voyages to and from Britain or other far-flung ports and garrisons of the Empire. Reinforcements such as the 57th Regiment began to depart India in late November 1860, but the first elements did not arrive in Taranaki until late January 1861, with further detachments disembarking over the ensuing months, and the last not arriving until June 1861. In January 1861 the 70th Regiment, also in India, departed in several contingents that did not arrive until May. The 14th Regiment in Ireland departed in several detachments in September 1860, some of which did not arrive until November and December of that year, with its last constituents only reaching their destination late February 1861.[72]

This lag determined the geographical and practical importance of the Australian colonies, and the material and manpower potential existing there, which could be despatched across the Tasman with relative ease and speed. New South Wales, Victoria, South Australia and Tasmania at this time all contributed war material for New Zealand's immediate military needs including the provision of quantities of arms, ammunition, commissariat stores, equipment and horses which would prove to be vital in allowing imperial and colonial forces at Taranaki to maintain, and then expand, defences around New Plymouth and neighbouring districts.

The Australian colonies were therefore pivotal in stemming any potential military collapse during the early stages of this crisis. Their importance is reinforced by the fact that other sizeable imperial reinforcements from elsewhere did not arrive in New Zealand until late 1860 onwards, many too late to be of any real service during the current war.

New South Wales and Victorian support

In early 1860, military affairs at Taranaki were not going well for the imperial and colonial forces. Just as in times of real or perceived crisis during the 1840s, the New Zealand governor or imperial officers appealed to the Australian colonies for a range of military support. In the early morning of 5 April Governor Denison in Sydney received a despatch from New Zealand's Governor Gore Browne, outlining the state of affairs in and around the settlement of New Plymouth and the ineffectual attacks upon the Maori by Colonel Gold and his limited forces.[73] Also included were documents adding weight to Browne's claims for prompt military assistance, which were borne to Sydney by a Mr Hall, a resident magistrate and former member of the New Zealand House of Representatives, whose task was to answer all inquiries Denison might have regarding the crisis.[74] One letter from Thomas Mould, commanding the garrison, applied for camp equipment for 250 troops.[75] This material was secured in Sydney, and appears to have been consigned along with the large quantity of ammunition, artillery, stores and troops shipped aboard the *City of Sydney* on 10 April.[76]

In a subsequent letter of thanks to New South Wales, Browne reaffirmed the critical nature of the situation and called for any serviceable arms to also help defend Auckland.[77] At this same time, Governor Denison received a request from the superintendent of Taranaki seeking 300 modern Enfield rifles so as to rearm local militia forces that were currently using outdated types.[78] Denison in reply could only inform the superintendent that he was unable to assist as there was simply 'not a single weapon of this kind' presently available.[79]

On 6 June, Denison received further correspondence from Browne calling for 1000 Enfield rifles. Although Denison remarked that he had been able to help source 400 rifles from South Australia, he still wasn't in any position to provide more weapons.[80] Following the military reverse at Waitara on 27 June, Browne took the opportunity to press again for more troops and any arms possible.[81] Denison received one further despatch from Browne on 14 November, forwarding a copy of the resolution of New Zealand's House of Representatives requesting a supply of rifles. But Denison's patience on this issue had worn thin: 'I do not see how we can spare any Rifles neither indeed can I imagine there is any urgent necessity for such a supply of arms while there are 2000 Troops and Marines in New Zealand and another Regiment expected.'[82]

New Zealand parliamentary papers also reveal that the New Zealand government purchased almost £1000 worth of arms and equipment direct from the government of New South Wales for its militia and volunteer forces during October and December 1860.[83] New Zealand, of course, did not limit itself to the Australian colonies as a source of its military requirements, as indicated by press news of orders placed direct to Britain for Calisher and Terry breech-loading rifles.[84] Apart from rifles and ammunition, New South Wales authorities also ensured that a quantity of revolvers was procured for the New Zealand government, and the shortfall not being available in Sydney was subsequently obtained in Melbourne.[85]

Shortly after the arrival in Melbourne of the news of war in Taranaki, the Victorian government warship HMCS *Victoria* was quickly fitted out for sailing to the conflict. Part of the vessel's orders included conveyance of 100,000 rounds of ball cartridges from stores in Melbourne, as well as 'a considerable quantity of commissariat stores for the use of the troops'. The *Victoria* sailed on 19 April, initially for Hobart, where a detachment of British troops and further commissariat stores were embarked for use in Taranaki.[86]

South Australian support

In Adelaide a telegram received in early May 1860 informed authorities of New Zealand's urgent requirement for rifles, and the South Australian government determined to assist by supplying '400 stand of arms'.[87] A board of officers from the 40th Regiment and Commissariat Department in Adelaide convened to inspect the condition of 400 Enfield rifles and accoutrements for New Zealand use, and transport to Melbourne was arranged.[88] The South Australian Treasurer Mr Duffield later stated to the House of Assembly that the government had evinced its 'sympathy for New Zealand' by providing these weapons.[89]

Later in August, South Australia received a request from the Victorian government for a large quantity of Enfield ammunition to be sent to both Melbourne and Sydney. This ammunition was needed to provide supplies for the magazines in these cities, replacing quantities already despatched to New Zealand, and to have quantities on hand to meet any future demands.[90] Captain Blyth, 40th Regiment, informed the governor on 22 August that orders had been issued to provide 500,000 rounds of rifle ammunition to Melbourne, and a vessel was advertised for to carry out this task.[91] The *South Australian Register* reported that the colony could easily part with this quantity as it had some 1,300,000 rounds in store, adding: 'the emergency which has arisen owing to the New Zealand rebellion has found South Australia alone prepared to meet it'.[92]

Despite South Australia's prompt generosity in supplying these Enfield rifles and large supply of ammunition, in certain circles this action was perceived as actually having an adverse impact on the colony's wavering volunteer movement.[93] News later received that both rifles and ammunition were going to be replaced by the imperial government was positively received, especially by volunteers in country regions who had not yet received equipment like that issued to their urban colleagues.[94]

Military horse trade with New Zealand

The Australian colonies were also the place from which horses were procured for war service, one example being the resupply of horses to 3/4 (after arrival referred to as C/4) Battery, Royal Artillery, which had been ordered to New Zealand. On account of the lengthy journey, this battery had to leave its original stable in England. To assist in replacing these animals, Veterinary Surgeon Anderson, Royal Artillery, sailed in advance to purchase appropriate horses ('walers') and have them forwarded from Australia to be ready for the battery once it landed in New Zealand.[95]

During February and early March 1861, 200 horses were specially selected and shipped to New Zealand aboard the *Light of the Age* on 8 March.[96] The *Sydney Morning Herald* opined that this consignment was one of the finest that had been made for a long time, 'well-bred powerful, upstanding horses, for the most part under four years old, and measuring from fourteen to sixteen hands ... purchased chiefly in the southern country', and which could not fail to produce a favourable impression of stock available in New South Wales.[97]

Despite the cessation of hostilities in Taranaki in early 1861, military authorities continued to obtain horses to accommodate logistical needs associated with the increasing imperial presence. In July the *Sydney Morning Herald* announced a contract for the supply of packhorses 'for the conveyance of munitions of war, and of human provender'.[98] A contract for 100 horses was granted to J.W. Cheesbrough, the son-in-law of a Sydney veterinary surgeon; the first draft of this consignment departing shortly after aboard the *City of Melbourne*. The *Herald* aptly concluded that it 'is pleasant, even in her difficulties, to see that New South Wales should be found, whether in animals or in minerals, the mother of the materials of locomotion for the sister colonies'.[99]

Imperial reinforcements from New South Wales

Governor Browne's despatch to New South Wales on 21 March 1860 included an appeal for strong troop reinforcements.[100] In Sydney, Governor Denison acted promptly, assuring Browne on 9 April that all necessary steps would be taken. Denison accordingly approached Major-General Pratt in Melbourne to ensure such support was forthcoming not only from the garrison in Sydney, but also from forces available in Victoria and Tasmania.[101]

Royal Navy vessels of the Australia Station at Sydney were also immediately prepared for sea. In March the vessels of this station comprised HMS *Iris* and HMS *Cordelia*, both in Sydney refitting; the survey ship HMS *Herald*, on a cruise of the northern coast; HMS *Pelorus* at Melbourne; and HMS *Niger*, already in New Zealand.[102] On 5 April all hands on both the *Cordelia* and *Iris* were busy 'bending sails and getting ready for sea'; the *Iris* even posting recruiting notices about the city calling for able seamen for the ship's company.[103] HMS *Cordelia* then departed Sydney on 6 April, the *Iris* the following day. The *Pelorus* left Melbourne for New Zealand on the 8th.[104]

By mid-April, four out of the five Royal Navy vessels on the Australia Station were serving in New Zealand waters. Orders arrived in Sydney during that month for the *Iris* to return to England, though this vessel would in fact be detained for use in New Zealand into 1861. Her replacement, HMS *Fawn*, arrived in Sydney later in April, and would soon see service across the Tasman.[105] By December 1860, five warships on the Australia Station would now be serving in New Zealand waters – the *Iris*, *Cordelia*, *Pelorus*, *Niger* and *Fawn*.[106] Clearly, the might of the Royal Navy available on the Australia Station was marshalled for the war effort in New Zealand.

The *Sydney Morning Herald* detailed the preparations under way in Sydney for the despatch of troop reinforcements, including four pieces of artillery, a considerable quantity of arms and munitions, and other equipment. These reinforcements departed on the *City of Sydney* on 10 April. The *Herald*, in reporting the departure of these 192 officers and men from the Royal Artillery, the 12th Regiment and some Royal Engineers, indicated that upwards of 2000 well-wishers, including the governor, were at Circular Quay to farewell this contingent.[107]

The departure of the battery of artillery aboard the *City of Sydney*, though, would elicit local concerns about the expense originally outlaid by New South Wales in bringing this force to the colony. Governor Denison was obliged to bring the issue to the attention of the Secretary of State for the Colonies, and in a despatch on 16 April 1860 outlined that this unit of Royal Artillery had been applied for, and all expenses met, by the colonial government 'for the express purpose of aiding in the defence of the harbor and city of Sydney'.[108] In light of the Taranaki crisis, Denison did not hesitate to suggest that General Pratt act promptly, although the governor was also careful about how the colony's Executive Council and legislature was informed of the matter, so as not to raise the question of the power of the general to dispose of the military force in the colonies.

Denison again wrote to the Secretary of State on this subject in June, advising the establishment of a definite principle which would clearly 'define the relations between the Mother Country and the Colonies . . . in such a manner as to leave them no just cause of complaint, either on the ground that sufficient attention is not paid to their defence, or that they are called upon to defray more than a just proportion of the expense of the Military force required for such a purpose'.[109] Following this correspondence, the imperial authorities acted to salve New South Wales's concerns, and agreed that it was proper in the circumstances to repay the colony's expenses for the artillery now serving in New Zealand.[110]

Further imperial reinforcements from New South Wales

In June 1860 Denison wrote to General Pratt outlining his opposition to further troops being sent to New Zealand, arguing that he perceived no real threat to Auckland at this time. Denison's concerns about political manoeuvrings in Europe and increasing French activity in New Caledonia dictated against further diminishing troop numbers in the Australian colonies.[111] The governor's attitude changed, however, during July when news from New Zealand revealed the necessity of sending additional soldiers following the failed attack on Puketakauere pa, Waitara, where British troops sustained sixty-four casualties. Denison described this disastrous assault as 'a piece of gross folly', and taking matters into his own hands, determined on a course of action to send more troops.[112] The captain of HMS *Fawn* offered to convey any reinforcements, and Denison decided these should sail for Taranaki immediately, with HMS *Niger* to follow in a week with whatever other personnel could be collected. He believed the effect of reinforcements following each other at short intervals would be beneficial to morale at Taranaki.

Denison also wrote to General Pratt in Melbourne on 11 July, updating him on events following the defeat at Waitara, and informing the general that he needed to go to New Zealand to take personal control. Here, while continuing to regret seeing the colonies denuded of imperial forces, Denison stated that he would 'have greater confidence in the effective handling of these men were you [General Pratt] on the spot – the mixed character of the Troops ... consisting ... Troops of the Line, Seamen from the Vessels of War, & Volunteers makes it more desirable that the officer in command shall be one whose rank and length of service will entitle him to claim an amount of authority'.[113]

The arrival of HMCS *Victoria* on the evening of 11 July with important news and despatches from Browne only re-emphasised to Denison the inevitability that all available forces needed to be sent with utmost haste.[114] HMCS *Victoria* was able to receive fresh supplies of coal from resources 'kindly supplied' from the Australian Steam Navigation Company's works at Pyrmont. Accordingly, the vessel was rapidly readied for departure for Melbourne to embark Major-General Pratt and as many of that city's 40th Regiment as could be carried, departing Sydney on 14 July.[115]

By this time HMS *Niger* had also returned from New Zealand to undergo necessary maintenance and repairs, which necessitated the vessel being dry docked for hull repairs carried out by a Mr Cuthbert, with the necessary engineering work and castings undertaken by the firm of P.N. Russell & Co.[116] Such naval works emphasised the importance of the port of Sydney as a refuge for shipping, though the connection with requirements for New Zealand is often overlooked. Sydney, as the base for the Australia Station with all its ancillary stores, workshops and dry dock facilities, played a significant role in maintaining the Royal Navy vessels serving in New Zealand waters. Once the works were completed the *Niger* was refloated and readied for return, departing for Auckland on 28 July.[117]

From available forces still in Sydney, an additional detachment of 111 officers and men of the 12th Regiment was prepared for despatch aboard HMS *Fawn*, which got under way on 15 July, as usual with a patriotic and enthusiastic send-off by Sydney residents.[118] Browne was quick to extend his colony's thanks for these Sydney reinforcements on 30 July, but in doing so did not miss the opportunity to apprise Denison of current affairs and the insufficient disposition of Auckland's defences now that all available sailors and marines were serving at Taranaki.[119]

Imperial reinforcements from Victoria

In Melbourne the dramatic intelligence of the outbreak of conflict in Taranaki was received on 5 April 1860. The governor was at that time at Queenscliff, but upon receipt of the news immediately returned to the city. Captain Seymour of HMS *Pelorus* received orders to prepare immediately for sea. That evening various communications passed between the naval, military and commissary-general in preparation for sending supplies, equipment and troops of the Victorian garrison of the 40th Regiment, as well as from Hobart Town, to New Zealand. HMS *Pelorus* set sail for New Zealand early on 8 April.[120]

The military authorities initially hoped to charter the *Wonga Wonga* to carry the 40th detachment, but problems arose and the *City of Hobart* was substituted.[121] As soon as this ship returned to Melbourne from Tasmania on 14 April it was immediately unloaded and coaled in preparation for the embarkation of 215 officers and men of the 40th Regiment, commanded by Captain Messenger. On 17 April a special train on the Hobson's Bay Railway shuttled these troops from Melbourne Station to the pier, where upwards of 4000 enthusiastic spectators witnessed this departure for the war in Taranaki.[122]

The service of HMCS *Victoria*

Victoria also assisted New Zealand even further and offered the service of its only warship, the screw steamer *Victoria*, following a request by the imperial military authorities for use of the vessel.[123] In response to questions about the deployment of the *Victoria* in the colony's Legislative Council, Mr Service indicated: 'He thought the House would be glad of having this small opportunity of showing our sympathy with our fellow-countrymen in New Zealand in the circumstances in which they are placed.'[124] The *Argus* on 7 April 1860 reported that the vessel's full crew complement had now been achieved, and preparations readying the *Victoria* for sea were accelerated because of the actions of Captain Seymour from HMS *Pelorus*, who placed his vessel's crew at the disposal of the Victorian government for this purpose.[125]

Captain W.H. Norman of the *Victoria* received orders on 16 April for the vessel's immediate departure.[126] The boat and her officers and crew had been placed under the 'disposal of the Crown' during the extent of this New Zealand service. Apart from taking on board all the necessary munitions for the steamer's heavy armament, the Victorian government also supplied it with breech-loading carbines and rifles for service ashore.[127] Norman and his crew thus constituted the first Australian colonial military unit to serve in an overseas conflict. As part of these arrangements it was agreed the imperial government would meet all expenses associated with the enterprise. Later, this vessel was considered to have been on continuous imperial service from 1 April 1860 to 30 April 1861, during which time maintenance and other costs totalled just over £18,465.[128]

On 19 April the *Victoria* departed for Hobart, where a detachment of troops and other military stores were embarked, before sailing on to Taranaki.[129] Governor Browne was quick to thank his Victorian counterpart on 26 May on the availability of the *Victoria*.[130] Secretary of State Newcastle also thanked Victoria for the 'measures adopted' in support of New Zealand at this time. This colony's 'cordial co-operation' with the imperial authorities was greatly appreciated at Downing Street.[131] In New Zealand the *Victoria* proved itself to be invaluable in ferrying troops and senior officers or government officials, supplies, refugees and messages between the various ports of the colony. Apart from these services there were numbers of the crew who volunteered for service ashore as part of the Naval Brigade.

One contemporary account of the war in Taranaki recalled that the *Victoria* had 'rendered the most valuable assistance as a transport; while at the same time her indefatigable and ever-ready commander . . . was always anxious to advance the interests of the State in every way, by furnishing such officers and men as he could spare for duty on shore; thus enabling them to share in the military operations of the campaign'.[132] The first instance of crew serving ashore occurred just prior to the *Victoria*'s departure from Auckland in July 1860, when some thirty crewmen under the command of Lieutenant G.A. Woods and Midshipman William Horn volunteered to remain behind as reinforcements, joining other volunteer seamen from HMS *Iris*, *Cordelia* and the *Niger*. These volunteer naval personnel were conveyed to Taranaki aboard the *Cordelia*, where on 9 July the thirty crewmen from the *Victoria* were landed in New Plymouth and marched to Naval Brigade camp at Fort Niger. The press reported that the *Victoria*'s crewmen were not only armed with breech-loading rifles but also equipped with revolvers and cutlasses.[133]

As part of the available military force, the crewmen from the *Victoria* serving in the Naval Brigade took part in the construction and manning of defences surrounding the settlement of New Plymouth. While undertaking these activities the *Victoria* suffered its only known casualty during the campaign – seaman Henry Serjeant dying on 6 August 1860 from complications associated with an accidental gunshot wound. Serjeant's injury required amputation of a limb on 15 July, which led to 'lock-jaw' (tetanus) and death. He was the first member of any Australian colonial military force to die on active service overseas.[134]

Crewmen from the *Victoria* also participated as part of the 'storming party' in the capture of the Matarikoriko pa, an action that took place over 29 and 30 December 1860. The *Victoria*'s contingent consisted of Lieutenant Woods,

Midshipman Horn and twenty-four other seamen.[135] Matarikoriko was actually abandoned by its Maori occupants on the eve of 30 December, though its 'capture' was actually viewed by certain British observers as a great victory. And it was during this engagement that General Pratt began systematically to apply the technique of sapping to assault and dislodge Maori defenders. Thereafter, this system dominated all further military operations at Taranaki until the ceasefire declared on 18 March 1861.[136]

Commodore Seymour, in a despatch from the Naval Camp at Waitara on 29 January 1861, conveyed to Victoria's governor his commendation and thanks in relation to the services of the crew of HMCS *Victoria*. This communication indicates that all crewmen serving ashore had now been re-embarked aboard the *Victoria*, and confirms that those who served ashore appear to have done so on separate occasions as required, rather than in one long period of service. The detachment serving at the engagement at Matarikoriko landed on 19 December; whereas the shore party left behind in July 1860 obviously returned aboard the *Victoria* some time after the vessel's return from Melbourne carrying General Pratt. Seymour's letter was subsequently presented to Victoria's Legislative Assembly on 27 February, as well as being published in the colony's newspapers for public interest.[137]

The service of HMCS *Victoria* in waters outside of Victoria's territorial limits is also important in relation to the Admiralty's disallowance of the colony's Armed Vessels Regulation Bill of 1860.[138] The Victorian government attempted to implement this legislation so as to maintain the authority of the captain and officers of the *Victoria*, and to indemnify the ship's company from any actions carried out while in colonial service, both in or out of Victoria's nautical jurisdiction. Although abortive, Victoria's legislative efforts were a sign of growing colonial maturity.

The *Victoria*'s war service also stimulated imperial authorities regarding the necessity for uniform regulations under which the various Australian colonial government vessels could operate as ships of war, but also to ensure they were legally recognised as such. The Colonial Naval Defence Act of 1865 would shortly allow the Australian colonies to provide their own warships, raise the required manpower, and operate such vessels with the appropriate legal status as ships of war. It also established principles of self-reliance in regard to local defences especially, which in turn aided in the reduction of imperial military expenditure.[139]

Further imperial reinforcements from Victoria

In the Victorian Legislative Assembly on 13 July 1860 it was announced that after HMCS *Victoria* returned to Melbourne the vessel would then convey Major-General Pratt, his staff, and as many of the 40th Regiment as could be carried, to Taranaki. This show of support for an increasing war involvement drew great applause throughout the House,[140] and also included inquiries about the welfare of families of seamen serving aboard the *Victoria*. The colonial treasurer was asked whether he 'was aware that the wives and families of some of the crew . . . were suffering great distress, in consequence of being unable to obtain any portion of the pay of their husbands'. In reply the treasurer stated that he was not aware of such cases but would ensure arrangements were carried out to see these wives received a portion of their husbands' pay.[141]

A message from Victoria's Governor Barkly was presented to the Legislative Council on 17 July about the necessity for the 'temporary withdrawal' from Melbourne of the Army Headquarters' staff and of the headquarters of the 40th Regiment for New Zealand service. The war simply required more and more of Victoria's available troops, and in this situation Barkly expressed reliance 'on the loyalty and prudence of the Legislature to make proper provision for guarding against any risk of aggression', whether from within or external, during the absence of the colony's imperial garrison.[142] In Victoria, as elsewhere, the imperial authorities relied on the colonial powers to ensure effective utilisation of both volunteer and police forces to temporarily make up for the shortfall in imperial troops and their former guard functions.

On 14 July a general parade of the various volunteer rifle companies of Melbourne and surrounding suburbs was held on the reserve facing the Prince's Bridge Barracks. The volunteers were here addressed by Colonel G.D. Pitt, who informed them all of their garrison duties.[143] The volunteers then relieved the 40th troops of all guard duties on 16 July, these including the governor's residence at Toorak, the treasury, powder magazine, and the main guard at the volunteer office in Bourke Street.[144]

Following an inspection preparatory to their departure, General Pratt addressed the men of the 40th at the Prince's Bridge Barracks on 17 July: 'Soldiers I am not going to make a long speech. I have just received a despatch from Taranaki, containing the names of your comrades that fell there. We are going to avenge them; and I shall be with you.'[145] The following day saw both the *Argus* and the *Age* publish a letter received by one of the soldiers awaiting departure, from a comrade already serving in Taranaki. This provided a list of heavy imperial casualties, adding moral weight to the necessity for the remainder of Melbourne's troops to be despatched as quickly as possible.[146]

The *City of Hobart* departed with this second consignment of reinforcements on 18 July. Again, thousands of Melbourne's citizens turned out for farewells, as many of these soldiers had been long-term Victorian residents. The *Argus* sadly noted that it was likely the 40th would not return to the colony, which was unfortunate as these troops had been 'resident amongst us for the last eight years', during which time the soldiers had come to be looked upon 'as colonists as much as ourselves'.[147] The *Age*, in one account of the patriotism displayed by the very large crowd attending this departure of 222 officers and men of the 40th, reported that no less than six to eight thousand people had assembled to bid them farewell.[148]

On 17 July HMCS *Victoria* returned to Melbourne from the vessel's first New Zealand tour of service. This allowed the *Argus* to report upon the achievements and activities of the colony's warship, noting that since departure back on 19 April, 'she has been under steam almost the entire time, and has visited nearly all the ports in the northern island . . . rendering most important services'.[149] The rigours of service in New Zealand waters also necessitated several days of immediate repairs now that the *Victoria* was back in its home port. By 23 July these had been completed and the vessel was again prepared for departure.[150] During this time large numbers of Melbourne citizens visited the vessel while moored at Williamstown, the *Argus* boasting how the *Victoria* 'has been of much use . . . and her services have been much appreciated by our brother-colonists of New Zealand. The colony may well be proud of the Victoria, and of the gallant behaviour of her officers and crew in the service in which they have been so early and so unexpectedly called to perform an important part.'[151]

Melbourne witnessed the departure on 24 July of the city's remaining 40th Regiment garrison and General Pratt and his staff for the war in Taranaki. This detachment aboard HMCS *Victoria* appears to have comprised fifty soldiers of the 40th.[152] The *Argus* reported at length on the departure of Australia's most senior imperial Army officer, off to take personal control of the war, noting the 'large concourse of spectators', including the governor, Melbourne's mayor and the colony's chief secretary, with the Volunteer Rifle Corps forming a guard of honour.

This leave-taking was no doubt made all the more of public interest, for Governor Barkly had just three days before married Blanche Pratt, the only daughter of General Pratt. As the general and governor boarded HMCS *Victoria* the Volunteer Artillery Corps fired a salute, and the vessel's deck was crowded with well-wishers 'who had come down to pay their respects'.[153] The *Argus* also drew attention to the appearance of the *Victoria* as having 'excited general admiration, and there was a pervading feeling of gratification that a British general officer and his staff should take his departure under our colonial flag, to vindicate the rule of our common empire'.[154]

Amongst Pratt's staff was his Adjutant-General, Lieutenant-Colonel Robert Carey, who later wrote an account of the Taranaki War entitled *Narrative of the Late War in New Zealand* (1863). Another officer aboard who commanded great respect was Captain Charles Pasley, who had volunteered to serve in Taranaki. Pasley is an important example of the role and place of a particular branch of the

British Army in the Australasian colonial context – the Royal Engineers; and particularly so for his strong connections with Victoria.[155]

Apart from these three contingents of 40th Regiment troops from Victoria, in August 1862 most of the detachment of Royal Engineers, who during the previous two years had been employed on construction of Melbourne's shore batteries, also departed for New Zealand. They joined the 6th Company, Royal Engineers, stationed at Auckland, where their technical and specialist assistance was on hand in the preparations for the Waikato campaign in 1863.[156]

Imperial reinforcements from Tasmania

Late on 16 April 1860 a telegram was received in Hobart by Colonel W.E.D. Broughton, ordering two companies of the 40th Regiment to embark immediately for Taranaki aboard HMCS *Victoria*, shortly expected from Melbourne.[157] The *Victoria* arrived on 21 April but was delayed for three days in order to be laden with a large quantity of military stores from the Hobart Commissariat. The 40th troops were embarked on 23 April to much public fanfare, and comprised 134 officers and men.[158] The *Victoria* sailed the next day, arriving at Taranaki 'after a fine run of five days from Hobart Town'.[159]

With the despatch of this detachment and the ongoing crisis at Taranaki, the remainder of the garrison troops in Tasmania were restructured and prepared for possible departure as reinforcements. This included troops of the 12th Regiment who had been garrisoned for some time at Launceston, and were now ordered to Hobart.[160] Later in July the continuing disastrous news from New Zealand saw the remaining 12th and 40th Regiment garrison troops being placed in a high state of readiness for immediate departure if orders arrived for their removal.[161] Although this scenario did not eventuate, the threat of Tasmania being denuded of its British troops still saw local efforts discussed for the maintenance of guard and other defence requirements. Tasmania, like other Australian colonies that saw elements of their garrison sent across the Tasman to stem the military crisis during 1860, never viewed such departures as permanent. In fact, the Australian colonies regarded this military support as a temporary measure and always believed such troops should be returned, particularly as open conflict at Taranaki ended in early 1861. Tasmania in early 1862, for example, was still corresponding in the hope of obtaining the return of all, or at least a portion, of the troops despatched during April 1860.[162]

On the day the 40th detachment sailed, the *Mercury* reported that the Volunteer Artillery Corps had offered their services to the government for mounting guard at government house, the magazine and the ordnance stores.[163] An editorial shortly after relayed that this offer was in fact an unfounded rumour.[164] The *Mercury* was initially opposed to the use of volunteers as guards but perceived the public display of support for the troops by the volunteers as 'manifest[ing] a sympathy with them which, under the circumstances, was peculiarly becoming, and imparted to the Volunteer movement itself a reality and a dignity which it could not so readily have obtained in any other way'.[165] The stance of this paper did not stifle thoughts towards possible use of the volunteers for guard duties, as news emerging by July revealed the poor state of affairs in Taranaki, which in turn fostered an expectation that the remaining garrison troops were about to depart. The *Mercury*, in a turnaround to its earlier position, responded accordingly by asserting that if it was 'deemed of sufficient urgency' to send more of the colony's imperial garrison troops, no doubt the 'Volunteer Corps will be called on to perform garrison duty' – in such circumstances expressing no doubt that 'the citizen soldiers of Tasmania will render their services with alacrity'; many of whom 'are already in a position to do this with credit to themselves and advantage to the Colony'.[166]

Chapter Three

THE HOME FRONT

ONE ASPECT of Australian involvement in New Zealand's wars escaping historical attention almost entirely is the organisation of and contributions to relief funds. Australian support in the 1860s for the Taranaki settler relief and British soldier family relief is in fact indicative of earlier relief efforts acknowledging the impact on settlers, civilians or families caught up in conflicts such as the Crimean War (1854–56) and 'Indian Mutiny' (1857–59).[1] The New Zealand precedent occurred in 1845 with concerns for Bay of Islands and other New Zealand settler refugees. Nonetheless, throughout the decade of the 1860s individuals and groups in the Australian colonies also exhibited concerns and carried out fundraising activities for a diverse array of humanitarian causes, many of which were war related.

The following list of funds provides an insight into the assortment of humanitarian relief or concerns prevalent in the Australian colonies during the 1860s. Although not claiming to be a comprehensive list, these entries do reveal a diversity of Australian awareness and involvement in worldwide events and issues. Relief associated with the New Zealand wars should therefore be acknowledged as part of a broader colonial experience.

One other relief fund which should be included within this phenomenon was established following the loss of HMS *Orpheus* – the flagship of the Sydney-based Australia Station – on the Manukau Bar in New Zealand's North Island in February 1863. This tragedy took the lives of the commodore of the Australia Station, W.F. Burnett, who was in the process of undertaking his first official visit, and some 187 officers and men from the ship's company. Only sixty-nine of the

Other relief funds found to be operating in Australia during the 1860s	**Date**
Papal Wars	1860
Syrian Massacres, and Syrian Relief	1860–61
Indian Famine, and Indian Famine Relief	1861
Donegal Relief Fund	1861
Lancashire distress, and the Lancashire and Cheshire Relief Fund	1862–64
Florence Nightingale (London Hospital and Nurses' training) Fund	1863
Irish distress, and Irish Relief Fund	1863
Polish Relief Fund	1863–64
Schleswig-Holstein War, and Schleswig-Holstein Relief Fund	1864–65
German War Relief	1866

ship's crew survived.[2] The enormity of the loss generated considerable public comment, which in turn stimulated substantial relief fundraising throughout Australasia for the many widows, orphans and other dependents associated with the perished crew. The Orpheus Relief Fund was particularly active in Tasmania, New South Wales, Victoria and New Zealand during 1863–64. The level of public sentiment exhibited towards this great loss even led to the erection of a memorial tablet in the Mariners' Church on the Hobart wharf in June 1864. By August 1863 the total amount of monies received from the Australasian colonies in aid of this relief fund was reported to amount to just over £4,310.[3] The Orpheus Relief Fund therefore showed an extension of concern for the welfare of the families of British servicemen killed in a line of duty not related to actual conflict. It was another example of deep Empire loyalty in the Australasian colonies, quite apart from those various funds directly motivated by the wars.

Often such relief activity was sponsored by or involved middle- and upper-class sections of communities, particularly women (and especially wives of imperial officers or officials), and received patronage by church, and socially or politically prominent persons within colonial society. The people involved were themselves usually imbued with the Christian or altruistic motivations so prevalent in this time of high Victorian values and culture. Nonetheless, the relief such individuals or groups so created was used to the benefit of those unfortunate enough to find themselves caught up in war or other tragedies. It is important to remember that, as colonial society had nothing like the system of social security or pensions we know today, those who found themselves in crisis following the loss of a breadwinner were forced to rely on handouts and charities. The relief funds that arose to deal with particular socio-economic hardships were thus of enormous consequence.

As part of this charitable experience we must also focus on one aspect that emerged as a result of regulations pertaining to marriage in the British Army. General orders in 1829 drew out the issue of the large numbers of women and children who appeared on regimental returns above limits instituted by regulations in 1824. The *United Service Journal* emphasised that efforts must be made to explain this issue to soldiers. Although 'their comforts, as soldiers' were increased by marriage, there was also 'inconvenience and the distress' attached to such marital and family connection, both 'serious and unavoidable, particularly when regiments are ordered to embark for foreign service, when only six women to one hundred men are allowed with their husbands'.[4]

It is this small ratio of men within a regiment who were permitted to marry with regimental approval which led to the need for family relief in the 1860s, when much of the 40th and 12th Regiments garrisoned throughout the Australian colonies were hastily despatched to New Zealand. Only approved wives were regarded as being 'on the strength' of a regiment and were provided for; those not 'on the strength' received no rations or sustenance. Economic and emotional hardship occurred when the troops were hastily sent to serve in the field as crises arose in 1860 and again in 1863, with many women and children left behind in Australian garrison cities neither provided for, nor allowed transport to accompany their menfolk. This serious charitable need in turn led to concerned inhabitants carrying out fundraising and distributing relief to assist these destitute Army families.

Their social dilemma was an especially sad one as these particular regiments had been in Australian garrison since arrival in the early 1850s and had established themselves very much as part of their various colonial communities. The first elements of the 40th Regiment began to arrive in Victoria in late 1852, and apart from this colony, detachments were also located in New South Wales, South Australia and Tasmania during the 1850s up to 1863. The first elements of the 12th Regiment began arriving in Melbourne in late 1854, with detachments thereafter variously located during the 1850s up to 1866 at Ballarat, Castlemaine and Sandhurst in Victoria, Hobart and Launceston in Tasmania, Adelaide, Swan River (Western Australia), Sydney and Brisbane.[5] The length of their stay saw many friendships and family connections fostered in the years leading up to the 1860s.

These British soldiers in garrison became integral parts of their colony of residence; and in fact, many detachments that went off to war in New Zealand during the 1860s were referred to in the Australian press as 'our troops'. War news often provided accounts of the progress of particular detachments such as 'our South Australians', or else published letters received by families or friends of these troops, as well as those received by editors of various Australian newspapers. It is one of the great contradictions of Australian history especially, where so much emphasis is placed on external war experience, that the lives, connections and very importance of these British soldiers and sailors, so much a component of colonial society, is either ignored or passed over as irrelevant.

The settlement of New Plymouth in Taranaki Province, from the *Illustrated London News*, 27 October 1860.

Taranaki relief in Victoria and New South Wales

William Swainson, in a book published shortly after the events occurring at Taranaki, detailed the great suffering of the European settler population caught up in the virtual siege at New Plymouth, during which the productive capacity of the province was completely brought to a halt. He described how the 'whole European population crowded together within the narrow limits of a small section of the town, suffered severely from sickness, anxiety, and harassing suspense. Both in men and money, and in the destruction of property, the cost of the war was by no means inconsiderable.... and the extraordinary amount of sickness, the result of over-crowding and other causes, carried off upwards of 100 of the Taranaki settlers.'[6] The destruction wrought in the province amounted to some two hundred houses burned, cattle, horses and sheep killed or driven off, fencing destroyed, noxious weeds allowed to overrun formerly cultivated lands, and the agricultural constituent of this Taranaki settler community deprived of its subsistence. In

Auckland during 1861 the commissioner for distributing the Taranaki Relief Fund reported the total amount of claims for actual losses of property sustained by Taranaki settlers brought before him by this date amounted to £181,693.[7]

The purpose of the Taranaki Relief Fund was to alleviate the suffering of these settlers, and in Australia was supported primarily in Victoria and New South Wales. In July 1861 the Victorian government voted to subscribe the sum of £1,000 to the fund.[8] Victoria's contributions had already elicited the thanks of the superintendent of New Plymouth in December 1860.[9] In debate on a vote of thanks by New Zealand's government, E.W. Stafford, in seconding Colonial Secretary William Fox's initial resolution, referred to efforts outside of Victoria and the unity of purpose and loyalty that was expressed among the Australasian colonies as a result of this war.[10]

Victorian public support and activities associated with Taranaki settler fundraising was especially evident during August–October 1860, and was still operative into June 1861. In 1867 the *Argus* reminded its readership of the exertions of Melbourne's inhabitants in their liberal subscriptions to this fund: 'The sum collected, amounting to nearly £3,000, was placed in the hands of a committee, formed of the most influential citizens of Melbourne . . . All claims, as we understand, having been satisfied.'[11]

Relief for the 'Taranaki sufferers' was not always simply a matter of supplying financial aid. In August 1860 a circular was forwarded from the Nelson merchant firm of Nash and Scaife to its Melbourne counterpart Lorimer, Mackie, and Company. Nash and Scaife had been alleviating conditions at New Plymouth as best it could by supplying goods and foodstuffs and other essentials. As Nelson and other South Island communities were too small to provide all that was required, this firm took the initiative to approach its 'richer neighbours' to contribute, and by naming the foodstuffs and clothing items 'necessary to mitigate the privations'. 'A further supply to supplement what has already been done was earnestly asked from the other colonies, among which Victoria naturally takes a first place.'[12] The Melbourne merchant firm acted upon Nash and Scaife's missive by immediately approaching the mayor and asking for a public meeting to address this humanitarian request. This took place on 7 September at the Town Hall and was chaired by Governor Barkly. Although attendance was not as large as expected, 'whatever deficiency there was in numbers, appeared to be made up in unanimity and enthusiasm', and from this gathering a committee was appointed to solicit funds for Taranaki relief.[13]

Relief subscriptions immediately began to be received and the committee held its first meeting at the Exchange Hall in William Street on 13 September. Thereafter other suburban municipalities held similar meetings and either formed committees to collect relief or expressed their sympathies with this relief movement. This municipal enthusiasm continued to spread outside of Melbourne and saw additional relief meetings, committees and fundraising in the nature of concerts, lectures and amateur performances take place in regional centres such as Kyneton, Geelong, Ararat, Creswick, Buninyong and Ballarat into 1861.[14]

At one meeting of the Melbourne committee in early October, the report from the subcommittee empowered to purchase and forward supplies provides an indication of the scale and complexity of the relief effort, including the diversity of goods and material being provided in aid of the Taranaki settlers. Here it was also noted that the supplies despatched aboard the *Wonga Wonga* were carried free of freight, lighterage, and labour charges courtesy of the generosity of the Australian Steam Navigation Company, the Hobson's Bay Railway Company, and Thos. Norton and Co.[15] In early November the *Argus* detailed further shipments of relief goods and supplies. In this case, apart from provisions stated as previously sent to Nelson where many New Plymouth settler refugees were temporarily evacuated, the Melbourne Taranaki Relief Fund Committee supplied goods totalling just over £734.[16]

Growing reports of the plight of settlers still in New Plymouth, and those who were departing as refugees to locations such as Nelson, generated concern in New South Wales in early September 1860. In this distressing news it was revealed that even HMCS *Victoria* was involved in the evacuation of settlers from New Plymouth, disembarking one group of approximately one hundred, mainly women and children, at Nelson on 12 August. 'The critical . . . moment has at length arrived, and New Plymouth, "the garden of New Zealand," is converted into a howling waste,' lamented the *Sydney Morning Herald*.[17] Taranaki relief was commenced by way of a preliminary meeting at Sydney's Municipal Council Chambers at Wynyard Square in early September. Those in attendance wanted to formalise a public expression of sympathy with the colonists of Taranaki and 'admiration of the conduct of the Taranaki volunteers'. This initial meeting confirmed a provisional committee and called for a public meeting to carry forward the creation of a relief fund and to invite the governor to preside.[18]

The planned public meeting was delayed, but finally took place on 1 October at the Hall of Temperance in Pitt Street.[19] The governor presided, and though it commenced with only a partially filled hall, it was gradually filled to capacity as the meeting progressed. Many speakers at this gathering strongly urged that the claims of suffering colonists should be met, and 'not only to sympathy but to material aid'.[20] The meeting confirmed a formal relief committee and also unanimously adopted all resolutions.[21] From this point the Taranaki Relief Fund in New South Wales began to carry out its task in earnest.

By 13 October over £300 had been collected in Sydney, apart from a quantity of goods and supplies. The Sydney committee held another well-attended meeting at the Municipal Council Chambers on 27 November. In December the Provincial Council of Taranaki responded to the support provided by New South Wales in a vote of thanks to this colony and Victoria for all that had been done to alleviate the suffering.[22] Later in January 1861 it was reported that £350 had already been remitted to Taranaki and a further £260 was in the hands of the treasurer. During April a detailed 'List of Subscribers' to the Taranaki Relief Fund was published in the *Sydney Morning Herald* providing details of persons actively involved, or from whom subscriptions were obtained. This statement indicates that just over £451 was raised in New South Wales and, as in Victoria, such contributions combined to form welcome relief to the war-torn and displaced settlers of the province.[23]

While considerable efforts towards this fund were under way in colonies such as New South Wales and Victoria, similar undertakings were also taking place in other parts of New Zealand itself during 1860. The Provincial Council of Otago, in a move similar to that of the Victorian government, allocated £1,000 towards Taranaki relief in April. And in September the Taranaki relief committee in Canterbury had reportedly received subscriptions totalling £1,130.[24]

Soldier family relief in New South Wales

It was not until July 1860 that letters to the *Sydney Morning Herald* drew attention to the plight of families of Sydney's 12th Regiment detachment whose husbands had been sent off to Taranaki. Letters from 'Inquirer', 'Homo', and 'Vox Humana' sought public action to alleviate the economic and emotional plight of these families, some of whom were accommodated in the military barracks at Paddington, where they were said to be largely cut off from the necessities of life. 'Surely something should be done to enable these women to exist, at all events. It is strange, in this young country, to reduce the dilemma to life or dishonour, especially when the circumstances causing the dilemma are the exigencies of one's country.'[25]

These correspondents also appealed for subscriptions to be opened for the collection of funds to assist these soldier families. A Queensland press column 'By A Sydney Man' reported that among the families of soldiers left behind in Sydney were twenty-three women married without military permission, all left to fend on their own, and with 'these poor creatures are 24 children'.[26] In chorus with such voices, the *Sydney Morning Herald* added its dismay at the lack of care for the wives and children of the troops left in Sydney.[27] This paper took the view that it was wrong to view the colonies as separate states having no mutual obligations, and nor was there any benefit from the British troops crossing 'the line which divides us from our neighbour'.[28]

Once subscriptions had commenced, the *Herald* became highly critical of the lack of effective government and public support in Sydney for the soldier families, especially in contrast to efforts being undertaken in Victoria.[29] On 4 August this paper expatiated upon the need to bolster support for the families of these troops: 'Although the subscription . . . is not altogether a failure . . . we cannot call it a success . . . It still remains a fact that while their husbands and fathers are risking their lives for the defence of the country they are left in a state of destitution.'[30] By late August less than £100 had been subscribed in Sydney for the relief of such soldier families – a poor record indeed when compared to those efforts instituted in Victoria.[31] Despite this situation, one British officer from Sydney's garrison serving at Taranaki relayed in a letter that although the troops were experiencing 'awfully severe duties', the knowledge of the family relief efforts being undertaken in New South Wales was of some comfort to them in their struggle.[32]

The New South Wales community was also able to assess the progress of the war from the publication of letters from soldiers in the field. Between April and August 1860, one Sydney resident, a brother of a 65th Regiment soldier serving in New Zealand, passed to the *Sydney Morning Herald* a series of accounts offering glimpses of the harsh life in camp and events associated with the war. These letters clearly depict the serious plight of all the civilians and military caught up in the conflict around the besieged settlement of New Plymouth.[33] The soldier concluded with signs of disillusionment exhibited among the troops, not only the result of poor weather conditions, but also because of the Maori method of warfare. British soldiers expected to face an enemy on open battlefields, and

The settlement of New Plymouth, looking from the camp of the 40th Regiment, from the *Illustrated London News*, 29 December 1860.

Maori hit-and-run tactics and pa fortifications were taking both a physical and mental toll on these imperial troops. 'The natives are now in their strongholds, north and south of us. They will rob and plunder, but will not give us the chance to meet them in the field, and to rush a pah is sheer madness. The weather is extremely wet and cold, and the roads next to impossible.'[34]

Public impressions could not fail to be affected by the grim content of such correspondence, and at the very least influenced involvement or financial contributions of some in the cause of the British soldier or Taranaki settler relief efforts.

Soldier family relief in Victoria

During late 1860 many letters received from Melbourne's 40th Regiment in New Zealand were published. These provided first-hand accounts of the fighting and conditions being encountered by 'their troops' in Taranaki. Other letters to family and friends vividly portrayed the appalling conditions experienced in New Plymouth by both civilian and military alike, including the shortages, horrendous weather, isolation and the fear of attack.[35] In addition, they also confirmed the high rate of casualties sustained among these troops, bringing home the realities of war to Victorian friends and family who would see the names of loved ones among the killed and wounded.[36] These letters also indicate that troops in the field, in turn, looked forward to receipt of news and papers from 'home'. One letter from Taranaki, dated 9 November, saw 'XL' confirm: 'It is with the greatest expectation that we always look forward to the arrival of the Melbourne mail, not only on account of receiving letters from our absent friends, but then the general cry is, "Who has *The Argus!*"'[37]

The fact remains that the public in Victoria considered 40th Regiment troops serving in New Zealand who had belonged to their garrison as still very much a part of their colony. In April 1861, 'M', in the false expectation of the return of these troops upon the cessation of hostilities, succinctly portrayed this bond: 'The termination of the war in New Zealand will allow the gallant 40th to return to Melbourne . . . As this glorious old regiment has been stationed . . . [here] for eight years and are looked on as "our own regiment," I would suggest that they receive a recognition of their services similar to what the Crimean army received on its return.'[38] Part of this connection with the soldiers of the 40th included concerns about the welfare of the wives and children of these troops in their absence.

In the Victorian Parliament questions were asked during July 1860 as to what provisions would be made for the widows and children of soldiers recently killed in Taranaki. No doubt the spur for these inquiries were the letters to the *Argus*, bringing this issue very much to public attention. For instance, 'A.B.C.' was keen to bring immediate notice to the plight of all the 40th soldiers' wives:

> By the kindness of Colonel Leslie, the men's wives who were married without leave have been allowed to go into barracks, but no provision whatever is made for their subsistence during the absence of the regiment. . . . the only means the men will have of sending to their families will be by mail from New Zealand. . . . what will the poor creatures do until their husbands have accumulated sufficient funds to send them something?[39]

Apart from the immediate financial hardships endured by the families of these departing troops, there was also the question of the welfare of widows and orphans of personnel killed or incapacitated. On this issue, 'Amicus' addressed the editor of the *Argus* on behalf of the families of the soldiers who were about to depart for the war:

> It will be no small consolation to them to know that there are some here ready to assist those they leave behind, and in the hour of mortal strife, it will nerve the arm, and calm the mind, then so distracted with thoughts of home. Let us . . . have our relief fund, on the principle of the Crimean and Indian relief funds. . . . The despatches . . . show the desperate nature of the fighting. In one of the two companies engaged, the dead outnumbered the wounded. One of the former has left us his widow and fatherless child.[40]

The government reply indicated there were currently three widows and three children in Melbourne. Mr Fellows for the government added that, because the troops did not belong to Victoria, and the war was not connected with the colony, any provision for the families of those who had fallen was a matter for the imperial government. The Victorian government therefore avoided responsibility for the welfare of these military families on financial terms, claiming it as an imperial matter, but some in Parliament saw this response as 'anything but satisfactory'.[41] Into this void of governmental support stepped the soldier family relief organisation.

In late July, following a petition, Melbourne's mayor convened the first public meeting to solicit funds and form a relief committee. Although also supported by some members of Parliament, it was not well attended, indicative perhaps that the public's pockets were somewhat shallower than their imperial fervour. The meeting was told that eighty-eight married women with 165 children were in need of assistance at the Spencer Street Barracks. Concerns were also raised for the families of crew of HMCS *Victoria*, whom it was believed should share equally in the benefits of the relief fund for the soldier families.[42] During August a ball was also organised by the Royal Victorian Volunteer Artillery Regiment to raise funds, as were a series of benefit performances by the Histrionic Society (including a lecture on 'Tom Brown's School-days' by prominent Victorian cricketer W.L. Rees). The ball was held at the Exhibition Building on 3 August under the patronage of Governor Barkly.[43]

By 18 August the relief committee determined that the greatest distress actually existed among the wives and children of those who were 'not married according to regimental regulations', and their needs were included in the appeal.[44] Later in October it was shown that all funds raised were nearly exhausted, although numbers of fresh cases of distress continued to arise, with more than twenty of the soldiers' children reported sick.[45]

The struggle to pursue its purpose saw renewed philanthropic activities in support of the soldier families take hold from October well into 1861. A lecture in aid of the relief fund on the history of the 40th Regiment by William Hull, member of the Legislative Council, though initially postponed, was held at the Mechanics' Institute on 1 November.[46] The Histrionic Society also continued to stage benefit performances, contributing a much-needed £50 in November. In an attempt to further stimulate public interest, the *Argus* reviewed these activities, making a plea for greater public involvement and contributions.[47] Public consciousness was awakened and led to organisation of a grand concert in aid of the soldier families at the Exhibition Building, a gala volunteer fête at the Cremorne Gardens, and early the next year an amateur concert at Brunswick at the courthouse under the patronage of the chief secretary, the local council, and the bench of magistrates.[48] Additional funds raised were used to continue assistance to these military families, and included an advance to 'widow Finigan', who was provided a passage to return to England.[49]

On 19 March 1861 a deputation from the 'committee of the Wives, Widows, and Orphans' Fund of H.M. 40th Regiment' called upon the Victorian treasurer, submitting a summary of the relief fund's activities over the previous nine months. They pointed out that the main objects of the relief committee had largely fallen upon their own shoulders, with the able assistance of the regimental schoolmaster; nonetheless, 'some 80 women and 70 children had been fed and aided by cash advances, and all misery from poverty had been averted. Some 15 children who had died had been respectably buried, and many comforts' were afforded to all those married outside of the military regulations.[50] The colonial treasurer promised to come to the assistance of the committee, for despite all the fundraising efforts, total expenditure was £408 but receipts themselves only amounted to £383. This shortfall reveals the struggle the fund had to contend with throughout its existence. Shortly thereafter the *Argus* commented that although little might be known publicly about the proceedings of this relief committee, 'many a voice can be found in the barracks at the present time to bear witness to the benefit conferred by them'.[51] Functions in aid of the widows and orphans of the 40th Regiment continued to be carried on beyond this time.[52]

Despite the difficulties the committee had in raising the funds needed for all relief purposes, Lieutenant-Colonel Arthur Leslie, commanding the 40th from Auckland in July 1862, conveyed his appreciation for all the efforts undertaken to support the wives of soldiers who were 'married without leave'. The public subscriptions raised in Melbourne had provided passage to Auckland for all wives and families not on the regimental strength who so desired it.[53]

Apart from this committee's tireless efforts, it should not be overlooked that a considerable number of other people assisted the relief drive by way of their organisation and participation in the various fundraising activities such as amateur performances, concerts and fêtes. Relief for these soldier families was generally successful, despite difficulties in having sufficient funds on hand. Similarly, as these efforts were being undertaken, they competed for contributions with like-minded fundraising and organisation for the Taranaki settlers, which to many colonists was perceived as a fund in greater need as a result of the enormity of destruction, suffering and numbers involved.

Relief efforts in Tasmania, South Australia and Queensland

The Tasmanian press during 1860–61 allotted considerable coverage to the predicament of settlers at New Plymouth or those evacuated to other locations such as Nelson. Such reportage also kept abreast of Taranaki Relief Fund activities carried out in the other Australian colonies, in New Zealand at Canterbury and Otago, as well as in London.[54] However, while the plight of the Taranaki sufferers was well known, no evidence has come to light of any organised government or public involvement in relation to their relief, although individuals may well have contributed money or goods via organisations in place in other colonies such as Victoria. Nor was there apparently any issue concerning destitute families of soldiers despatched to New Zealand during 1860–61. Tasmanian concerns about the welfare of such soldier families only became evident later in 1863 – no doubt the result of the majority of troops actually remaining in garrison during 1860–61, apart from two companies of the 40th who departed during April 1860.

Of course this did not mean that the welfare of the troops who did leave Tasmania was forgotten. Tasmanians, apart from constant coverage of the war itself, were kept informed of the condition and service of the 40th soldiers through published correspondence received by family and friends, and in July a number of such letters were included in the pages of the *Mercury*. One from Taranaki, dated 21 June 1860, describes the appalling living conditions of the troops in the field and the siege-like military situation:

> I would have written to you before were it not for the manner in which I have been situated since I left Hobart Town. After we landed . . . we were put into tents and there remained for a month, relieving every day, nine men in each tent, . . . We can only get a mail once a month, . . . We have obtained a little comfort lately by getting into huts, though miserably situated.
>
> Major Nelson landed about the middle of May, and took command of the 40th. . . . It is a good thing for us to have the Major. I can assure you Nelson is opening some of their eyes. We have only had one night in bed since we landed, and have been up to our knees in water.
>
> There are about 300 men found for guard every day in the garrison of Taranaki, exclusive of a night patrol of 50 men . . .
>
> We have a chain of sentries about fifteen yards apart inland from one sea beach to the other, for fear the Maories should come and take Taranaki, as they have threatened they would, and their time would be at the dawn . . .[55]

Another letter arrived in Hobart from a soldier named Quinn at Camp Waitara, dated 30 June. This described the vicious hand-to-hand fighting which had occurred on 27 June and this soldier's feelings at surviving the engagement:

> Dear William, – I am happy to inform you of my safe escape on the morning of the 27th when we made an attack upon one of Kingi's pahs. We lost 32 killed and 32 wounded; our men fought like lions, hand to hand in six feet high of fern. Any of our men the Maories came across when wounded, they tomahawked, and of one officer of the name Lieutenant Brook they did not leave one inch together, but they cut and hacked him to pieces, and a Serjeant who was trying to save him met with the same fate. . . . We left . . . camp 300 men strong . . . and returned . . . with sixty-four casualties, so you may imagine the destructive fire we were under, for four hours surrounded on all sides by hundreds who held a position strong enough to hold against ten thousand troops . . .[56]

Quinn's correspondence in fact reinforces the true nature of the attachment such troops developed while in garrison locations like Hobart. The publication of such letters provided family and friends and other concerned colonists with some grasp of conditions endured by their particular troops serving across the Tasman. There was clearly a sense amongst Australian colonists of their place as a 'home front'.[57]

One other related arrival in Hobart from the troops in Taranaki was a series of drawings made by Captain J.E.D. McCarthy who commanded the 40th Regiment detachment from Tasmania. They were reproduced as photographs by a Mr Frith of Murray Street, Hobart in early 1861. These images were presumably made available for inspection and sale and were reported to consist of several Maori chiefs and various views of military camps and fortifications and the battlefield, thereby adding to Tasmanian public imagery of the war beyond the available press accounts.[58]

Queenslanders and South Australians were also aware of the efforts being undertaken in other colonies for soldier family and Taranaki relief, and although no indication was found of actual involvement in Queensland, limited activity appears to have occurred in South Australia. No doubt the scale of trade and communications between particular colonies impacted upon the nature of public responses to such issues, where long-established colonies such as New South Wales and Victoria had greater interaction and reaction to events unfolding in Taranaki. Press coverage in both Queensland and South Australia nonetheless described the activities and progress in other colonies.[59]

In an editorial on 'Assistance to New Zealand', the *South Australian Register* detailed efforts of support in Melbourne, and suggested similar efforts be made in Adelaide. The *Register* concluded that if no government or public action could be stimulated as had occurred in Melbourne, individuals could still play a role.[60] The Sydney press shortly hereafter reported that the South Australian governor had contributed £25 to the Taranaki Relief Fund. Monies were also provided by a number of financial institutions, including £25 from the Union Bank, and just over £10 from the English and Scottish Chartered Bank. As well, a relief committee was reported established and active, including a subcommittee to take charge of any contribution in goods.[61]

Victoria triumphant: the return of HMCS *Victoria* and General Pratt

The Victorian warship HMCS *Victoria* with Major-General Pratt and staff departed New Zealand on 3 April 1861. Just prior to departure the *Victoria*'s final task was to proceed to the Waitara with Governor Browne, the Native Secretary, and two other ministers for peace negotiations. On 11 April the *Victoria* moored at the Sandridge Railway Pier, Melbourne to much public acclaim. The returning general was widely perceived as both saviour and hero at Taranaki. On arrival, Governor Barkly proceeded on board to welcome (his father-in-law) the general, and as this party landed they received a salute from the Volunteer Artillery, while the crew of the *Victoria* manned the rigging as the general left the vessel.[62]

Both public and government in Melbourne fêted the general and the officers and crew of the *Victoria* for their services in Taranaki. In the Legislative Assembly, Pratt received an address congratulating him and all the soldiers and sailors who served under him in New Zealand, expressing as well the government's sympathies for the widows and children of those troops who fell during the conflict.[63] On 13 April, Melbourne's Lord Mayor visited the *Victoria* and invited the crew to a public dinner in the name of the corporation of Melbourne – the first ever welcome-home function for an Australian colonial military unit.[64] This reception took place on 18 April at the Bull and Mouth Hotel in Bourke Street attended by between '60 and 70 of the crew'.[65] A deputation from the Melbourne City Council also presented General Pratt with a congratulatory address, while other events saw him entertained at the Melbourne Club, and take part in a volunteer levee where he received the officers of the various participating volunteer corps.[66]

During April, Victoria's Governor Barkly received a despatch from New Zealand conveying that government's thanks for the services rendered by the *Victoria* and the vessel's officers and crew. Governor Browne relayed that the return of the *Victoria* to Melbourne afforded an opportunity of acknowledging 'the deep obligation under which the New Zealand Government feels itself to the Government of Victoria for the valuable services rendered to this Colony for nearly a year' by this warship. These responsibilities were at all times performed 'in the most satisfactory manner', with the men performing duties 'of an arduous and harassing nature'.[67] Overall, Victoria could well feel proud of the services rendered to New Zealand and in its patriotic support for imperial interests throughout the Taranaki crisis. Not only had the colony acceded to a diminution of its available imperial garrison, its only colonial warship and crew had participated throughout the conflict in a most admirable manner.

Following the cessation of hostilities in 1861, some elements of Victoria's former 40th Regiment garrison were returned, though only as a temporary measure, as in 1863 these soldiers would depart for New Zealand shores again, marking the withdrawal of this regiment from Australia.[68] Victoria's response during 1860–61 readily placed it in a position to render like-minded support when the call of the Empire came once more in 1863.

During 1861 some of the military forces also began to return to New South Wales. On 15 July HMS *Cordelia* arrived in Sydney with the latest gloomy New Zealand news, where up to 23 June 'the general impression appeared to be that hostilities would commence throughout the island at no very distant date'.[69] It was not until 16 October that the *Henry F. Fernie* arrived in Sydney bringing some of the colony's 12th Regiment troops despatched the previous year.[70] Despite the arrival of these troops, the governor was still corresponding with his New Zealand counterpart into 1862, requesting the return of all troops in order to re-establish New South Wales's allotted military strength. Governor Young emphasised that the original force despatched was 'in the expectation that they would have been permitted to return long before this'.[71] Governor Grey, though, was reluctant to diminish any further the soldiery he now had on hand, arguing instead 'that nothing could operate more prejudicially upon the Native mind than the weakening of our Forces at the present moment', on account of the 'difficulties prevailing'.[72] In fact, Grey was already looking to the expansion of military forces available to him in preparation for the invasion of the Waikato.

Another important arrival aboard the *Henry F. Fernie* was Colonel Gore Browne, the former governor of New Zealand. Browne, having been replaced in this post by Sir George Grey, would subsequently take up the governorship of Tasmania, where in 1863 he would continue an involvement in New Zealand affairs when he promptly reacted in support of New Zealand's renewed calls for military assistance in the prelude to the Waikato campaign.

Chapter Four

A REAL WAR

THE INCONCLUSIVE OUTCOME of the Taranaki War of 1860–61 merely allowed for a short breathing space during which both Maori and British began preparations for further clashes. During this lull before the storm, imperial authorities asserted their determination to force their domination into the Maori-controlled interior of the North Island by constructing the Great South Road as a communications and supply line. The purpose of this road was not lost on the European settlers of the Auckland frontier. Stephen White, a farm labourer working south of Auckland, and a former Australian resident, wrote to his sons in Adelaide in 1862: 'I am happy to say that War is quiet at present [though] the English are making a rode [*sic*] through the Bush now so that they can get to the Mowry's.'[1] But at Tataraimaka in Taranaki Province on 4 May 1863, violence once again flared when a party of the 57th Regiment was ambushed and killed. Events quickly escalated, and on 11 July Governor Grey issued a poorly veiled ultimatum to the 'Chiefs of the Waikato'.[2] The next day the first elements of General Cameron's force to invade the region crossed the Mangatawhiri, a tributary of the Waikato marking the northern Kingite Maori border, signalling the beginnings of 'the largest and most ambitious campaign' of the New Zealand wars.[3]

The year 1863 marks the high-water mark in Australian military involvement in New Zealand. It was the events of this year – though less so in 1864 (particularly when looking at reactions to the second military settler recruiting mission) – that were supported by majority public sentiment in the Australian colonies, as well as by both the colonial and imperial authorities. The co-operation New Zealand

The Great South Road between Drury and the Waikato, emphasising the difficult forested terrain faced by imperial and colonial forces, from the *Illustrated London News*, 7 November 1863.

received from Australia's imperial military and civil representatives enabled the scale and success of the campaigns that took place during 1863–64. This willingness, though again sometimes grudging and with an eye to colonial self-interest evident in 1860–61, saw Australian colonial administrations once more interact with the imperial authorities and New Zealand government, ensuring a diverse array of military, commissariat and logistical support.[4]

The Great South Road near Shepherd's Bush, where Maori forces ambushed a British convoy, from the *Illustrated London News*, 7 November 1863.

Australian manpower contributions

One myth associated with the four Waikato Military Settler Regiments raised during 1863 and 1864 is that they were all from the Australian colonies. This is simply incorrect. The Australian-born or -recruited members actually make up varying proportions of the individual strengths of each of the four regiments comprising this force – as they did the (often overlooked) Taranaki Military Settlers. Another popular misconception is that the largest proportion of Australian enlistees is found in the 1st Waikato Regiment, when in fact this was only the case with the last-formed, 4th Waikato Regiment, and the Taranaki Military Settlers.[5]

In reference to the Taranaki Military Settlers, a review of the roll of the 'Melbourne Contingent' of this corps reveals a total of at least 557 men of enlisted rank enrolled in Victoria and South Australia in January 1864.[6] One member of this 'Melbourne Contingent' was Francis Sire. In Victoria he enrolled as No. 790, Taranaki Military Settlers, at Geelong on 23 January 1864 aged 26, stating his trade as labourer. He departed Melbourne aboard the *Gresham* and arrived at New Plymouth, Taranaki on 17 February 1864. Serving in No. 8 Company, he saw action on the west coast in engagements at Sentry Hill (April 1864) and the siege at Pipiriki (July 1865), and was also a member of the East Coast Expeditionary Force (which included Nos. 8 & 10 Companies of the Taranaki Military Settlers) where he saw further action at Opotiki during November 1865.[7] Upon return from the East Coast, the period of service for these Taranaki Military Settlers had expired and disagreement over pay and other entitlements caused a number of the men to claim their discharge, but this stand led to them losing their military settler land entitlements.[8] Sire was one of this number, and after his service, like many other military settlers, moved on in search of other opportunities and employment. He had returned to Victoria by 1872 when he applied for the New Zealand War Medal, and where he also appears to have become involved in that colony's volunteer movement.[9]

Evidence also indicates certain individuals made the trip across the Tasman to enlist in the New Zealand colonial forces on their own initiative or travelled there with informal small groups. Individuals such as these therefore entered service in military settler or other units in New Zealand, and as a result their Australian origins often go unrecognised. One such was William Fraser, former drill instructor of the Reedbeds Cavalry, a South Australian volunteer unit, who went on to serve in the 2nd Waikato Regiment and the Colonial Defence Force.[10] On 28 September 1863 the *South Australian Register* reported that he had departed for the war, 'and Captain Egerton and Serjeant-Major Hawke, formerly of the Kapunda Rifles, are said to have left with the same gallant intention'.[11] These men left Adelaide off their own bat, as no formal military settler recruiting took place in that city until January 1864. This particular band of South Australian volunteer officers and non-commissioned officers thus provides an excellent example of the military fervour of some Australian colonial volunteers who saw the wars in New Zealand as their opportunity for real action and to do their bit for the Empire. In late 1863 Fraser wrote back to South Australia to announce that he had joined the 2nd Waikato Regiment and had been promoted to sergeant.[12] A later letter received by the *Register* provided an account of his service and experiences under the heading of 'A South Australian in the New Zealand War'. He was then serving in the Colonial Defence Force cavalry at Tauranga and provided an account of an engagement, presumably at Te Ranga, on 21 June 1864. Here his horse was shot from underneath him, but he managed to extricate himself and joined with the infantry until the end of the battle.[13]

Another example is Walter Vernon Herford, an Adelaide solicitor who was involved in South Australia's volunteer movement, serving as captain of the Kent Rifles.[14] Herford migrated to Australia sometime in the early 1850s, and met and married Annie McNee, with whom he had two daughters.[15] He was a person imbued with martial fervour and imperial patriotism, and departed for New Zealand to offer his services on his own initiative, no doubt encouraged in this action by coverage in South Australia's press of the commencement of military settler recruiting in other Australian colonies. Such news also detailed the arrival of Colonel Pitt to organise the recruiting and the military settler terms and conditions being offered, as well as offers of service and associated enthusiasm emanating from the volunteer movement of these other colonies.[16] The *South Australian Register* on 29 December 1863 reported on 'Adelaideans in New Zealand', noting not just Herford's presence, but that of other South Australians now serving in the colony such as Alexander Kirkland, who had re-enlisted and was now a colour-sergeant in the 12th Regiment. Kirkland, a former soldier and veteran of the Crimean War and 'Indian Mutiny', had been drill instructor to South Australia's volunteers.[17] This account also relayed details from another 'late resident' of Adelaide who had witnessed the battle of Rangiriri.[18]

On 20 October 1863 Herford was appointed captain in the Auckland Militia, serving in the 3rd Waikato Regiment.[19] In order to confirm his entitlement to this captain's commission and the bounty for obtaining the requisite recruits, he undertook the enrolment of a company of military settlers for the 3rd Waikato Regiment at Nelson and neighbouring areas in the South Island.[20] He later volunteered for service with the Imperial Commissariat Transport Corps, no doubt to avoid the tedium of garrison duty and increase the opportunity to be in locations where fighting was taking place. It was in this latter capacity that his reckless desire for action led to his demise. During the siege of the Maori pa at Orakau (30 March–2 April 1864) he received a mortal gunshot wound to the head while leading a party trying to pierce the Maori fortifications. William Race, a 1st Waikato Regiment militiaman from Melbourne and later a member of the Forest Rangers, who was present at this engagement, left an account of these events in a record of his war service.[21] Though incorrect about the actual manner of wounding, Race's reminiscences recount the atmosphere in which Herford received his severe injuries, when 'he almost sought it by the very indiscreet manner in which he exposed himself . . . no less than attacking the pallisading [*sic*] single handed with a view to effect a breach by cutting some down; of course the Maories very soon observed him'.[22]

Before his death at Otahuhu on 28 June 1864, Herford was mentioned in General Cameron's despatches for Orakau and brought to the notice of the governor, who directed his promotion to the rank of major for distinguished services in the field.[23] Afterwards a subscription was raised for his widow and children and an amount of just over £335 was gathered. Annie and the children had remained at Adelaide, where she received her husband's war medal in 1877. She was also granted an annual pension from the New Zealand government, which amounted to £130 per annum in 1888.[24]

Apart from colonial enlistments into garrison regiments such as the 12th and 40th, other members of the British Army serving in Australasia were Australian-born who appear to have enlisted in Great Britain or other parts of the Empire. Many such men may well have been sons of British soldiers who had been in garrison in these colonies in earlier periods. An 1864 obituary for Captain Donald Maclean Fraser, a young officer of the 70th Regiment who saw service in New Zealand, reveals not only apparent Australian birth, but his family connection via his mother from Sydney, who married an officer of the 80th Regiment.[25] The 80th had been in garrison in Australia and New Zealand from 1836–44 before departing Sydney for duty in India where it was soon on active service during the Sutlej Campaign of 1845–46. This particular family lost their father and husband during the battle of Ferozeshuhur in December 1845, their plight also revealing the path into the military that orphaned sons often followed, as in this case, via a deceased father's regiment.[26]

Another Australian-born officer serving in the British Army was Captain John Shaw Phelps, 14th Regiment, who in New Zealand died of wounds sustained during an attack on Maori fortifications at Rangiriri on 20 November 1863. Phelps was born in Sydney and grew up on his parents' property on the Paterson River in northern New South Wales. He studied medicine in Sydney, and in the early 1850s sailed for England to join the British Army. His motivations were probably patriotic, acted upon after receipt of news of the outbreak of the Crimean War.

Initially appointed assistant surgeon in the 57th Regiment in 1854, he served in Crimea, after which he was appointed to the 2nd Battalion of the 14th Regiment, which later served in New Zealand during 1860–66.[27]

It should not be forgotten that the Royal Navy also recruited in Australia for those of its warships serving on the Australia Station. Considerable problems had existed in establishing experience and expertise in the Royal Navy during the 1840s as a result of paying off ships' companies upon the expiration of the three-year commission. The decision in 1853 to introduce a new system of continuous service eased this situation, and by 1857 almost half of the men then serving in the Royal Navy were serving under the new regulations.[28] As requirements arose aboard Royal Navy vessels on the Australia Station, naval authorities in Sydney often recruited for seamen throughout the 1840s into the 1860s. The involvement of these individuals, as either Australian-born or -recruited individuals who played a role in New Zealand's wars, must also be taken into account.

The most significant contribution of Australian colonials to New Zealand's wars, though, was made by those recruited as military settlers in 1863 and 1864. These men derived largely from Victoria, New South Wales and Tasmania, while smaller numbers were also enlisted in South Australia and Queensland. Others were drawn from places such as Otago in the South Island of New Zealand, where many had ventured in search of gold, but are often unable to be identified effectively as Australian colonists. Among those who enlisted for service on the nominal roll of the 'Otago Contingent' of the Taranaki Military Settlers are ten Australian-born recruits, including one Western Australian.[29] Other men who were either Australian-born, or else had prior Australian experience, residence or family connections, were already in the North Island where they joined in localities such as Auckland or New Plymouth. One such was Campbell Stevens, who was born at Redfern, Sydney. He enlisted in Auckland in the 3rd Waikato Military Settler Regiment as Regt. No. 1352 on 11 December 1863. On enlistment he stated his occupation as 'Bushman', which may account for his presence in the North Island plying this trade. He served in No. 10 Company during 1863–66 and became entitled to the New Zealand War Medal after coming under fire in a skirmish when he was a member of a small party of six or seven Waikato militiamen and British regulars. This party was on a reconnaissance when they discovered the Maori constructing the Orakau pa, which led to the siege of this fortification. Upon completion of service, Stevens was granted a military settler town lot and farmland in the Waiterimo Valley, Cambridge. It is not known when or why he departed New Zealand, but much of the military settler scheme was unsuccessful, and many had either left or sold their lands by the late 1860s. Stevens, as a bushman obviously, sought different horizons, which in time found him residing on Lord Howe Island off the coast of New South Wales. Here in

1888 he applied for the war medal to which he had only recently learned he was entitled, finally receiving it in 1892.[30]

What these biographical cameos illustrate is the frequency of cross-Tasman travel during this period. And although precise figures are impossible to ascertain, it is clear that upwards of 2500 men enlisted for service as military settlers during the formal recruiting missions to Australia in 1863 and 1864.[31] In addition, an unknown number, but possibly around several hundred, departed Australian shores independently or else were already in New Zealand but still had definite Australian origins, experience or connections. These men clearly made a substantial contribution to the military forces available in the country. Such men were not only invaluable for front-line service, but as became more common, worked as personnel assisting in the commissariat and logistical services which kept imperial and colonial forces clothed, fed and armed throughout the difficult and diverse terrain of New Zealand's North Island.

Australian humanitarianism, 1863–65

Australian colonial communities again expressed concern for the welfare of soldiers' families. Such solicitude also found expression in the extension of sympathies and relief to the widows and children of soldiers who were killed in this major period of imperial campaigning during 1863–64. The issue was also taken up in New Zealand itself, including the New Zealand government appropriating £2,000 for the support of wives and families of British soldiers and sailors killed during the war.[32] Such efforts towards a patriotic fund saw like-minded efforts in Australia. In Sydney in July 1864 a benefit night for the widows and orphans of the seamen and Royal Marines killed at the disastrous Gate Pa engagement presented amateur performances by the officers and crew of HMS *Curacoa* at the Prince of Wales Theatre.[33] A large audience including Governor Young and many naval and military officers attended this occasion, which by all accounts was very successful.[34]

South Australian relief efforts

With the departure of South Australia's 40th Regiment garrison to New Zealand in October 1863, Adelaide residents soon became aware of the plight of the families of these troops still in their midst. In particular, those families not formally recognised as part of the regimental strength were in immediate danger of economic distress. On the eve of his departure on 29 September, Lieutenant Lucas of the 40th wrote to Major Bowdler on the issue of allowances provided to families via the South Australian government.[35] Bowdler immediately brought before Governor Daly for his 'favourable consideration' the supplication that allowances be granted this officer's wife in his absence. He also handed the governor a petition requesting the provision of pay, free quarters and rations to the wives and children of all ranks of the 40th detachment while absent on war service.[36]

During October the *South Australian Register* received various letters to the editor on the issue of the soldiers' families. Not all were in support of moves to establish charity or a soldiers' bazaar for such families, although 'Industrious', the author of such comments, was soundly countered by subsequent letters in reply.[37] Later in November the *Register* dedicated an editorial to the issue of the 'Soldiers' Families'. Although commending the efforts of the persons involved in the relief efforts, the paper also raised the question of whether the imperial authorities should in fact be responsible for the welfare of these families.[38]

'A Lady' from North Adelaide, through the medium of the *Register*, wanted to draw the immediate attention of 'the wives and daughters of South Australia' to the plight of the families of the troops about to depart. This correspondent suggested that the initiative of the ladies of Tasmania, who were reportedly already preparing themselves to assist their own military families, should be mimicked.[39] In support of this issue the *Register* provided details of the numbers of women and children who would be affected by the departure, pointing out that only eight families would be going to New Zealand. Eighteen wives and thirty-five children, most of whom would then be without their usual means of support, would remain in Adelaide.[40] 'Colonist' directed attention to the fact 'that out of the 18 soldiers' wives and families who are left behind only three are allowed quarters in the barracks'. As the remainder would soon face prospects of destitution, 'Colonist' suggested the government allow the remainder of the soldiers' families without quarters the temporary use of the barracks 'until their husbands and fathers return, or until they embark from New Zealand . . . for England in case they are so ordered'.[41]

Within days of this suggestion the South Australian government declared it would only provide quarters and rations for the three families (three wives and nine children) of soldiers who were married in accordance with army regulations. The remaining fifteen wives and thirty-five children were accordingly left to fend for themselves. Into this charitable gap sallied forth a small group of dedicated Adelaide citizens who were prepared to organise fundraising activities, and on 15 October an advertisement announced a 'dramatic entertainment' to this end.[42] The impoverished circumstances of these soldier families were not long after related in the *Register* as having 'awakened something more than sympathy in the minds of some of our more fortunate fellow-colonists'. Here, a Mr Edwards and other amateur musicians kindly offered their services. The governor and a number of influential gentlemen also came forward to give their names as patrons.[43]

The preliminary meeting for the organisation of this relief took place on 28 October at the Armoury in Adelaide. At this meeting Colonel Biggs, Lieutenant-Colonel Mayo, Inspector G. Hamilton JP, Neville Blyth MP, Sergeant Clarke the barrack-master, and Mr F. Downie the armourer formed themselves into a committee to obtain subscriptions.[44] Two days later Clarke reported that he had already acted to relieve three wives from pressure from landlords, as well as guaranteeing payment of rents for all those who required such assistance. Clarke also detailed the arrangements made with various tradesmen, by which 'he could supply rations for each woman and every five children per week at a rate of 5s. 1½d., and with rent 17s. 6d. weekly; this would make a total sum of £5 6s. 9d. required per week'. The committee agreed to relief on this scale, with rent to be paid from the date of departure of the detachment, and rations to commence the following day.[45]

At a meeting in early November the total amount of donations received amounted to just over £52. In seeking additional funds, Inspector Hamilton informed the committee he had subscription lists forwarded to all police stations, and the Honorary Secretary F. Downie likewise reported forwarding of lists to all volunteer captains to try and stimulate assistance from those quarters. Extensive advertisements and press commentary reminding the public of the amateur performance in aid of this fund also appeared during this month. It was held at the Victoria Theatre on 23 November under the patronage of Governor Daly and was reported a great success.[46] By 16 December the committee of the Soldier Family Relief Fund reported receiving a total of just over £210 in donations. Subscriptions from various sources continued to be received well into 1864.[47] The committee also approached the touring Lancashire Bellringers who were in Adelaide in March 1864. Their performance attracted a large audience, adding over £24 to the fund.[48]

At a committee meeting in May 1864 Colonel Biggs produced a document signed by the whole of the 40th soldiers now in New Zealand who had been part of the Adelaide detachment, making it clear that all the men wanted their families to remain in Adelaide at this time because of the lack of sufficient accommodation in Auckland.[49] In recognition of this wish the committee continued to dispense its services to those families still requiring assistance from June into September of that year.[50]

One of the last recorded subscriptions provided occurred in September 1864 from a benefit performance by the Christy Minstrels. During this month there was a special meeting of the committee at which it was unanimously resolved the fund would continue to disperse relief only until the end of September. After this time the only relief offered would be for those willing to proceed to New Zealand as soon as the committee was able to provide passage. Later, at a full meeting of the committee on 3 October, it was reported that only two of the soldiers' wives and families were prepared to take up the offer of passages to New Zealand. Thereupon it was unanimously resolved to abide by their previous decision and no longer provide relief to those who had declined to rejoin their husbands.[51] Apart from learning that the Auckland accommodation problems had since dissipated, part of this decision was no doubt prompted by the knowledge that the 40th Regiment would not be returning to Australia. Thereafter, the affairs of the South Australian Soldier Family Relief Fund were wound up.

Adelaide's committee proved to be the longest and most efficiently run of any of those whose purpose was the relief of military families during the 1860s. This committee carried out its brief to care for the basic needs of the wives and children of Adelaide's 40th troops in some form or other for over a year. Not only was this a substantial commitment from all those involved, but obviously of immeasurable value both to the families concerned as well as the soldiers on active service across the Tasman.

Tasmanian relief efforts

Tasmania's philanthropic efforts were similarly motivated in the support of the families of troops despatched in 1863. Commencing in August, this relief effort proved both popular and successful. The *Mercury* published an advertisement for a 'Fancy Bazaar' to be held at the military barracks on 6 and 7 October, with proceeds to be applied to the relief of the families of soldiers now on active service in New Zealand. This charity work was organised by the governor's wife, Mrs Gore Browne, Mrs Major Eagar, Lady Smith, Mrs Cole, Mrs Scott, and other leading women. To assist with the bazaar they had applied to the Tasmanian volunteer unit the Second Rifles for use of their band, which was granted, and the *Mercury* proclaimed its certainty that the efforts of these ladies would be praised in 'so laudable a work'.[52] Large attendances were acknowledged during the two days of the bazaar, the event raising a total of £350.[53] The *Mercury* was able to relay the success of this endeavour, acknowledging in turn the crucial role of Hobart's women and the importance of the significant sum of money so raised at a time of economic downturn, the paper also observing, 'what a prominent part the wives of the officers of the men now in New Zealand' had taken in this fundraising.[54]

A unique particular of Tasmania's public concern for the welfare of the British forces serving in New Zealand was the offer to provide quarters in Hobart for troops with the onset of winter during April 1864. This offer came in response to news that there were not adequate timber supplies for the construction of sufficient huts for the troops. An editorial in the *Mercury* brought this issue to the attention of readers, indicating that it was a 'question of no small importance' to ensure troops obtain suitable winter quarters, and declaring: 'There is no place in this hemisphere, in which there is finer barrack accommodation, than in Hobart Town.'[55] The *Mercury* took it upon itself to obtain two photographic images of Hobart's barracks by a well-known Hobart artist Mr Cherry. These were then despatched to General Cameron, including copies of the paper's editorial on the subject.[56] The *Mercury* also reaffirmed the early and decisive support displayed by Tasmania at the commencement of conflict in 1863, this proposal to house troops with winter coming on being merely an extension of Tasmania's willingness to assist her sister colony at this time.[57] The photograph of the barracks was briefly put on public display at Mr Cherry's Hobart studio, before being sent off to New Zealand on 6 April.[58] One Tasmanian resident, 'ALPLA', wrote to the *Mercury* with the additional suggestion of employing Royal Navy steamers serving in New Zealand to transport troops to Tasmania for winter quarters.[59] This concern for both the welfare of the troops in the field, and their families still residing in Hobart, illustrates, once again, substantial public interest in and support of the war effort in the Australian colonies.

Military settler family relief

On 22 September 1863 the New Zealand government issued a notice for 'New Zealand Volunteer Militiamen enlisted in the Neighbouring Colonies', allowing privates to remit a portion of their pay to families residing in the colony from which they were enlisted, and free of any charge and postage.[60] Though these arrangements were advertised in the Australian press, this of course still relied on the soldier in question to inform the military pay authorities of this requirement, and in a minority of cases the use of false names and family abandonment created social and economic problems.[61]

Following concerns voiced about the welfare of families of military settlers in both the Australian colonies and New Zealand, the issue was discussed in New Zealand's House of Representatives in November 1863. The government was asked whether it would take steps against those men arriving who had left wives and families unprovided for in the colonies from which they had enlisted. In response, the government outlined that no legislation 'could empower the backing of warrants to run through other colonies in cases of misdemeanour. . . . It was almost impossible that, for persons at a distance, any remedy should be provided, unless they could come to New Zealand to prove their case.' The government, though, was still confident that before long most wives and families would be following their husbands with little or no inconvenience.[62] Despite such assurances, alarm over the actual plight of certain military settler families in colonies such as Tasmania and Victoria demanded public and government intervention to alleviate their suffering.

Consequently, from late 1863 to early 1865, Tasmanian colonists expressed concerns and participated in relief to assist wives and children of Tasmanian-enlisted military settlers. On 26 December 1863, 'Z.W.D.', in a highly critical letter to the *Mercury*, used the example of one aged and widowed mother whose only son had enlisted leaving her destitute in Tasmania.[63] Families of such military settlers were to be at least for the short term at an economic disadvantage until remittances from the pay of their sons or husbands arrived. A wife of one of the volunteers, 'M. Evans' of Campbell Town, shortly after wrote on 'the utter impossibility of the volunteer's wife following her husband to New Zealand, without assistance', despite being eager to follow him 'even to the battle-field, if necessary'.[64] It was quickly becoming realised that the financial costs of moving family and material possessions across the Tasman to join already departed husbands was a burden many of the wives were unable to meet without either New Zealand or Tasmanian government assistance.[65]

For some families, remittances soon began to arrive through the paymaster of the forces in New Zealand from their husbands serving in the 3rd Waikato

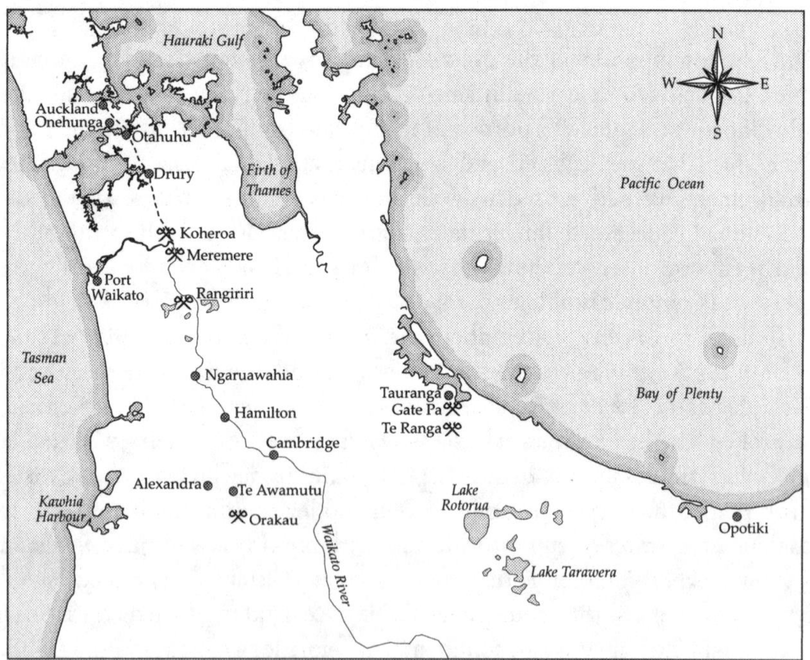

The Waikato and Bay of Plenty regionsof the North Island of New Zealand, showing the Great South Road from Auckland into the heart of the Waikato.

Regiment, allowing them to cope till transport was properly arranged. On 1 January 1864 a list of husbands' names was published and the families concerned were requested to come forward to obtain payment of monies remitted for their care.[66] Colonel Chesney at the Volunteer Office at the Hobart Military Barracks worked to ensure these remittances were accessible to the relevant families, as well as organising transport for some families during January and February before his own departure to join the Royal Engineers in New Zealand. The *Reliance* departed on 26 February taking wives and families of a number of Hobart volunteers now serving in the 3rd Waikato Regiment amongst its passengers.[67]

In April, 'Humanity' used the pages of the *Mercury* to ask whether provisions were made either by the Tasmanian or New Zealand governments, before volunteers were allowed to enlist, to force them to provide for their families left behind. This correspondent felt compelled to take the action after coming into contact with one woman and her children who had been 'deserted' – a state of affairs made all the worse by ill health which prevented her from providing for her children.[68] On this plea for information, the newspaper commented that these were not new questions, but nonetheless outlined in detail the relevant persons, offices and other steps that could be taken in order to assist any others who might find themselves in a similar predicament.[69]

The necessity for such military settler family relief was not only obvious in and around Hobart. At the annual meeting of the Launceston Benevolent Society held in December 1864 it was recounted that the relief activities brought before the committee for the previous year included several cases involving military settler families.[70] And from 1864 into April 1865, Tasmanian government correspondence with New Zealand documents efforts to ensure the welfare of the families of two Tasmanian military settler volunteers – Mrs McKinnon with four children, and Mrs Tynan with six. This involved providing passages and other travelling expenses involved in getting these families to New Zealand.[71]

In Victoria a minority of military settler families confronted much the same scenario. In early December 1863 the *Argus* reported that Colonel Pitt was about to facilitate arrangements for the conveyance of some of the wives and families of the Australian-enlisted military settlers. To aid in this process he distributed circulars to the commanding officers of every corps, which also included providing a blank form which asked men to confirm whether they were married, and if so the extent of their family and dependents, as such families would be provided lodgings and rations at the same rate as those of imperial troops.[72] Despite such news, cases of financial hardship and abandonment continued to exist for some families. An extreme example was that of Charlotte Lloyd, a mother of three children, brought before the Sandridge Police Court in February 1864, where she was charged with attempted suicide after having tried to throw herself from a railway pier.[73]

Surviving correspondence between the Bendigo Benevolent Asylum, Victoria's chief secretary and New Zealand's colonial secretary for the period June–August 1864 reveals the additional support and travel provisions certain families required in order to join their husbands and fathers. The military settlers and families concerned in these instances were Daniel Dillon, wife and three children; Daniel Mahoney, wife and three children; Frank Johnson, wife and six children; and Charles Wetherby, wife and children (number not cited).[74] The Bendigo Benevolent Asylum sought the aid of the Victorian government in communicating with its New Zealand counterpart to secure transport of these particular families to New Zealand, as they had been recipients of aid from this charity for some time.[75] Such dependents were no doubt finally able to travel to New Zealand on one of the vessels organised to convey them in July and August 1864, which carried families of Victorian-enlisted Taranaki Military Settlers.[76]

Prohibiting warlike stores to New Zealand, 1863–65

The Australian colonies again combined in aid of New Zealand in 1863, mimicking assistance rendered in the 1840s and 1860–61, by the enactment or continuance of regulations prohibiting exports of warlike stores. In late July 1863 the New Zealand government itself proclaimed what items it deemed to be warlike stores and so restricted under its earlier Arms Act 1860.[77] The Australian press reported upon these efforts by New Zealand authorities to restrict Maori obtaining arms and ammunition prior to, and after, its July 1863 proclamation. Such news also indicated sentences handed out for persons convicted of such illegal trade, and even detailed the maritime blockade put in place on the East Coast to try to combat the illicit trade in early 1864.[78] One of the avenues through which the Maori were believed to be obtaining quantities of arms and munitions was again from American whaling vessels.[79] In December 1863 the American whaler *Mercury* was reported as having gotten under way from King George Sound for New Zealand with a supply of gunpowder for traffic with 'rebel' Maori.[80] News of such alleged activities by American whalers continued into 1864, when they were reported as quite active off the East Coast of New Zealand's North Island.[81]

Apart from supplies of arms and ammunition arriving from outside sources the press also reported the Maori manufacture of cartridges. Just prior to the commencement of the Waikato campaign the *Sydney Morning Herald* noted that during the Taranaki War Maori living at 'Mangarei' [Mangere] near Auckland had manufactured large quantities of cartridges, 'most of which undoubtedly found their way to Taranaki'. It was also reported that a cartridge factory had more recently been established at Putaki, near Mangarei, where 'operations are carried on . . . without let or hindrance'.[82] 'Maori Ingenuity' in utilising seemingly unrelated household materials to manufacture these munitions was also remarked upon. Maori were said to be using 'eyelets and lucifer tops as percussion caps', as well as marbles, wooden plugs and copper coins as substitutes for bullets.[83] The *Argus*'s special correspondent, Howard Willoughby, in a lengthy report on 'The Hostile Maories' in January 1864, provided a detailed account of this Maori know-how, their munitions industry, and the diversity of weaponry being used:

> The natives are armed principally with double-barrelled guns. They have also revolvers, and the . . . possession of a number of rifles. They manufacture powder, themselves. It is coarse-grained . . . and is weak. It is believed, however that supplies of good powder are obtained from the American whalers . . . It is not known where the Maories make their powder now, but before the war broke out there was a station near the Bay of Islands, and three in the Waikato district. . . . It is asserted . . . that one native was a hired servant in a mill near Sydney . . . [where] he learned the art of making powder . . . and brought over with him a complete apparatus for . . . [its manufacture].[84]

Within Australia concerns were raised on a number of occasions about shipments of gunpowder to New Zealand. In June–July 1863 the authorities in Sydney were informed of a shipment of six tons for use by Maori.[85] Governor Young subsequently sent a despatch to New Zealand warning of this large consignment. On 10 July the governor declared that he had initially disallowed the shipment but that the person concerned produced official New Zealand documentation which permitted the transaction to take place.[86] In December 1863 he was to again warn Governor Grey of a cargo of gunpowder that arrived in Sydney aboard a German barque *Steinwarder*. Young was concerned about the nature of this freight with respect to the ongoing war and tried to detain it.[87]

In August 1863 South Australia also proclaimed prohibitions on the export of warlike stores except under licence issued from the governor.[88] In New South Wales the amended restrictions proclaimed in October 1862 were still in force and were pursued by this colony until their expiry on 12 October 1864. In April 1865 the governor of New South Wales assented to renewed restrictions (Gunpowder Export Restriction Act of 1865), which in turn saw such restrictions continue in force into 1868.[89]

In Victoria during July 1863 the firm of M'Ewan & Co. was charged with offences relating to gunpowder and caps being exported to New Zealand. This company answered in the Melbourne Police Court to charges initiated by the New Zealand government, but here the defendant proved there had been no attempt at concealment and that these materials were only intended for the mining industry. Its only penalty was a nominal fine imposed by the Bench.[90] To clarify the situation for merchants and others, on 31 July the Victorian Department of Trade and Customs republished the 1860 warlike stores exportation restrictions which were still in force. In doing so, the Commissioner of Trade and Customs emphasised that 'the provisions of the law will be strictly enforced'.[91] Within a few days, the *Argus* reported that the Commissioner of Customs had officiously refused to allow the departure of a cargo of five tons of blasting gunpowder from a Melbourne firm destined for railway contractors in Canterbury, as no shipping order or documentation had arrived from New Zealand. With efforts undertaken by all parties to resolve the apparent impasse, the *Argus* concluded by acknowledging, to the credit of the minister in charge, 'we have not always had such a vigorous administration of the affairs of the Customs department'.[92]

Australia's first war correspondents

A unique aspect of Australian coverage of the conflicts during 1863–64 was the despatch of war correspondents from Melbourne and Sydney by the *Argus* and the *Sydney Morning Herald*. Previously the Australian press utilised correspondents resident in New Zealand for the supply of news and views, or else relied heavily on the arrival of New Zealand despatches and newspapers, eagerly awaited with every shipping arrival. During the 1840s conflicts, the press relied totally on what was available in New Zealand's newspapers, but especially on the arrival of military despatches, or even accounts from returning officers and men and other colonists. The reminiscences of an officer of the 99th Regiment who served in the wars of the 1840s include a lament on the lack of war reporters to detail the actions and service of the troops in the field: 'Alas! in those days we had no war correspondents, or those who fought and fell in tough struggles with the Maoris would have lived in history.'[93]

In 1863 the *Argus* and *Sydney Morning Herald* undertook to send their own reporters to the war. Their reportage thus ushered in a new era in Australian journalism – Australian reporters were able to report first hand on the experience and service of the military settler volunteers and British troops from their respective colonies. Howard Willoughby was selected by the *Argus* to act as this paper's special correspondent to the Waikato War. Recognised as a remarkable writer and journalist throughout his career, on his death in March 1908 the *Argus* eulogised that Willoughby 'was the most remarkable journalist who has yet appeared in Australia. In energy, keenness, versatility, equability of temperament, readiness, and skill in writing, he combined qualities which placed him in a class by himself.'[94] Willoughby was born in Birmingham, England in 1839, where he commenced his education. In 1857 he arrived in Melbourne and in 1861 as a junior reporter initially joined the staff of the *Age*, but the next year commenced his association with the *Argus*. After returning from New Zealand in 1864, his proven abilities and descriptive style were rewarded by despatch to Western Australia to undertake an investigation for the *Argus* of this colony's convict system, resulting in a series of articles opposing the ills of convict transportation.[95]

As the *Argus*'s 'special reporter', Willoughby left Melbourne aboard the troopship *Himalaya* on 7 November 1863.[96] It was not till 7 December that the paper was able to publish his first reports containing a detailed account of the vessel's departure from Melbourne, and the voyage, activities and spirits of the 50th Regiment troops aboard. After arrival at Auckland he lost no time in getting into the field by becoming attached to the forces of the Thames Expedition in mid-November, where he reported that the troops were 'in great hopes of having a brush with the enemy'.[97] One review of Willoughby's New Zealand wars journalistic talents has commented that his 'words have a descriptive vitality and an economy of language, which reads better than many war correspondents of a century later'. His reports are said to have provided an Australian audience with a 'descriptive word picture of Imperials and Australians serving in the redoubts, stockades, camps and gunboats' in a manner not experienced in the war reportage up to that time.[98]

Willoughby's correspondence continued until early April 1864.[99] In what appears to be the last of his New Zealand reports, 'The Maories and the Maori Question', he provided a personal assessment of their conditions. While astute in many ways, his analysis is nevertheless beset with attitudes of British racial superiority and associated stereotypes. In the following extract he attempted to make sense of the various imagery associated with the Maori and to separate fact from fiction for an Australian audience:

> Frequently as the aboriginal inhabitants of New Zealand have been brought before the public, it is questionable whether people generally have at all a correct idea of the Maori of the present day. While one class are accustomed to regard the civilization as an accomplished fact, another see him chiefly through the medium of fancy war sketches, depicting him arrayed in feather and girdle like a Red Indian of the West, or they know him only through stage representations, in which he passes an existence of frantic singing and still more frantic dancing. The second, though partly true of the time "When wild in the woods the noble savage ran," applies no longer.[100]

Willoughby may also be making a direct reference here to the very popular and well-attended (and reported) Maori travelling troupe that toured Australia between the Taranaki and Waikato wars. This troupe performed in Sydney during June–August 1862, before departing for Victoria where it performed in Melbourne and regional goldfield areas during September and October 1862. The Australian public, no doubt, were left with particular imagery of the Maori as a people, and greatly impressed by the warlike dances, regalia and weaponry utilised during their performances. Willoughby, in 1864, now presented a picture of the Maori and their society in the midst of war – a time of conflict where there was no united front of resistance, and where Maori took up arms on either side or not at all. He concluded by asserting that the Maori were

> a brave, honest, light-hearted people, inclined to be lazy, greedy, and dirty, but half-civilized, and, there is some ground for fearing, but half Christianized. Few who have lived in their midst – except those by whom they have been wronged – fail to express a warm affection for them, while a mournful interest attaches to them in the eyes of all as signs and symptoms point unerringly to their extinction as a people. Let us still hope, however, that chasm between civilization and barbarism, may not prove impassable, but that a goodly remnant of the tribes may be spared – not to fulfil the historic prediction of surveying the ruins of the British Empire, but to form one of that empire's contented and prosperous provinces.[101]

Despite returning to Victoria, Willoughby was again to show his flair for war-related reporting following the arrival of HMS *Curacoa* on an official visit in September 1864. This vessel's commanding officer, Sir William Wiseman, and the crew took a very active part in the campaigns during 1863 and 1864, where many of the complement served ashore with the Naval Brigade. The *Sydney Morning Herald* republished his lively depiction of this vessel and crew, and in so doing noted its author as the *Argus*'s special correspondent to New Zealand, 'who accompanied the troops throughout the whole of the summer campaign'.[102]

The *Sydney Morning Herald* also sent its own correspondent, whose name unfortunately has yet to be uncovered. It is not known when he departed for New Zealand, but his reports show he arrived prior to Willoughby and seem to begin in issues of the *Herald* from 12 September 1863 and then feature periodically throughout 1864.[103] The *Herald*'s reporter appears to have visited the Waikato front line and various regimental camps, though many of his reports actually look to be written from Auckland.[104] The report 'From Our Own Correspondent' published on 21 September provides a detailed description of General Cameron's complex and extended military front from Auckland into the Waikato country. This in turn helped to explain to some degree the reasons for the apparent 'lull' in the advance of the imperial and colonial forces at this stage of the Waikato campaign which, 'I suppose, has excited some surprise in Australia'.[105] The *Argus*'s Howard

Willoughby, though, in a report compiled at General Cameron's headquarters at 'Te Rori' in January 1864, asserted that he was the only press reporter to have actually ventured beyond Auckland to the Waikato front:

> Nothing should be taken with greater caution than an Auckland rumour. Brilliant statements of our actual operations may always be believed when they are not communicated by responsible correspondents from head-quarters; and I may mention that your journal is the only one out of Auckland represented at the front.[106]

The real importance of both the *Argus* and *Herald* war correspondents is that for the first time the press of Australia sought to obtain war news on its own behalf and initiative – heralding the birth of Australian war reporting. Instead of waiting for copies of military or governmental correspondence, or second-hand news extracted from external newspaper sources, these publications proactively sought out news and views and did so with an Australian colonial audience's thinking or interests in mind.

Attitudes to New Zealand's wars

In Australia the radical intellectual and literary circles, as in the 1840s, adopted a critical stance towards the processes of military imperialism taking place in New Zealand. The Maori struggle again offered literary comparisons praising like-minded struggles for liberation and freedom from imperial oppression. An important contributor to this radical counterpoint was Daniel Henry Deniehy (1828–1865), a Sydney-born orator, man of letters, lawyer and politician. Steeped in the cause of the Young Ireland Party and its leaders, Deniehy had been a fervent supporter of Reverend J.D. Lang's Australian League, and a contemporary and associate of other literary and intellectual figures such as Charles Harpur, whom he greatly admired. In 1862 he went to Melbourne where he edited the Catholic weekly newspaper the *Victorian*. During 1863–64 this position afforded him the opportunity to espouse opposition to the war in New Zealand and the recruiting of military settlers in Victoria. He viewed the military settler recruiting in particular as simply a tool to assist the process of extinguishing Maori 'Antipodean nationality'.[107] Deniehy, of course, also appealed to idealised notions earlier issued in verse during the 1840s:

> The present war . . . exhibits the characteristics which have marked all the Maori's hostilities with the Pakeha, namely great courage and much rude, but effective military skill on the part of the semi-civilised warrior, . . .

> If the Maories are a fierce and blood-thirsty race, reckless of life, and cruel in their resentments – they are also brave men and born soldiers, who, in their contests with the British remind us often of the well-fought combats sustained by the Gauls of old against the legions of Rome.[108]

Such sentiments certainly exhibited opposition to the war effort, but the emphasis was generally sympathy with the Maori right and ability to prosecute their cause. Nonetheless, these utterances form components in colonial Australian attitudes to war.

Even as late as 1869, when the worst extremes on both sides in New Zealand's ongoing conflict were being witnessed, another Australian published poet, Benjamin Hoare, would pen verse in praise of the Maori and their ongoing struggle.[109] Hoare later went on to become a well-known Melbourne journalist, producing a number of works including *War Things That Matter*,[110] and died in 1932. In *The Maori* he displayed his admiration for the Maori and in so doing compared them with the nationalistic struggle of Boadicea and the Britons against the Romans.[111] If not truly part of an anti-war movement, such encomiums are surely pinpricks of colonial conscience in reaction to events unfolding across the Tasman.

Chapter Five

THE BUSINESS OF WARFARE

DURING 1863–64 the Australian colonies again demonstrated their geographical and practical importance by being able to supply quantities of arms, ammunitions, and a vast array of commissariat and logistical material to satisfy New Zealand's war needs. This ability was vital in the early stages of the developing conflict when taking into account the 'tyranny' of distance and time involved in seeking sources of manpower and military paraphernalia from Britain or other far-flung points of the Empire. In New Zealand the scale of military mobilisation undertaken during 1863 can easily be gauged from the ministerial statement to the New Zealand House of Representatives on 3 November. This also made reference to the Colonial Defence Force, not only indicating its size at this time, but also the Australian origins of many of its personnel, although there is no evidence of any formal recruiting carried out for this force in any of the Australian colonies during 1863–64 as is inferred.[1]

Nevertheless, the colonial press did inform the public early in 1863 of the measures associated with the expansion of this New Zealand force, including its conditions of service, pay and enlistment details.[2] This no doubt proved an inducement for some individuals to travel across the Tasman to enlist. The Australian personnel in the Colonial Defence Force either arrived in New Zealand on their own initiative, or else had actually transferred from those troops who had already arrived as part of the military settler recruiting missions.[3] By early November 1863 the growing colonial forces being raised in New Zealand's North Island comprised 5937 men (including the Waikato Military Settlers) in

Auckland; in Wellington (including Wanganui), 1768; in Taranaki, 812 (the whole of the male population); in Hawke's Bay, approximately 750 (also the whole of the male population); and the Colonial Defence Force, then numbering 375.[4]

While all these military preparations were taking place, the war also created a demand for a range of imports such as oats and 'breadstuffs', to the benefit of Australian commercial activities and shipping.[5] In December 1863 the *Launceston Examiner*, via New Zealand news, provided some explanation for these initial commercial fortunes and the demand for Australian exports across the Tasman: 'whilst our population is increased by continual arrivals, our supplies of grain and produce from the native districts have almost ceased since the commencement of the war, and many of the European settlers have been prevented from tilling their lands, as well as by the inroads of the natives, as by the necessary demands upon them for military service'.[6]

The enormous scale of the military operations compounded this situation, creating an ever-increasing demand for imported foodstuffs into 1864. In March of that year Tasmanian newspapers pointed out that there was a huge demand for grain in Auckland by the New Zealand Commissariat, with this department's current consumption reported as 25,000 bushels per month, while the consumption of oats exceeded one million pounds per month.[7] The Australian colonies were therefore in the fortunate geographic and economic position to benefit from the vast commercial demands of New Zealand's wars. This diverse and conveniently located Australian support also enabled the war effort to proceed at a faster pace – something not possible if New Zealand had relied solely on Britain or other imperial outposts to meet its needs.

During this process of rapid militarisation during 1863 the New Zealand government was to find itself deficient in a whole range of military materials such as uniforms, equipment, tents, weaponry, accoutrements and ammunitions. Australia also became the convenient locale from which to obtain the requisite military materials to supply the newly created and expanded Colonial Defence Force, military settler and other units, with initial needs being to equip some 3000 men. 'It was impossible to procure these supplies by the ordinary means of purchase. All that could be got, in Auckland, were procured; and additional supplies of the best available substitutes were obtained from Dunedin and the Australian Colonies.'[8] William Fox commented upon this situation in 1866, confirming that New Zealand obtained a 'great part of the supplies . . . [needed] direct from other countries . . . flour from Adelaide, horses from Sydney, hay . . . and corn from England, while the meat contract was held for a long time by a grazier' from Victoria.[9]

Nonetheless, Britain did become an important arsenal from which New Zealand received military logistical and manpower assistance, so integral to the large-scale military campaigns of 1863–64 and the associated influx of imperial military force.[10] Yet, as before, the Australian colonies were vital in the overall expansion of military capability, especially evident in the initial stages of campaigning. Examples of New Zealand turning to its Australian neighbours may be found in the tenders published in the *Sydney Morning Herald* in September 1863 for 3000 forage caps and 100 military circular tents.[11] Similarly, in January 1864 the New Zealand Office in Melbourne authorised the publication of tenders for New Zealand colonial forces for 7000 pairs of boots, 6000 blankets, 3000 pairs of blue serge trousers, 5000 blue serge shirts, 5000 haversacks, 2000 forage caps, 500 waterproof coats and 200 tents.[12] Such military requirements even extended to the musical needs of the New Zealand Militia for forty bugles and twenty cavalry trumpets in 1863, ordered from the Sydney Music Merchant Robert Gilfallan.[13]

Tasmanian support

Brigadier-General Chute and other officers arrived in Hobart from Melbourne on 30 May 1863 on an official tour of inspection. To assist in the military build-up in New Zealand, a number of officers of the Ordnance and Commissariat Departments were ordered to depart as soon as possible, along with 100 tons of commissariat stores including a quantity of canvas tents, foodstuffs and building materials.[14] Shortly after, the *Louisa*, carrying Ordnance Officers A.C. McDuff and H. Potter, was loaded with these stores and sailed for Auckland on 15 June.[15]

Tasmania, South Australia, Victoria and New South Wales were locations from where quantities of ammunitions, thousands of rifles, carbines, pistols and revolvers and associated accoutrements were also made available. On 31 July 1863 the Tasmanian colonial secretary received a request from the New Zealand colonial secretary's office for 500 Enfield rifles and accoutrements as well as any revolvers that might be obtainable. He quickly brought this petition before Tasmania's military authorities who acted to fulfil its requests. Five hundred rifles and accoutrements were able to be provided promptly, but only a quantity of smoothbore pistols, as no revolvers were available. The *Reliance* received this consignment of weapons, and departed for Auckland on 5 August.[16]

It is important to acknowledge another request for Tasmanian military assistance that came from the office of the superintendent of Otago in June 1863. External defence fears were felt throughout the Australasian colonies as a result of the American Civil War (1861–65) and Britain's ambiguous attitude to the Confederacy and tensions with the Union, apart from concerns about other events fomenting in Europe and the Pacific.[17] The provincial authorities at Otago felt particularly vulnerable, and wanted to establish defences for the harbour as well as the town of Dunedin to ward off possible attacks by privateer vessels. The superintendent of the province approached the Tasmanian governor seeking 'two or three useful pieces of Ordnance of the largest size and the most approved construction that can be spared, together with the necessary shot and other material'.[18] A reply on 16 July pointed out that as Hobart Town and Launceston 'are very imperfectly defended' it was regretted in this instance that Tasmania was unable to comply with Otago's wishes.[19]

During February 1864 the Commissariat Department in Hobart supplied additional stores for New Zealand. The schooner *Annie* was loaded with these commissariat stores at Constitution Dock with the aid of a gang of prisoners, taking several days to complete the loading before clearing for the Waikato on 5 February.[20] Following this vessel's return to Hobart, the *Mercury* provided an account of the *Annie*'s arrival at Port Waikato and the intense activity being carried out at this vital facility. Captain Fisher of this vessel also spoke highly of the ability of the officials in charge at this New Zealand port, allowing him to unload nearly 300 tons of cargo in five days. In addition, he detailed the presence of about 100 people employed in the dockyards, along with the stationing of a further 100 men and three officers of the 1st Waikato Regiment. This port was a hive of activity, with extensive wharves and several very large storehouses in the course of construction, 'as it is expected that fully 10,000 tons of provisions will shortly arrive at Waikato, which is to be the principal commissariat depot'.[21]

Further evidence of the quantity and variety of materials made available for use by Tasmanian authorities is evident in early April 1864 when the Hobart Commissariat Office advertised for tenders for commissariat supplies. This was not only to supply 10,000 bushels of feed oats, five tons of fine flour, and 2000 bushels of quality bran, but also to provide shipping direct to the Commissariat facilities at Manukau Harbour before the end of the month.[22] The Hobart Commissariat Office called additional tenders towards the end of April. One was for the conveyance from Hobart to the Commissariat Depot at Onehunga of 75 tons of flour, 4000 bushels of oats, 3000 bushels of bran, and two tons of biscuits, while another was for the conveyance of approximately 180 tons of military stores from Hobart to Auckland, comprising 3200 loose shells, shot and shells packed in boxes, and some '18 to 20 tons of filled cannon cartridges, packed in metal boxes'. This consignment also required the Royal Engineers Department in Hobart to install a purpose-built magazine in the vessel selected.[23]

New South Wales support

Following correspondence with Brigadier-General Chute on New Zealand's 6 June request for more troops and Armstrong artillery pieces, Governor Young responded to Governor Grey on 9 July outlining the colony's current position after learning that 'disturbances of a serious nature' had again broken out. Concluding that no further troops could be spared from Sydney's garrison, Young reminded Grey that 'half the Infantry and more than half the Artillery' had previously been sent.[24] This initial reticence to provide additional troops and arms, especially in light of the large contributions made during 1860, softened in August 1863 after the arrival of an official New Zealand government party headed by the Native Minister F.D. Bell.[25] The arrival of such a formal delegation tasked to obtain a range of military and logistical supplies and to commence the recruitment of military settlers stirred New South Wales authorities to support the endeavour. In correspondence to Grey on 18 August, Young was now able to state that in accordance with the formal request for aid brought by Bell, he was now providing all the 'aid and countenance' in his power. Government ministers were also supplying 'arms and ammunition from the Colonial Magazines' and according him 'every facility for recruiting', and a detachment of fifty troops from the 12th Regiment was embarking this same day for New Zealand.[26]

In August the New South Wales government directed the colonial storekeeper to send 1000 rifles and 200 breech-loading carbines to New Zealand.[27] These weapons were conveyed on the *Claud Hamilton* that was transporting Lieutenant-Colonel Carey and a detachment of the 12th Regiment. Before proceeding to sea this ship also took on board 150 barrels of cartridge powder from the powder magazine at Goat Island.[28] On 24 September the *Novelty* departed Sydney for Auckland with another seventy-two packages of ammunition.[29] Then, on 25 September, the *Lord Ashley*, conveying from Sydney to Auckland the New Zealand government officials and recruiters and forty military settler volunteers, carried a further forty cases of firearms from the colonial storekeeper.[30]

Governor Young also saw that two Armstrong artillery pieces were prepared for despatch. On 16 September he asked Commodore Wiseman of HMS *Curacoa* whether, apart from the 12th Regiment reinforcements from the Sydney garrison, he could also transport these guns with the requisite ammunition, which the New South Wales government was prepared to place at the disposal of the forces in New Zealand.[31] The *Curacoa* departed Sydney on 22 September in company of another Royal Navy vessel, HMS *Eclipse*, which was towing the Sydney-constructed gunboat *Waikato*.[32] Aside from the 12th reinforcements and artillery pieces aboard this small New Zealand-bound convoy, the gunboat itself was loaded with a considerable quantity of military stores.[33] The two 40-pounder Armstrong guns were soon in action after they were placed in position to command the landing place at Meremere in late October 1863.[34]

New South Wales was also a location with the requisite maritime construction capabilities to supply some of New Zealand's requirements for purpose-built shallow-draught and highly manoeuvrable vessels capable of operating on the difficult waterways of the North Island. These river gunboats became the first Australian-built and -exported vessels of war. The first was the iron stern-wheel paddle steamer initially known as Gunboat No. 3 (also as *Waikato*), but after arrival in New Zealand named *Pioneer*. This vessel was reported as costing £9,000 to complete, and during July to September 1863 the progress of its construction by the Australian Steam Navigation Company works in Sydney, as well as its unique characteristics for defence, attracted much reportage in Australia.[35] On 15 September the *Sydney Morning Herald* reviewed events in a detailed account of the completion of this gunboat. The New Zealand government, through Mr E.O. Moriarty, the Engineer for Rivers and Harbours, commissioned the A.S.N. Company to construct a gunboat to its specifications. In Sydney, this company's chief engineer, Mr T. Macarthur, was entrusted with the project, which saw the gunboat completed in seventeen weeks. It was also observed that it was gratifying that New South Wales possessed 'a firm capable of building a vessel like this to meet such an urgent emergency, when we consider that it would require some sixteen to eighteen months to import one from the mother country'.[36]

The Sydney-built gunboat *Pioneer*, from the *Illustrated London News*, 28 November 1863.

Preparations were also undertaken for obtaining crew for this vessel, which included the New Zealand defence minister issuing instructions to Captain Mayne, commanding HMS *Eclipse*, to proceed to Sydney to supervise the completion, arming and crewing of the gunboat. As a result of selecting crew from

Sydney, many of whom had prior Royal Navy experience, 'New Zealand's river gunboats were not only built by Australians but also had at least one crewed by them'.[37] As part of this process, advertisements for a chief officer were placed in Sydney during August, and in the following month tenders were called from insurance companies and underwriters willing to insure the *Waikato* for its maiden voyage.[38] The complement for the trans-Tasman crossing was to comprise Captain G.R. Breton, Lieutenant W.G.P. O'Callaghan, Chief Engineer Mr Jeffrey, and a crew of twenty-five other officers and men. Apart from the various armour and associated defensive superstructure installed on this vessel, the crew were each supplied with a breech-loading rifle, revolver and a cutlass.[39] Later in November a letter to Sydney from Chief Engineer Jeffrey detailed events that unfolded subsequent to the vessel's takeover by the Royal Navy shortly after its arrival in New Zealand. After being officially handed over to the imperial authorities on 16 October, following some debate between the New Zealand government, the governor and the imperial authorities over control of the *Pioneer*, all the Sydney-enlisted crew were discharged, except for Mr Jeffrey, who was apparently asked to remain. In the end, he declined to do so, not only because of disillusionment with the original crews' treatment, but as a result of apparently drastic changes to the boat's structure and equipment and damage carried out in the lead up to the commencement of the vessel's Waikato service.[40]

On 21 September a considerable variety of munitions was loaded aboard the gunboat. Later that morning Sir Henry Barkly, Governor Young and Commodore

The Sydney-built gunboat *Pioneer* under fire at Meremere, from the *Illustrated London News*, 30 January 1864.

Wiseman inspected the vessel – an event heralded by a thirteen-gun salute from HMS *Curacoa* as this party boarded. The next day the *Waikato* departed Sydney, under tow by HMS *Eclipse*. Despite a stormy and eventful voyage, both vessels arrived safely at Manukau on 3 October.[41] The *Sydney Morning Herald*'s 'Own Correspondent' was soon to report upon the successful performance of the *Pioneer* in action at Meremere when the vessel came under fire from Maori cannon:

> I am happy to be able to bear testimony to the excellent qualities of the Pioneer. . . . She stood a heavy fire for upwards of two hours from the natives at Meremere, including being battered with the cannon, but showed no signs of injury. She steams well against the stream, doing from seven to eight miles an hour up the river. . . . Her chief fault being her length, which must certainly prove unwieldy when as in the height of summer the stream is almost confined to a narrow and tortuous channel.[42]

Following the reconnaissance at Meremere on 29 October the *Pioneer* carried out a further mission as far as Rangiriri on 31 October, and thereafter continued providing transportation for troops, stores and artillery wherever required. In December 1866 it was berthed at Port Waikato when it slipped its moorings and drifted out to sea before being detected. An attempt was made to retrieve the vessel, but despite some efforts these failed and the *Pioneer* was wrecked on the Manukau Bar.[43]

To add to the fleet being assembled for the water transport services, the New Zealand government decided upon the construction of two further iron gunboats. The tender for these vessels was awarded to the Sydney firm of P.N. Russell and Co., and to allow for prompt delivery they were to be supplied as prefabricated sections which could be assembled on site in New Zealand. James Stewart, a civil engineer from Auckland who designed them, arrived in Sydney in October 1863 to superintend their construction. Stewart's design of these vessels took into account the need to turn easily in waters little more than their own projected lengths. They would also have a single paddle wheel so as to reduce their beam, as well as armament and superstructures arranged to offer the best possible cover of both the river and its banks.[44] The *Sydney Morning Herald* noted that these boats were 'of a smaller size than the last one built by the A.S.N. Co. These boats are to be about eighty feet long by twenty feet wide, to be propelled by steam (stern wheel)'.[45]

The P.N. Russell Engineering and Foundry works in Sydney manufactured the prefabricated sections for these two gunboats during late 1863 and early 1864. Established by Peter Nicol Russell in Sydney in 1842, by the 1860s this firm had developed into a leading engineering and foundry business. It was capable of major iron and brass foundry, had engineering, boilermaker and blacksmith works, and possessed various branch works and wharves, manufacturing goods from dredges to railway rolling stock.[46] Earlier in 1845 the works had been of assistance to the imperial forces being amassed for service in the Bay of Islands by manufacturing a small batch of Coehorn mortars.

The first of these prefabricated paddle steamers to be constructed was the *Koheroa*, which was ready for shipment after a mere six weeks. On 15 December 1863 the *Beautiful Star* departed Sydney, carrying the sections of the *Koheroa* and a shipment of coal for New Zealand, with engineer James Stewart as passenger, arriving in the Waikato eight days later. The *Koheroa*'s prefabricated sections were then assembled at the dockyard facilities at Port Waikato.[47] Stewart also brought with him from Sydney additional tradesmen for the construction work. The *Herald*'s 'Own Correspondent' reported the *Koheroa* 'being rapidly put together by the citizens brought over' by Stewart at Port Waikato.[48]

However, completion of the *Koheroa* did not take place as rapidly as expected.[49] It was not until early February 1864 before the boat was in a state of readiness to undertake its first trial, but pressures to have this vessel ready were greatly increased when the gunboat *Avon* hit a submerged tree and sank on the Waipa River early that month. This setback necessitated the *Koheroa* being hastily readied in an incomplete manner as a replacement to ease any potential supply crisis caused by General Cameron's advancing troops.[50] During March 1864 the importance of the riverboats was evidenced when the *Koheroa* and the refloated *Avon* were able to penetrate the Horotiu River in the immediate neighbourhood of the major Maori defensive positions at Pikopiko and Paterangi. This feat was rendered the more remarkable as 'the drought . . . has rendered the Waipa barely navigable, even for the Koheroa, to any where near Te Awamutu. The cannon and ammunition for the troops in the attacking column have been conveyed in the steamers, as also the provisions.'[51] Although the *Koheroa* foundered near Rahuipokeka (Huntly) in November 1865, and was raised in October the following year, its engines were removed and it was hulked at Port Waikato.[52]

The second of the Sydney prefabricated gunboats was the *Rangiriri*. The sections of this vessel were also loaded aboard the *Beautiful Star*, departing Sydney in February 1864. Upon arrival and assembly at Port Waikato the *Rangiriri* was finally able to join the *Koheroa* in March. In August the *Rangiriri* and the *Pioneer* brought up personnel of the 4th Waikato Regiment to the location where the military settler community of Hamilton was to be established. The *Rangiriri* remained in New Zealand government service until 1870. In 1890 this vessel was abandoned alongside the riverbank at Hamilton, but in 1982 its remains were raised and placed as a historic monument at this spot.[53]

The prefabricated Sydney-built gunboat *Rangiriri*, from the *Illustrated London News*, 4 June 1864.

Victorian and South Australian support

In 1863 Victoria became a source for additional artillery pieces when a battery of Armstrong artillery, the property of the Victorian government, was transferred to New Zealand. This transaction occurred following negotiations initiated in Melbourne after the arrival of Colonel Pitt (via Sydney) with the New Zealand government party.[54] The *Argus* revealed on 25 August that Governor Grey had already submitted a number of requests for military assistance since June. Following the third such request in early August, Major-General Chute recommended that half of the Royal Artillery (including half the battery of Armstrong guns) and infantry force in Victoria be despatched.[55] Victorian government ministers, however, went further and proposed sending the whole of the imperial garrison, and that the entire battery of six guns should be loaned to the New Zealand government if so requested. Orders were subsequently issued on 27 August for the immediate despatch of the majority of the 40th Regiment and Royal Artillery personnel stationed in Victoria. The Royal Artillery battery was also ordered to take the six Armstrong 12-pounder guns together with all necessary equipment and ammunition so as to be ready for immediate service once landed.[56] But it was not until November that the terms of sale were finalised, allowing this complete artillery battery to be despatched aboard the troopship *Himalaya*.[57] Almost £3,600 was paid to the Victorian government for these guns through New Zealand's Crown Agent in London later in 1864.[58]

Following a written request from New Zealand, the South Australian government in November 1863 consented to supply 500 long Enfield rifles which were on hand in the Adelaide Armoury.[59] In January 1864 a further 120 rifles were reportedly sent to New Zealand aboard the *Coorong*.[60] Later in June 1866 the superintendent of the Adelaide Armoury tabled a report to the South Australian Legislative Council, indicating that 525 Enfield rifles and one Westley Richards breech-loading carbine had been made available to New Zealand.[61]

South Australian riverboats and the services of Captain Cadell

South Australia also became important as a source for the purchase of riverboats for use in the vast waterways that were so heavily impacting on military campaigning in the Waikato and other North Island regions. Some of the riverboats in action with New Zealand's River Transport Service arrived indirectly, while others were purchased specifically for war requirements. Apart from useful riverboats, New Zealand was able to enlist the services and inland waterway expertise of Captain Francis Cadell – one of the principal pioneers of river navigation and transport on the Murray River – to operate its growing flotilla of river craft.

Certain South Australian riverboats were initially purchased for employment in trade and communication services for South Island interests, such as the 120-ton steamer *Sturt*. In June 1863 the *Sturt* underwent alterations before departure for use by the Nelson and Marlborough Steam Navigation Company. The vessel was despatched from Adelaide on 16 June and arrived at Nelson twelve days later.[62] In March 1864 New Zealand decided to purchase the steamers *Sturt* and *Prince Alfred* for government service on the Waikato and Waipa rivers.[63] The *South Australian Register*, in reporting the purchase of these two vessels in April, also pointed out 'that orders for further purchases of small steamers have been sent to the Australian colonies'.[64] The *Sturt* continued in service with the New Zealand government until 1870 when it was wrecked on the Kaiapoi Bar.[65]

On 23 February 1864 Mr J.C. Firth, a New Zealand government representative, arrived in South Australia (via Melbourne) looking to purchase steamers. The 90-ton iron paddle steamer *Gundagai*, which had been involved in the Murray River trade, was subsequently chosen and purchased for £4,250. The *Gundagai* arrived in Adelaide from Goolwa on 13 March where it was overhauled and repaired. The vessel was able to depart on 18 May, travelling first to Launceston, before finally arriving in the Waikato on 9 June,[66] where it proved to be one of the most useful boats in the New Zealand government's River Transport Service. In January 1865 this riverboat's valued services on the Waikato River ended, where it reportedly had been more successful than any other craft employed, and it was then despatched to penetrate the Whanganui River in support of 'the troops on the march' in this west coast region.[67] In a report to Governor Grey about military affairs on the west coast, General Cameron acknowledged the role played by the *Gundagai* as well as the services of Captain Cadell:

> Both the Waitotara and Patea can be entered by steamers of very light draught, and the two camps [at these locations] are supplied by sea from Whanganui, by the Colonial steamers "Gundagai" and "Sandfly."
>
> I am greatly indebted to the officers in charge of these two vessels, . . . Mr. Cadell and Mr. Marks, for affording me the means of reconnoitering the coast, and for the zeal and good will with which they perform the important duties of supplying the troops, and keeping up the communications with Whanganui.[68]

The *Gundagai* continued in military and commissariat service on the west coast during 1865–66 until wrecked while crossing the Patea Bar on 25 June 1866.[69]

New Zealand's enlistment of the expertise of Captain Francis Cadell was South Australia's other significant contribution to that country's water transport services. Born in Britain in 1822, Cadell was educated at Edinburgh and Germany before becoming a midshipman aboard an East India Company vessel, including service during the first China War. By age 22 he was commanding a vessel, before visiting the shipbuilding yards of the Tyne and Clyde, where he gained 'a thorough knowledge of naval architecture and the construction of steam engines. He studied the subject of river navigation after a visit to the Amazon; and in 1848, when he arrived in Australia, his attention was drawn to the practicability of navigating the Murray and its tributaries.'[70]

In June 1863 Cadell sold his last remaining riverboat *Wakool* to New Zealand, most probably for financial reasons, although this vessel was not utilised for military purposes and was later wrecked in the South Island in 1865.[71] On 15 February 1864 he received a telegram from Colonel Pitt who had arrived in Victoria to recommence military settler recruiting. Pitt requested he see J.C. Firth once he arrived from New Zealand, no doubt to seek advice on securing additional riverboats, but also to obtain his services in the Waikato. As a result, Cadell departed Melbourne for New Zealand on 27 February.[72] In New Zealand his appointment as superintendent of the River Transport Service was confirmed as commencing from 15 February 1864, in which capacity he served until 31 January 1866.[73]

The River Transport Service and the Commissariat Transport Corps utilised a flotilla of various craft which quickly proved crucial for their ability to ferry troops and supplies as well as for communications throughout the difficult waterways traversed during the Waikato campaign. The motley collection of vessels involved included armoured barges, purpose-built gunboats, armed steamers or schooners, and other small craft. This 'fleet' was operated by a variety of personnel from Royal Navy ships, the British Army, volunteers from the Waikato regiments serving under the guise of the Imperial Commissariat Transport Corps, as well as civilians. The vessels and their crews ensured that imperial and colonial troops could be rapidly moved, and while in the field were able to be fed, clothed and equipped, as well as providing a water route into the heart of Maori-held territory in the Waikato and elsewhere.[74]

During the initial stages of his superintendence in June–July 1864, Cadell was an instrumental figure in the selection of sites for the various military settlements of the men and families of the Waikato regiments. The colonial defence minister, writing to Colonel Haultain commanding the 2nd Waikato Regiment, outlined the object behind the selection of township locations based on navigable river sites, which would ensure the growth and development of these centres 'where travellers to the interior of the country leave the steamers and where the produce of the Upper Waikato districts would be shipped'. Cadell was instructed to provide his assistance in these aims, and advise at which point the rivers ceased to be navigable for steamers.[75] Although he returned to Australia following the termination of his services as superintendent of the River Transport Service,[76] his invaluable contributions had led to the development of an efficient river transport service, which greatly assisted the day-to-day logistical needs of both imperial and colonial forces during 1864–66.

Another individual who saw service as part of New Zealand's maritime services, George Gregory, unsuccessfully attempted to obtain a New Zealand War Medal in 1901–02 as a token of his contribution. Born in England in 1836, Gregory came to Australia aged fourteen. During his first five years in the colonies he pursued a seafaring life, serving aboard a vessel trading between Australia and New Zealand. Temporarily relinquishing the nautical life, he went to Namoi, New South Wales, purchased land and settled at Wee Waa. He is said to have later journeyed through Queensland, arriving back in Sydney during the outbreak of war in New Zealand, from where he journeyed to Auckland (possibly in 1864). In New Zealand he served as a deckhand and fireman aboard the government steamer *Sturt* commanded by Captain Fairchild. During this service he became involved both at sea and ashore at Patea and Wanganui on the west coast, as well as in the aftermath of the Poverty Bay Massacre on the east. Later returning to New South Wales, he took up land at Narrabri in 1870, where he raised a large family, and died in 1913. Because of bias associated with colonial entitlements (as opposed to imperial issuance) and the stipulation to prove either conspicuous service or having come under fire, Gregory, like many others, failed to obtain a medal. His correspondence acknowledges disappointment over this fact, especially in light of his participation during the years of renewed conflict for which he failed to obtain this small gesture of gratitude from the New Zealand government.[77]

Naval coal, chandlery, and other shipping tenders and services

As with the supply of various Army needs during the 1860s, commissariat requirements for the Royal Navy were met through the Australian colonies. For example, in December 1864 the Commissariat in Sydney advertised for tenders for supplying 'sundry articles of Ship Chandler's Store' for HMS *Miranda*.[78] In early 1865, contracts were issued by the Commissariat for supplies for both the Army and Navy services at Sydney.[79] Apart from stores, the Royal Navy and other shipping firms utilised Australian coal for their steam vessels. Despite unfavourable results of experiments using Australian coal carried out by Commodore Seymour in 1862 aboard HMS *Pelorus*, 'Perfect Combustion', in a letter to the *Sydney Morning Herald* in August 1863, defended the Australian product.[80] Next day the *Herald* provided further commentary on Australian coal, maintaining its worth and value for money, as 'colonial coal is the cheapest for use on this station . . . [its] utility . . . is sufficiently evidenced, not only by its uniform use in all colonial furnaces, both ashore and afloat, but by the preference given to it by the P. and O. Company'.[81] The supply of such diverse naval needs enabled vessels to operate efficiently on the Australia Station as well as to maintain a constant presence in New Zealand waters throughout the 1860s.

Another way in which the Australian colonies were important was as a location from where shipping for a variety of military purposes could be procured. Apart from the despatch of the various contingents of imperial troops in 1860 and 1863, shipping was also required for miscellaneous military needs. Tenders were called and charters agreed to for the return of wounded or invalided troops and their families from New Zealand to Australia, and then on to England. Shipping was also required to return regiments to England as they were being gradually withdrawn from the New Zealand theatre of operations during 1864–66.

In April 1860 the Tasmanian Steam Navigation Company was reported to be in negotiations with the Victorian government for the conveyance of troops and ammunitions from Melbourne to New Zealand aboard the *City of Hobart*, offered by the firm's directors at £3,500. The company was successful in obtaining the charter and on arrival in Melbourne from Tasmania this vessel embarked a strong detachment of the 40th Regiment bound for Taranaki.[82] In August 1863 the Commissariat in Melbourne again called for tenders to transport 173 officers and men (and families) of the 40th Regiment from Melbourne to Auckland.[83]

Australian ports and facilities were also utilised for military shipping coming to and from England or other destinations – either for repairs, re-supply and fuel materials, and even as a temporary place for troops to disembark before continuing on to New Zealand. Such events attended the arrival of the troopship

Himalaya in Melbourne in November 1863. This vessel transported the 50th Regiment from Colombo en route for New Zealand, and required re-coaling in Melbourne. During their very brief stay, the officers of this regiment received offers of hospitality, but the necessity to get under way as soon as possible prevented acceptance.[84] In late December 1863 the transport *Australian* from Rangoon also arrived in Melbourne carrying the headquarters elements of the 68th Regiment. This vessel similarly required coaling before continuing on to Auckland, but these few days in port allowed a number of officers and men time to disembark and visit the sights of the city.[85] Later, in December 1864, the *Roxburgh Castle* arrived in Melbourne from London with troops and families of the 7th Battery, 2nd Brigade, Royal Artillery, who were disembarked and temporarily quartered at the Prince's Bridge Barracks, before continuing on to New Zealand.[86]

In December 1863 Adelaide witnessed the arrival of the troopship *Armenian* from Rangoon with four companies of the 68th Regiment. This vessel had suffered damage in a severe gale, necessitating repairs and a refit before proceeding. Its captain presented himself to the South Australian government, which issued instructions 'for the prompt supply of his wants, so that no time might be lost in getting his vessel to sea again'.[87] The 68th troops were permitted to disembark and to pitch their tents on Torrens Island while the ship was repaired. Major Kirby, commanding the detachment, noted that the public response was such 'that the colonists may kill his men with kindness'. While in Adelaide these troops were shown an array of hospitality, which included a cricket match organised between the 68th and a team of eleven players representing South Australia at the Thebarton Racecourse, including organised catering, entertainment and additional coach services for the day. The *Armenian* was finally able to get under way for Auckland on 4 January 1864.[88]

Shipping arrangements were also made in Australia for the conveyance of sick or wounded soldiers from New Zealand. On 9 September 1864 two Royal Navy officers, Captain David Spain and Lieutenant Jones, arrived in Sydney to arrange for a charter for the return of sick and wounded troops to England. The Melbourne firm of Bright Brothers became the successful contractors.[89] On 2 November the *Hero* arrived in Melbourne with a contingent of several officers and 125 wounded or invalided soldiers from various regiments serving in New Zealand. The *Argus* reported that these troops would then proceed to England in the Black Ball Company ship *Royal Dane*, which had been chartered for this role.[90]

In August 1864 it was reported that the detachment of Royal Artillery that had been despatched from Sydney to New Zealand in 1860 had been ordered to prepare to return to Sydney. HMS *Esk* brought these troops back on 8 August.[91] Later in December the Sydney Commissariat issued a tender notice for the conveyance from Sydney to England of seventy-two officers and men (and families) of the Royal Artillery, most of whom had recently returned from New Zealand service.[92]

Tenders were also advertised in Australia calling for shipping to be able to provide transport for troops of the 68th and 43rd Regiments and their families from Auckland to England in December 1865. In January 1866 the Sydney Commissariat chartered the steamer *Great Victoria* to convey troops from Auckland, and in February the vessel *Maori* was chartered in Adelaide to convey some more of these troops from New Zealand.[93] In March 1866 the Admiralty Transport Office in Auckland issued an additional tender for the conveyance of the 40th Regiment, a Royal Artillery battery, and about one hundred military invalids and wounded men, including families, to England.[94] Australian shipping and contracting firms were therefore in an enviable position throughout the 1860s to fulfil the imperial shipping requirements for the commissariat, logistical and troop transports associated with the New Zealand campaigns, which in turn stimulated the Australian shipping industry.

Military stores and the New Zealand commissariat service

The sheer volume of military stores flooding into New Zealand during 1863–64 necessitated a vast commissariat network to deal effectively with the requirements of the expanding imperial and colonial war machine. Emphasising this complex infrastructure, on 26 March 1864 the *Mercury* reported that few in Australia 'are aware of the magnitude of the Military Store Department in Auckland':

> The large reinforcements of troops that have been received have of course necessitated a commensurate supply of munitions of war, and the Military Store becoming inconveniently crowded, it was found necessary to erect new buildings . . . Fort Britomart, is the grand depot for these supplies from which they are distributed over the country, as the exigencies of the war may demand. It may well be imagined that the duty of issuing these stores is a very onerous and important one . . .[95]

In assessing this logistical component of New Zealand's commissariat organisation, it is important to remember the contribution of the men who enlisted for service as military settlers, both in New Zealand and the Australian colonies. Many of these individuals were to provide a vital, yet generally unrecognised, service to the overall war effort as volunteer personnel in the Imperial Commissariat. Examples of Australian-enlisted military settlers who saw service in the Imperial Commissariat are Jacob Cheshire and Henriques DeLeon.

Jacob Cheshire enlisted in the 2nd Waikato Regiment in Sydney on

11 September 1863. In New Zealand he also served in the 3rd Waikato Regiment, and from this unit volunteered for service with the Imperial Commissariat Transport Corps. After military service, he had a varied career in New Zealand and then later Queensland, where he and his family finally settled in Inglewood in 1884.[96] Henriques DeLeon enrolled in the 2nd Waikato Regiment in Sydney on 21 August 1863.[97] In New Zealand he served with the 2nd Waikato Regiment until January 1864, when he transferred into the 3rd Waikato Regiment, before again transferring into the 1st Waikato Regiment in February 1865. Whilst serving in the 1st Waikato Regiment he volunteered for service with the Imperial Commissariat. After his military service De Leon embarked on a career in education (specialising in languages), firstly in Otago, briefly in Melbourne, and later in Hobart.[98]

In order to try and see early action, or to escape the mundane routine of redoubt life and the garrison duty most military settlers found they faced upon arrival in New Zealand, some Australian-recruited military settlers applied to join the Colonial Defence Force cavalry.[99] Similarly, small numbers transferred to the Forest Rangers, while the largest number volunteered for service with the Imperial Commissariat Transport Corps.[100] Volunteering for service in the Transport Corps was a common option for men of the four Waikato regiments. This was especially the case with the 3rd Waikato Regiment, which had at least 616 officers and men from its total complement volunteering for duty with the Imperial Commissariat. From assessment of New Zealand government papers it seems that a total of 1942 colonials (excluding British Army or Royal Navy personnel) served in some role as part of the Imperial Commissariat Transport Corps, and of these, approximately 1397 came from the four Waikato regiments.[101] The logistical aspect of the wars was of crucial importance to military operations. Without the exertions of this corps the combat troops and various garrisons and redoubts could not have been effectively armed, clothed and fed under some of the most trying physical conditions. Australian-derived men such as Cheshire and DeLeon served in a role usually not glamorous, sometimes monotonous or arduous, and often not seeing combat, but nonetheless were extremely important to the overall success of the various campaigns. This force was sometimes referred to as the 'Commissariat Transport Corps', the 'Colonial Transport Corps', or simply as 'C.T.C.', as well as earning the nickname of the 'Mokes'.[102]

Military horse trade with New Zealand, 1863–64

In relation to the Colonial Defence Force and the Commissariat Transport Corps especially, the Australian colonies were also the place from which draught and cavalry horses were procured. This particular horse trade may not have been as large and long-lived as that which took place with India, but constituted a significant market nonetheless.[103] The arrival of the New Zealand government party headed by F.D. Bell to Sydney in August 1863 heralded the beginnings of the horse trade in this period. Among this government party were several individuals whose purpose was 'to purchase horses for the military defence corps'.[104] In late 1863 a contract was also let to a Sydney saddlery firm to supply saddles and other associated mounted troop equipment.[105]

The New Zealand government selected Edward Mayne to be their remount agent in Sydney, and he appears to have arrived as part of Bell's government party.[106] Mayne commenced this work in August by attending the Burt & Co's Horse Bazaar. The initial advertisement in the *Sydney Morning Herald* on 20 August sought 'Troop Horses', noting Mayne's job to select for purchase horses suited for 'cavalry work'. Geldings were preferred, apart from requirements that they be quiet to ride, of sound condition, not less than fifteen hands in height, nor older than seven years.[107] Further advertisements over the ensuing days continued to seek 'Troop Horses' but at the same time also sought animals adaptable for cavalry purposes. Here, mounts needed to be already broken in for riding, of good weight and action, and aged between four and six years.[108] Another advertisement appeared at this time seeking 100 horses for the New Zealand government. In this instance, eligible animals were required to be well bred, active and compact, sound, quiet to ride, between fifteen and fifteen hands two inches in height, and aged between five and seven years. Persons with such horses were invited to apply daily to Mr Armstrong, veterinary surgeon of Pitt Street, Sydney.[109]

On 15 September the *Claud Hamilton* departed Sydney for Auckland with eighty horses in its cargo exported under the authority of F.D. Bell.[110] Such animals were presumably made available for the Colonial Defence Force or the Commissariat Transport Corps. William Morgan's journal entry dated Drury, Saturday night, 31 October 1863, for instance, recounts the arrival of a long procession of horses and drays: 'On enquiry I found it was No. 5 company of the Transport Corps on the march from Penrose with commissariat stores. There were 131 men, 140 horses, [and] 43 drays ... Most of the horses seemed first class, many of them being those lately imported from Sydney.'[111]

To assist in the purchase of suitable horses for the imperial forces in New Zealand, Mr Anderson, a Royal Artillery veterinary surgeon, arrived in Sydney from Auckland in October 1863.[112] Such a visitation did not always sit well with Sydney residents already accredited and engaged in such work. In a letter to the *Sydney Morning Herald*, 'S. Wooller' addressed fraudulent horse-selling practices:

> It must be patent to the employers of these gentlemen that our Government are large purchasers of horses for their own requirements, ... enquiry should

> have satisfied them that the individual at present thus serving acquits himself to the satisfaction of his superiors . . . [and] the veterinary surgeon of our police is the gentleman on whose shoulders should have devolved the nice task of procuring suitable animals for the New Zealand Government.[113]

In early 1864 the Commissariat Department offices in Melbourne, Sydney and Hobart Town were notified of the requirements for sound horses for both draught and lighter types for riding or pack animals.[114] The full extent of the trade which emerged out of Tasmania is not clear but it may have been affected by the stipulation that horse 'purchases would be made in New Zealand, the owners shipping at their own risk, the Department not being bound to purchase'.[115] It was reported that the *Chrishna* at Hobart had been 'rapidly fitted up for the conveyance of horses' to New Zealand.[116]

In February–March 1864, advertisements in the *Sydney Morning Herald* by the 'Inspector of Horses for the Colonial Defence Force at Auckland' again sought horses, this time specifically for the Colonial Defence Force cavalry.[117] The trade and supply of various types of horses from the Australian colonies was obviously of enormous value to the military operations being undertaken during 1863–64. The volume of this trade out of Sydney alone can be ascertained from a summary of the Sydney horse market on 23 May 1864:

> At present there are numerous orders for horse teams . . . It is, however, difficult to meet these requirements, nearly all our available cart stock having been cleared off to meet the New Zealand demand in the summer months, and our own carriers who were tempted by prices then to sell out have a difficulty to replenish their teams. We estimate that one thousand horses were shipped to New Zealand in the first four months of the present year, of which 800 were cart stock, and would leave £30 per head here. The other 200 would cost about £20; adding freight and forage, not less in round numbers than £30,000 for horse stock alone.[118]

Meat and cattle trade with New Zealand, 1863–66

The Australian colonies were similarly a major source of beef and mutton, as well as live cattle and sheep, for New Zealand's military and public requirements, as was particularly evident in the period 1863–66. The availability of Australian beef ensured adequate supplies to feed the needs of large numbers of imperial and colonial troops serving in the field. In early July 1863 the *South Australian Register* directed attention to the scarcity – and as a consequence, high price –

of meat in New Zealand. This situation led to a relaxation of sheep and cattle importation regulations in relation to Britain, Ireland, and the colonies of South Australia and Tasmania, although there was some indignation 'at the relaxation not having been extended to New South Wales, Queensland, and Victoria', where supplies were likely to be obtained.[119]

In Tasmania the *Mercury* drew attention to the cattle trade to New Zealand being 'of no small importance' to the colony. This particular traffic commenced in 1862 with the discovery of the Otago goldfields, which led to quantities of horses and sheep being sent from Hobart, and horses, sheep, horned cattle and pigs from Launceston. The *Mercury* stated that since this time 'this trade has increased, and it promises to be a flourishing one. Steam, direct to New Zealand, is about to be laid on, and this will, in all probability assist it, indirectly, if not directly.'[120]

In September 1863 the *Sydney Morning Herald* reported that a mob of cattle from Warrah Station passed through Singleton for shipment at Newcastle. This station also supplied a 'mob of 3000 fat sheep', and it was noted arrangements had been made so 'that continuous drafts of stock can be sent from this well-known station'.[121] By December 1863 the shipping of cattle was improved by technological innovation, when instead of the usual horse-power being used to hoist individual cattle over a vessel's side, the steamer *Xanthe* commenced using a steam derrick for the same purpose.[122]

In December 1863 the *Mercury* pointed to difficulties in competing in the shipment of cattle to New Zealand. The lack of proper wharf facilities with appropriate accommodation for stock, depth of water for vessels, and associated loading infrastructure 'militates against operations of that nature here'. It was revealed how Gippsland pastoralists were assisted by the Victorian government, which apparently aided 'stockholders by erecting yards and other appliances at the port whence cattle are shipped, and at present a large number are taken from that port of the colony'.[123] This governmental support was crucial to certain Gippsland pastoralists being able to secure the imperial meat contracts for New Zealand forces in 1864.

In August 1864 the New Zealand Commissary-General began accepting fresh meat tenders from any of the Australian colonies and not limiting them to New Zealand, as had occurred previously.[124] In October it was reported that Mr J. Johnson of Gippsland was successful in obtaining the contract to supply fresh meat for imperial forces in Auckland Province:

> We need hardly say that Mr. Johnson has been largely engaged in the importation of cattle to this province, and that some of the finest stock brought here have been imported by him. He has a large cattle station in Gipps Land, Victoria, and owns the Kate Waters, Eclipse, and Lombard,

> which are all vessels exceedingly well adapted for carrying stock. The Kate Waters has made several successful attempts here, having lost very few cattle indeed.[125]

During late 1864 the Auckland Commissary-General advertised again for fresh meat for the imperial forces in Auckland, this time for April 1865 – March 1866. Johnson is believed to have also secured this tender.[126]

Press reports suggest that a considerable trade in cattle and other livestock to New Zealand occurred during 1864, particularly from Newcastle.[127] This included working bullocks, a resource greatly in demand by the Imperial Commissariat Transport Corps. In March 1864 the vessel *Dudbrook* left Newcastle for Auckland with a freight of cattle consisting mainly of 175 working bullocks. A John Chadwick of Auckland had selected these beasts, and this shipment also included all 'the necessary gear to equip perfect teams'.[128] By late 1865 it became evident that the difficulties in getting cattle brought down country in reasonable time and in sufficient numbers to meet requirements necessitated those involved seeking alternative sources for their stock. This obstacle saw a proportion of the trade move to more northern ports in Queensland and even affected Johnson's ability to fulfil his meat contract. Information originally taken from the *Newcastle Telegraph* stated:

> we learn that several other vessels which have been engaged for some time past as regular traders between . . . [Newcastle] and New Zealand are about to leave us for Rockhampton [in Queensland]. Among others we hear that the Kate Waters, the Lombard, and Eclipse, all of which are under charter to Messrs. Johnson and Co., who have a contract with the New Zealand Government, are to be taken off this line, and henceforth to proceed to Rockhampton to take in cargo.[129]

Banking and the wars

Capital and banking institutions in Victoria and New South Wales were extremely important in the maintenance and operation of New Zealand's financial dealings from the early nineteenth century.[130] Although the goldfields of the 1860s were an important source of reinvestment in New Zealand, most money still came from overseas, mainly from the Australian colonies or England. New Zealand gold actually allowed established Australian banks to spread themselves further afield and increase their business across the Tasman. The Bank of New South Wales doubled its volume of business during the period 1861–66, and the Bank of

Australasia opened branches in Auckland, Christchurch and Dunedin in 1864.[131] Capital also came via the 'nest eggs' of immigrants, but more importantly through 'the capacity of some migrants to pull more money in after them in the form of loans and investments from Britain or Australia – the chain migration of money'.[132] British and Australian trading banks established themselves in New Zealand during the 1840s, but the banking system only became fully pervasive in the 1860s. In this decade a local counterpart, the Bank of New Zealand, joined overseas financial institutions. Nonetheless, all these banks borrowed money in Britain and Australia for internal purposes in New Zealand.[133]

The wars during the 1860s did have an effect on Australian banking interests. Economic progress in the North Island was retarded by these conflicts, while that of the goldfields-rich South Island prospered by comparison.[134] The enormous costs the fighting placed upon the coffers of the New Zealand government also become evident by June 1864 when the Australian press began to report 'public finances are deficient, the Bank refuses to increase overdraft, and Ministers are resorting to forced sales of surveyed and unsurveyed lands'.[135] In January 1865 the *Sydney Morning Herald* detailed the financial drain of the wars, which now saw New Zealand seeking loans in Australia to rectify its economic woes, with this colony sending an agent to New South Wales to negotiate a temporary loan. 'The enormous expense incurred . . . in dealing with the rebellion has rendered this course necessary.'[136] The New Zealand government's decision to seek temporary loans in Australia led to publication of notices advertising 'New Zealand General Government.-Eight Per. Cent. Debentures'. Persons interested in these bonds were advised to apply to the manager of either the Sydney or Melbourne branches of the Oriental Bank.[137]

Railway technology and tenders, and advertisements for surveyors, 1863–66

Australia also provided New Zealand with railway technology and equipment, including experienced contractors and engineers to carry out rail projects in both the South and North Islands.[138] One by-product of the military successes associated with the Waikato campaign was advertisements in Australia for a railway engineer for the Auckland and Drury Railway in February 1864.[139] The construction of this line was also stimulated by the expected demands of both military and free settlement to make use of confiscated Maori lands in the Waikato. It was reported that railway engineers Stewart and Harding had been appointed to work on the line, and as the work was being pushed on rapidly it was suggested 'some Australian contractor' should place a tender.[140] In August and September 1864 the commissioners of the Auckland and Drury Railway in fact sought tenders in Australia for the construction of the twenty-four miles of track. This included a branch line to Onehunga where a large commissariat depot and military base for imperial and colonial forces was located.[141] Australian press news suggests this project was going to be awarded to a Melbourne firm, as despite a local contractor having submitted the lowest tender, difficulties for this firm in securing the required sizeable deposit were likely to see the contract go to Melbourne instead.[142]

The need for surveyors from Australia was particularly vital in relation to vast areas of Maori lands confiscated in the Waikato and Taranaki. Surveying was also crucial to the creation of military settler land divisions and settlements for the men of the Waikato and Taranaki regiments. In order to fulfil such enormous undertakings properly, in June 1864 the New Zealand government advertised for surveyors in New South Wales.[143] Surveyors were especially in demand during the 1864–65 period when the government needed to diminish its growing war debt. The subdivision of huge tracts of confiscated Maori lands, not only for military settlements, but also for sale to a fresh wave of settler immigrants, generated revenue with which to try and counterbalance the colony's war debts.[144]

The New Zealand government was looking for settlers to fill the now 'open land' behind General Cameron's forces as early as March 1864. Instructions had been issued to the government agent in England as to the terms to be offered to prospective immigrants to the Waikato.[145] Later, during August–October, the sale of the first portion of confiscated land in the Waikato-Ngaruawahia area was similarly reported upon in Australia.[146] In May 1866 the Auckland Commissioner of Waste Lands instigated public notices in Australia advertising the availability of large numbers 'of Allotments situated in the towns of Hamilton, Cambridge, Alexandra, and Harapipi [Harapepe], in the district of Waikato, and Country Allotments in Paparata Valley and Wangatawhiri [Mangatawhiri] Valley, Auckland district' which were soon to be offered by public auction.[147] Apart from the role of surveyors in preparing the availability of lands for sale, such sales allowed people in Australia an opportunity to purchase confiscated Maori lands – lands which in a real sense had been won by the involvement of the imperial forces and military settler volunteers from that country.

The picture emerging thus far is of an integrated Australasian effort to maintain and provide the logistics for the actual war in New Zealand and the subsequent division of Maori lands. Clearly, these were never just New Zealand wars. They were wars fought by British settlers in all of the Australasian colonies. Commissariat supplies, transport, and finances all depended on the Australian colonies. The British and colonial New Zealand wars of the early 1860s simply could not have been waged successfully without the proximity, and support, of the Australian colonies.

Chapter Six

THE FLOODGATES OPEN

NEW ZEALAND'S REQUESTS for military assistance during 1863 led to the bulk of the remaining imperial garrisons in the Australian colonies departing for service across the Tasman. Although the Australian colonies' support for their despatch would seem, on the face of it, imperial duty in aid of a fellow British colony, this response was very much balanced by colonial self-interest and each colony's respective concerns about internal and external defence. There were varying levels of resistance to further diminishment of troop numbers. As evident during the Taranaki War, total military support was not possible when taking into account the tensions associated with individual colonial interests, especially noticeable with New South Wales's responses during June–September 1863. Genuine defence fears associated with growing French interests in the Pacific, as well as the possibility of war with the United States, also need to be weighed up in this respect. No Australian colonial governor could ignore their own colony's defences entirely, despite the increasing military demands emanating from New Zealand.

Imperial soldiers and sailors, along with the military settlers, represent Australia's total manpower contribution to the forces being amassed during 1863–64. Although only around 683 imperial troops were sent during August–October 1863, it should be remembered that most Australian garrisons had not witnessed the return of the majority of the troops despatched during 1860. Similarly, those soldiers made available in 1863 constitute a military force able to be put into the field promptly, whereas many of the imperial reinforcements coming from other parts of the Empire did not arrive until late 1863 or early 1864. The 50th Regiment from Ceylon arrived in Auckland mid-November 1863, while the 43rd at Calcutta was ordered (as was the 68th) to New Zealand in September 1863, of which its major elements arrived in December (though some smaller detachments from India and England did not arrive until January and March 1864). The 68th departed Rangoon (Burma) in three contingents during October–November 1863, all of which arrived in Auckland in January 1864.[1]

Australian reinforcements therefore had an importance beyond their actual number during the initial stages of the military campaigns, reinforcing the geographical and practical consequence of the Australian colonies to New Zealand's military affairs. And apart from the extensive Australian press coverage of the wars, numerous correspondence was also received, and published, from both former imperial soldiers and military settler volunteers, which provides glimpses into their varied war experiences. This record in turn indicates that colonial Australians were well informed about events taking place, and confirms the responsiveness of this Australian home front to events unfolding across the Tasman.

New South Wales reinforcements

Brigadier-General Chute arrived in Sydney from Army Headquarters in Melbourne in late June 1863 on an inspection tour of the colony's garrison. As a result of this visit it was soon rumoured in the press that 100 officers and men of the 12th Regiment would shortly proceed to New Zealand.[2] Governor Young had also just received (via Army Headquarters) General Cameron's request 'for a detachment of troops and for the Armstrong Guns which the Colonial Government has just procured'. Young in response informed Chute on 30 June of the 'great inconvenience and heavy expense to which the Colony has already been put by the withdrawal for a long period of more than half its quota of soldiers'. He feared that 'the number present scarcely suffice' the colony's requirements, and advised that with the concurrence of the Executive Council this request for more troops could not be complied with. The Armstrong guns, ordered because of fear of war with America, and taking into account 'public opinion' in the colony, similarly could not be surrendered to New Zealand at this time.[3]

On 14 August an official New Zealand government party headed by the Native Minister F.D. Bell, J.E. Gorst, the civil commissioner for the Waikato, Colonel G.D. Pitt and Captain Rogers-Harrison of the New Zealand Militia, and other officials arrived in Sydney aboard the *Claud Hamilton*. The appearance of this government party bearing a further request for military aid to the New South Wales authorities resulted in an array of imperial and colonial support being set in motion. Apart from supplies of commissariat stores, artillery, arms

Satirical Victorian cartoon directed towards motivations of some of the members of this colony's volunteer movement as to whether or not to enlist as military settlers at the commencement of the first Australian recruiting mission. *Melbourne Punch*, 3 September 1863.

and ammunitions, this assistance included 'every facility' for the recruitment of military settlers. Such a response enabled recruiting to commence in Sydney during August, as well as preparations for the despatch of the first contingent of imperial troops to depart during 1863.[4]

On 15 August the *Sydney Morning Herald* reported that there were insufficient numbers of troops currently in New Zealand to be able to hold all 'the necessary posts' or to mount any offensive operations, 'and the natives are now thoroughly determined to test the strength of our arms'. This situation was compounded by the drafting in Auckland province of all young men into the militia, with Auckland itself only defended by second-class militiamen. Under these circumstances the government now sought 'two thousand young men qualified for bush warfare' for enrolment as military settlers, the *Herald* concluding that the 'Two races are brought face to face with each other; the question of supremacy must be finally resolved. Retreat is utterly impossible.'[5] These wars were clearly perceived as conflict between the races, with the exhortation that all the 'Australian colonies should comprehend their common interest in the final settlement of the Maori difficulty, and rendering New Zealand as strong by its internal resources as it is important by its geographical position'.[6]

On 18 August in the New South Wales Legislative Assembly, the colonial secretary replied to a question about the government's stance on the availability of troops, and the contention of the press that his government objected to their departure. Mr Cowper reminded the Assembly that the colony had previously supplied a large portion of its garrison of Royal Artillery as well as infantry during the Taranaki War, 'thus showing a desire to help New Zealand as much as we could'.[7] However, the government's reluctance was not well received by some in Sydney, nor in New Zealand. 'A Sydney Merchant' passed on a stinging critique he had received from Auckland: '"I hope you are thoroughly ashamed of your Government, for not sending every soldier you have. The only way to touch the Sydney people is through their pockets . . . You have had millions of money from New Zealand, and yet you will not help us all you can, in this our time of great need."'[8]

Despite public concerns raised over the apparent half-hearted provision of military aid, behind the scenes Governor Young penned a supportive reply to Governor Grey, informing him that 'all the aid and countenance in my power', including the active support of the colonial government, was now being mustered to assist New Zealand.[9] The following day a detachment comprising fifty-five officers and men of the 12th Regiment, accompanied by Lieutenant-Colonel Carey, embarked aboard the *Claud Hamilton* and sailed for Auckland. This vessel also carried a large quantity of military stores, weapons, ammunition, and other commissariat materials. The *Sydney Morning Herald* reported 'the wharf and the approaches to it were crowded with spectators' to see the departure.[10] With this reduction of Sydney's garrison, Lieutenant-Colonel H.M. Hamilton, 12th Regiment, recommended the withdrawal of the Mint Guard from the number of posts currently mounted. Young therefore requested the colonial secretary take steps to create a replacement guard formed from either the volunteers or police.[11]

Over the ensuing weeks, the New South Wales government's attitude was transformed from one of reticence to willingness to provide the bulk of the colony's imperial garrison to New Zealand – public and parliamentary pressure aiding this change of heart considerably. Mr Moriarty moved a motion in the Legislative Assembly on 11 September that the government without delay give every available assistance, criticising it for sending a mere fifty men and not a full company of troops. New Zealand had requested military aid from all the neighbouring Australian colonies, reaffirming the urgent nature of this call for help, but Moriarty noted that 'New South Wales had the unenviable notoriety of being the only colony that had refused to comply with that application'. Such comments led to debate concerning any further role in assisting New Zealand, and despite the colonial secretary condemning the motion, the resolution was passed. New South Wales was deemed able to dispense with the troops, and, as one member pointed out, such additional military force would express the colony's public and official sympathies with New Zealand.[12]

The arrival of a draft of ninety-eight officers and men of the 12th Regiment from London aboard the *City of Sydney* on 12 September enabled the *Herald* to indicate that these troops would likely be New Zealand bound.[13] Two days later the same paper reported that the entirety of the colony's available 12th Regiment troops, including those just arrived from England, would be conveyed aboard HMS *Curacoa*.[14] Hamilton would depart in command of this detachment, leaving Lieutenant-Colonel J.F. Kempt and about 100 men in Sydney for garrison duties.[15]

Preparations were immediately set in motion to organise these troops for departure for Auckland, and the Sydney Volunteer Rifles, Volunteer Artillery and the Volunteer Rifle Band were ordered to participate in the send-off.[16] The departure of this large troop reinforcement again necessitated replacements for guard duties throughout Sydney. Young informed Hamilton that the 12th would remain in charge of the guards at the naval base on Cockatoo Island, but the duty at Government House would be for the time being undertaken by the artillery. The police were instructed to guard the Mint, the 'Main Guard' and Goat Island.[17]

On the eve of the troops' departure, Hamilton delivered a farewell address to the colony's volunteers, during which he made a call to members of the volunteer movement who were willing to venture across the Tasman to serve.[18] Another officer of the 12th, similarly active with the colony's volunteers, was Captain Robert Laver. His departure elicited some regret among the volunteers at the loss of his 'valuable services', as he had served the movement for nearly three years as brigade adjutant and assistant inspecting field officer of the New South Wales Rifles. The volunteers organised a committee to take subscriptions so as to provide Laver with a testimonial before departure, which they presented on 21 September.[19]

The 12th troops departed on 22 September under Colonel Hamilton, with fourteen other officers and 274 other ranks. The *Sydney Morning Herald* reported that the 'general interest which the departure . . . excited was shown in the crowds of persons who followed them as they marched through the city, or who assembled at the Circular Quay, at Fort Macquarie, and at the other points to witness, their embarkation'. Sympathies were also acknowledged for these troops, 'a large number of whom have left wives and families in Sydney, and many hopes were expressed that the speedy termination of the war would enable them to return to their homes'.[20] This send-off, though, was marred by the deaths by drowning of three women while they were trying to view the departure.[21]

Governor Young sent a despatch for Grey with HMS *Curacoa*, outlining the details of this 'strong reinforcement', in which it was made clear what the colony's position was in making these troops temporarily available: 'I trust your Excellency will bear in mind that they are sent on the honorable understanding of their return as soon as the crisis ... is at an end or earlier should any' situation arise which would require a demand for their return.[22] Despite recognition of the colony's participation in aiding New Zealand, New South Wales nonetheless remained concerned about the 'paucity of British Troops' available for its own needs.[23] In January 1864 Young corresponded with Brigadier-General Chute in Melbourne to ascertain whether the Artillery at least could be returned. 'The troops are quite insufficient for the necessary guards and Policemen are obliged to be employed in aid at the Convict Depot at Cockatoo Island at a very heavy cost.'[24] Shortly after, news of large reinforcements of troops having arrived in New Zealand prompted another letter informing Chute of the colony's desire to have the half battery of Royal Artillery, originally lent to New Zealand at the time of the Taranaki War, returned.[25] This Artillery detachment was not to return to Sydney until 8 August 1864.

Despite the exodus of many of the colony's imperial garrison, the people of New South Wales were kept abreast of events surrounding their former soldiers in service across the Tasman. Apart from extensive press reportage of the Waikato campaign during late 1863 and into 1864, letters received from the soldiers were published, providing greater appreciation of their experiences and impressions of the Maori and the conflicts taking place. One resident, a former imperial officer himself, who had served during the first Burmese War (1824–25), suggested in November that General Cameron 'will act with respect to this fortified position of the Maories as a countryman of his successively did during the first Burmese war'. This strategy, he suggested, would ensure the successful storming of the Maori rifle pits at Meremere.[26]

Other correspondence detailed the difficulties and human toll such assaults against Maori fortifications would involve. In December the *Sydney Morning Herald* published a letter that Mr Teale, a lieutenant in the Sydney Volunteer Rifles, had received from Captain Laver of the 12th. This was a detailed account of Laver's participation aboard the gunboat *Pioneer* during the attack at Rangiriri, where he was in a unique position to witness the failed frontal assaults that took place against this Maori pa on 20 November.[27] Laver discussed the surrender of the Maori defenders and the carnage and death evident on both sides in and around the fortifications afterwards. He also took the opportunity to pass on martial sentiments for Teale to inculcate into the colony's volunteers, to encourage them to pursue their purpose with vigour:

> I would beg of you to tell them ... that it is no light duty they have undertaken, but one that every man has a right to for the protection of their homes. But they have no idea of the horrors attending a sharp engagement with an

> entrenched enemy, and I beg that they will make themselves as proficient as possible . . . Let your brave fellows not scorn the steady step of the soldier, nor the exercise of the rifle . . . [and] [t]ell our champion shots what fine game they would have had . . . here. Lots of black cock, and game black cock too.[28]

Another letter received in Sydney by a brother of a soldier present at Rangiriri, and who had been severely wounded by gunshot during the assault, was reported in the *Sydney Morning Herald*. This soldier acknowledged how Meremere had been viewed as a strong defensive position, but that Rangiriri by comparison was not only stronger, but quite difficult to get at.[29]

The Australia Station

The receipt of news that conflict had broken out again in Taranaki caused 'great excitement' in Sydney in May 1863. As a result, the Royal Navy vessels HMS *Harrier* and *Miranda* were prepared for immediate despatch, with the crew of the former working all day on 26 May to load all the necessary ammunition and stores before departure for Taranaki.[30] The developments taking place across the Tasman led to all warships available on the Australia Station – the *Harrier*, *Miranda*, and the *Eclipse* – serving in New Zealand waters by August 1863.[31] HMS *Eclipse* returned to Sydney on 30 August, and while in the port underwent repairs and a hull inspection when dry docked, before being refloated on 12 September. The *Eclipse* then returned to New Zealand towing the Sydney-manufactured gunboat *Waikato*, departing on 22 September.[32] By October these three warships were complemented by the arrival in New Zealand of HMS *Curacoa* and HMS *Sandfly*, with HMS *Esk* expected to arrive shortly – the fleet described as 'the most numerous as well as the finest squadron that has ever yet assembled under the Australian command'.[33]

After the new commodore of the Australia Station, Sir William Wiseman, arrived in New Zealand aboard HMS *Curacoa* in late September 1863 he had 365 men from the *Curacoa*, *Harrier* and *Eclipse* landed ashore. These Royal Navy personnel assisted with the manning and operation of the Waikato River flotilla of vessels that were of invaluable assistance in the movement of troops, weapons and supplies during the course of the Waikato campaign.[34] Prior to Wiseman's arrival, personnel from HMS *Harrier* had already established a valuable presence ashore since July.[35] Apart from these roles, Royal Navy personnel, as they had during the Taranaki War, also served on shore as an additional fighting force in the Naval Brigade. In was in this capacity that the Royal Navy suffered heavy casualties during the disastrous Gate Pa attack on 29 April 1864.[36]

Victorian reinforcements

The receipt of news in Victoria of the ambush of British troops in Taranaki immediately stimulated martial fervour and the expectation that the troops would 'be removed to the seat of warfare, and the defence of the colony entrusted once more entirely to our volunteers'.[37] On 23 May 'A Rifleman', a North Melbourne member of the Victorian volunteer movement, suggested using volunteers for New Zealand: 'I trust that some of the Victorians will form a corps to proceed there . . . I for one would gladly (and I know many more who would do the same) volunteer if the Government would undertake to defray all expenses of transport, and give the same pay as the regular regiments.'[38] Despite such interest it was not until August, following the receipt of New Zealand's request for military aid and the arrival of members of that colony's government party, that preparations for despatching the majority of the imperial garrison were undertaken.[39]

In the Victorian Legislative Council on 2 September, Dr Evans asked the colonial treasury whether it was the intention of the government that the detachment of artillery and the battery of Armstrong guns now in the colony were to be retained or despatched to New Zealand. Mr Verdon for the government in reply outlined discussions and decisions between the government, the governor and the military authorities headquartered in Melbourne. The government decided that if any troops were to be retained, it would be preferable to keep the artillery, and let the whole of the 40th detachment go.[40] The Commissariat in Melbourne issued a tender in late August for the transport of the Victorian 40th troops and regimental families to Auckland, chartering the Black Ball Company vessel *Queen of the South* for this task.[41]

The final decision to send only the 40th Regiment garrison did not meet with every Victorian's satisfaction. 'C.M.S.' was of the opinion that despite the numbers of 40th troops being despatched, a number were invalids and many had already seen upwards of twenty years' service. Instead, 'C.M.S.' believed the more useful decision would be to send ninety men from the Royal Artillery, and ninety of the 40th Regiment.[42] In reply, 'R.M.' pointed out that New Zealand already had a force of nearly 400 Royal Artillery personnel, who for the most part were being employed as cavalry because of 'the nature of the country not permitting the free use of field guns'. Under these circumstances, the government had 'exercised a wise discretion in retaining the battery of Royal Artillery' and sending the 40th instead.[43]

When the 40th detachment embarked on 4 September the *Argus* noted this regiment had served 'now nearly eleven years' in Victoria. These troops had very much become a feature of Victorian life over this time, and their departure 'occasioned no little excitement. The regiment arrived here in . . . 1852, and though head-quarters were transferred to New Zealand upon the outbreak of the late Maori war [in 1860], the presence of the companies then left behind served to keep up' the connection between this regiment and Victoria.[44] At the same time as these troops were embarking, military settler volunteers were also embarked aboard the *Caduceus* which was awaiting departure to New Zealand.[45] This 40th contingent comprised 158 officers and men, their departure witnessed by a very large public turnout of Melbourne's citizenry. The *Argus* acknowledged that 'the attraction which had brought the majority down seemed to be the national impulse in favour of the "redcoats" – a desire to see the last of the troops who have so long represented Her Majesty's regulars in the colony'.[46]

South Australian reinforcements

In June 1863 the *South Australian Register* reported on growing numbers of imperial troops embarking from Australia and other locations in the Empire to augment forces across the Tasman. As part of this troop redistribution, elements of the 12th and 40th Regiments still in Australian garrisons were believed to be under orders to embark as soon as possible, although no orders had been received in Adelaide with respect to its own 40th detachment.[47] After receiving a despatch in August from the British government, which had determined that the Australian colonies must see towards their own defences in the coming years, the *Register* announced that 'the general feeling will be that the withdrawal of the military from this colony should be taken advantage of in the way of developing and improving the volunteer system as it now exists'.[48] South Australia's volunteer movement had already been utilised to temporarily mount guards in Adelaide in place of the regular troops during March 1863, when the 40th garrison were undergoing a period of training.[49]

It was not till September that discussions for despatching the colony's imperial garrison became more evident. The news of the support being rendered by other Australian colonies no doubt stirred a desire for like-minded assistance from South Australia. On 3 September the *Register*, on the subject of colonial defence, questioned, 'why the fine detachment of troops now stationed in this colony are not called upon by the authorities . . . to proceed to New Zealand. It is painful to read the urgent appeals of Sir George Grey, and to know that experienced soldiers are remaining idle in South Australia.'[50] Treasurer Dutton proposed that an address be presented to the governor that these troops should be made available during this crisis.[51]

Brevet-Major G.W. Bowdler, 40th Regiment, reported the 'Duty State' of South Australia's garrison to Governor Daly on 4 September. Thirty-six men were on duty in Adelaide and fourteen at the Stockade, and numbers of these could be dispensed with if the governor approved the reduction of the Stockade detachment, and Bowdler himself did away with the regimental guard. If carried out, thirty men were all that would be required to retain, and twenty could be despatched to New Zealand under Lieutenant Moller.[52] With the belief the troops were 'already as good as decided that they are to go', the *Register* offered the suggestion that the colony imitate Victoria and use volunteers to mount the necessary guards. 'But as a permanent arrangement it would . . . be better to employ men on purpose for this work . . . a dozen policemen would be sufficient to perform the duties . . . in Adelaide and at the Stockade . . . therefore, it is absurd to retain a little "standing army".'[53] Following upon Bowdler's report, Governor Daly informed this officer that he had his 'full concurrence to place the entire detachment at the disposal of the General Commanding'.[54] Bowdler therefore made immediate arrangements for their despatch, commencing with the withdrawal of the Dry Creek detachment to rejoin the rest of the garrison in Adelaide on 30 September.[55]

As these preparations were in train, public reaction to the imminent departure of the 40th revealed how these soldiers had endeared themselves to the people of South Australia during their garrison stay.[56] On 20 September, Canon Farr at the Trinity Church preached to the congregation, '"Young man, I say unto thee, arise;" and in the course of his sermon turned to the garrison and encouraged the men to live the lives of those warriors for whom the death on the Battle-field had no terrors.'[57] The members of the Adelaide Lodge of Oddfellows held a dinner for all members of Adelaide's 40th detachment at the Freemasons' Tavern on 24 September, which was also attended by members of the Reedbeds Cavalry and officers and men of other volunteer companies.[58] Another tribute to these soldiers saw an attempt to raise a subscription in order to provide each soldier of the garrison with a revolver for personal protection for their New Zealand service.[59] Shortly after, the officers of the 40th were fêted by 350 guests, including the governor and his daughter and numerous members of both houses of parliament, at a bachelors' ball on 2 October.[60] Sergeant Clarke, the Adelaide Barrack-Master, made a personal gift by presenting each soldier with a Bible.[61] Clarke was also a highly active participant and a committee member in the soldier family relief organisation during October 1863 into 1864.

Upon news of the 40th being readied for departure, the First Adelaide Rifles Band offered their services to accompany the troops on the day of embarkation, which Major Bowdler readily accepted. The vessel *Nightingale*, a regular trader between Adelaide and Auckland, was engaged for their conveyance.[62] The departure of the three officers and fifty soldiers of the 40th on 10 October was accompanied by considerable public fanfare in both Adelaide and Port Adelaide, the *Register* acknowledging the fact that the detachment, so long stationed in Adelaide, by leaving for the war 'created considerable excitement'.[63] 'Small as the detachment was it presented varieties of the British soldier. There was in it the bronzed veteran who had seen service in many lands . . . There was also boy soldiers eager to smell powder in battle . . . The majority, however, were of the steady rank and file, who can be relied on in all the dread exigencies of warfare.'[64]

The send-off that this imperial contingent received illustrates the bond the colonial public had with many of its garrisons. Nor did their departure end that connection, as becomes obvious with the soldier family relief organisation, but also in the press monitoring of the service of these troops in New Zealand.[65] South Australians were soon made aware that some of their former soldiers became casualties during the failed assaults against Rangiriri on 20 November 1863:

> We regret . . . that one of the privates . . . recently stationed in Adelaide, Private Usher, has been killed in the attack . . . Usher will be remembered by many as the servant to Lieutenant Lucas, and marker on many occasions for the Adelaide Rifle Club. We perceive, also, that Private Jones, the pioneer of the Adelaide detachment, has been wounded. He has left a wife and three children in Adelaide, who are in receipt of rations from the Relief Committee. Usher's wife and two children accompanied him to New Zealand.[66]

During early 1864, anxieties were also held as to the names of the casualties in an ambush of a bathing party of 40th troops at Waiari on the Mangapiko River on 11 February.[67] Details on this engagement appear in a letter from a sergeant of the former South Australian garrison, sent to a friend in Adelaide (dated Camp Paterangi, 24 February):

> Dear Friend . . . I write this . . . squatting on the ground on an outlying picket, surrounded by Maories . . . On last Friday a party of men were going to a creek to bathe. When about to get into the water a party of Maories from the other side of the bank poured in a volley from double-barrelled rifles . . . Major Blyth and Major Bowdler moved out with about 50 men, for the Maories had got a strong reinforcement from the stronghold, and the work commenced now in right good earnest. Lieutenant Lucas was ordered to go with 30 men, and cut off the retreat of the Maories to their position. They now fought almost hand to hand for about two minutes . . . They fought bravely, but finding that our men were getting round them they retired into an old Maori pa . . . where Larner and McCarty and several of the detachment lately at Adelaide were opposed to a very unequal number

> of the enemy. We now found that some of our poor comrades were getting killed and wounded.[68]

In another letter published in April, the same sergeant continued to outline the experiences met with by the troops during the campaign to outflank the sophisticated Maori fortifications at Paterangi and Pikopiko:

> Paterangi was one of the strongest of the Maori positions, and Pikopiko was the other; they are situated seven miles apart, but in sight of each other. I will give you a description of one of them:- The position stands in about seven acres of ground; there are five redoubts, and a perfect labyrinth of rifle-pits with communication trenches, so that the Maories could go from one redoubt to the other without exposing themselves. There were small covered loopholes to fire from, and in front of the works there were, at about five yards distance, stakes driven into the ground, and six feet-high, sufficient to check a charge. In front of the stakes, and about three yards from them, a trench so covered as not to be seen extended of a depth sufficient to break the legs of men who fell into it advancing, . . . Fortunately it was abandoned . . .[69]

This letter not only vividly described the complexity and brilliance of the Kingite Maori fortifications, but also referred to military settler volunteers with South Australian origins.[70]

Artist's impression of the engagement on the Mangapiko River, involving elements of the 40th Regiment, from the *Illustrated London News*, 28 May 1864.

The absence of all troops in New Zealand saw government consideration towards South Australia's defence leading to a request to the Secretary of State for the Colonies for a company of infantry in December 1863.[71] However, the implications of the decision of the imperial authorities to gradually reduce military strengths in Australasia, compounded by the ongoing New Zealand conflict, prevented troops being made available until 1866.[72]

Queensland reinforcements

The impact of the Taranaki War had already delayed Queensland receiving a portion of its allotted imperial garrison. The arrival of the first elements of the 12th Regiment commanded by Lieutenant D.T. Seymour in January 1861 was followed by a further small contingent of thirteen soldiers in July 1862, though these additional troops merely replaced those who had deserted in Brisbane during 1861–62.[73] This still left Queensland with a woefully inadequate garrison, and Governor Bowen continued to correspond on the subject through 1862 and 1863 in the hope of procuring more troops for the colony's defence.[74]

In March 1862 Major-General Pratt informed Bowen that troop numbers in Sydney were below those sanctioned by 'the Home Authorities to be stationed there', but additional troops had been asked by the New South Wales government from New Zealand. Pratt concluded by stating he would not fail to send the additional force for Queensland whenever it was possible to do so.[75] Despite this apparent optimism, the commencement of renewed conflict in 1863 dampened such prospects. The exigencies of New Zealand's wars far outweighed Queensland's right to a complete garrison.

On 1 September the *Courier* reported a communication received from Sydney to hold the Brisbane detachment of the 12th Regiment in readiness to proceed to New Zealand at short notice, their departure depending on 'news received by the next boat from New Zealand'.[76] On 7 September Seymour laid before Bowen a letter received from Brigadier-General Chute in Melbourne urging the 'immediate Despatch to New Zealand of as many Officers and Men as can possibly be dispensed with'. In response, Bowen outlined Queensland's position, emphasising that the colony's detachment was less than half the number allocated:

> Queensland is ... in a different position from the older and more populous colonies of the Australian group. This young community is necessarily as yet without the numerous and efficient Volunteer Companies of Victoria and New South Wales; and it is felt that even the present detachment is too weak to form the nucleus of, and to supply drill instructors ... [for the volunteers.]

> However, after consultation with my Executive Council, I am under all the circumstances of the case ready to concur in the immediate despatch of one of the two Officers here, and all of the Men, with the exception of about thirty (30) fit for duty. This is, I think, all that can be expected from this Colony; the capital of which would be practically defenceless without a guard of regular soldiers.[77]

Bowen concluded by offering thoughts towards the Brisbane detachment being 'restored to at least its present strength' as soon as the situation across the Tasman would permit troop redistributions to occur.[78] Arrangements to send the available 12th troops were to take place immediately, but a telegram from the military authorities was received 'directing the Officer Commanding the Troops at Brisbane to suspend all action until further orders'. Shortly after, further orders were received and Bowen consented to Ensign A.H. Brittain proceeding to Sydney, 'taking with him every man that can possibly be spared'. Queensland's small imperial contribution would comprise one officer and ten other ranks of the 12th Regiment.[79] These troops departed together with Brisbane's military settler volunteers on 10 October.

With regard to Queensland's remaining 12th Regiment detachment, it should not be forgotten that they too departed for New Zealand service in late 1866. This event took place with the arrival of a relief detachment of one company of the 50th Regiment in October, direct from Auckland, following the completion of that regiment's war service. The *Alice Cameron* cleared Brisbane on 16 October for Sydney carrying Captain Mair and seventeen men (and families) of the 12th.[80] Arriving on 22 October, these Brisbane troops awaited the arrival of a small contingent of their regiment from Tasmania before embarking together aboard the *Alice Cameron* on 31 October.[81] Just prior to the arrival of the small Queensland and Tasmanian 12th detachments, those remaining elements of this regiment in Sydney, comprising sixty-seven officers and men (and families), also departed, aboard the *Auckland*, on 17 October. An account of this Sydney troop departure again reveals the public fanfare evoked by such events.[82] These former Queensland, Tasmanian, and New South Wales personnel landed at Tauranga in the Bay of Plenty where they participated in the last operations in which elements of the British Army undertook active field operations in New Zealand. Here, sections of the 12th assisted colonial forces, including the 1st Waikato Regiment, in what became known as the Tauranga Bush Campaign (December 1866–February 1867).[83]

Tasmanian reinforcements

In late July 1863 Tasmania's Governor Gore Browne received a despatch from his New Zealand counterpart George Grey, requesting 'all the available troops in Tasmania transferred to Auckland with the least possible delay, to aid and assist there in the war'.[84] Browne immediately sought advice from Major E.H. Eagar, 40th Regiment, to ascertain how many troops could be made available. Eagar, who would command this contingent, reported that 116 officers and men were ready to be conveyed to Auckland, while thirty other soldiers and Captain Sillery would stay behind to maintain guard duties in Hobart and at the Port Arthur penal establishment. Captain Chesney, Royal Engineers, would also remain to command the garrison in Eager's absence.[85] Tasmania's prompt and ready action in determining to aid New Zealand, as had occurred in 1860, endeared it yet again to its sister colony:

> We learn that the Tasmanian Government... have at once taken order for aiding our necessities, ... We return our hearty and heartfelt acknowledgements for this noble demonstration of Tasmanian generosity. They who, like ourselves, are aware of the military requirements at such settlements as Port Arthur, and the surveillance demanded in a country so recently disentangled from the thrall of convictism, can thoroughly appreciate the value of the sacrifice, Tasmania, like Victoria, approves herself a friend in need.[86]

Because of the 'urgent demand' for troops, Major Eagar even approached the Tasmanian colonial secretary and the governor about several cases relating to military witnesses in a civil case, and a military prisoner. The three soldiers involved were all to be allowed to depart for New Zealand.[87]

As part of the preparations leading up to the troops' departure, Eagar also brought to the attention of the colonial government the circumstance that various military guards would be withdrawn on the embarkation of the majority of the garrison for active service in New Zealand.[88] It therefore devolved upon Tasmanian authorities to resort to 'other means, municipal, or Departmental' to provide the appropriate protection at these locations, and on 11 August the government reported all such arrangements had now been established.[89] Reliance on Tasmania's volunteer movement and constabulary to meet many contingencies in this situation was not unexpected, for the *Mercury* had already alluded to such eventualities.[90] At Port Arthur, in place of the military, a guard of constabulary was formed from men specially selected by the Inspector of Police.[91]

During early August various shipping arrangements for the conveyance of the troops were reported, before the *Isabella* was chosen for the task after successful chartering arrangements set at £900 were negotiated. This vessel was rapidly fitted out and was visited by various 'officers and ladies' as these tasks were being completed, including the loading of a large quantity of stores.[92] The *Mercury* outlined plans to accompany the departure of the military but in doing so relayed the sense of belonging that these soldiers had with the Tasmanian community they were about to leave.[93] The departing contingent comprised 117 officers and men of the 40th and 12th Regiments.[94] The *Mercury* estimated that between 4000 and 5000 people attended their departure on 13 August – a day of considerable outpourings of patriotic enthusiasm.[95] The *Isabella* sailed on 14 August and reached Auckland on 2 September, but Tasmanian interest in their former imperial soldiers continued.[96] The first fatality among the garrison actually occurred during *Isabella*'s voyage. On 26 August, Private William Woolley of the 12th was in the process of drawing a bucket of water over the vessel's side when he was somehow dragged overboard and was lost.[97]

On 13 October the *Reliance* arrived bringing Major Eagar back to Hobart, who was then able to specify the location of the colony's former troops, indicating that the men of the 40th were at the Queen's Redoubt, and the 12th at 'Wangornia [*sic*]'.[98] These troops were soon in action in the Waikato, participating in the failed assaults against Rangiriri on 20 November 1863. The *Mercury* pointed out that among the names of the British casualties was one man killed and five wounded from the colony's former garrison, and published further details on Rangiriri containing a description of the defences at this Maori stronghold:

> The writer, a sergeant-major of one of the line regiments which took part . . . having served . . . in the Crimea . . . He says:—"The guns kept up a fire for half-an-hour not doing much, as the earth here is very sandy, and they went right through it. When the order to charge was given, at it we all went for a distance of 600 or 700 yards; arrived at the outer rifle pits, and cleared them in no time, . . . But an unexpected obstacle presented itself in the form of an irregular redoubt, stronger than anything I ever saw, even in the Crimea. The renowned Redan was nothing to it. I will tell you why. In all regular fortifications, the salient angles can be guessed at, but Rangariri was rendered strong by its irregularity."[99]

The troops in 1863 were not the last to depart from Tasmania. Captain F.R. Chesney, Royal Engineers, was also summoned in February 1864,[100] and in September 1866 the final elements of the 12th Regiment were ordered to prepare to depart for Sydney en route for New Zealand. This detachment comprising Captain Sillery and six men (and one family) left for Sydney in late October,

An artist's impression of the Queen's Redoubt on the Waikato River, from the *Illustrated London News*, 30 January 1864.

where they departed shortly after with the Brisbane detachment of the 12th for the Bay of Plenty.[101]

Tasmanian authorities during 1865–66 endeavoured to obtain the proper allotment of troops prescribed for the colony.[102] Hearing in September 1866 that Queensland was to receive the first elements of the 50th Regiment returning from New Zealand service, the Tasmanian colonial secretary bitterly complained to Governor Browne. This restoration was made all the worse in his opinion on account of the ready support Tasmania had always previously shown New Zealand, as well as the colony's more pressing internal defence needs.[103] Despite this, Tasmania shortly received a detachment of three companies of the 2/14th Regiment, also returning from New Zealand service.[104]

Over two years, 1863–64, the Australian colonies were stripped of their imperial forces to defend their sister colony across the Tasman. Despite fears that this left the colonies vulnerable to attack, no major problems occurred and the small numbers remaining were able to perform adequately their guard and ceremonial duties. If circumstances had been different – if the United States or a European power had chosen these years of vulnerability to attack any major Australian port – the colonists would have been defenceless. However, the events in New Zealand were considered so momentous that the risk was worthwhile.

Chapter Seven

IN RETURN FOR SERVICE

THE MILITARY SETTLER recruiting mission experience in Victoria and New South Wales has received some limited treatment by historians, but analysis of its operation in other Australian colonies is almost non-existent.[1] Because New Zealand's government enlisted these men and they departed to serve across the Tasman, they have been dismissed as no longer having an Australian historical significance. In New Zealand, the place of a whole range of Australian support, including imperial and colonial manpower, has yet to be recognised for its full impact upon the wars. In that country, as in Australia, there is still a tendency to ignore cross-Tasman connections. Yet New Zealand's wars have a very real Australian context, of which the military settlers enlisted during 1863 and 1864 are a major element.

In a memorandum to Governor Grey on 31 July 1863, Alfred Domett outlined reasons behind the New Zealand government's plans to form military settlements in the North Island, including suggested sources for the requisite manpower which could be harnessed on the goldfields of Australia and Otago, where men 'tired of a diggers' life' could be induced by the 'liberal terms' of the scheme. Sought were 'men, hardy, self-reliant, accustomed to a bush life, expert in the use of fire-arms; and, as a body, fully impressed with the necessity of the maintenance of law and order'.[2] Later in October, Grey, in a speech to the House of Representatives, clarified the long-term expectations which the military settler scheme was designed to fulfil. It would provide a force for the future protection of the settlers, as well as leave the regular troops free for offensive operations by

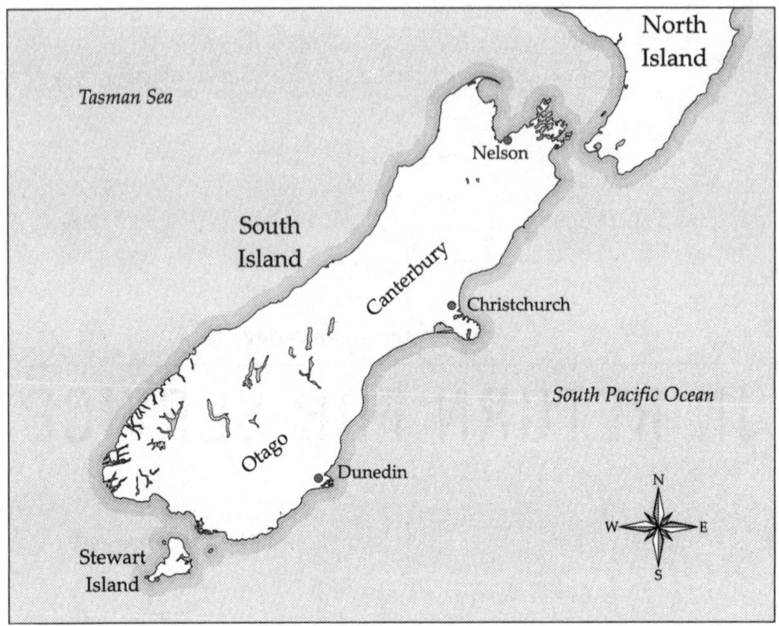

The South Island of New Zealand.

releasing them from their current garrison duties, and thus able to undertake those operations at an early date. To pursue this aim, a large number of volunteers were to be introduced from Australia and the South Island to serve for a certain period as militia, before forming military settlements.[3]

Apart from these factors, the geographical proximity of the Australian colonies again was most crucial, especially when looking at the distances and time involved in getting a similar scheme up and running in Britain. This circumstance was brought home during debate in the New Zealand Legislative Council in November 1863, when Mr Whitaker for the government stated that it was proposed to raise a force of 5000 from Otago and Australia. 'He considered that they were greatly indebted to the Australian Colonies for the drafts of Volunteers', whereas to try and obtain settlers from England would take eight or nine months before any could arrive, and 'in the meantime the country might be abandoned', necessitating it to be reconquered.[4] Settlement therefore played a crucial part in the act of conquest in the Waikato and Taranaki.

The first of the military settlement schemes established was for the province of Taranaki. The New Zealand Colonial Secretary's Office issued conditions of military settler service for this province, located between Omata and Tataraimaka, on 6 July 1863.[5] The discussions were extensively followed in the Australian press, including republication of the full details of the conditions of service as detailed in the *New Zealand Gazette*.[6] In September the *Launceston Examiner* reported on news received from Otago which indicated that recruiting for the Taranaki Militia and the Wellington Colonial Defence Force was progressing well, especially for the former, due to the inducement of land grants for military settler service.[7] No doubt the publication of these conditions of service, and the associated offer of land, caused some individuals to travel to Taranaki to enlist well before any formal recruiting missions took place in Australia.

One of the officers selected during July to commence recruitment in Otago for Taranaki military settlers was Ensign F.J. Mace, Taranaki Militia. From Dunedin, he informed the government he had enrolled 150 men, of which 110 were sworn in and despatched on 17 August, the remainder soon to be forwarded.[8] This first contingent of Otago military settlers was quickly being drilled, and within a month would be ready 'to occupy the ground at Oakura, and defend themselves against the Natives'.[9] Among such Otago recruits were numbers of men, especially miners, who were either Australian-born or -derived.

On 3 August the New Zealand government issued the conditions of service for 'Volunteer Militia Settlers', 'Military and Naval Settlers', and 'Settlers Generally' for the Waikato District in the province of Auckland.[10] Again some of the initial recruiting for military settlers destined for the Waikato occurred in Otago during August–September. On 6 August the colonial secretary informed Mr W. Mason at Dunedin of the government's desire to raise 500 recruits from this province, as the government had no doubt that this number of men could be recruited from the various goldfields.[11] But what quickly became realised with these separate conditions of service for Taranaki and Auckland provinces was that they were somewhat restrictive, with men enlisted on these terms only able to serve in those specific localities. Domett advised Governor Grey of this situation, and the steps being taken to rectify these limitations, on 7 September.[12] Shortly after, the revised conditions upon which land in the North Island would be granted for military service were published in the *Gazette*.[13]

In Australia the men being enlisted during 1863 were utilised in the formation of the first three Waikato military settler regiments for deployment in Auckland Province. The objective of the second recruiting mission, in early 1864, was largely to obtain additional men to assist in raising a further, fourth, regiment of Waikato military settlers and the large 'Melbourne Contingent' component of the Taranaki military settlers. In September 1863 New Zealand's colonial secretary reported that it was agreed that an additional number of military settlers should be raised to serve in the province of Wellington, or elsewhere in the southern part of the North Island. But this was 'not to impede' the raising of 2000 men for

Auckland Province, which was deemed the priority.[14] In early 1864 the *Mercury* revealed that military settler units were being formed for other locations in the North Island, though personnel for these were not directly sought in Australia.[15]

One important figure in both Australian recruiting missions was Lieutenant-Colonel George Dean Pitt, an imperial officer in the 80th Regiment, and eldest son of Major-General George Dean Pitt (1781–1851) who had also served in the 80th Regiment. Following appointment as inspecting officer for the Leeds recruiting district in March 1837, Pitt (senior) relinquished command of the 80th. In 1847 New Zealand became a separate Army command and the first general officer commanding appointed was Major-General Pitt, who also became lieutenant-governor of the New Ulster Province (1848–51). To assist him, his eldest son George Dean Pitt, a junior officer in the 80th Regiment, would serve as his private secretary.[16] Captain G.D. Pitt may have also assisted his father during his role as a senior recruiting officer in England, or at least was imbued with his father's service and organisational expertise in that capacity.[17]

As a captain in the 80th, G.D. Pitt was also to gain an intimacy with the colony of Victoria in the 1850s and early 1860s. As an imperial staff officer stationed in this colony he served as inspector of musketry and acting deputy adjutant general. In July 1859 he also became the first commandant of the Victorian volunteer force with the local rank of colonel of volunteers. Over the years 1859–62 he became instrumental in revitalising and expanding the Victorian volunteers, and was widely recognised as 'a good soldier and an able organiser'. In February 1862 he received orders from England to leave Victoria for New Zealand command, departed for Auckland in March, and was promoted major.[18]

In June 1863 the New Zealand government appointed G.D. Pitt lieutenant-colonel 'for special service' in the 1st Battalion Auckland Regiment of Militia.[19] The *Argus* shortly after commented: 'We are sure the volunteers . . . from among the Auckland Militia will be gratified to learn that this officer, so long and favourably known in Auckland, and who earned a worldwide popularity among the volunteers of Victoria, has been nominated to the command of the 400 men called out for active service.'[20] In this capacity as commander of 'Pitt's 400', which would form the nucleus of the 1st Waikato Regiment, he shortly found himself responsible for the mission to enlist military settlers in Australia.[21] Upon returning to Victoria, his thorough knowledge of the place, the people, and the various officers and units of the volunteer movement of this colony would see him play a highly public role in the recruiting that was to take place.

It is not the intention here to explore the progress of the military settlements established in the Waikato, Bay of Plenty, Taranaki or other locations in the North Island from 1864. Suffice it to say that New Zealand's military settlement schemes were generally a failure, and by the time of the formal disbandment of the military settler units on 22 October 1867, social and economic depression had fallen 'over the sparsely settled European claim on the Waikato. By 1868 in Tauranga there were barely 10 military settlers farming land, hundreds of others having taken their leave.'[22] In Taranaki, such hardships were not as obvious, as the established provincial government was sustaining the requirements of the eleven scattered settlements in this province. Although some military settlers established themselves, many were simply not equipped with proper farming expertise, nor had they received sufficient government support and the infrastructure necessary to succeed. By the late 1860s many military settlers had either abandoned their lands or sold up and moved on to other activities such as the Thames goldfields, while others returned to Australia.

The First Military Settler Recruiting Mission

New South Wales recruiting

The arrival of a New Zealand government party comprising F.D. Bell, J.E. Gorst, Colonel Pitt and Captain Rogers-Harrison on 14 August 1863 marks the commencement of the first military settler recruiting mission to the Australian colonies.[23] The *Sydney Morning Herald* emphasised the need for united Australian support in this great crisis, as this was 'the first time in our history when the common interest of the Southern world has made Australians brethren in arms. It will be seen whether our young men fond of adventure, and fearless of danger, will muster to the rescue of their colonial brethren in this great trial and peril.'[24]

Advertisements detailing the New Zealand government's 'Waikato country' military settler service conditions commenced on 15 August and ran extensively throughout this month until the departure of the first contingent of volunteers. These advertisements also indicated Gorst had established recruiting offices on Bridge Street, Sydney.[25] The *Herald* reported that the promotion 'seems to be regarded with some degree of favour, as already more than eighty eligible candidates for military service have been accepted by the Sydney agent, and it is understood that many applications, from persons resident in the interior, have also been received'.[26] In charge of recruiting in Sydney was Captain J.H. Rogers-Harrison, a former 58th Regiment officer. In his later capacity as captain on the Auckland Militia staff, he was involved in the Waikato military settler recruiting, before arriving with the New Zealand government party to commence efforts in New South Wales.[27]

By 20 August over 150 persons had registered their names for service, and over the next couple of days these men underwent medical examinations, from which

'The New Zealand Difficulty', a satirical cartoon about the experiences which one Victorian military settler volunteer was about to face on service in New Zealand. *Melbourne Punch*, 22 October 1863.

sixty-five were accepted.[28] Despite the tempting land offers advertised, some initial concerns were raised which pointed out that the New Zealand government was 'not in a position to give land that is offered, and that the promise made to the effect may be repudiated'.[29] The *Herald* elaborated upon this apprehension, including a detailed letter from 'H.C.' on the subject,[30] which in turn received a response from 'One Who Knows', who countered by stating that New Zealand's government 'does not pretend to have the land offered actually in possession. It is native land in the Waikato district, belonging to tribes now in rebellion, which has to be taken before it can be occupied.'[31]

The opportunity of active military service nonetheless stirred interest among members of the Sydney volunteers. One of these stated he was 'disposed to offer' his services but was concerned that he could not afford to pay for his government-issued volunteer uniform if he enlisted. 'I think it would be a graceful act on the part of our Government were they to sanction the formation of at least one company to proceed to New Zealand (of course under New Zealand regulations) armed and dressed as they are.'[32] 'Rifleman', a member of the Sydney Volunteer Rifles, on 22 August inquired whether Mr Gorst would reply to his queries, including whether 'a Volunteer, having satisfactorily served the full period of three years, can then sell his land and return to New South Wales, or is bound to remain in New Zealand and cultivate it?'[33] Such an inquiry perhaps indicates that some volunteers harboured the intention to return to New South Wales rather than stay and settle, and looked for direction on the New Zealand government's position. Yet the offer of land, although a great inducement for many, was not the sole reason for enlistment. A chance to take part in one of the Empire's wars was apparently also a significant motivating factor. Seemingly, plain martial interest enticed a good number of men to enlist. The *Sydney Morning Herald*, on the hundreds recruited in Sydney, noted that they were a fine body of men, 'many of them already acquainted with drill, and a dozen members of our Rifle corps, to one of whom an Ensign's commission has been given. A large proportion have an acquaintance with the use of firearms, and are adapted to bush action.'[34]

As the first contingent of military settlers was finalised, it was announced that the *Kate* was being prepared for their departure.[35] They were to muster on 27 August on the Patent Slip Wharf for embarkation, though much 'regret is felt that, notwithstanding the military and Volunteer bands' offering their services, the New Zealand officer in charge reportedly did not want any public fanfare. This 'created some disappointment on the part of those about to leave as well as amongst their friends', no doubt because it was a major contrast to the public spectacle attending the send-off of the imperial contingents, though as it turned out, this was not to be the case.[36] The *Herald* reported that the wharf

> was so crowded that it was only by ... considerable tact that people were able to keep from falling into the water.... There were a great number of people on ... the wharves and other places ... [trying to catch] a glimpse of the men ... altogether there could not have been less than five thousand persons assembled to witness the departure.... The roll was called, and the men who answered to their names were drafted on board one at a time ... When the Kate was hauled off, cheers were given by the men on board and their friends on the wharf, the band at the same time playing "Speed the Plough."[37]

This contingent of eighty volunteers was commanded by Ensign R.J. Coulter, a former member of the Sydney Volunteer Rifles, and accompanied by Dr Drake as medical superintendent.[38] The *Kate* arrived at Auckland on 3 September.[39]

To mark the vessel's departure, within a few short days the Sydney photographic firm of Freeman Brothers of George Street had published a large print of this 'spirit-stirring scene', which was presumably made available for purchase.[40] From news received from Auckland, several weeks later the *Herald* was able to recount some impressions of these Sydney volunteers:

> They are really a fine body of men, and such as could scarcely ever be found, as a rule, amongst new settlers. If all who come are of the same sort as these, Auckland will wish for twenty-thousand rather than five, as they could not fail of providing most admirable settlers when their military duties are at an end. The uniform adopted for the Sydney regiment of Volunteers is a most serviceable looking one, consisting of a blue shirt, dark grey trousers, tucked at the bottom, inside knee-boots.[41]

Despite 'somewhat unnecessarily' being detained in Auckland, this first contingent of Sydney volunteers commenced for the front on 28 September.[42]

Recruiting efforts continued in Sydney following this contingent's departure, and during August–September advertisements again appeared detailing the conditions of service.[43] These efforts continued to attract men and preparations were commenced to despatch a second contingent aboard the *Charlotte Andrews*. On 12 September this vessel prepared to depart Sydney after a contingent under the command of former 12th Regiment officer and South Australian resident Lieutenant H.L. Williams, a 'Sergeant Brennan', and 116 other rank volunteers.[44] Captain G.E. Elliot, another Auckland Militia recruiting officer who arrived with the government party, accompanied them.[45] Just prior to departure, two officers and thirty-three other rank military settler volunteers from Brisbane transshipped aboard the *Charlotte Andrews* for Auckland as well.

Following the departure of the *Charlotte Andrews* further contingents continued to sail from Sydney. Recruiting efforts were maintained in and around the city and advertisements were again carried in the colony's press from 14 September.[46] The *Claud Hamilton* is believed to have conveyed a further twenty-five military settlers when it departed on 15 September.[47] Four days later, the *Herald* reported that conditions of military service were still 'regarded with some degree of favour, as already more than eighty eligible candidates . . . have been accepted'. Enthusiasm to enlist also extended outside of Sydney, with numbers of applications being received by the recruiting officers 'from persons resident in the interior'.[48]

On 25 September the *Lord Ashley* departed Sydney with various government officials returning to Auckland accompanied by a further forty military settler volunteers.[49] By 6 October another forty men had come forward and enrolled.[50] The contingent destined for the *Kate* in October was commanded by James Holt,[51] a former New Zealand resident, and 'Ensign Brown', believed to be Duncan

Michie Brown, later killed in action in January 1869 while serving as an officer in the Armed Constabulary.[52] The *Herald* also suggests that former members of the colony's volunteer or police forces continued to be found amongst those being selected.[53] This final contingent from New South Wales during 1863 (reported as totalling either seventy-seven or seventy-eight) departed for Auckland aboard the *Kate* on 10 October.[54] The *Herald* was later able to offer advice for those family and friends remaining in the colony after being handed an 'excellent map of the seat of war in the Waikato country'. Produced by the Tasmanian firm of Walch & Sons, this was available in Sydney, allowing residents to trace the military movements taking place across the Tasman.[55]

As would occur with all the Australian colonies, letters received from military settlers, or those handed in by friends and families, would shed light on the experiences of these men in New Zealand. In October 1864 the *Sydney Morning Herald* detailed one such example from a military settler who had enlisted in Sydney during 1863. Thomas Joseph Willis, a private serving in the No. 2 Company, 2nd Waikato Regiment, at Alexandra Redoubt in the Upper Waipa, was originally from Parramatta in Sydney.[56] Willis used this opportunity to express a highly critical and illuminating appraisal of New Zealand's military settlement scheme:

An artist's impression of the Alexandra Redoubt on the Waikato River, from the *Illustrated London News*, 5 December 1863.

> You are of course well aware of the enthusiasm that was manifested in Sydney with regard to the enrolment of Volunteers for this island, and the ardour with which the cause was embraced by many a promising young man, who like myself unheedingly bartered his liberty and reputation to become the scapegoat and lacquey of his superior (?) officers, many of whom had difficulty in earning a livelihood even by their wits, in the mature colony of New South Wales. . . . And the reward from this liberal and Crœsus-like Government is fifty acres of farming land and one acre town allotment; the land may be good, the land may be bad, the land may be rich (but in a swamp or on a mountain), a man may be shot, but one thing I know . . . [is] the land is quite far enough from civilisation in every case so as not to interfere with the Government Land Sales hereafter; the fact of the matter is simply this, that the military settlers are deluded, and become the victims of a vile and unmitigated imposture, it is impossible that this Government can much longer withstand the enormous drain, upon its finances that this cruel and bungled war entails. I know not what the mass will do when the militia pay is stopped, but many have foreseen the crisis that must surely come; and, consequently, have provided for it by saving as much as will take them back to old Sydney.[57]

In this astute commentary, Willis pinpoints many of the factors that would eventually contribute to the failure of the military settler scheme by the late 1860s.

Victorian recruiting

On 15 August the *Argus* announced the expected arrival of Colonel Pitt 'to raise a regiment of Volunteers' for service in New Zealand. Now the young men of Victoria would have an 'opportunity of distinguishing themselves' in the war 'by the liberal offer held out' by the government of New Zealand.[58] This same day the following advertisement, initiated by R.D. Harte, of 2 Queen Street, Melbourne, marked the beginning of recruiting in Victoria:

> AUCKLAND MILITIA. – PERSONS desirous of accepting the liberal offer made by the New Zealand Government, which entitles each Volunteer to one town allotment, and one country section of 50 acres, will please COMMUNICATE with the under signed by letter without delay, stating address, age, &c.[59]

Advertisements by Harte were repeated in league with the publication of the full conditions of military settlement in the Waikato country, up until the arrival of Colonel Pitt in Melbourne on 21 August, after which fresh advertisements were commenced the following day.[60] On the day of his arrival, Pitt's first act was to seek an interview with the governor to present his credentials and elicit support from Victoria's authorities for his government's recruiting activities. The Port Phillip Hotel on Flinders Street where Pitt obtained accommodation was also chosen as the venue for the commencement of recruiting.[61]

The Victorian press quickly responded in support of aid to New Zealand, reinforcing the thread of blood and kinship that connected all the Australasian colonies. The *Argus*, for instance, asserted that the war in New Zealand brought home 'forcibly the vitality of that common bond of interest and of race which connects the Australian system'.[62] Several days later this paper expressed confidence at the prospects of a successful outcome to Pitt's mission in Victoria: 'It is not unlikely, indeed, that he will suffer from an *embarras de richesse*, and that he will be perplexed with the number of applicants for the shilling.' In reaffirming the patriotic duty being required at this time of crisis, the *Argus* concluded: 'In spite of the national reputation with which Napoleon stamped the English character, there are occasions when the blood of an Englishman courses along the channel of his veins as rebelliously as any Frenchman's. The New Zealand war is just one of them.'[63]

Throughout August and September, Victorian papers also kept their readers well informed of the military aid and recruitment efforts taking place in other colonies such as New South Wales, Queensland and Tasmania. No doubt this coverage also provided additional interest or enthusiasm via the ever-present undercurrents of inter-colonial rivalry evident amongst the Australian colonies, but especially between Victoria and its northern neighbour New South Wales.[64]

Commencing on 17 August, the *Argus* carried the full advertisement detailing the conditions of military settlement in the Waikato country.[65] Now that Colonel Pitt had arrived, new advertisements sought recruits not only for service but also called for candidates as officers and non-commissioned officers. From 25 August, Pitt ensured that his advertisements were accompanied by extracts from his government's Militia Act Amendment Bill, which furnished information regarding pensions for wounds or to widows in the event of the death of a militiaman. A separate advertisement also notified potential applicants to ensure they brought written character references with them to assist in the selection process.[66] On the first day of recruiting for officers and non-commissioned officers, 'no less than sixty-five candidates' presented themselves.[67]

In the Victorian Parliament on 25 August the debate centred on the nature of assistance that could be offered. Part of these discussions revealed the government would place no obstacles in the way of Pitt's recruiting mission, though at the same time would not offer 'any extraordinary facilities' to assist in recruiting for Pitt's regiment of military settlers.[68] In defence of the government and Pitt's objectives, the *Argus* stated: 'In the midst of mercy, there will be self-interest, and we cannot blame the Government for maintaining a position of neutrality in a matter involving the emigration of its citizens.'[69] The government's initial reservations were allayed, however, when the New Zealand Native Minister F.D. Bell, who had delayed in Sydney, now arrived in Melbourne to elaborate on his government's plans, and legitimise Colonel Pitt's credentials.[70]

Another concern raised in the Victorian Legislative Assembly during August pertained to the welfare of the families of military settlers. Mr A.J. Smith asked the Chief Secretary Mr McCulloch whether the government would inquire into the numbers involved, as it was reported that many recruits 'were leaving their wives and families totally unprovided for'. Smith wanted the government to make arrangements whereby either these men, or the New Zealand government, would be 'obliged to give a guarantee' that such families would be neither left destitute nor dependent on this colony to provide support. McCulloch responded that the government would try to do something to prevent this situation occurring, but conceded that 'there were considerable difficulties in the way of dealing with such a question', and the government really had no powers to act.[71]

Such concerns about the welfare of wives or families of military settler volunteers were certainly well founded in particular instances. The *Victorian* shortly reported its belief that the departure of military settler volunteers would lead to many cases of wife desertion. The first such instance came before the Melbourne City Court on 1 September, when a woman named Isabella Jones complained that her husband had departed the previous day without leaving her any means.[72] Despite such issues, an officer from the 'Victorian Contingent' from South Yarra soon after wrote in defence of Pitt and the responsible married men who had volunteered: 'Victoria need not be afraid of being overwhelmed with what you call a legacy of poverty, as there is not a married man among us who will not take advantage of the arrangement with the Oriental Bank [for remittance of pay for wives and families].'[73]

As would occur in other Australian colonies, it was from among the ranks of Victoria's volunteer movement that many men stepped forward offering their services. One of the first examples was reported on 17 August, when the 'martial ardour' of four members of the Geelong Troop of the Prince of Wales's Victoria Volunteer Light Horse impelled their offer of service.[74] By 18 August Mr Harte reported he had been besieged by potential applicants and had 'registered 127 eligible candidates, many of them of the Victorian volunteers'.[75] Despite the initial response, after arrival Colonel Pitt felt obliged to state that he did not desire that the regiment 'should be formed of trained volunteers alone. All who are disposed to accept the liberal conditions offered... however little they may know of military matters, are invited to join the force.'[76] In this sentiment Pitt makes it clear that his government did not simply require just military men, as enlistees could be trained. It was settlers with farming experience, who could fulfil the long-term expectations of the military settlement scheme, that were greatly desired.

At Geelong, William Fraser, a lieutenant in the local troop of the Victoria Volunteer Light Horse, was appointed to enrol volunteers by Colonel Pitt.[77] At the end of the first day of enrolments Fraser had obtained twenty-seven names, but the *Argus*'s Geelong correspondent reported that fifteen members of the Light Horse also promised to enlist.[78] On the eve of departure for New Zealand, Captain Bell of the Geelong Troop of Light Horse, in the presence of friends and members of this volunteer unit, presented Fraser with a sword as a token of respect.[79]

At Ballarat, Pitt designated Major Robert Wallace, a former officer in the 60th Regiment and now commanding the 1st Ballarat Rifle Corps, as authorised to accept applications. By 26 August Wallace had received twenty-five applications, one of which was from a member of the local Rifle Corps, but this candidate was rejected – not only was he under the age of twenty-one, but his father strongly opposed his enlistment. It was also reported that several members of the Ballarat Rifle Corps had expressed a readiness to volunteer for active service, providing the major would have the command. Days later it was reported that enrolments were being discontinued at Ballarat after Wallace received a telegram from Victoria's attorney-general, which advised him, that as a Victorian public servant, it would be inappropriate for him to be engaged in recruiting for Colonel Pitt.[80]

Pitt's recruiting office was kept very busy, and by 26 August had registered 241 men for service. A great deal of time was actually taken up in examining the qualifications of potential candidates, with many being rejected as unsuitable, while others were declared medically unfit.[81] The next day the *Argus* was able to announce that the first detachment of volunteers, comprising 'Nos. 1, 2, 3, and 4 companies', would depart 'for the scene of war on Monday first'.[82] On the eve of their departure, Colonel Pitt called these volunteers together to address them on the duties and tasks they were about to embark upon. They were reassured of his government's abilities to meet its land grant offers following the completion of their service.[83] During early September, Pitt and Minister Bell also visited the regional centres of Castlemaine and Sandhurst, followed by Geelong and Ballarat, in search of further recruits. To facilitate these regional moves, a Lieutenant Rickards arrived at Ballarat in late August, commencing enrolment activities at Craig's Royal Hotel.[84]

This first Victorian contingent comprised a total of 405 privates and non-commissioned officers and was placed under the command of four officer appointees. These included Captain H.G. Smith (former captain, Victorian Volunteer Engineers), and Lieutenants W.A. Smith (former lieutenant and senior drill instructor, Pentridge Volunteer Rifle Company), H.B. Lomax, and William

Nunnington (former drill instructor, Fitzroy Volunteer Rifle Company).[85] On the composition of the men making up this contingent, the *Argus* reported that the volunteers, despite including 'many specimens of the genus "loafer," ... were altogether a fine body of men', and 'not at all likely to reflect shame on the colony they are leaving'. The majority were believed to be labourers and miners, plus a number of tradesmen, artisans and clerks.[86]

Before departure, Native Minister Bell addressed the volunteers of the 'Victorian Contingent' aboard the *Star of India*, thanking them all 'on behalf of the Government and colonists of New Zealand, for the prompt manner in which they have come forward to aid that colony in its difficulties'.[87] He also took the opportunity to again reassure these recruits of his government's good faith in regard to land grants, as well as appealing to their imperial patriotism as inspiration.[88] The *Star of India* then sailed for Auckland on 1 September.[89]

With this departure the *Victorian* acknowledged that the 'New Zealand difficulty' had created considerable interest not only in Melbourne but throughout the colony, with recruiting 'going on briskly', although prospective volunteers were warned to be wary:

> It would be unjust to repress the outflow of our sympathy for the British settlers in New Zealand, but it is only right to caution enthusiastic would-be-volunteers ... [as] they will find soldiering there a very different sort of amusement from the powder-play of Collingwood [volunteer rifle] butts; and not a few will curse the day they left Victoria – beguiled by the Will-o'-the Wisp promise of their "own vine and own fig tree" kind which will eventuate in a very different way for many of them. Let those who think of going consider well what they are about, for once on the saltwater off Sandridge their regrets will be in vain.[90]

Continued recruitment in Melbourne and surrounding regional centres required Pitt to charter the *Caduceus* for conveying the second contingent of Victorian volunteers. Advertisements for the 'New Zealand Militia', and for candidates for officers or non-commissioned officers, were also recommenced in the press.[91] One of these successful applicants was Captain James Skene at Bendigo, who had previously commanded the Bendigo Volunteer Rifle Corps, and was a familiar figure in the area.[92] By the evening of 31 August, Skene had received applications from nearly 100 men.[93] He signed on seventy-six as volunteers, as well as attracting two sergeants from the Bendigo Volunteer Rifle Corps. Before departure on 16 September, Captain Skene was presented with an honour sword and illuminated address from his former volunteer unit. The Sandhurst Volunteer Band similarly presented Skene with an illuminated address, along with a ring made of Bendigo gold, in appreciation of his services to the region's volunteers.[94]

On 4 September a number of volunteers boarded the *Caduceus*. Morning trains brought men from Sandhurst and Castlemaine – Colonel Pitt having enrolled 150 men at the first regional centre and forty-five at the second[95] – while others arrived in Melbourne during the afternoon. A further twenty-five were enrolled in Melbourne this same day, with more expected to follow from Pitt's visit to Geelong and Ballarat on 5 September. Two former imperial Army officers were selected to command this second contingent of Victorian military settlers.[96] These were Lieutenants J.J. Dunn and J.S. Perceval (late 55th Regiment), who were joined by Ballarat enlistee and officer appointee Lieutenant Robert Wallace.[97] Perceval and three other Victorian enlistees serving in the 1st Waikato Regiment were shortly to be killed in action in New Zealand at Wheeler's Farm, Titi Hill, near Mauku on 23 October 1863 – the first fatalities among the Australian-enlisted military settlers.[98]

Following a visit to Geelong and Ballarat, Pitt accepted the services of twenty-three men at the former location and twenty-seven at the latter. He had arrived in Ballarat on 5 September accompanied by Lieutenant Rickards, with recruiting taking place in Craig's Royal Hotel.[99] Back in Melbourne on 7 September, Pitt enrolled another fifty-three men, who were all then embarked aboard the *Caduceus* in preparation for completing the complement of 400 wanted before departure.[100] The *Caduceus* cleared for Auckland on 8 September with 'upwards of 400' Victorian volunteers.[101]

Pitt continued his recruiting activities at Melbourne's Port Phillip Hotel, while in regional centres was assisted by Lieutenant Fraser at Geelong, Captain Skene at Sandhurst, Lieutenant Walker[102] at Castlemaine, and Lieutenant Rickards at Ballarat.[103] Rickards is believed to be the same officer who arrived in Hobart to undertake recruiting in Tasmania, but whose name is often incorrectly referred to as Richards. The *Golden Age* was chartered for conveying a projected third contingent of volunteers, while recruiting efforts continued to attract almost twenty volunteers per day.[104] By mid-September some 112 volunteers had embarked aboard the *Golden Age*, and enrolments were taken right up to the day of departure.[105] On 19 September the third and final contingent of '180 volunteers' (though a review of Victorian recruiting provides a different figure) cleared Melbourne, but it was not until the 23rd that the vessel sailed for Auckland.[106]

Overall, 1429 applicants had offered themselves during 1863, 380 of whom were rejected on medical or other grounds. A total of 932 volunteers of enlisted rank were embarked in the three contingents despatched to Auckland, and a further 117 enrolled individuals failed to embark. The reasons behind the failure of some men to turn up are unclear, but no doubt a number had a change of

'The New Zealand Difficulty – No. 2', another satirical cartoon about the experiences which one Victorian military settler volunteer was about to face in New Zealand. *Melbourne Punch*, 5 November 1863.

heart about their decision to enlist. Others may have simply failed to arrive in time, or had not completed family or business arrangements, but nonetheless may still have departed on their own initiative individually thereafter. The *Star of India* conveyed 'four officers and 406 men', the *Caduceus* 'three officers and 386 men', the *Golden Age* 'four officers and 140 men', and three other officers sailed 'by way of Otago or Sydney', comprising a total force embarked of fourteen officers and 932 men. Of all these volunteers, thirty-five per cent were said to be 'drilled men' – presumably former members of colonial volunteer forces or former imperial soldiers or sailors; nine per cent were married. The average age was twenty-seven and the average height was 5 ft 7½ in. Colonel Pitt accompanied the final contingent of volunteers, departing Melbourne aboard the *Golden Age*, while Bell was reported having sailed from Sydney.[107]

Through the medium of the press Victorians were to be provided glimpses into the experience, expectations and eventual disillusionment of their military settler volunteers. One letter from a member of the first contingent, dated Otahuhu, 30 September 1863, recounted their initial reception:

> As soon as we had landed we were marched direct through Auckland to this camp ... There are upwards of 8,000 men in this camp, and volunteers from all the neighbouring colonies are daily arriving, but chiefly from Victoria and Otago. The first detachment of the Sydney Volunteer Militia came a week before us, and, after four days' drill, volunteered for the front.... The militia and colonial volunteers ... are simply taught, first of all, obedience to orders, the manual and platoon exercises, and skirmishing – all intricate military evolutions being of no possible use in fighting in the bush with the Maories.[108]

This military settler noted that the officers and non-commissioned officers of the military settler regiments were 'for the most part old soldiers, who thoroughly understand their duties', whereas their drill instructors were imperial soldiers stationed at Otahuhu Military Camp. This writer also indicated his prior service in the volunteer movement, and acknowledged that his New Zealand experience was quite different to that of his former volunteering days.[109]

Another glimpse of military settler life came from William Moore serving in the 3rd Waikato Regiment at Queen's Redoubt on 10 May 1864.[110] Moore appears to be one of the many members of the 3rd Waikato Regiment who volunteered for service with the Imperial Commissariat Transport Corps, and here not only wrote of 'his disgust with the Land Transport Service into which he had drafted', but also related a very narrow escape he had whilst stationed at Ngaruawahia:

> ... I found, on going to feed my horses ... that one of them was missing. On reporting my loss to the commanding officer, he ordered me to take my remaining horse and look for the other, telling me, however, "not to go too far from camp." As I did not suppose that the missing animal was more than a mile or so away, I rode carelessly off, totally unarmed.... and proceeded onwards a good deal absorbed in thought, and without observing how far I was from camp. When ... about four miles from camp, my meditations were suddenly interrupted by the sharp ring of a bullet in unpleasant proximity to my head. I assure you that I did not wait for another hint, but ... galloped homewards followed by a volley and loud Maori yells and curses.[111]

Moore also gave thought to the nature of the conflict with the Maori, emphasising that conquest, and the government keeping faith with its land agreements with the military settlers, would lead to successful European settlement and control of the Waikato.[112]

Queensland recruiting

The Queensland press reported on the initial efforts to recruit military settlers in Sydney and Melbourne from mid-August.[113] Shortly after the arrival of the New Zealand government party in Sydney, a telegram was received on 19 August by the 'head of the military department in Queensland' – Captain H.D. Pitt, Royal Artillery[114] – requesting he commence enrolling in Brisbane 'as many volunteers as are willing to offer themselves'. The *Courier* concluded by stating, the 'war is now assuming a serious aspect, and it is anticipated that a strong succession to the force at present there may be received from Queensland'.[115]

The news of the commencement of recruiting in the city elicited some interest amongst members of the local volunteers, 'as many who were willing to do so could enrol' for New Zealand. The offer of land grants for service was viewed as a significant incentive for many to 'emigrate to the seat of war' in the other colonies, and it was 'rumoured that a few will be found willing to go' from Queensland, including some recently arrived German immigrants.[116] The Germans in question had only just arrived in the colony aboard the immigrant vessels *La Rochelle* and *Alster* in early August. A body of these immigrants, unable to find immediate employment and disgruntled at what they found upon reaching Moreton Bay, saw military settler service as an option and were to become a feature of the recruiting experience that took place in Brisbane.[117] In the Queensland Parliament on 19 August Dr Challinor asked the colonial secretary whether he was aware German immigrants who had been 'brought here at the expense of this colony' had now enlisted for New Zealand military service. In reply the colonial secretary stated the government had no information on the matter, but remarked that he hoped this was not the case.[118]

During the evening of 22 August another telegram arrived from Sydney for the officer commanding the colony's troops. This permitted enrolment of volunteers for New Zealand to be undertaken at the military barracks on Queen Street, and stated that the rules and regulations would shortly be issued and a recruiting officer would arrive and medical inspections of prospective recruits then be carried out.[119] On 26 August the *Courier* published the first of the advertisements detailing the conditions of service.[120] Despite 'liberal' land entitlements after three years' military service, the realisation that such settlers could in fact be killed caused the *Courier* to observe: 'The settler under such conditions may never enjoy the fruits of his militia labors. That is merely a "chance," however; and judging from the accounts we have received from Sydney it is a "chance" hardly considered when compared with the Inducements held out for incurring it.'[121] And on the progress of the first week's recruiting, this paper also confirmed that 'considerable excitement of a martial nature' prevailed in Queensland, as had occurred in other colonies, as a 'consequence of the liberal offers' made to volunteers for New Zealand. 'In the course of a few days an agent is expected to arrive, and from current rumour it is believed his errand will not be fruitless.'[122]

The New Zealand government recruiting agent, Mr R.C. Mainwaring, arrived in Brisbane aboard the *Telegraph* from Sydney on 30 August.[123] With his arrival, the Brisbane recruiting task commenced in earnest, though tentative voices of concern were raised. On 3 September, for instance, the *Queensland Daily Guardian* pointed out that in financial terms Queensland was more involved than other colonies. 'It must be remembered . . . that as the introduction of each immigrant to Queensland costs the Colony a land order worth £18, Queensland actually contributes more by the sending of twenty volunteers to New Zealand than either New South Wales or Victoria by furnishing 1000 men.'[124]

On the eve of the departure of a portion of Brisbane's small imperial contingent and the military settler volunteers the *Courier* asserted that 'some fine manly corps could be selected' from Victoria, New South Wales, 'and "little" Queensland', despite those in opposition to the scheme who 'express a belief that "not many" will be found to go' from this colony. 'That such a supposition is incorrect will be proved in a few days, and it has been contradicted by the events which have taken place in the neighbouring colonies. . . . To suppose that one tenth of the men who will leave . . . are filled with military enthusiasm is absurd. Acres of land . . . form the bait which allures them away from settled occupations.'[125] The *Courier* also drew attention to expense incurred by Queensland bringing in immigrants, such as the recently arrived Germans, only to now see them being lured across the Tasman:

> We do not wish to be understood as desiring to discourage the movement . . . made in answer to the appeal of Captain Pitt. In fact, the response has proved that Anglo-Saxon courage is not weakened by the influence of a tropical climate. We should, however like to know what is the intention of the government with regard to the land orders of those immigrants, who . . . intend to leave it for one less attractive.[126]

It was reported that seventy-four New Zealand volunteers were expected to muster, although a larger number had enrolled, at the military barracks on 9 September for transport via Sydney aboard the A.S.N. Company's steamer *Clarence*. These volunteers – of whom 'the greater part . . . are composed of Germans' – would be accompanied by the small 12th Regiment contingent commanded by Ensign Brittain.[127] Although these optimistic figures were not fulfilled, interest amongst Queensland's volunteer movement nonetheless saw Captain Pitt make certain inquiries with the colonial secretary on 2 September. 'As it is probable that some of the Members of the Volunteer Force may wish to join the Volunteer Militia being raised here', he asked that such persons should not be expected to repay the cost of the volunteer uniforms provided by the government. The government responded by approving his recommendation.[128]

Prior to arrival in Queensland, Captain Henry Dowdeswell Pitt was active in the New South Wales volunteer movement during 1860–62. While serving in that colony he had commanded the Royal Artillery detachment sent from Sydney with the second military contingent to quell civil unrest at the Lambing Flats goldfields in July 1861.[129] The following year he was appointed private secretary and aide-de-camp to Queensland's first governor, G.F. Bowen.[130] In Queensland, Pitt fostered renewed interest in the volunteer movement when he was appointed captain-commandant of the Volunteer Artillery in August 1862, as well as becoming major of brigade of the Volunteer Rifle Brigade.[131]

An interesting aspect to Captain Pitt's involvement in the recruiting in Brisbane was unspecified activity in New Zealand undertaken later during 1864. During January of that year he requested three months' leave of absence 'for the purpose of visiting the adjacent colonies on urgent private affairs', which was promptly granted, and departed for Sydney, arriving on the 21st.[132] Although it is not clear what these 'urgent private affairs' were, he did travel to New Zealand, where he no doubt witnessed the military operations under way. Providing evidence before a select committee gathering information on Queensland's defences in 1866, he acknowledged witnessing New Zealand's militia and volunteers system during his 1864 period of leave. He also outlined in evidence his personal opinion on the military settler system and other New Zealand colonial irregular units such as the Forest Rangers.[133] While it is unfortunate that much of his activities during this period remain unknown, as a serving imperial officer he no doubt ensured some degree of personal involvement in the conflict taking place across the Tasman.

On the day of the departure of the Brisbane volunteers the *Queensland Daily Guardian* proclaimed its judgement on the 'regrettable' race struggle in New Zealand. In doing so, the *Guardian* indicated that amongst these volunteers were a few who possessed prior combat or field experience which would be of some use, offering as well suggestions for combating the Maori on their own terms, including Aboriginal trackers:

> But New Zealand is a rough rugged country; the natives crouch in the fern, and rely frequently on ambuscades for the success of their attacks. It would be . . . wise to meet them with their own tactics, to follow them into their fastnesses . . . The North American Indians have long been celebrated as trackers, but the Australian blacks are more acute and reliable trackers than they. The presence of a few of them . . . would greatly facilitate the operations of our army, would hasten the termination of the war, and would prevent any unnecessary shedding of blood.[134]

On 10 September this paper provided an account of the departure of the Brisbane volunteers, but was also scornful of the total lack of public fanfare to see them off:

> A fine body of volunteers, numbering about forty-five, were marched down Queen-street yesterday . . .They are a picked lot from a number of applicants, and there are among them as fine soldiers as ever handled a musket. In Melbourne and Sydney the . . . Volunteers were accompanied to the place of embarkation with military music and a guard of honour; but here they were marched off with freezing coldness, without one friendly cheer or shake of the hand.[135]

The *Courier* also noted that as these volunteers marched through the town, one 'attempted to make his escape, but was quickly brought back and compelled to proceed with the others'.[136] Later these volunteers were reported being under the command of 'Brevet Ensign Reilly'.[137] As they boarded, each was issued a pair of blankets, and the recruiting agent Mr Mainwaring accompanied them on the *Clarence*'s departure.[138]

In Sydney the second New South Wales military settler contingent scheduled to depart aboard the *Charlotte Andrews* was delayed so as to take on board these Queensland volunteers. The *Clarence* arrived in Sydney on 12 September with '35 Volunteers', mooring temporarily below Garden Island so that these men could be transshipped to the *Charlotte Andrews*, which then departed for Auckland.[139] In summary of these Queensland events, the *Courier* proudly surmised that despite the colony having 'not much interest in common with . . . New Zealand, its people have already proved themselves most willing to make a sacrifice in order to aid in putting an end to a war which has now for some years been a blight upon that splendid portion of Australasia'.[140]

One of these Brisbane-recruited Waikato military settlers was civil servant and volunteer artilleryman Henry J. Glassock. In the formation of Queensland's volunteer movement in 1860, he can be found amongst those who enrolled in the Brisbane Volunteer Rifles Corps in September, before later involvement with the Volunteer Artillery Corps (1862–63). He had also obtained employment as a clerk in the Queensland Registrar-General's Office in January 1862.[141] The *Courier* later relayed news from New Zealand that all the Brisbane volunteers arrived safely in Auckland during September 1863 and that Henry Glassock, 'late of the Queensland Volunteer Artillery, has been appointed ensign'.[142] He served in the 2nd Waikato Military Settler Regiment, receiving his ensigncy in September 1863. From this regiment he volunteered for service in the Imperial Commissariat Transport Corps, and later resigned his commission in July 1865.[143]

Tasmanian recruiting

On 28 August the *Mercury* heralded the commencement of recruiting that would now take place in Tasmania.[144] Native Minister Bell was expected in a few days, and Captain F.R. Chesney, the officer in command of the troops in Tasmania, would accept applications from prospective volunteers in the meantime. Also published this same day were the full conditions of military settler service for the Waikato country.[145] During the initial stages of Tasmanian recruiting the colony's papers voiced concerns about the ability of the New Zealand government to offer the land grants being advertised, as had already been expressed in Sydney and Melbourne.[146] Such reservations led the *Mercury* to be cautious, yet still supportive, of Tasmanian involvement in New Zealand's war:

> The . . . war is no longer one of the pleasantest, if it ever was so. It does not partake of the character of "playing at soldiers," but it consists of hard fighting, and of work at the trenches. This should be well understood by those who volunteer for this service. And they should be prepared for the worst. The men that are wanted are not men, that are only "fit food for powder," . . . but men that will fight, and that take an interest in bringing war to a successful issue . . .[147]

By 22 September, around 200 applicants, including several from Tasmania's volunteer movement, had applied to Chesney, and of these, 130 were 'accepted conditionally'. To assist in this recruiting, two Auckland Militia officers, Lieutenants P.O. Rickards and William Percival, were sent from Melbourne to Hobart.[148]

With these recruiting officers in place, the formal enrolment of volunteers commenced in late September at the Hobart Military Barracks. All candidates who had already sent their names to Chesney were asked to call and produce character certificates and to pass a medical examination. They also had to prove the Immigration Agent had no claim on them, and if married, that they had made leave for an order for a portion of their pay to be set aside for their wives and children during their absence.[149] By a recent Act of the Tasmanian Parliament, no member of the volunteer force could enrol, although such men continued to do so. Rickards recruited in Launceston, while Percival continued activities in Hobart.[150] On 1 October a fresh advertisement provided details on the pensions available for wounded militiamen and for widowed wives and families.[151] Rickards carried out the enrolment of volunteers at the Launceston Barracks over 2 and 3 October, with individuals enrolled then travelling overland to Hobart.[152] Meanwhile in Hobart enrolments continued during the first week of October, but despite the numbers of men coming forward, a large proportion were being rejected because they failed the medical examination.[153]

On 6 October all the selected volunteers assembled at the Hobart Town Barracks for embarkation aboard the *Derwent Hunter*.[154] The *Mercury* detailed the public spectacle that accompanied the departure of this first 'Tasmanian Contingent' on this day: 'The unusual character of the event excited a great amount of interest, and a very large concourse of spectators were present to witness the departure of the gallant Volunteers.' The contingent was commanded by Lieutenants Rickards, Percival, and George Ashton, who was appointed in Hobart.[155] It comprised eighty-three volunteers, twenty of whom were from Launceston, with their ages 'reported as ranging from 18 to 39 years – the average being 30. Of the sixty-three men passed in Hobart Town, nine were married.'[156] Before the *Derwent Hunter* sailed on the afternoon of 7 October, an official party, including 'Dr. Hall, Vicar-General, Major Wilkinson, Captain Chesney and other gentlemen', visited the volunteers aboard ship and addressed them with 'a few words of encouragement'. Just prior to departure their numbers were reduced to seventy-nine after two were taken off the vessel under orders 'from the magistrates' and another two were discharged. This first contingent of Tasmanian volunteers arrived in Auckland on 22 October.[157]

On 12 October advertisements announced that 'Volunteers for Auckland' would continue to be enrolled in Hobart at the military barracks and the Adelaide Inn.[158] This resulted in more applicants coming forward.[159] Lieutenant A.K. Gregson of the Hobart City Guards was provisionally appointed lieutenant to command the second contingent of volunteers.[160] Gregson also acted as enrolling officer and visited Richmond, New Norfolk and Kingston seeking recruits.[161] He also carried out this regional recruiting accompanied by the Immigration Officer Mr Smith, who was also a lieutenant in the City Guards. These officers visited New Norfolk and Glenorchy, enrolling several men at each location. By 23 October the enrolment for the second contingent of volunteers was 'rapidly progressing', with fifty men enlisted. All candidates were informed to be ready to board the *Reliance* at Constitution Dock on 24 October. This contingent was reported as 'nearly all single and . . . able bodied, active fellows'.[162]

'The New Zealand Difficulty No. 3', a further satirical cartoon about the experiences which one Victorian military settler volunteer would face in New Zealand. *Melbourne Punch*, 19 November 1863.

The departure of the second Tasmanian contingent on 24 October was reported as not attracting many spectators in Hobart, though no explanation for this relative disinterest is offered in the press. After the roll was called at the military barracks only forty-eight out of the fifty-five men who had signed on had presented, although five of the missing seven turned up at the last minute. Chesney accepted the services of two of them to complete the complement of fifty required. 'The men are on the whole a well selected body, and, we believe, they will prove themselves staunch and determined in the field.'[163] The *Mercury* also provided analysis of the type of men who made up this second contingent: 'Their ages vary from 17 years to 39 years, the average being about 25 years. The majority are, however, young men, ranging between 17 and 24 years. Six of the number . . . are married.'[164]

Because a small number of men missed their passage aboard the *Reliance* it was determined to send one further detachment. Advertisements announced that recruiting would recommence at the military barracks and the Queen Adelaide Hotel in Hobart on 4 November, with T.T. de Burgh Miller chosen as the enrolling officer and commander of this third contingent.[165]

Indicative of a degree of public interest in the events unfolding across the Tasman, in late October the Hobart- and Launceston-based firm of Walch & Sons produced 'A Map of the Seat of War in New Zealand' for sale. Printed in a limited run, these maps were compiled by the Government Survey Office in Hobart from plans and related information supplied by Governor Browne.[166] Even so, by October–November the *Mercury* was becoming uneasy about the continuation of recruiting, revealing in turn the undercurrents of colonial competitiveness versus co-operation on the issue. In early November this paper asserted:

> . . . with the war in the North, and the reported discovery of new gold-fields in the Middle Island, we are placed between two fires. This must now be patent to everybody . . . Auckland is attempting to swindle us out of our populations by her Military Settlement "dodge," and Dunedin, by her exaggerated accounts of the productiveness of the neighboring gold-fields. . . .
>
> More than once before have we "hinted a doubt and hesitated dislike" to the Auckland Military Settlement project . . . When we looked at it merely as a project for increasing the available number of troops . . . we gave it our hearty assent, and were not . . . slack in our endeavors to promote it. But now that British troops have been poured into Auckland from all parts of the world in sufficient numbers, and that this Military Settlement project has assumed the startling dimensions of a demand for thousands and tens of thousands, in place of hundreds and tens of hundreds, we feel bound to protest against any further assistance to it by Tasmania.[167]

These Tasmanian concerns about New Zealand 'stealing' its settlers would grow in volume with the commencement of Colonel Pitt's second recruiting mission in January 1864, pre-dating vocal sentiments that would soon also be heard in Victoria and elsewhere.

Nevertheless, efforts continued in and around Hobart to recruit more military settlers. On 9 December the *Mercury* again decried these activities:

> . . . it is quite time that the farce . . . was at an end. . . . Supposing these men to be immigrants; they have cost us at the rate of £14 to £16 per head for their introduction, or, in the supposition of their being native-born, it either has,

> or will still cost us at the same rate per head for others to supply their places. And if we allow this system of drafting to go on unchecked, we shall soon be made aware of the immense loss we are sustaining by the pressure on our labor market.[168]

Ten days later this same paper brought to notice another aspect of concern – the maintenance of care and support of wives and families left behind, after being made aware that 'wives of some of the volunteers from the Huon district having been left in a state of great destitution, . . . these poor women are [now] thrown entirely upon the charity of their neighbors'.[169]

The men enrolled for this third and final contingent of Tasmanian volunteers were notified to muster at the military barracks for departure on the *Reliance*.[170] Wet weather delayed the departure but they embarked on 17 December, the contingent comprising Lieutenant de Burgh Miller, Ensign A.G. Pogue, A.F. Smith (former 99th Regiment officer, and captain Hobart Town Volunteer Artillery), and twenty-nine enlisted rank volunteers.[171] With this last departure New Zealand had acquired a total of 162 volunteer officers and men from Tasmania.[172] These personnel mainly assisted with the raising of the 3rd Waikato Regiment, though some, like Ensign Pogue, served in the 4th Waikato Regiment. Now that this body of volunteers had left to become part of New Zealand's military settlement scheme, as had the bulk of the colony's garrison troops been made available, the *Mercury* confirmed, 'we are beginning to grow weary of the movement' . . . 'we think our full quantum, considering the present aspect of affairs [has been reached]'.[173]

The Tasmanian newspapers also kept their readership well informed of the service and experience of the 'Tasmanian Volunteers'. In a letter to a Hobart resident, one 'Tasmanian Volunteer now serving in New Zealand' provided an early depiction of 'Volunteer Life' during the initial stages of the difficult bush fighting on the Auckland–Waikato front during July–August 1863:

> I have just returned from the scene of action, which we designate the "front" . . . We scoured all round and after four hours' fruitless searching returned to our camp chagrined and disappointed. Imagine yourself in the thickest bush at the Huon, and you will have a faint conception of the hardships we must have endured. . . . We were out three times, but could never come across the beggars though we could hear their yells distinctly. We . . . start again to take the battlefield in a week. . . . I hope when I write again to be able to inform you that Tasman's sons have not been behind the rest in quelling an unprincipled insurrection and bringing into subjection a rebellious race.[174]

The letter was dated Auckland, 25 August 1863, indicating this individual enrolled prior to any formal recruiting taking place in Tasmania. He either travelled across the Tasman on his own initiative (or enrolled in another Australian colony), or was already in New Zealand and possibly serving in some of the companies first raised for the 1st Waikato Regiment. A letter published shortly after was made available by friends of another military settler who had left for Auckland. This man was also serving well before formal recruiting commenced in Tasmania, so no doubt is a further example of an individual travelling across the Tasman to enlist independently.[175]

'The New Zealand Poacher', a satirical Victorian cartoon attacking the commencement of the second military settler recruiting mission to Australia. *Melbourne Punch*, 21 January 1864.

In January 1864 a letter was received via Hobart's Detective Brennan, from a friend in New Zealand who was one of the volunteers from the first contingent raised. This military settler stationed at St John's Redoubt reported having not yet heard an enemy's shot since arrival, and had been largely employed in escort duty.[176] And in April a letter from a member of the 'Tasmanian Contingent' at Camp Te Awamutu detailed the redoubt life many Australian enlistees contended with during their New Zealand service. This Tasmanian sarcastically stated: 'When one first joins the service he is led to think that he will lead a regular miserable life, but after a little experience and gentle starvation, you become reconciled to your fate and get along swimmingly. . . . The duties . . . are various and often-time arduous.'[177] During May a lengthy letter from another Tasmanian enlistee in the 3rd Waikato Regiment to his father described his experiences in combat against the Maori during the siege at Orakau.[178] Apart from various press coverage of the wars, the publication of such correspondence shows the considerable exposure of friends, family and the general public to information dealing with the experiences of their Tasmanian military settler volunteers serving during 1863–64.

The Second Military Settler Recruiting Mission

The commencement of a second recruiting mission by Colonel Pitt elicited a much different reaction in the Australian colonies, and especially in Victoria, to the largely responsive experience of 1863. In Tasmania, where recruiting continued until December 1863, the beginnings of serious misgivings and opposition to New Zealand's military settlement plans were clearly evident. News of a second mission in 1864 would lead to the *Mercury* continuing its opposition to the scheme.[179] On 20 January this paper pointed out:

> If there had been necessity for this fresh recruiting for the subjugation of the Maories . . . we should have been the last in the world to have breathed a whisper against it. But there is not the pretence of more people being required for any such purpose. At this moment, the Maories are suing in all directions for peace. . . .Or, it were not so, we still have a force of 8,000 regular troops there, exclusive of all the militia and volunteers to compel them in that course.[180]

No attempt at recruiting would take place in Tasmania for this second mission, no doubt in part due to the early cancellation of efforts in Victoria and South Australia which prevented any thoughts of expansion. With the receipt of news from Victoria that Pitt had put a halt to recruiting, the *Mercury* reminded its readers in February that: 'As yet we have not quite done with the matter. . . . We are glad to see that all further enlistment is to be stopped, but what of the wives and children of those who have been enlisted?'[181] By the following month the *Mercury* begun referring to the military settler missions as a 'kidnapping scheme' – a far cry from the patriotic overtones ringing in support of New Zealand plans in August and September 1863.[182] But despite these sentiments and the short-lived nature of recruiting in Victoria, South Australia and New South Wales, New Zealand was still able to procure a large body of military settler recruits, and many with families. This subscription demonstrates a continuation of significant Australian manpower involvement in events across the Tasman.

Victorian recruiting

On 14 January 1864 the steamship *Hero* brought Colonel Pitt once more to Melbourne.[183] He was accompanied by Captains W.M. Hunter, Jackson Keddell and William Fraser (former Geelong volunteer officer), as well as Lieutenants William Percival and C.D. Pitt.[184] Colonel Pitt established himself in Hockin's Hotel, on the corner of Elizabeth and Lonsdale Streets, and immediately advertised for candidates for appointments as non-commissioned officers as well as detailing the full conditions of service for military settlers for land in the North Island of New Zealand.[185] Pitt also took the extra precaution of including additional information with these terms to circumvent criticisms and problems associated with his first mission. These provisions included free passages for the families of married men provided by the New Zealand government; an advance of pay for three months from the date of embarkation to every man who requested it; and all married men to be sent to Auckland in the same ships as their families. Plans for a limited number of single men to be sent to Taranaki and Napier, rather than to Waikato, to be military settlers were also notified.[186] The *Argus* added that the New Zealand government would be providing accommodation and rations for the families of married volunteers until these men were located on their lands. It also acknowledged Pitt's efforts to alleviate financial hardship encountered by volunteers enlisted the previous year, who had been promised pay from their date of arrival, but which he had managed to obtain for them from their date of embarkation.[187]

Nevertheless, the *Argus* was quick to scrutinise this second recruiting mission, indicating that resistance to Pitt's activities was quickly being marshalled in Victoria. On 20 January this paper asserted:

> The second appearance of Colonel Pitt . . . is hardly likely to be so successful as his first. We must confess that these visits of the recruiting-sergeant are getting quite too frequent in this colony. We cannot perceive the necessity of a second mission of this sort, within so short a space of time. . . . It is one

> thing to assist the colonies of the Northern Island in waging a difficult war against the Maories – it is quite another to help the Auckland Government in its new scheme of colonization. We may supply soldiers, but it is surely a little too much that we should be asked to contribute colonists.[188]

This paper concluded that it was clear Pitt had returned to Victoria 'not so much as a recruiting-sergeant [but] as an emigration agent. The war is put forward merely as a cloak to his real purpose. The New Zealand Government finds itself suddenly the owner of a vast territory, and it desires, not unnaturally, to people it.'[189]

The Victorian public were also quick to pass negative judgement upon Pitt's return for more volunteers. 'Uncle Toby', for instance, writing that it becomes 'a question for very grave consideration how far the Government of Victoria is justified in permitting or in any way encouraging [Pitt's recruiting] . . . and the question is one deserving [its] serious attention.'[190] 'Caution' posed the issue of pay for the military settlers, pointing out there were no guarantees whatsoever that a volunteer would receive three years of pay: 'It may be for six months – perhaps a week after he lands. This I had from Colonel Pitt himself.'[191] Others such as 'R.B.' from Hawthorn perceived Pitt's mission as one merely seeking colonists 'under the guise of recruits for the Northern Island'.[192]

Despite expectations that numbers enlisted would not be numerous, combined with a short-lived advertising campaign due to the negative public and government response, Pitt quickly attracted hundreds of volunteers, many with families, during January 1864.[193] It would seem that the offer of land was indeed too tempting for some Victorian colonists. Nor should it be overlooked that the officers involved in the recruiting carried out a widespread advertising campaign, albeit of short duration. By the evening of 21 January, 353 men had been formally enrolled – 114 of whom were married and 239 single. The *Argus* reported that the assembly rooms at Hockin's Hotel where recruiting was taking place had in fact 'been thronged each day'. Those men coming forward were, with few exceptions, stated to be 'fine, healthy, active looking men – decidedly above the average type of aspirants for military fame'. Only about twenty per cent of applicants were rejected.[194]

Again among those enlisting were members of the Victorian volunteer forces, which, apart from the land offers, shows that the call of Empire was still a factor in enlistment. One such prominent individual was A.W. East, an officer of the Prahran and South Yarra Battery of the Volunteer Artillery, who Colonel Pitt appointed to be captain and would subsequently serve in the 4th Waikato Regiment.[195] Other officer appointments, most of whom were destined for the Taranaki Military Settlers, included Lieutenants Cecil, Daniel (also as David) Pennefather, and Jackson.[196] On such members of the Victorian volunteer forces being lured into New Zealand service, 'HY.M.M.' cynically outlined concerns, making a case in point regarding East's appointment by Colonel Pitt:

> [who] succeeded in cajoling Captain East from his allegiance to this colony. Captain East has been receiving the public money of Victoria for six years – he has become in that time sufficiently experienced to aid us in turning to some useful account our expensive volunteer establishment . . . His quality is known to Colonel Pitt, who avails himself of his experience of our volunteer corps to seduce from the colony one of our most useful men. Is the Government utterly powerless? Can no stay be put upon this disreputable system of wholesale spoliation of one neighbouring colony upon another, under the flimsiest of shams, the most transparent of delusions? As you truly say, a British officer, disguised as a recruiting-sergeant, to do the work of an emigration agent; and worse still, using the knowledge he acquired in our service to filch from us that which the people of this colony are heavily taxed to procure.[197]

In a later correspondence 'H.M.M.' again drew attention to this issue, stating Pitt had no scruples whatsoever 'to enlist some of our volunteers – men who have taken the oath of allegiance to this colony, who wear its uniform, and receive its pay'.[198]

The Victorian government reacted adversely to this second recruiting mission and put pressure on Pitt to end his activities, though the government was to admit that it had no legal powers to bring them to a halt.[199] The Victorian Chief Secretary, James McCulloch, urged upon Pitt 'the impropriety of his coming to this colony, as the representative of another Government, and offering bounty for the purpose of inducing persons to leave'. In parliament on 26 January, McCulloch recounted how he had pressed Pitt in their interview on 'the necessity of staying his hand from further action' until he had an opportunity of laying the case before the New Zealand government. Pitt, after considering the matter, refused, and instead stated that 'his orders were to pursue a certain course'.[200] The chief secretary then asked Pitt 'to refrain from any further action in the matter of enrolling men'. At this juncture Pitt again refused, stating that this was not consistent with what he conceived to be his duty in the matter, but adding that he would contact his government as soon as possible to inform them of Victoria's concerns.[201]

The intervention of the New Zealand Colonial Treasurer Reader Wood, who then happened to be in Melbourne on his way to England, led to Colonel Pitt being ordered 'to immediately discontinue the enrolment' in Victoria.[202] Pitt accordingly inserted a public notice in the *Argus* on 26 January announcing there would be no further enrolment.[203] The Victorian government took the matter seriously nonetheless and continued to press its point:

> I would . . . hope that the . . . New Zealand [government] will . . . see the necessity of putting a stop to the . . . attempt to introduce settlers at the cost of a neighbouring Colony who devotes so large a portion of her revenue to the purpose of Immigration.
>
> . . . I would remind you that Victoria has always proved herself ready to afford every assistance to New Zealand in her time of need and would even now cheerfully give her aid by providing the present movement if the exigencies of war required it. But the manifest object . . . being merely to introduce settlers to a newly acquired territory at the expense of Victoria this Government feels bound to protest against it.[204]

The *Victorian* was glad to note that Pitt's 'crimping operations have received a *quietus*, and the Recruiting Sergeant and Emigration Agent is ordered to "stand at ease".' It asserted, however, that the press and government had made too much of his activities, as his 'doings were not illegal, and if . . . our colonists are satisfied in such a country, for half-a-crown a-day and chance of a fifty-acre farm of a very precarious kind, better let them go, and most of whom will soon wish themselves back again'.[205]

Of those men actually enrolled, the single men, and those married men who did not intend taking their families immediately, were organised for departure aboard the *Gresham* for conveyance to Taranaki. In the intervening days before departure, recruiting had continued – and it was 'intended to prosecute it actively in the country districts' – and on 20 January opened at Kyneton 'where twenty-two men were enlisted', as well as in Geelong. Recruiting officers continued activities at Ballarat and Castlemaine on 21 January, followed by visits to Creswick and Sandhurst.[206] At Castlemaine, 'Captain Langden, another of Colonel Pitt's accredited agents, was almost mobbed at his hotel by the eager recruits'.[207]

On 23 January the *Argus* stated the total number of volunteers enrolled both in Melbourne and from country districts numbered 632, including 210 married men, though figures for Sandhurst were not yet known.[208] This same day the first of the Victorian volunteer contingents for 1864 was scheduled for departure aboard the *Gresham*. The contingent comprised Lieutenants Daniel Pennefather, C.P. Sisson and J.H. Clarke (also known as Clark), and 356 other ranks.[209] Figures for this *Gresham* contingent also vary, with one 1878 history of Taranaki stating that apart from one other officer, Ensign M.G. Roddy, the total was in fact 420.[210]

The *Thomas Fletcher* was chartered to convey the wives and families of Victorian military settlers recruited during 1863. Pitt wrote asking them to assemble at Sandridge on 28 January for embarkation. Married men who had just recently enrolled were also requested to assemble with their families for boarding the vessels provided. The *Thomas Fletcher* cleared Melbourne on

A further satirical Victorian cartoon in 'The New Zealand Difficulty' series, this time depicting the plight of the Australian recruited military settler and family in New Zealand. *Melbourne Punch*, 28 January 1864.

3 February 1864 with a contingent of seventy-three volunteers under the command of Captain East and Ensign J.R. Horne, including eighty-seven women and 107 children (although the *Victorian* reported eighty-two men and 188 women and children).[211]

On 1 February the *Aldinga* from Adelaide brought twenty-eight South Australian military settler volunteers enrolled by Captain Hunter to Melbourne where they would have transshipped onto one of the vessels engaged for New Zealand.[212] The other vessels chartered by Pitt were the *Swiftsure* bound to Auckland, and the *Brilliant* destined for Taranaki.[213] The *Swiftsure* sailed on 6 February carrying a contingent commanded by Captain Allan Stewart, consisting of 168 volunteers, 231 women and 471 children.[214] Many of these volunteers were destined to serve in the 4th Waikato Regiment. During the *Swiftsure*'s voyage one young child fell overboard, but the ship was travelling so fast that efforts to save the child proved fruitless.[215] The *Brilliant* sailed for Taranaki on 7 February carrying Lieutenants J.T.V. Kirkby, J.H. Clarke, Bamber Gascoigne, J.R. Jackson, and 128 other rank volunteers for the Taranaki Military Settlers (although the *Victorian* reported 172 men).[216] Pitt's second recruiting mission thus resulted in nearly 800 military settlers from Victoria and South Australia. The total number including women and children amounted to 'nearly

2,000 souls' departing Victoria for New Zealand during January and February 1864 – a considerable achievement despite the widespread opposition and criticisms the enterprise evoked.[217]

Through the medium of the press, Victorians were again provided further glimpses into the experience, expectations and disillusionment of Victorian military settlers enlisted during 1864. This is clearly evident in one letter received by a resident of Daylesford, Victoria from a brother who enlisted at Castlemaine and was now serving in the Taranaki Military Settlers at Fort Niger, New Plymouth, dated 28 February. This account provides a detailed insight into the initial experience and conditions that Victorian-enlisted Taranaki Military Settlers faced upon arrival at New Plymouth:

> As we landed, we marched off to an office, and were sworn in, a dozen at a time. We then had a bit of a run down into the town, and were very much surprised to find ... quite a large town, and well laid out – good wide streets, and in blocks, same as Castlemaine.... As the embankment on this side of the town has only been down about eight months, the Maories used to come so close in that the people had to leave their houses and live in the town. Even now ... no people [live] ... beyond a mile. It seems a pity that the houses ... stand empty, and everything go to rack and ruin; but it is not considered safe. ... There were about 800 ashore ... we all fell in and marched off ... to our camp, about one mile from town, where we found the tents pitched ... they are all bell tents, and accommodate thirteen men.[218]

After an initial weekend of relative freedom, this military settler detailed the work involved in training to become soldiers and aiding in the local defences in Taranaki. He also noted the arrival of a further 150 Australian volunteers from the *Brilliant*, which brought numbers at camp to 600. The following week, drilling and the distribution of the military settlers, who were now available to man various defences, took place:

> The company I was in were drafted to those nearest town. I am in Fort Niger, I must say the most dangerous place, though very comfortable, after being in tents, as it generally gets cold towards evening.... Our fort is in a delightful situation; to the front, Mount Egmont; behind, the sea beach; about three-quarters of a mile distant to our right, the town of New Plymouth; one and a half miles away, to our left, deserted homesteads and gardens; and we being on the top of a small hill, can see to a great distance ... It has, a parapet all round, and a deep ditch outside.... The clothes are a blue serge jumper, forage cap with M in front, a pair of Sydney tweed trousers, and a pair of

great hob-nailed blucher boots.[219]

South Australian recruiting

Initial details of Colonel Pitt's first recruiting mission had become known in South Australia on 19 August 1863.[220] Although it was initially thought the offer of land and pay would elicit some favour among South Australians, and despite the size and enthusiasm shown for the 'volunteer movement in Victoria for service in New Zealand', newspapers reported that no real interest was exhibited in this colony.[221] Neither evidence of any formal recruiting taking place in South Australia nor the arrival of a recruiting officer or advertisements for military settler service during August–September, as occurred in Queensland, New South Wales, Victoria and Tasmania, has come to light. The lack of enthusiasm was probably more the result of South Australia not being directly targeted at this time; there was simply no recruiting structure or officers involved for men to enlist.

Even so, individuals chose to depart for neighbouring colonies or New Zealand on their own initiative during the latter months of 1863. On 28 September the *South Australian Register* directed attention towards Lieutenant H.L. Williams, a former imperial officer and South Australian resident:[222] 'We see . . . that the Charlotte Andrews takes . . . volunteers to New Zealand. There is reason to believe that Lieut. Williams, . . . formerly of the South Australian Staff, and a J.P. of this province, has been appointed Captain of this company.'[223] Others included William Fraser, former drill instructor to the Reedbeds Cavalry, a South Australian volunteer unit, who went on to serve in the 2nd Waikato Regiment and the Colonial Defence Force. Other members of the colony's volunteer movement departing included Captain Egerton and Sergeant-Major Hawke from the Kapunda Rifles, as well as Adelaide solicitor and captain of the Kent Rifles W.V. Herford, who served in the 3rd Waikato Regiment and was to die from wounds sustained at Orakau in 1864.[224]

In Adelaide it was announced on 7 December 1863 that Pitt was about to embark on a second recruiting mission.[225] Only in the following month were South Australians for the first time specifically targeted. A formal New Zealand government advertisement for military settlers began to appear in the *South Australian Register* on 15 January. This advertisement outlined all the conditions of service 'upon which Land in the Northern Island' would be granted, and was authorised by Colonel Pitt in Melbourne.[226] An editorial in the *South Australian Register* stated that the 'Maori war will be the making of New Zealand':

> The rebellious natives are to be ousted by emigrants from Australia, and a British population – the pick of all the colonies – is to be settled, amidst towns and farms, upon the now sparsely occupied lands of the Northern Island. . . . We suppose that this call upon South Australia has been made in consequence of the number of enrolments in Victoria, New South Wales, and Tasmania not being equal to the demand.[227]

This commentary indicates that apathy exceeded enthusiasm for this second military settler mission. As with other colonies, there was also clearly a belief that New Zealand's colonisation of the North Island was being carried out to the detriment of the Australian colonies, which in turn were similarly hungry to attract migrants to cater for their own settlement schemes.

Shortly after, it was announced that a Captain Hunter was selected to be the South Australian recruiting officer, and would be undertaking activities at the Globe Hotel on Rundle Street, Adelaide, as well as planning to visit Kapunda. The *Register* was pessimistic about the expected results of this recruiting mission: 'We hardly think his mission will be a very successful one, as we believe the people in this colony will decidedly prefer the one certain bird in the hand to the two doubtful ones in the bush.'[228]

Captain W.M. Hunter, adjutant of the 1st Waikato Regiment, arrived in Adelaide aboard the *Alexandra* from Melbourne on 22 January and promptly set about his recruiting mission the following day.[229] His initial advertising was aimed at attracting suitable candidates for appointment as non-commissioned officers.[230] He also issued from his 'New Zealand Office' in the Globe Hotel a tender for '300 pairs Blankets, Knife, Fork, Spoon, Tin Plate, and Pannikin' for use by New Zealand local forces.[231] On 25 January he placed further advertisements stating that 'Men wishing to Enrol themselves' should attend his office over the coming days.[232] But news of this recruiting mission saw resistance to these activities evident in both editorials and letters received by the *Register*,[233] one 'Mark Tapley' contributing a humorous caution:

> Sir, That ere advertisement wich you prints in your paper about wolunteers for New Zealand rayther reminds me of a wery jolly journey wich I made once in company with a nice young man, wich his name was Chuzzlewit. We went to that blessed land of liberty, America, to make our fortunes, and then to come home rich and marry our dears. You may have read of a place called Eden, a fine juicy country, where land was a precious deal scarcer nor water. There was one Scudder, who were a smart man, and one of the most remarkable men in that ere remarkable country. He were an oily cove – he were. How he did do that innocent young man Chuzzlewit, with his Banks

> and Institoots, all to be built under the superintendence of Chuzzlewit & Co. . . . Wen we got to Eden we found snakes, fever-stricken settlers . . . and tobacco-chewing, wood-whittling, bowie-knife-using, and revolver-firing loafers . . .
>
> Now, Mr. Editor, wot I says to persons . . . who may be thinking of going to New Zealand – wot I says is this – Remember Eden, think of Scudder, and don't forget the eventful history of young Chuzzlewit and his friend.[234]

'C.J.' even suggested publication of the names of those being recruited in order to avoid 'tradesmen from being duped' and lost to the colony, as well as in the hope of avoiding wives and children being left destitute by men who might use enlistment to avoid family obligations.[235]

On 25 January forty prospective applicants showed up at the Globe Hotel, although many of these men proved ineligible. By the close of the first formal day's recruiting Hunter had enlisted twenty-eight recruits, several being married men. The next day only thirteen more men were enlisted, before Hunter received orders from Melbourne to discontinue enrolments. Consequently he advertised that all enrolment would cease from 26 January.[236]

Despite this short-lived recruiting mission the *Register* was able to insert a nominal list of forty men engaged over these few days.[237] Hunter organised for these recruits to travel to Melbourne aboard the *Aldinga* on 30 January, with married men to be accompanied by their families.[238] A large number of people had assembled at the station to see off what they thought would be a contingent of forty volunteers, but when Hunter called the roll it became obvious that all were not present.[239] The *South Australian Register* concluded that those men who presented themselves 'did not appear in very high spirits, and judging from the number who attended . . . it would appear that many who had given in their names as recruits thought better on the subject before it was too late'.[240] When the *Aldinga* arrived in Melbourne on 1 February 1864 the total South Australian contingent comprised twenty-eight volunteers and associated families.[241] The abortive nature of the recruiting effort in Adelaide as a result of the halt to affairs in Victoria, combined with the opposition to this recruiting evident in the colony's press, saw but a token body of recruits obtained.

Several months after their departure, the *South Australian Register* detailed the experiences of one 'Adelaidean in New Zealand'. This was William Ewart who was serving in the Taranaki Military Settlers:

> It states that upon their landing the volunteers were placed under canvas and were drilled for eight days. On the 2nd March they were sent to the front, where they joined a detachment of the 57th Regiment. Corporal Ewart was

> present at the taking of the Kaitake pa, and was on the 10th April . . . attached to the 10th Company . . . He describes the country as very beautiful, the cultivated land taken from the Maories being in his opinion worth £10 an acre. He describes the camp life as laborious and the fare rough, but declares that £100 would not attempt him to abandon a soldier's life.[242]

Ewart's correspondence reveals an obvious enthusiasm for soldiering, a talent observed earlier when he was appointed acting corporal in charge of the volunteers departing Adelaide. His letter also indicated that some Australian volunteers experienced combat against the Maori shortly after arrival, and after only rudimentary military training.

New South Wales recruiting

Late in December 1863 the *Sydney Morning Herald* reported that Colonel Pitt was about to embark for Victoria to undertake a second recruiting mission.[243] Though he did not travel to Sydney as part of this renewed effort, another Auckland Militia officer did arrive to undertake renewed recruiting in New South Wales. This was Lieutenant William Steele, an officer who had already seen active service around Auckland during 1863.[244] After completing his recruiting mission he was appointed captain in the 4th Waikato Regiment in March 1864.[245] One history documenting the founding of Hamilton by the 4th Waikato Regiment describes the selection of Steele for the position of Sydney recruiter as a good choice. 'He was thirty-two years old, personable, and had some farming experience. He had left England . . . and had followed the gold rushes in New South Wales, Victoria and California. He was a judge of men, and it was to choose settlers rather than soldiers that he was sent.'[246] The New Zealand authorities issued instructions on 31 December to guide Steele in this Sydney recruiting task, from which many of the men enlisted were to be used to help form the newly created 4th Waikato Regiment.[247] His instructions stated that he was to proceed to Sydney to enrol a company of military settlers under the conditions gazetted on 5 August 1863: 'The Government . . . [desire] men with wives and families, who . . . are more likely than unmarried men to become permanent settlers. I am therefore to impress upon you the necessity of choosing respectable men with families in preference to all others.'[248] Steele arrived in Sydney in January 1864 and immediately set about recruiting by placing an advertisement in Sydney papers:

> A number of married men with their families are required to proceed to Auckland (passage free); also a limited number of single men to complete a

> settlement. None need apply who cannot produce testimonials of industry and sobriety.
>
> Lieutenant Steele will, on and after Monday 18th January, be in attendance to make engagements and give any information that may be required. For the present apply to Soper and Steele, Market Wharf.[249]

Unfortunately, Sydney press information on shipping is somewhat vague as to the size or make-up of contingents departing during February–March 1864, and it is impossible to ascertain accurate numbers associated with the Sydney volunteers despatched. Comparison with various other sources, though, gives an indication of some of the contingents and the numbers of volunteers and families involved.

On 3 February the *Kate* left Sydney for Auckland with a contingent believed to number upwards of fifty-five, although a proportion of this number may actually have been families of military settlers.[250] This first draft of Sydney volunteers shipped on the *Kate* with a William Rudland 'as drill instructor'.[251] Further detachments from Sydney took place on 13 February when '31 men [also cited as 24], single or without their families' departed aboard the *Claud Hamilton*. The *Alice Cameron* had already left for Auckland in early February carrying forty volunteers and associated families comprising 145 women and children. On 25 February the *Novelty* had also departed with eleven (also cited as twelve) military settlers and their families.

Steele reported his return to Auckland aboard the *Bella Marina* on 24 March 1864, 'bringing with him the remainder of the men whom he had engaged as military settlers, 33 in all, of whom six were married with families'.[252] One source provides a figure of 144 volunteers who were to serve in the 4th Waikato Regiment as the total number recruited by Steele during January–March 1864. Other evidence suggests that upwards of 170 military settlers were actually enlisted in Sydney in this period. Some of these men presumably served in units other than the 4th Waikato Regiment.[253]

Informal Queensland recruiting

The winding up of the second recruiting mission in Victoria was similarly welcomed in Queensland's press, which asserted that when 'New Zealand colonists were in immediate danger, an impulse of generosity prompted a ready response to the call for aid'. But now that some 10,000 regular troops had arrived in New Zealand, apart from colonial forces, there no longer seemed any pressing need for more military settlers. 'For the subjugation of this peaceful land we need the ploughshare, and it ought not to be wantonly turned into a sword for the chastisement of a people who, whatever their crimes, have done to us no

Yet 'Another New Zealand Difficulty' cartoon, lampooning the service experiences of Australian recruited military settlers in New Zealand. *Melbourne Punch*, 10 March 1864.

wrong.'[254] Despite such sentiments and the cessation of recruiting in Victoria and South Australia, an informal recruiting effort took place in Brisbane during late February and March of 1864.

On 29 February an advertisement appeared in the *Courier* for 'Volunteers for New Zealand' to meet this same day at M'Adam's Sovereign Hotel. 'All persons willing to volunteer on the terms offered by the New Zealand Government are requested to attend.'[255] Captain H.D. Pitt, the senior military officer in Queensland, did not initiate this effort nor had he received any instructions to seek further volunteers.[256] This was an informal undertaking initiated by private individuals with former British Army backgrounds. A letter to the *Courier* by 'Dragoon Guards' in early March related the events associated with the meeting that had taken place:

> Sir, – I am an old soldier, and, as I have a liking for the profession, I desire to be a soldier again. As there is a war of races in New Zealand, I, in common with many others, would willingly volunteer to aid in settling it. An advertisement . . . [called] a meeting of such persons as myself.

> Amongst the number I attended, but took no part in the proceedings further than expressing my entire approval of them. Twenty-five names were taken down by the Secretary, Mr. Lang, who was appointed on the occasion, and many others were refused. The twenty-five were drilled men who had served in her Majesty's cavalry and infantry regiments in different parts of the world. There were officers of various corps, men who had been dragoons, men of the 60th Rifles, and men of various regiments of foot. We determined to pursue certain plans, but the officious interference of certain parties who had nothing to do with the movement, and whose officiousness might defeat it altogether has prevented our carrying out our plans as we desired to do.
>
> We have been accustomed to fighting, and we want to fight again, but we will not consent to be sent hence to New Zealand under the auspices of an officious recruiting sergeant who is self-appointed.[257]

It appears that particular individuals (possibly referring to Captain Pitt, or else Lieutenant Seymour, commanding Brisbane's 12th Regiment detachment) who were involved with the recruiting during 1863 did so in such a manner as to disillusion or gain the disapproval of potential enlistees. This situation may in fact account for the small number of volunteers who departed at that time, despite the larger numbers reported having engaged.

'Dragoon Guards' went on to explain that a few of these selected former military men, possibly twenty-five in total, were to depart aboard the *Telegraph* for Sydney en route for New Zealand, but that many more would have gone 'had the military authorities only withheld their countenance and support'. For 'every efficient soldier who is sent down under the auspices of the military, ten will be left behind, simply because their voluntary movement has been taken advantage of':

> I can safely assert, that if the New Zealand government signified its willingness to pay the passages of settlers arriving direct from Queensland, the 250 disappointed drilled men left behind now . . . would go down and the few who have volunteered for rations would have been left behind.
>
> I regret that, I, with many others, cannot go to New Zealand . . . I think . . . that for every recruit obtained to go by the Telegraph, five could be got to go direct under auspices of the committee which originated the movement, and that committee could continue to send volunteers long after the military authorities had failed to find any who would have anything to do with them.[258]

'Dragoon Guards' here indicates the existence of an informal recruiting committee awaiting a reply from the New Zealand government about organising a body of upwards of 250 recruits direct from Queensland. It is possible such a communication accompanied the initial group of volunteers aboard the *Telegraph*, but this is not clear. This correspondent also seems to infer that a considerable number of men originally wanted to enlist during 1863, but for varying reasons were not pleased by the reception they received at the military barracks where recruiting took place. Many of these men were probably also involved in Queensland's volunteer movement.

The *Telegraph* departed on 8 March, but we have no specific names or numbers to confirm the identities of the informal volunteers it carried, though there is a Colonel H.S. Russell listed.[259] Departing from Sydney, these volunteers presumably enlisted in military settler regiments, particularly the last-formed, 4th Waikato Regiment, or other New Zealand colonial units such as the Colonial Defence Force. Once again we are unlikely ever to ascertain names and numbers, for their place of enlistment would most likely be given as New Zealand, and their Queensland origins obscured. This seemingly unique informal Queensland recruiting experience may indicate similar undertakings elsewhere. At the very least it emphasises the fact that many men who cannot be identified in surviving records did in fact travel across to fight in New Zealand's wars on their own initiative and not as part of the recognised military settler recruiting missions – some, as indicated by the evidence of this Brisbane example, fostered by groups of former soldiers or sailors seeking to renew old professions and take part in another of the Empire's wars.

Australian military settler contributions

The primary purpose of this history has been to investigate the Australian perspective, contributions, and home-front experience associated with New Zealand's wars, and not to provide detailed accounts of the many campaigns and actions in which Australian-derived military settlers were participants. With this in mind, it should still be emphasised that military settlers played important roles throughout 1863–64 and into 1867 when these, and other colonial units, were disbanded.[260]

The first recorded engagement involving a detachment of the 1st Waikato Regiment ('Pitt's Militia') took place on 14 September 1863 at Pukekohe East, several miles south-west of Drury on the Great South Road in Auckland Province. The detachment of 'Pitt's Militia' which participated in this engagement comprised one captain, one sergeant and twenty-five other ranks. These troops were then assisted by another sergeant and twelve men of the Commissariat Transport Corps – presumably all 'Pitt's Militia' themselves – who all remained at Pukekohe and formed part of the defence of the stockade.[261] This detachment was commanded by Captain William Moir, an ex-58th Regiment sergeant-major with prior New Zealand war service (1845–47).[262] Although the origins of the Waikato militiamen involved are unclear, some Australian volunteers are believed to be amongst their number, including one who was wounded.[263]

The first recorded deaths in action involving Australian-derived Waikato militiamen occurred on 23 October 1863 at Wheeler's Farm on Titi Hill, near Mauku Stockade. These men and other 1st Waikato Regiment casualties on this day are memorialised in a monument still standing in the churchyard of St John's Anglican Church at Drury.[264] And one of the last field campaigns involving elements of the Waikato military settlers was the 1st Waikato Regiment's involvement in the Tauranga Bush Campaign during January–March 1867. Amongst the casualties sustained during this campaign were three Australian-enlisted privates killed in action.[265]

The first active service of the Australian-enlisted component of the Taranaki Military Settlers occurred on 11 March 1864. Supported by elements of the 'Melbourne Volunteers' (also known as 'The Melbourne Contingent'), Taranaki Military Settlers, the 57th Regiment carried out a successful reconnaissance of Maori positions at Kaitake in Taranaki Province.[266] On this occasion those 'Melbourne Volunteers' involved were largely held in reserve in redoubts or in support and no casualties were sustained. 'Melbourne Volunteers' were again shortly in action on 25 March, taking part in the attack and capture of Kaitake pa. One company of 'Melbourne and Otago Volunteers' under Captain Corbett was here engaged for the first time 'and distinguished themselves by the spirited manner in which they assaulted and took one of the stockades, considered to be the key of the enemy's position'.[267] Captains James McKellar and Andrew Page's two companies of Taranaki Military Settlers also took part in this attack, and the total complement of 'Melbourne and Otago Volunteers' involved comprised 240 officers and men.[268]

Again no fatalities were sustained amongst the ranks of the 'Melbourne Volunteers' of the Taranaki Military Settlers – but this was to change suddenly on 6 April 1864. In a Maori ambush of elements of the 57th Regiment and a detachment of Taranaki Military Settlers at Te Ahuahu near Kaitake, among those troops killed, decapitated or otherwise mutilated were four Victorian-enlisted personnel, and four other Victorians were wounded.[269] The search-and-destroy operations that ensued in the district south of Tataraimaka following Te Ahuahu involved imperial troops of the 57th, Royal Artillery and Royal Engineers, as well 'Melbourne Volunteers' and Taranaki Volunteers. Despite these horrors, and shortly after compounded by the discovery of missing Private Gallagher's ('Melbourne Volunteers') mutilated and ritually cannibalised remains, it was reported that the 'new levies from Melbourne and Otago, who take their share of the labour of this harassing warfare [do so] with cheerfulness and zeal'.[270]

One of the last active field operations involving the Taranaki Military Settlers took place in an attack on the Maori village of Pokaikai in the Patea District on 2 August 1866, involving Taranaki Military Settlers from Nos. 8 and 10 Companies, Patea and Wanganui Rangers, and Wanganui Cavalry. During this attack, Private Denis Spain, a Melbourne-enlisted private in the 'Melbourne Contingent', was accidentally killed. The last Australian-derived Taranaki Military Settlers to be killed were Lieutenant Bamber Gascoigne (and his whole family) and Privates John Milne and Edward Richards in the White Cliffs (Pukearuhe) Massacre, Taranaki District on 13 February 1869 – all of whom hold the dubious honour of being the only Australians actually killed on their military settler land entitlements.[271]

Again it must be remembered that many of the military settlers also served in a variety of other New Zealand colonial units during 1863–67. These include the Colonial Defence Force, Patea Rangers, Patea Rifle Volunteers, and then especially from October 1867, the Armed Constabulary when this force was established. For example, during 1868–69, among the fourteen fatalities sustained by Australian-enlisted or -derived Armed Constabulary casualties, at least eleven of these were former Australian-enlisted Waikato or Taranaki military settlers. In fact, the last known Australian military settler volunteer who was killed in action appears to be Donald McDonald. McDonald had enlisted in the 3rd Waikato Regiment in Launceston, Tasmania in October 1863, and was killed in action in an ambush in June 1869 while serving as a trooper in the Bay of Plenty Volunteer Cavalry.[272]

Chapter Eight

FROM ONE COAST TO ANOTHER

FACING ANOTHER CRISIS during 1868–69, New Zealand authorities again sought assistance from Australia. But despite concerns about events unfolding across the Tasman, the Australian colonies did not provide aid in either the form or quantity granted in 1860 or 1863. Nonetheless, there was important Australian involvement in this late conflict period. The *Argus* in October 1868 gloomily predicted a repeat of the earlier settler disaster in Taranaki: '. . . by the visible fact that the Government has no sufficient number of white troops capable of real service in the bush. . . . It is not impossible that what happened in Taranaki in 1860 and 1861 – when the colonials fled en masse [is about to happen again].'[1]

Australian support derived primarily from recruiting in Melbourne for the Armed Constabulary, which saw 205 men embarked in five contingents during December 1868 and January 1869. Concern about events is also evident with the depth of press coverage, including the death of G.F. von Tempsky and the associated Von Tempsky Fund, which appears to be the last relief fund associated with the New Zealand wars. Several Australian colonies also maintained legislation prohibiting the export of warlike stores, and at the same time there were several 'volunteer' offers as well as appeals for imperial garrison troops and Royal Navy vessels to be made readily available.

Similarly, from within New Zealand came appeals for the maintenance or even increase in the numbers of imperial troops – a reversal of the gradual withdrawal

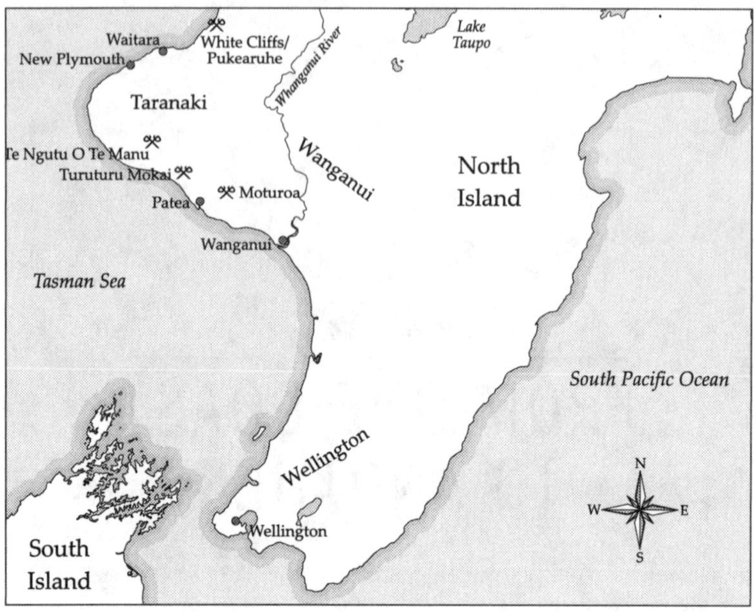

The West Coast and southern regions of the North Island of New Zealand.

of such forces then taking place throughout all the Australasian colonies. On these calls the *Sydney Morning Herald* in November 1868 countered and passed its own judgement:

> When we compare the numerical strength of the combatants in these several wars it is quite evident that the advantage can never have been on the side of the natives. Making all the allowances for their instinctive courage, the superiority they have sometimes shewn must be ascribed to the want of adaptation in the force employed against them and the strength of the country for a war of defence. . . . Without reckoning the local Volunteer forces, it is estimated that there were at least five soldiers to each Maori. It has been said that the . . . [Maori] were never more than 2000 in the field at one time. . . . it is now useless to look for the conquest of the Maori race by employing large masses of soldiers.[2]

The *Herald* went further here and offered suggestions for the imitation of past practices of conquest and civilisation, and interestingly compared the New Zealand situation with that experienced in the bloody race conflict in the Moreton Bay region of Queensland:

> The losses of life in New Zealand by rebellion, except as in actual conflict, is less than the destruction of life occasioned by the settlement of squatting stations.... it is calculated that from the commencement... at Moreton Bay, not less than 600 whites have been murdered. The calculated loss of life by the English in New Zealand... by the hands of the Maories... [is] not greater than this.[3]

Impetus to colonisation rather than military victory – 'conquest not so much by arms as by the pick and spade – by a road which should always be accessible' – was the *Herald*'s contribution towards obtaining a final solution to New Zealand's ongoing race conflict.[4]

New Zealand's crisis and Australian reactions

On the west coast of the North Island, New Zealand government troops suffered a series of dramatic military reverses against Titokowaru and his forces in the South Taranaki and Wanganui regions during 1868.[5] These routs occurred at Turuturu Mokai (12 July), Te Ngutu o te Manu (7 September), and Moturoa (7 November). On the opposite coast, Te Kooti and his followers created similar difficulties for government forces following his escape from the Chatham Islands. Initially with several actions in July 1868 in the Poverty Bay and Hawke's Bay area, the impact of Te Kooti was dramatically reinforced in what became known as the 'Poverty Bay Massacre' on 10 November.[6] By this date 'the successive heavy blows of Te Ngutu, Moturoa, and Poverty Bay... [became] a serious threat to European dominance'.[7]

The crisis developing on the west coast, for the first time since the 1840s, brought war to the doorsteps of the European settlers of the southern part of the North Island.[8] The *Argus* in early December confirmed the ever-widening scale of the crisis:

> the whole country, up to the town of Wanganui, has been abandoned... Everywhere the farms are deserted. The colonial military are under cover, and Tito Kowaru and his bands stalk about unopposed. Half of Wellington Province and the whole of Taranaki are doomed to be laid waste by this war – a far wider extent of territory than was desolated in 1861.[9]

The *Argus* also found it hard to believe that the crises on both coasts of New Zealand were being fomented by such small numbers of Maori when compared to the far grander scale of campaigns and combatant numbers that had been confronted in previous years:

> It has been variously estimated that Tito Kowaru has with him 600 or 800 men, and the lesser number has been heretofore considered the closer approach to the truth.... On the east coast, TE KOTI has increased his band to about 500 men... We see, then, that less than 800 men on one side of the island, and 500 on the other, march about and do as they please, in face of the greatly superior numbers of the colonial troops and their native allies.[10]

Press statements such as these also coincided with the arrival of Captain W.G. Stack in Melbourne to begin recruiting for the Armed Constabulary. This air of crisis was no doubt a stimulus for some of the men who came forward to offer their services in December 1868 and January 1869, and especially those who already had prior New Zealand military service, or even family and friends residing in this colony.

Of course, opinions in the Australian colonies were not solely influenced by press reportage, but came via correspondence received from family and friends residing across the Tasman.[11] In a letter from Auckland dated 23 November 1868, Edward Deas-Thomson wrote to his father in Sydney. Apart from a discussion of the mining field and its prospects, his tidings focused on the horrors of the Poverty Bay Massacre and the general New Zealand political and military situation:

> The settlers have lost all their stock and other property. The Maories destroyed every thing they could lay hands on, burnt the houses and other buildings, & stole all the stores.... The Constabulary are really of very little use... About a month ago 150 recruits were taken from the Thames goldfield straight into the field... [where] they were beaten to pieces. Some certainly had been in the line before, but they had never been trained together.[12]

Some of these letters were also disseminated amongst the press in order to show the 'adventures and hardships which have to be encountered by the settlers'.[13]

Another avenue for obtaining New Zealand information was public lectures. As in earlier periods, these were undertaken by persons with New Zealand experience and took place in churches or Mechanics' Institutes. One such example occurred on 7 December 1868 at Rev. Kininmont's Presbyterian Church, North Melbourne, where Reverend R. Laishley, who was reported as having many years' residence in that colony, undertook a lecture on 'New Zealand'. This was well attended by an audience 'who listened with interest to his descriptive account of this colony'.[14]

The fact that fighting in these wars was being carried out more on the guerilla level, with few set-piece battles, and massacres taking place on either side, left the Australian public numb and horrified. An editorial in the *Sydney Morning*

Herald in December 1868 contended it was 'impossible to read over the accounts of the recent massacres without deep emotion'. Tidings of the 'industrious settlers whose habitations were assailed by night, and whose wives and children were destroyed before their eyes', left people deeply concerned.[15] Some even thirsted for revenge. News of the horrors occurring also drew commentaries on how such a situation could have been allowed to develop, and in this search for answers drew comparisons with the frontier bloodshed of the North American continent.[16] In Queensland, a colony familiar with frontier horrors and settler retribution, the *Brisbane Courier* in March 1869 foretold considerable struggle ahead for New Zealand forces against an enemy at home on the land and equal in military talents:

> [I]t is not a war with a civilised nation...but with a band of daring bloodthirsty savages, nearly as well armed and as capable in the use of their weapons as the men sent out against them. Every success... is only a success to the extent of the number of rebel Maories which are killed or made prisoners. Every Maori who escapes remains unconquered.[17]

The White Cliffs (Pukearuhe) Massacre on 13 February 1869 in the Taranaki District would also elicit similar responses and expressions of regret at this further instance of tragic loss. The *Sydney Morning Herald* sadly contended: 'There is nothing new in the character of the Massacre at New Zealand. The same unprovoked cruelty, pursued with the subtlety and treachery characteristic of the race, has marked this sacrifice.... They are parts of a system of warfare which ... is seeking the destruction of the English race.'[18] Among those killed on this occasion was a former Melbourne-recruited Taranaki Military Settler officer, his wife and family, and two other former Melbourne enlistees. The deaths of these three military settlers are some of the last known casualties, apart from personnel serving in the Armed Constabulary, to be documented from among those men and families who came from Australia as military settlers during 1863–64.[19] The European victims at White Cliffs were the former Melbourne-enlisted officer Lieutenant Bamber Gascoigne, his wife Annie, and their three children.[20] Also killed were the long-serving Wesleyan Minister Rev. John Whiteley and two others, John Milne and Edward Richards, both former 'Melbourne Contingent' Taranaki Military Settlers.[21] These former military settlers have the unfortunate distinction of being the only known Australian-enlisted military settlers to have lost their lives on their land.[22]

Reports of the human and material cost of the war in 1868–69 elicited two sorts of reaction from the Australian public – one for retribution (some even calling for the extermination of the Maori), the other more placating (urging that the Maori viewpoint be heard). A column in December 1868 by 'A Sydney

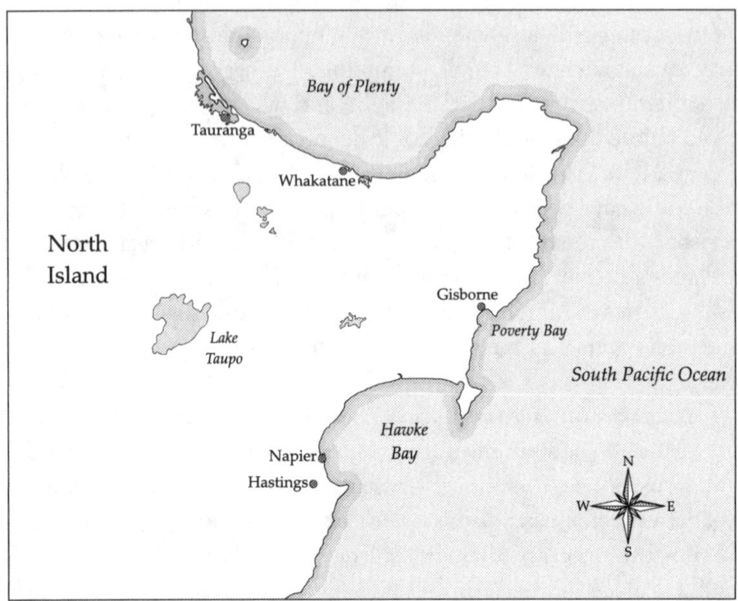

The East Coast region of the the North Island of New Zealand, showing Hawke Bay, Poverty Bay and Bay of Plenty.

Man' propounded meting timely punishment for the outrages carried out: 'The murdering savages were threatening Wanganui, and there is really nothing outrageous in the supposition that they might soon compel . . . [Governor] Bowen to vacate Wellington if not held in check. . . . The "noble savage" has . . . had it all his own way, and it is surely time for a little wholesome retribution.'[23]

On 17 December the *Sydney Morning Herald* announced that the 'policy of exterminating the natives of New Zealand, is being discussed in the Auckland papers with considerable vigour', but noted that thankfully the 'objectors are in the majority'.[24] Such debate was no doubt stimulated upon receipt from England of an article entitled 'Exterminating Natives', which during October and November of 1868 was republished and discussed throughout the colonies. The *Argus* carried this article which originated in the *Pall Mall Gazette*: 'There should be a war "of vigorous measures; it should be complete and final." Whimpering appeals to spare the cannibals should be disregarded.'[25] The *Argus* thereafter republished a discussion following on from this proposition, citing another English paper *The Standard*, which replied to the *Pall Mall Gazette*'s strong stance.[26]

The fact that only a very few people responded to the New Zealand crisis by publicly calling to hear the Maori perspective is evident from a letter to the *Argus* in October 1868 wherein 'Tarapipipi' pleaded for more balance to the reportage of New Zealand affairs: 'Only now and then . . . has any line been written in favour of those "blood-thirsty miscreants" (the New Zealanders), while every action of theirs has been exaggerated. Fair-play is the motto of Britons, and if the writers in your columns, and in those of your contemporaries, will wait "a wee," the other side of the picture may be shown.'[27]

On occasion information disseminated portrayed Maori in the image of the 'noble savage' – a native people valiantly making a stand against great adversity whilst defending their country from the invaders. The *Sydney Morning Herald* in January 1869, for instance, published a letter reputedly written by Titokowaru to Colonel Whitmore at Wanganui:

> You were made a pakeha, and England was made for you. I was made a Maori, and New Zealand was made for me. You did not recollect that a great division (gulf) was between us, the great sea. You ceased to remember this fact, and crossed over from that place to this.... My word to you – move out of my place to your own place in the midst of the sea.[28]

Of course, amongst many colonials, the Maori, like the Aborigines, were perceived to be a dying race – a seemingly inevitable fate in the light of indigenous population decline and the advance of the 'superior' British race and civilisation throughout Australasia in the 1860s. The Reverend Dr Bromley, lecturing on 'Pre-Historic Man', confirmed such sentiments in Melbourne when he provided 'evidence' for the belief in a hierarchy of races.[29] The doomed race theory could also be affirmed by dissemination of a Maori lament heralding the inevitable demise of the Maori and their way of life. The *Illustrated Australian News* saw these 'mournful words . . . as prophetic of the fate to which the native race of New Zealand is doomed':

> As the Pakeha fly has driven out the Maori fly:
> As the Pakeha grass has killed the Maori grass:
> As the Pakeha rat has slain the Maori rat:
> As the Pakeha clover has starved the Maori fern
> So will the Pakeha destroy the Maori.[30]

This belief in the inevitable demise of the Maori was reinforced by the influx of immigrants to New Zealand during the 1860s. It must have seemed then that the Maori were simply going to be swamped by 'Pakeha' arrivals. Census figures for 1861 show a European population numbering 97,904, and an estimated Maori population of 55,336. In 1867 the settler population reached 217,437, whereas the Maori population had declined to an estimated 38,540; by 1869, settler numbers had risen to 237,249 (including 1020 British regulars).[31]

Prohibiting warlike stores to New Zealand, 1867–69

As often happened earlier, Australian colonial authorities continued to restrict the export of arms and other warlike stores to New Zealand. In February 1867 the *Argus* drew attention to the sale in New Zealand of 'old military stores', of which some 2000 military bayonets, many in near perfect order, were sold. These arms were then readvertised for sale, and the *Argus* asserted fears they might fall 'into unpatriotic hands' and be used 'against the breasts' of British soldiers.[32] In December 1867 Victoria gazetted for public attention what items were deemed warlike stores and the restrictions upon exports of such materials, to reinforce the earlier notice from August 1863.[33]

New Zealand's new governor, Sir George Ferguson Bowen, fresh from Queensland where settlers and the Native Police had been steadily decimating its own indigenous population, received various reports in early 1868 to provide him with assessments of the social and political state of the Maori population throughout the colony. One report on Auckland Province mentioned an illegal arms trade, and referred specifically to Maori in the northern regions of the North Island, but pointed out difficulties in totally eradicating this illegal trade due to the willingness of American whaling vessels to continue participating in the activity.[34] Shortly after this report the New Zealand colonial secretary sent circular despatches to the various Australian colonial governments anxiously inquiring if any shipments of arms had recently been sent to New Zealand. This missive also requested the various customs officials to give 'early intimation of any such' shipments. Following its receipt in Queensland, the matter was directed to the Brisbane collector of customs, who in reply on 5 May stated that no arms or ammunition had been shipped in the last twelve months, but that he would promptly respond to the proper authorities if news of any such came to hand.[35]

Other Australian colonies followed Queensland's promptitude. On 8 July 1868 Victoria responded once more by issuing a further proclamation on the 'Restriction on Exportation of Arms and Gunpowder and Other Warlike Stores'. This limited exports to New Zealand to only those under written licence from the commissioner of trade and customs, and then only under very stringent guidelines in the event permission was granted.[36] This proclamation was distributed amongst the other Australian colonies, which in turn assisted Victoria by disseminating information on these restrictions to their own citizens.[37]

Calls for the despatch of imperial forces

Following receipt of the 'disastrous intelligence' of the Poverty Bay Massacre, the *Argus* commented that it was suggested imperial forces in Australia should immediately be despatched 'unless the hands of the commander-in-chief are so tied by his instructions from home that they cannot be so sent. The emergency at Poverty Bay and Wanganui is evidently a grave one.'[38] It was also stated that HMS *Challenger* was expected to sail immediately from Sydney. On 23 November HMS *Blanche* was similarly reported as having departed Sydney for Auckland.[39] In Melbourne shortly after, the *Argus* was able to better inform the public that rumours of the imminent despatch of the city's 14th Regiment garrison to the seat of war were unfounded.[40]

The government of Victoria did not in fact totally rule out a willingness to allow for the departure of its troop garrison, as is revealed in the *Argus*'s lengthy commentary on events associated with the arrival of Captain Stack to recruit for the Armed Constabulary. The Victorian government proposed allowing the troops to be sent, but Stack was not in a position to accept such an offer. His primary task was to recruit for the Armed Constabulary – he simply had no other instructions from his government on seeking such imperial aid.[41] However, the imperial government's decision to withdraw all British troops from Australasia was not to be rescinded, nor would the available troops in Australia and the 18th Regiment still in New Zealand be embroiled in any further fighting against the Maori. Its expenditure of men, money, and effort of the earlier 1860s was not to be repeated. Britain was determined that New Zealand became 'self-reliant', despite this latest military crisis.[42]

As part of the contingency preparations for possible New Zealand assistance, Sydney's naval authorities ensured that available Royal Navy warships, HMS *Blanche*, *Rosario*, *Challenger* and *Charybdis*, were nonetheless ready for despatch at short notice. The *Challenger* departed Sydney for Melbourne in early December 1868 to await news from New Zealand, which also offered an opportunity for senior Royal Navy officers to discuss first-hand any requirements with their senior Army counterparts at Army Headquarters in Melbourne.[43] The *Argus* noted the arrival of HMS *Challenger* on 11 December flying the flag of Rowley Lambert, commodore of the Australia Station.[44]

On 14 December the *Argus* announced that news had come to hand following the arrival of the *Rangitoto*, noting the conflicting nature of much of the information previously received in Melbourne. Consequently, the newspaper found it difficult to present an accurate summary of the actual state of affairs in New Zealand.[45] The following day the *Argus* confirmed that the military authorities in Melbourne had not yet decided whether to transfer the troops in Victoria to New Zealand; nor had such a request been received from the New Zealand government by the last mail. The arrival of HMS *Challenger* in Melbourne also allowed for a prompt visit by Major-General Trevor Chute, commander-in-chief of forces in Australia and New Zealand, to Commodore Lambert aboard his flagship.[46] No news was reported as to what these senior imperial officers discussed, but New Zealand affairs were obviously high on the agenda. On 23 December HMS *Challenger* left her Melbourne anchorage for New Zealand.[47]

In relation to the possible despatch of Australian garrison troops, it is interesting to note New Zealand public resolutions directed at Governor Bowen on this issue of military assistance. A public meeting in Wellington on 3 December addressed three resolutions relating to the 'native war', the third being to urge the governor 'to apply for the assistance of the Imperial troops stationed in Australia, on the grounds that the colonial forces were unable to cope with the rebellion'. An amendment to this resolution was then brought forward which in contradiction advised 'adherence to the policy of self-reliance'. Numbers proposing the third resolution and those supporting the amendment were reported as nearly even, necessitating a vote which carried the later amendment.[48] Despite the outcome of this Wellington meeting, Bowen received a memorial signed by 261 residents requesting an appeal for additional imperial troops from the Australian colonies. As so often before, Australia was regarded as the place from which imperial troops could be quickly acquired in times of crisis.[49]

On 9 January 1869 a military party consisting of Chute and Colonel H. Page, also coinciding with the departure of Captain Stack following his successful completion of recruiting for the Armed Constabulary, left Melbourne for New Zealand (via Sydney).[50] Despite the fact that Chute's visit was reported as a routine inspection of the British troops in that country, it was also an obvious opportunity for the most senior imperial officer in Australasia to judge first-hand the seriousness of the situation across the Tasman. Chute's decision temporarily to delay the removal of the 18th Regiment then stationed in New Zealand was later reported as having a beneficial effect on the colony's public affairs, with the reassuring presence of 'redcoats' bolstering morale in threatened townships such as Wanganui.[51]

Australian offers of assistance

Apart from the contribution to the personnel of the Armed Constabulary, offers of support or suggestions on how to assist New Zealand at this time were also heard from other quarters in Australia. In November 1868 'A Sydney Man' commented on the urgent need to aid New Zealand following receipt of the 'horrible intelligence' of the Poverty Bay massacre. Apart from sending imperial forces, this correspondent went further by suggesting the government 'sweep the streets of Sydney of the hundreds of lubberly, blackguard young men and hobbledehoys who swarm them on a Sunday night, fighting, swearing, and insulting every respectable person, and I would ship them off to Poverty Bay, and land them there with rifles in their hands'.[52]

From Sydney came another unusual proposal by a resident and former Army officer. He advocated the New Zealand government raise 'a force of 630 Australasian blacks, officered and accompanied by 120 whites, principally good bushmen, and 1,200 dogs'.[53] It is possible this former officer had served in Cape Colony and was proposing a military force similar to those raised in that part of the Empire to cope with native insurrection. A similar force – the Native Mounted Police – had long existed in New South Wales and Victoria and was now operating in Queensland, systematically and brutally eliminating all Aboriginal resistance.[54]

From among the ranks of the Australian volunteer movement emanated stirrings of martial fervour and willingness to assist as had occurred during 1860 and 1863. Volunteers in New South Wales were reported as having made offers of assistance.[55] In Brisbane, a 'Volunteer' not only indicated having followed the serious events overtaking New Zealand in recent months, but asserted a readiness, with others of similar mind, to help if supported by the provision of transport: 'I am acquainted with many myself that would jump at the chance of going to the war in New Zealand, but getting there is the great difficulty.'[56]

From Queensland's Gympie goldfields would also come an offer by John Hamilton to form a special unit with men of the right calibre and experience to go to New Zealand's aid. Hamilton was born in 1841 in Melbourne where he was educated at Scotch College and by private tutor. In his early twenties he departed for Rockhampton, Queensland to undertake a career in the pastoral industry, but on the way was attracted to the gold rushes in Calliope during 1862, and thereafter to Gympie in 1867. The next year he became magistrate of Gympie's mining court, and later a long-serving member of Queensland's Legislative Assembly representing Gympie (1878–83) and Cook (1883–1904).[57] In January 1869 the *Gympie Times* reported the beginnings of his volunteer endeavours: 'It is rumoured that a recruiting agent has arrived on Gympie for the purpose of enlisting men to serve in the colonial army at the seat of war . . . [but] we are induced to believe that either the recruiting agent is not acting under proper authority, or that there is actually no foundation for the report.'[58]

What appears to have occurred is that Hamilton and other individuals following events in New Zealand and the Melbourne recruiting for the Armed Constabulary were themselves inspired to act. Hamilton, in a letter on 20 January

1869, offered to form with other Gympie goldfields residents a 'guerilla corps' to assist New Zealand forces in their struggle against the Maori. The *Gympie Times* also indicated it had received communications from a number of Gympie goldfields residents who indicated a desire to serve with the 'colonial forces in the present war'.[59] On 1 May this newspaper was able to report that the New Zealand defence minister replied to Hamilton that his government 'do not require more men at the present time to serve against the rebel Maories'.[60] Though unsuccessful, Hamilton's offer demonstrated that the spirit of volunteering, whether to aid the Empire or a sister colony in trouble, was very much alive in the Australian colonies. It is also important to note that the Queensland goldfields were a great attraction to many former British military, as well as New Zealand colonial forces (such as former Waikato or Taranaki Military Settlers), personnel in the late 1860s and 1870s. John Hamilton no doubt knew numerous military and/or New Zealand experienced men from whom enthusiasm and concern about events across the Tasman was channelled into fresh service in this later period of strife.[61]

The Von Tempsky Fund

Apart from reactions and coverage of events as they unfolded during 1868–69, there exists another expression of Australian public interest (and limited support) in the form of the Von Tempsky Fund – the last example of fundraising associated with New Zealand's wars. Gustavus Ferdinand von Tempsky served as an officer in the Prussian Army before the thirst for adventure led to his departure to South America. Here he developed skills as a linguist, and also wrote a popularly read book about his travels and adventures.[62] From South America his travels first led him to the Californian goldfields, and thereafter to Victoria in 1858. Here the von Tempsky family already had connections via the sister of his wife. The lack of success on Victoria's goldfields saw him then lured to New Zealand's Coromandel goldfields in 1862, and during 1862–63 Australians became aware of the state of the New Zealand gold rushes through his letters to the editor, and later appointment as 'Coromandel Correspondent'.[63] But it was his subsequent military service, particularly with the famed Forest Rangers, that familiarised Australians with his exploits against the Maori during 1863–68.[64]

Gustavus von Tempsky's successes against the Maori ended on 7 September 1868 in the disastrous engagement at Te Ngutu o te Manu. As an inspector in the Armed Constabulary, he and eighteen others were killed in action and thirty-one were wounded while attempting to breach the brilliantly designed and defended fortifications of Titokowaru and his forces.[65] His death was a considerable blow to the New Zealand colonial public, as it was a shock in Australia – the *Brisbane Courier* in a column on the 'Defeat of the Troops by the Maories' asserting that his 'death will cause a great sensation throughout New Zealand'.[66] His widow Emilia became entitled to an annual New Zealand government pension under the Military Pensions Act 1866.[67]

Despite this provision for their welfare, von Tempsky's fame and popularity saw a process commence whereby monies were raised from both government and public sources to care for his widow and young family. In an obituary in the *Illustrated Sydney News*, specific reference to his prior Victorian residence and family relationship was made.[68] This same newspaper shortly after reported the establishment of the Von Tempsky Fund in New Zealand.[69] The *Brisbane Courier* wryly observed that:

> [he] fell with his back to the field and his feet to the foe, and in consideration of his long services, his tried courage, his gallant leadership, . . . a grateful and generous country has transmitted to his sorrowing widow a splendid solatium of £20! Let that widow dry her eyes and cease troubling. If she be not consoled, she ought to be.[70]

A subsequent response from the New Zealand government necessitated this newspaper to later correct itself on the actual contributions offered to von Tempsky's widow. Apart from an annual pension of £180, she also received a further donation of £200 from the New Zealand government.[71]

In Victoria, Howard Willoughby, the *Argus*'s special correspondent to the New Zealand war in 1863–64, contributed a donation of just over £2 in November 1868 on behalf of himself and the proprietors of the *Argus* towards this fund.[72] Presumably the reverence in which von Tempsky was held in Australia, but particularly in Victoria where he had resided and still had relatives, would have generated other sums being similarly forwarded. The progress of this fund was followed in Australia's press into 1869, where even a contribution of fifteen guineas by the Maori congregation at Kaipara was acknowledged.[73]

George Vowles, a Queensland-born poet and former Waikato Military Settler, also immortalised von Tempsky. In October 1863, at the age of 19, Vowles enlisted in Sydney in the 2nd Waikato Regiment, but his military service was cut short after being discharged due to 'disability' on 31 December the same year.[74] On return from New Zealand he enjoyed a lengthy teaching career in Queensland (1869–1917), dying in Brisbane in 1926. Not much else is known about his military experiences (nor whether he even knew or had met von Tempsky in person), though the *Queenslander* in his 1928 obituary stated that he 'was one of the Queenslanders to volunteer for service in the Maori War, where he had some exciting experiences'.[75] In 1870 Vowles published a book of poetry entitled *Sunbeams in Queensland* – the first book of verse published by a native-born

Queenslander.[76] Aside from containing a number of poems on martial themes, presumably influenced to some degree by his own personal military experiences,[77] one is specifically dedicated to von Tempsky.[78]

Governor Bowen and Father Bucas

In correspondence from the Secretary of State for the Colonies in August 1867, Queensland's Governor Bowen was informed of his appointment to succeed George Grey in New Zealand.[79] Bowen subsequently left Brisbane on 4 January 1868 accompanied by his long-serving Queensland aide-de-camp and private secretary Captain H.D. Pitt, RA.[80] Ironically, while Queensland governor, Bowen undertook a long campaign to ensure the colony was provided with its allotted garrison of imperial troops.[81] New Zealand's wars of 1860–61 and 1863–64, as well as New South Wales's despatch of a large proportion of its own imperial garrison and subsequent reluctance to countenance any further drain for Queensland's needs, had a direct impact on Queensland's defences throughout 1860–66. With developments that occurred in New Zealand in the latter part of 1868, Bowen now found himself in a contrary position, where although large numbers of imperial troops were present, from 1866 these were being gradually withdrawn, and now only one regiment, the 18th, remained. The crises then emerging on both the east and west coasts drew calls from private and government circles for the retention of what limited British troops were still stationed in the colony, as well as appeals for fresh regiments to help contain the situation. Bowen's hands in this instance were tied by the Home Office's determined decision to continue with the total withdrawal of British troops from Australasia. A reply from the Secretary of State for the Colonies in January 1869 confirmed that New Zealand had to deal with the situation on its own, and that no imperial assistance would be forthcoming. Even the 18th Regiment must depart as scheduled.[82]

Just prior to Bowen's departure from Brisbane he was fortunate to have contact with a unique French Catholic priest, Pierre Marie Bucas, who had recently arrived from New Zealand. During his career Bucas was to establish himself as a considerable linguist, first with Maori in the Waikato, and later with the Aboriginal peoples in the Mackay region of North Queensland.[83] He appears to have arrived in Brisbane in September 1867, not long before Bowen received word of his New Zealand appointment. In Brisbane in preparation for Bowen's departure, Bucas would tutor him in the basic elements of the Maori language.

Bucas was born in St Jean, Poterie, Brittany in 1840 – the eleventh in a family of twelve. He commenced his education at the Sorbonne and St-Sulpice, initially with an interest in medicine, but thereafter devoting his energies towards the priesthood. An obituary for Father Bucas, who died in Queensland in October

1930 (aged 90), detailed aspects of his early military experiences during the Papal Wars in 1861, which indirectly led him to serve the Catholic faith in New Zealand in the mid-1860s. He had served as a corporal in the Papal Zouaves until a bullet wound above the knee incapacitated him, and led to his return to Paris where he resumed his studies. In 1865 he was ordained deacon, and in the same year went to New Zealand.[84] While in New Zealand Bucas was either deported or asked to leave because of firearms training of local Maori. After meeting Bishop Quinn (Queensland's first Roman Catholic bishop), he found employment at St Stephen's in Brisbane during 1867–69, before undertaking a lengthy career in North Queensland. Whatever the exact nature of this cleric's New Zealand troubles and departure, his knowledge of the Maori language and culture was to be of some practical worth to Bowen on the eve of his new governorship.[85]

Australia and New Zealand's Armed Constabulary

On 19 October 1867 Governor Grey proclaimed the inception of New Zealand's Armed Constabulary, which was to come into operation on 1 November.[86] This newly raised body became New Zealand's first colony-wide police force. The initial personnel largely transferred from (or had prior service in) other New Zealand colonial forces such as the Forest Rangers, and the Taranaki and Waikato Military Settler regiments, as well as discharged soldiers from imperial regiments. During its first years of operation 'the armed constables' duties more nearly resembled those of soldiers than of civil police'.[87] This was especially true throughout the unrest and conflict during 1868–69 on the east and west coasts, and the sporadic fighting thereafter into 1872. It is from within the ranks of this force that significant Australian involvement, including the Melbourne recruitment of 205 men – the last specifically targeted Australian recruits – continued.[88]

The Armed Constabulary was conceived as a 'combined standing army and occupation/pacification police' essentially for use in the North Island, though its 'brief as a mobile militarised constabulary however covered the entire colony'. Nevertheless it was always intended to be more a constabulary proper, rather than a military fighting force.[89] It was comparable to New South Wales's Border Police (1839–50), as well as Canada's own frontier force, the North-West Mounted Police.[90]

There are numerous examples of individuals who had varied imperial or colonial experiences, such as former British regular and New Zealand colonial forces service, before their employment in the Armed Constabulary. One individual with both Australian and New Zealand colonial experience was Stuart Newall. Born in Scotland in 1843, he came to New Zealand from the colony of Victoria in 1863. After trying his hand at gold mining in Otago he then enlisted as a military settler in Dunedin in December 1863 and served in the 3rd Waikato Regiment.[91] Subsequently he joined the Armed Constabulary and proceeded to Wanganui in February 1869, where he took part in the campaign against Titokowaru on the west coast. He continued to serve in the Armed Constabulary until 1883 when he transferred to the New Zealand Defence Force, and in this continued military role later commanded the 5th New Zealand Contingent to the war in South Africa in 1900.[92]

Another individual whose family and personal career had both Australian and New Zealand connections was Cholwell Dean Pitt. Pitt's father was Lieutenant-Colonel G.D. Pitt, an officer prominent firstly in Victoria, then New Zealand, who returned to Australia to enlist military settlers for the New Zealand government in 1863 and 1864. Cholwell continued his family's military traditions by following his father to New Zealand. In July 1863 he was commissioned ensign in the 1st Battalion, Auckland Regiment of Militia, and served with the initial group of military settlers raised by his father, commonly known as 'Pitt's Militia', the nucleus of the 1st Waikato Regiment.[93] Following the disbandment of the military settler regiments in 1867, he followed a professional soldier's life and enlisted in the newly formed Armed Constabulary, and in October was commissioned sub-inspector.[94] He resigned in 1874 after eleven years' military service, nine of which were on active duty in the field.[95]

One should remember that the Australian colonies were also the locale from which personnel were similarly obtained in the 1840s. Among the various civil service and other government personnel supplied by New South Wales to assist with the establishment and policing of New Zealand in 1840, there was one sergeant and four troopers of the New South Wales Mounted Police.[96] This small detachment was later placed under the command of Lieutenant H.D. Smart, 28th Regiment, formerly commander of the Mounted Police division stationed at Bathurst, who arrived in New Zealand in March 1840 with additional Mounted Police personnel and troop horses aboard the storeship *Westminster*.[97] This detachment was utilised as part of a force, including a detachment of the 80th Regiment, despatched by Lieutenant-Governor Hobson to Port Nicholson to restore the sovereignty of the Queen and to subordinate the New Zealand Company to his government in May 1840.[98] These mounted troopers were volunteers selected from various regiments, such as the 80th, then garrisoned in New South Wales.[99] Thus, even in this initial period of colonial emergence, New Zealand relied upon Australia for some of its policing requirements.[100]

A further aspect of Australian involvement in New Zealand that rarely merits acknowledgement is the role and influence of former police officers. This cross-Tasman migration of police personnel saw individuals (particularly from Victoria, but also from other colonies such as New South Wales) sought for the creation and development of New Zealand's provincial police forces. These experienced men were of great importance to the emergence and expansion of such forces, especially on South Island goldfields such as Otago during the early 1860s. Important examples in this vein include William James who served in the Victorian Police (1852–63) before being encouraged to join the Canterbury Armed Police Force in 1863, and who continued a New Zealand police career until 1888.[101] Another is Robert Clarke Shearman who served in the Victorian Police from 1851, before later appointment as Commissioner of the Canterbury Armed Police in 1862. By the time the New Zealand Police Force was created in 1886, he was appointed Inspector, the second-highest rank in this new force, and finally, Officer-in-Charge Auckland Police 1887–88.[102]

What is not then recognised is that some of these cross-Tasman police also tended to serve in other New Zealand colonial forces, or else were absorbed from their provincial police forces into the newly created Armed Constabulary from 1867 onwards. In this manner some also played a role in the wars of the late 1860s. Similarly, the conditions of service and pay of the restructured Armed Constabulary appears to have continued to draw recruits from Australia, and again mainly from the police force of Victoria up to the early 1870s at least.[103]

One such individual with cross-Tasman police and military service was Jackson Keddell. Keddell was a former Victorian policeman who went to Otago to assist Commissioner St John Branigan, another former Victorian police officer colleague and friend. His career mirrored that of his superior: 'army service, Victorian police, rapid rise to commissioned officer rank'. While on leave of absence from Victoria, he came to Otago with Branigan to sound out prospects. Branigan secured his appointment as sub-inspector, backdated to August 1861.[104] In November 1863 Keddell was appointed captain in the 4th Waikato Regiment, later becoming second-in-command to Colonel Moule.[105] In January 1864 he accompanied Colonel Pitt to Victoria to assist in the second military settler recruiting mission. After his return in early 1864, and now a major, he commanded and cared for some seventy families at Otahuhu while their menfolk were serving in the field with the 4th Waikato Regiment. In October 1864 he took over at Onehunga.[106] One historian of the town of Hamilton notes that although Keddell's name was rarely recognised, 'his special qualities and ability no doubt were useful in the early days' of this military settler township. William Seed, the under secretary for defence, confirmed Keddell's reputation as an efficient and zealous officer.[107] Keddell later sold his lands acquired for military settler service in and around the military settlement of Hamilton, and thereafter found appointments as a resident magistrate and warden in various New Zealand goldfields.[108]

The Melbourne Armed Constabulary recruiting mission

Analysis of the personnel of the Armed Constabulary reveals that Captain William Griffin Stack recruited 205 men in Melbourne during December 1868 and January 1869. This particular Australian contribution to New Zealand's military forces has largely been forgotten, despite these recruits again illustrating the importance of Australia as a place from which to obtain military personnel at times of New Zealand crisis.[109] Although considerably smaller in number to the thousands of men and families obtained during the military settler recruiting efforts in 1863 and 1864, these later recruits were nonetheless a vital contribution to the forces available to the New Zealand government. They arrived at a time when authorities were desperately scrambling to outfit and deploy adequate forces to contend with the disastrous military situations transpiring on both coasts of the North Island.

Captain Stack arrived in Melbourne aboard the steamship *Omeo* on 28 November 1868.[110] His arrival in Victoria marked the commencement of this fresh recruitment drive by the New Zealand government. In June 1863 he had been appointed captain in the 1st Battalion, Auckland Regiment of Militia, and then commanded a company of the 1st Waikato Military Settler Regiment.[111] During the Waikato campaign his company initially moved from headquarters at Otahuhu to Drury, before departing for the front in October 1863.[112] After seeing later active service in the Tauranga Bush Campaign (January–February 1867), he was appointed paymaster for Colonial Defence Services at Tauranga and Opotiki in the Bay of Plenty in December 1867.[113] It was in this region that the establishment of military settlements for many of the members of the 1st Waikato Regiment took place. Review of Stack's military service clearly shows he was an experienced officer with considerable involvement with the Australian volunteer component of the 1st Waikato Regiment. This experience no doubt stood him in good stead when ordered to Victoria to recruit for the Armed Constabulary in 1868. Following his services in the recruitment of personnel in Melbourne, he continued to have connections with the Armed Constabulary into the 1870s.[114]

The Melbourne *Argus* provided a very lengthy commentary on the events associated with Stack and his Victorian recruiting mission: 'This is the third effort of the kind ... [in] the two previous instances Colonel Pitt ... came here to enrol men to serve as ... military settlers. ... The present recruiting officer ... [hopes] to raise a force of 200 men to join the armed constabulary force now engaged in coping with the rebellious Maories.' His government's instructions have apparently 'directed him to start at once, and expressly stated that the attempt to raise recruits was to be made "with the sanction of the Victorian Government".'[115] At their first meeting it was also reported that Victoria's Chief Secretary James McCulloch asked Stack to return in one day so as to allow the cabinet time to deliberate upon its position. When they met again Captain Stack was informed that the Victorian government 'had decided upon adopting a memorandum setting forth their willingness' to despatch 400 men of the 14th Regiment for service in New Zealand, but as noted earlier, Stack simply possessed no authority from his government to act upon such an offer.[116]

To assist Stack in recruiting, a Doctor Dermott was despatched from Hokitika to provide medical inspections of prospective recruits, arriving in Melbourne on 4 December.[117] Despite this provision of a medical practitioner, later New Zealand press reports indicate that some Melbourne recruits may not have been truly fit for service and were discharged in Wanganui.[118] Unfortunately, the reportage of this situation supplies no analysis of how many of the men discharged as medically unfit were actually Melbourne recruits, as opposed to those obtained from other recruiting missions around the North and South Islands.

One other individual, Joseph Tuckwell, was also to be involved in the process of selection of men in Melbourne. Tuckwell, a former detective in the Victoria Police, departed for Otago in November 1861 after having been asked to organise a detective force for this province.[119] Tuckwell is yet another example of former Victorian police personnel who departed to assist with the development of New Zealand's provincial police forces.[120] In December 1868 he was now reported as a private investigator engaged by Stack 'to aid him in selecting the right men'.[121] This requirement was especially necessary as the Victorian government denied Stack any formal recognition or assistance from its own detective force in weeding out any criminal elements that might try to engage for New Zealand. Tuckwell, the former Victorian and Otago detective and more recently gaoler at Auckland's Mt Eden Prison, was to prove an important component in the procurement of personnel in Melbourne.[122]

The *Argus* on 5 December 1868 mentioned that the location for recruiting was Meagher's Hotel on the corner of Lonsdale and Swanston Streets, Melbourne, and any recruits enlisted would embark the following week.[123] Later this same day the *Argus Supplement* became available in which a very detailed, near full-page, advertisement was taken out by Stack: '200 unmarried MEN, of good character, under 40 years of age, and of sound health, are REQUIRED, for the above force, to serve for three years [under the provisions of the 1867 Armed Constabulary Act].'[124] This lengthy advertisement went on to outline in full the 'Act to Provide for the Establishment and Maintenance of an Armed Constabulary' (10 October 1867), the associated Governor's Order (issued by Governor Bowen, Auckland, 7 May 1868), the Regulations for the Armed Constabulary, as well as the Military

Pensions Act 1866. These moves left no doubts about the nature, benefits and conditions associated with this force.[125]

The commencement of recruiting in Melbourne did not escape the scrutiny of the *Melbourne Punch*, which provided its readers with its own satirical interpretation of New Zealand's needs: 'Wanted immediately, . . . some men able to take their own part, none of the white inhabitants being troubled with this complaint.'[126] This paper also alluded to the lack of direct imperial involvement at this time as 'Manly Independence', and parodied the current Victorian recruiting as '[s]nubbing the Imperial Government, and then whining for Victorian immigrants to fight New Zealand battles'.[127] Such commentary manifests a distinct degree of disdain in Victoria for New Zealand's seeming unwillingness to organise its own settlers to fight, and instead once more seeking men from Australia.

Captain Stack began to receive applications on 5 December. The *Argus*, despite initially reporting that his mission was probably going to be 'a fruitless one', now confirmed almost 100 men had presented themselves, and of these, fifty-eight passed the medical examination, five only being rejected, with the others still to be examined.[128] This paper also passed judgement on the class and quality of the men seeking to enrol. Though he was likely to take 'a few who can well be spared', the 'class of applicants is generally better than it is desirable to see leaving the colony. Some will go probably from mere love of change; yet is was clear that many' now besieging Stack's recruiting rooms 'found the 5s. a day, without rations' a very strong inducement.[129] An *Argus* editorial therefore confidently predicted that within a week Captain Stack would be able to despatch 200 men.[130]

On 9 December the *Argus* reviewed the results of the previous four days of recruiting as clearly indicating substantial headway made towards obtaining the total number of men being sought. 'Up to yesterday he had succeeded in enrolling 107 men . . . and there seems no doubt that the men engaged are a loss to us, being desirable colonists.'[131] This same day the *Alhambra* cleared Hobson's Bay for Wellington with the first contingent of ninety-nine Melbourne recruits.[132] On the events associated with this initial departure, the *Argus* noted 'that some of them took the opportunity of "bolting" at the last minute', though only eight out of the 107 men enlisted were missing, and several of these were actually detained by circumstances that had nothing to do with any unwillingness to go.[133] Accompanying this contingent was Stack's report which included 'a descriptive return of the men, and an agreement signed by them', because he had been made aware by legal advice that the oath prescribed by the New Zealand Armed Constabulary Act could not be legally administered while in Victoria.[134] Because of these problems, he therefore sought the intermediate option of getting all the selected applicants to sign an agreement, whereby each confirmed that he had applied and been selected to serve in the Armed Constabulary, and on arrival in New Zealand would immediately take the required oath.[135] This procedure was carried out with all the men of the five contingents selected for New Zealand service.

We have a glimpse into the initial reactions of many of the Melbourne recruits who departed aboard the *Alhambra* just prior to their being sent to Wanganui in December 1868. Upon arrival in Wellington these recruits, including others from the South Island, like so many soldiers before them on the eve of departure for the front, took solace in alcohol, the *Argus* republishing a not so glowing account of their behaviour. Although these recruits had 'looked a very fine body of men as they marched up to the militia-office', they soon 'gave ample proof of their rowdy character before they left in the evening'. They had gotten so thoroughly drunk that 'when the hour of embarkation approached very few of them were in a condition to traverse unaided the short distance' to the wharf.[136]

An aspect to consider when looking at those who volunteered in Melbourne is the large number who had prior military service. The rolls of the five contingents indicate many individuals with previous service in the British Army or Navy, various police forces, as well as British and Australian volunteer or militia units. Similarly, attention should be directed to the significant number of Melbourne recruits who had already served in New Zealand as either Taranaki or Waikato Military Settlers. At least seventeen per cent of those embarked were former military settlers, while a good twenty per cent indicated prior service in the British Army or Navy, the East India Company Army or Navy, or other Indian military forces. Moreover, six per cent recorded service with British, Australian or Indian police forces and approximately thirteen per cent had prior service in various volunteer or militia units from throughout the Empire. These are all conservative statistics because 'previous service' details were not recorded with every enlistee, and are likely to have been higher in all categories.[137]

The presence, contributions, and therefore significance of these former military and police personnel within New Zealand colonial forces has neither been fully appreciated nor explored. In both Australia and New Zealand, most volunteer corps included a small cadre of retired or discharged military personnel who provided the experience, enthusiasm and structure around which colonial units were formed, trained and operated.[138] The Armed Constabulary is simply another force that gained invaluable knowledge, experience and leadership from personnel within its ranks who had such prior military, as well as police, experience, and which was to prove particularly crucial during the period 1868–72.

The recruiting in Melbourne again revealed some prevailing societal ills following the departure of the first contingent aboard the *Alhambra*. As with the earlier military settler volunteers, some men appear to have enlisted for New Zealand service to avoid family responsibilities, as it transpired that one recruit had left a wife and family behind. Victoria's colonial secretary contacted

Captain Stack on this matter, but Stack defended his actions by pointing out that 'the first question he put to every applicant was, whether he was married or not, if married, he would be refused, however eligible. In one case a man who declared himself unmarried' was discovered to have a wife, and despite having already enrolled, was refused. Where applicants were minors, the consent of parents or relatives was also a condition of enrolment.[139] By the time of the departure of the third contingent, the *Argus* warned of the dangers of absconding under any guise as a recruit for New Zealand's Armed Constabulary.[140] No doubt this admonition was influenced by memory of the public burden and concerns raised in relation to the number of wives and families of military settlers during 1863–64 who were either abandoned or else temporarily left destitute until transport could be arranged for them to rejoin their husbands in New Zealand.

Following a brief cessation in recruiting associated with the departure of the first group of recruits, enrolments recommenced on 10 December. Men continued to come forward to apply on this day, with the press commenting that 'it appears that a better class of men have become candidates', including one individual noted for his 'former Imperial service having been engaged in the construction of the military engineering work' during the very recent war in Abyssinia.[141]

Editorials in the *Argus* suggested a degree of public support in Victoria for New Zealand at this time of renewed crisis, similar to that which arose in 1860 and 1863. This endorsement extended to countenance of Captain Stack's recruiting activities, though tempered by concern about the employment and apparent lack of effective training which these prospective Victorian recruits were to receive:

> Among the recruits . . . are plenty of fine young fellows . . . sure to do their duty if they get a chance. But will they get a chance? They will be sent to the front at once, devoid of that training without which bodies of men, no matter how brave individually, are simply useless against an enemy who is not a novice in his business.[142]

The *Melbourne Punch*, reflecting on events associated with Victorian recruiting for military settlers in 1863 and 1864, once again provided a counterpoint to the *Argus*'s stance with its own sarcastic vision of the situation involving these latest Victorian recruits for New Zealand's present difficulties with Maori:

> The military tactics hitherto followed . . . have lamentably failed. Each step taken since the more recent disturbances have occurred has proved a *faux pas* . . .
>
> One man alone, possessing experience in the peculiar warfare of the country, would render greater service than a whole regiment of well-trained

> soldiers, and in Victoria that *one* man is to be found! The incorruptible patriot, the man of many parts, the true COLOSSUS of *roads*, the pride of Melbourne, our own JONES!
>
> In former times JONES had much practice *in the breeching of Pa(h)s*, a fact which many respectable Victorians affirm with considerable satisfaction. The fame of his skill has been noised abroad. Our sister colony, in her dire extremity, calls JONES to her rescue . . .[143]

By 12 December some forty additional men had been enrolled.[144] This same day saw the *Otago* depart Hobson's Bay with the second contingent numbering forty-one recruits.[145] After several days' intermission following the departure of the *Otago* contingent, Stack again recommenced recruiting. Starting on 16 December, he placed a further advertisement in the Melbourne papers and began to receive fresh applications.[146] In the first two days he received thirty-six. Those men selected were formally enrolled and then departed aboard the *Rangitoto* for Wellington on 19 December. This third contingent totalled thirty recruits.[147] The *Argus* reported that Stack would now 'attempt to complete his tale of 200 men elsewhere' as the rush of applications in Melbourne had dwindled, with Ballarat suggested as his next probable destination.[148]

But on 23 December it was announced that Stack's recruiting mission would soon cease, although the recruiting office at the Royal Hotel would remain open daily, as men were still urgently needed.[149] The *Melbourne Punch* humorously offered the helpful advice that, 'as we have an abundance of majors in the volunteer service, we can better spare for New Zealand our majors than our miners'.[150] A continual trickle of applicants allowed for the embarkation of a fourth contingent of nineteen recruits aboard the *Gothenburg*, which cleared on 26 December.[151] The *Argus* deemed Stack's recruiting mission through December a success.[152]

The fifth and final contingent of sixteen recruits departed Melbourne aboard the steamship *Omeo* on 5 January 1869, bringing to 205 the total number sent to Wellington.[153] Stack had been 'as successful as he could have wished in his mission', attaining just over the full complement sought.[154] This *Omeo* contingent therefore marked the end of the Melbourne recruiting, though Stack temporarily remained in the city on related military business seeking to procure ammunition for breech-loading rifles currently in short supply in New Zealand.[155]

Captain Stack finally departed Melbourne for New Zealand aboard the *Hero* on 9 January 1869. His departure coincided with that of the military party of General Chute and Colonel Page.[156] It was no mere coincidence that Stack returned to New Zealand with this party. As the official New Zealand government agent recruiting for the Armed Constabulary, and also seeking arms and munitions, he no doubt had discussions with imperial officers both in Melbourne and en route to New Zealand. In addition, there was considerable public awareness of New Zealand's military crisis, which saw the Victorian government proposing to despatch 400 men of the 14th Regiment to bolster the available forces if required. Obviously such factors would be an impetus for Chute's inspection to see for himself whether any further assistance was necessary.[157]

One other way to gauge an Australian contribution to New Zealand's Armed Constabulary is from analysis of personnel who were killed in action or died of wounds during 1868–70. It appears some fourteen men (approximately one fifth) can be confirmed as being either Australian-born, former Australian-recruited Waikato or Taranaki Military Settlers, or 1868–69 Melbourne-recruited personnel, out of a total believed to be sixty-four Armed Constabulary deaths during 1868–70.[158] As regards former military settlers, their Australian origins are often passed over, ignored, or lost in the historical record, but their very reason for being in New Zealand and familiar with local events and experiences is because of their original recruitment in Australia during 1863 or 1864. After 1867 and the disbandment of the military settler regiments, many military settlers went on to serve in the Armed Constabulary, joined by others because of the large-scale failure of the military settlement scheme. Some also enlisted in the Armed Constabulary to continue their military careers, and others merely sought to ensure a form of future employment in the uncertain social and economic times of late 1860s Australasia.

Conclusion

A FRIEND INDEED – THE ANZAC GENESIS

IN 1968, communist publicist and amateur labour historian Rupert Lockwood traced a connection between conscription in Australia and the White Australia policy. In doing so he began with the 1840s wars in New Zealand, viewing Australia's role as 'her initiation as an imperial *place d'armes*'. These so-called 'Maori Wars' had in fact 'ushered Australia into the world as a base for colonial military expeditions'.[1] Although imbued with the radical left's perspectives of both Australian and world history, Lockwood nonetheless touched upon the depth of Australian involvement in New Zealand's internal conflicts, largely missed by other historians. He also emphasised that these wars were a conflict between two races – Maori versus British – in which racism, as we now understand the term, was to play a role in the attitudes and actions of the participants. Furthermore, he viewed these wars as 'an important turn in Anglo-Australian relations', wherein Australia was clearly established as a suitable 'supplier of manpower for colonial wars' – a scenario which would repeat itself throughout the remainder of the nineteenth century and into the twentieth.[2]

What the present history has shown, as Lockwood earlier observed, is that Australian involvement in supplying both material and manpower was of considerable importance to the outcomes of the wars that plagued New Zealand throughout the period under discussion. From 1834 through to the late 1860s, Australia was continuously involved in New Zealand affairs in ways that have not been fully taken into account. This exploration of the Australian context to these wars should provide opportunities for fresh perspectives and instil greater understanding of shared Australian–New Zealand social, economic and military perspectives, as well as opportunities for delving into the complexities of Australian public reactions to the conflicts taking place across the Tasman. An Australian home front undoubtedly existed for the New Zealand wars and this experience warrants greater reincorporation into the histories of both countries.

Today, much historical effort seeks to further explore or reaffirm the 'Anzac legend', whereas relatively little or no research is devoted to investigating Australian–New Zealand connections prior to 1915, when surely these earlier aspects are crucial to the ease with which the legend was formed from World War I. The New Zealand wars are in fact one of the most complex and detailed aspects of the Australian–New Zealand experience. Australia and New Zealand possess a unity which is forged in blood and conflict – first during the New Zealand wars, and reaffirmed thereafter in later conflicts, wars and peacekeeping efforts.

Nor should it be forgotten that both Australia and New Zealand emerged as British settler societies, and that all 'European colonies were mostly born in and "enveloped" with violence'.[3] In Australian colonies such as Queensland the Native Police brutally and methodically 'dispersed' the Aboriginal peoples and pacified the expanding colonial frontiers. In New Zealand, the wars marking that colony's period of violence underpinned the settler society that rose up from the ashes of the conflicts during the 1840s and 1860s.

Australian involvement during 1834–1847

Australian military involvement in New Zealand affairs was established by the events that took place between 1834 and 1845. In this period the Australian colonies were confirmed as a base for military operations, and of easy-to-hand Army and Royal Navy reinforcements and vital logistic and commissariat needs when required. The wars that broke out in the north, and then later in the south, of the North Island during 1845 and continuing until 1847 saw New Zealand able to take advantage of a process already well established. This major Australian involvement, though largely forgotten, ensured an overall outcome in favour of the imperial and colonial authorities, although the Maori were far from a defeated people, as events in the 1860s were to demonstrate.

Throughout 1845–46 especially, Australia became a major contributor towards New Zealand's logistic and commissariat requirements. Australian stores and arsenals provided a considerable array of weapons and artillery, ammunitions, and associated military equipment. Manufacture of a type of Coehorn mortar in Sydney also signified the beginnings of an Australian arms industry. Other war material included stores and foodstuffs, camp equipment, drays, working bullocks, horses and cattle, manufactured 24-pounder gun carriages, and coal from Newcastle for use by the Royal Navy in New Zealand waters. Sydney's port facilities were also vital in both victualling and the maintenance and repair of warships and other supply vessels throughout the conflicts, as well as being a place from which additional crew were recruited.

Australian garrisons also provided some 1560 soldiers from the 58th, 99th, 96th and 65th Regiments for New Zealand service between March 1845 and November 1846. Numbers were augmented with available Australian-based Royal Navy ships, and the many sailors and Royal Marines who served ashore as part of the available military personnel. Part of this force included a stopgap trained artillery component and volunteers, until proper Royal Artillery units arrived in 1846. The imperial garrisons of Australia therefore provided the bulk of the military force able to be put into the field against the Maori during the campaigns of 1845–47.[4] But New Zealand's wars in turn also had a direct impact upon Australian colonial defence. Authorities in these colonies had to contend with a major redistribution of imperial troops throughout 1845–47, and some tentative thoughts were even entertained towards greater self-reliance and the raising of volunteers or militia.

The ability to carry out the scale of campaigning undertaken in New Zealand by imperial forces at this time was due to the geographical proximity and military capacity offered by New South Wales and Van Diemen's Land. Military assistance from other locations of the Empire took considerable time to be marshalled, and arrived late. In the meantime, the ready and willing responses of the imperial and colonial representatives in Australia to New Zealand's repeated calls for assistance met the needs of immediate crisis – whether real or imagined. The strong sense of duty to the Empire and to fellow colonists in need even outweighed New South Wales' cries against further troop losses during 1847.

Governor Grey's requests for assistance in particular were always accommodated in some form, and his ability to repeatedly procure and maintain a vast imperial military force was to be replicated upon his return to the New Zealand stage in the 1860s. Indeed, Grey's experience during the 1840s no doubt instilled him with confidence that the Australian colonies could be relied upon to comply with his later diverse military requirements. And he was not to be disappointed in this expectation, for the experience of the 1840s clearly set the stage for Australia's equally crucial role in New Zealand's wars in the 1860s.

During 1845, Australian humanitarian efforts for the first time were inspired by the displacement of Bay of Islands settlers and others fleeing in panic from Auckland and Nelson. These colonies also contributed to slowing the arms trade to the Maori by support of New Zealand's restrictions on the trade of warlike stores, and enacting similar legislation to add force to such aims. Van Diemen's Land even became a destination for the imprisonment of Maori political prisoners associated with the Wellington–Hutt Valley conflict during 1846. What all these various elements indicate is that Australian involvement in the New Zealand campaigns of 1845–47 was crucial to overall outcomes and should not be underestimated. This in turn has ramifications for understanding of Australian–New Zealand affairs throughout the 1830s and the 1840s.

Australian involvement in the Taranaki War, 1860–1861

During the Taranaki War of 1860–61, New Zealand received support from the Australian colonies that was vital in stemming the military and social crisis faced in and around the province's major settlement of New Plymouth. In a situation reminiscent of the 1845–47 conflicts, the Australian colonies again became a major supplier for New Zealand's immediate logistic and commissariat needs. Geographical proximity and ease of supply saw Australian commissariat stores and arsenals provide much-needed camp equipment, modern rifles, revolvers, artillery, various munitions and other military equipment. This assistance extended to stores and foodstuffs to feed the military force assembling in this New Zealand province, and even the horses to carry these supplies.

The Australian imperial and colonial authorities again took steps to limit any trade in arms and ammunitions to the Maori by various legislative restrictions instituted during 1860. This conflict in turn had a direct impact on defence in these colonies. The departure of portions of the Australian imperial garrisons lent an impetus to existing volunteer movements, or in New South Wales's case, resulted in considerable pressure to resurrect such a force. With this redeployment came a realisation that a degree of self-reliance and more long-term planning was essential beyond the short-term immediacy of the Taranaki crisis. While many volunteers also expressed desires to serve against the Maori, at this date this manpower potential was not tapped, although it provides a clear indication of the support and martial fervour the military settler recruiting missions would elicit during 1863–64, and accounts for many of the subsequent recruits.

Renewed Australian humanitarianism also saw money and material goods collected for the alleviation of the sufferings of the Taranaki settlers, and although not on the scale of the Taranaki Relief Fund, other Australian colonists contributed to the relief of families of British troops sent to fight across the Tasman. Both these relief efforts are indications of loyalty to the Empire and concern for fellow colonists, so important when assessing the social experience of nineteenth-century Australasia.

New Zealand's war needs also saw the majority of the available vessels of the Royal Navy's Australia Station serve in New Zealand waters, and hundreds of its personnel in turn serve ashore as part of the Naval Brigade; as did HMCS *Victoria* and constituents of its crew.[5] The service of Victoria's only colonial warship is highly significant, not only as the first Australian colonial military unit to serve in an overseas conflict, but also because of the occurrence of the first Australian colonial military force casualty with the death of seaman Henry Serjeant in New Plymouth during 1860. Sydney's port facilities, naval supply and maintenance capabilities also ensured the efficient service of the Royal Navy vessels serving across the Tasman throughout 1860–61.

The Australian colonies, apart from despatching Australasia's most senior military officer, Major-General Pratt, to take personal command in July 1860, also contributed a considerable supplement to available forces in Taranaki. Between April and July 1860 at least 926 additional regular officers and men from the Royal Artillery, 40th and 12th Regiments, and Royal Engineers were conveyed from Sydney, Melbourne and Hobart for war service.[6] The suspension of hostilities in early 1861 was simply a lull before the renewal of conflict in 1863. Australian military involvement in New Zealand, initiated in 1834–47 and extended during 1860–61, would now develop on a far grander scale during 1863–64. This would enable a vast imperial and colonial war machine to be unleashed in the Waikato and on both coasts of New Zealand's North Island. Australia was truly a major player in New Zealand's wars.

Australian involvement, 1863–1864

The high-water mark in Australian military involvement in New Zealand took place during 1863–64. The Australian colonies in this period supplied a considerable array of commissariat and logistic material ensuring the magnitude of the imperial and colonial war machine that rolled through the Waikato, Taranaki, and other locations of the North Island. Australian commissariat stores and arsenals once again contributed rifles and carbines, munitions, artillery and other associated ordnance material, while the trade in military horses also greatly increased at this time. Armoured river gunboats were manufactured in Sydney to New Zealand's orders, and existing riverboats were purchased from South Australia. These colonies also contributed naval coal and chandlery supplies and services, apart from the shipping utilised for a variety of military or commissariat purposes. Australian pastoralists successfully tendered for meat and cattle contracts for imperial forces in New Zealand, and other colonial enterprises and industries supplied many foodstuffs, military clothing and other equipment for the war effort.

While such supplies of war material and foodstuffs flowed across the Tasman, Australian imperial and colonial authorities continued their legislative restrictions aimed at reducing any trade in arms and ammunition to Maori. The importance of events under way in New Zealand also led to major Australian newspapers deeming it necessary to despatch their own correspondents to ensure effective coverage of the wars, and so heralding the beginnings of Australian war reporting. These first Australian war reporters in turn provided an Australian colonial perspective to occurrences as well as the human story. This development was important in disseminating information to the Australian 'home front' that had itself contributed large numbers of imperial soldiers and military settler volunteers. New Zealand's wars have a very real Australian context.

A related aspect to this Australian home front was the continuation of humanitarian efforts contributing towards the maintenance of welfare to families of British troops despatched for New Zealand service. Such efforts extended to assistance for widows and orphans of Army or Royal Navy or Marine personnel killed. Similarly, families of some military settlers also relied on Australian charity or colonial government assistance, which ensured their welfare and eventual departure to rejoin military settler husbands and fathers.

Again, the nearness of the Australian colonies also enabled the successful harnessing of the manpower potential, particularly in Victoria. This enlistment benefited to some degree from the spirit of volunteerism evident throughout the volunteer movements of the Australian colonies (and most noticeable during 1863), quite apart from the incentive of land in exchange for military service. It is impossible to ascertain the number of individuals or those small informal groups of men who left Australia during 1863–64 to enlist in New Zealand colonial forces separate to those obtained during the two formal military settler recruiting missions. Their origins are largely lost, although numbers of these men are revealed to be members of the Australian volunteer movement, or else former British Army personnel. Nonetheless, evidence presented here would seem to allow estimates in the hundreds as reasonable approximations for these unrecognised Australian-derived individual or small group volunteers. It is therefore not unrealistic to postulate upwards of 3000 men – combining totals from formal recruiting (2500) with those estimated from informal individual or small groups – as a more accurate figure for the total Australian contribution to the military settler regiments and other colonial units.

What did the first Australian recruiting mission achieve? New Zealand, through its initial 1863 recruiting mission, was able to draw upwards of 1500 men as military settlers away from the Australian colonies. Rumblings of discontent at government level were beginning to be heard by late 1863, as the financial costs of this exodus were calculated. Quite distinctly, a different tone emerges in the records from that of the patriotic fervour displayed only a few months earlier. The matter was complex. New Zealand did need help to defeat the Maori, but was this supremacy being gained at the expense of Australia's east coast colonies? Was the recruiting mission for military settlers really a competitive (or covert) move to steal migrants, already paid for by sister colonies, away to New Zealand? The necessity for, and the directives behind, a fresh wave of recruiting in early 1864 were no longer as clear-cut as had appeared during 1863. In turn, this change of heart also led to the early termination of Colonel Pitt's second recruiting mission during early 1864.

British garrisons in Australia similarly contributed at least 683 troops to General Cameron's available forces during 1863. These soldiers should also be seen alongside those supplied during 1860, many of whom had not been returned to their former Australian stations after the conclusion of the Taranaki War. The following breakdown of effective Army strengths in Australia and New Zealand during 1860–69 clearly shows the ebb and flow of troops back and forth across the Tasman during 1860–61 and 1863–64. Totals in 1867 also show the withdrawal of the bulk of imperial troops from New Zealand, and the return of garrison strengths in the Australian colonies. Further figures into 1869 reveal the diminution of imperial garrisons throughout Australasia in accordance with the British government's decision to withdraw all such forces; their total removal was completed in 1870.[7]

Effective Army strengths in Australia and New Zealand, 1860–69

Year	Australia	New Zealand
1860	1695	1120
1861	1044	4451 (including Royal Marines & Naval Brigade)
1862	1154	5708
1863	1000	5275
1864	369	10,336
1865	405	10,036
1866	359	6692
1867	1651	2820
1868	1901	911
1869	994	797

Similarly, the bulk of the Royal Navy vessels available on the Australia Station headquartered at Sydney were heavily involved in New Zealand – supplying an additional force of many hundreds of sailors and Royal Marines who were utilised on land and at sea. Australia was quite clearly a major supplier of imperial and colonial manpower to New Zealand's war effort during 1863–64. These Australian-derived imperial soldiers and military settlers were integral components of the outcome to the various campaigns that took place not only during 1863–64, but also through into 1866–67.

The picture that emerges is of an integrated Australasian effort to maintain and provide the logistics for the actual war in New Zealand and the subsequent division of Maori lands. These were never just New Zealand wars. They were wars fought by British settlers in *all* of the Australasian colonies. Commissariat supplies, transport, and finances all depended on these colonies. It is reasonable therefore to conclude that the British and colonial New Zealand wars of the early 1860s could not have been progressed successfully without the proximity of, and support from, the Australian colonies.

During the early 1860s the Australian colonies were stripped of their imperial forces to defend their sister colony across the Tasman. Despite fears that this left them vulnerable to attack, no major problems occurred and the small numbers remaining were able to adequately perform the required guard and ceremonial duties. If circumstances had been different – if the United States or a European nation, say, had chosen these years of vulnerability to attack any major Australian port – the colonists would have been defenceless. However, the events unfolding in New Zealand were considered momentous enough to justify the risk.

The New Zealand crisis and the Australian response, 1868–1869

The period 1868–69 marks the end of direct Australian involvement in wars in New Zealand, although many personnel from Australia continued to serve in the colony's Armed Constabulary and other volunteer or militia forces. While Australia did not supply the logistic or commissariat material, or imperial troops, it had during the early- to mid-1860s, it remained the place from which vessels of the Royal Navy were victualled while on station in New Zealand waters throughout the continuing turmoil.

However, it is from within the ranks of the Armed Constabulary that significant Australian involvement, especially the Melbourne recruitment of personnel – the last specifically targeted Australian recruits – continued to prove Australia's importance to New Zealand manpower requirements. Captain Stack enlisted the services of 205 men who were despatched to Wellington in five contingents. These New Zealand recruiting activities, although rekindling some of the criticisms earlier levelled at Colonel Pitt's military settler recruiting, were nonetheless an overall success in Melbourne. Although this mission only sought 200 men, 205 were enrolled, and it should not be forgotten that far more came forward offering their services but were rejected on medical or other grounds.

The political situation, both with respect to imperial relations and the expectations of colonial self-reliance throughout Australasia, demanded that New Zealand ride out this renewed crisis. Despite the severity of New Zealand's internal strife, the imperial authorities maintained their withdrawal of all Army regiments from Australasia. However, Australian colonial governments continued to provide assistance by maintaining legislation prohibiting exports of warlike stores. Albeit an indirect involvement, such actions were greatly appreciated by New Zealand authorities. Despite limited overall Australian support, calls for imperial troops to be despatched once more resounded throughout the Australian colonies, as did expressions to volunteer for service. As before, Australian colonials were clearly concerned about affairs unfolding across the Tasman, which in turn reaffirmed the crimson thread of kinship uniting Australasia throughout the conflicts that arose during the 1840s and 1860s, and again reinforcing the significance of Australian involvement throughout that period.

Australia, New Zealand, and issues of memory and forgetting the wars

Remembrance of the Australian involvement in the New Zealand wars was lost early to the collective memories of people on both sides of the Tasman. But why was this so? One reason is that no colonial or British regiments returned to Australia after service in the 1860s. Of course, some Australian-enlisted or -derived military settlers and their families drifted back to Australian colonies as individuals or small groups from the late 1860s into the 1870s and thereafter. The military settler scheme was largely a failure, and few were able to make a success of their land grants, so many either sold up or walked off their lands and sought other means. Many returned to Australian family or friends, or else tried their luck in other colonial locations or endeavours. However, for the 12th and 40th Regiments, long resident in Australian colonies, the end of their tours of service in New Zealand during 1866–67 did not see them return to their former Australian garrisons. Although many in Australia looked upon the men of these particular regiments as 'their' troops, with numerous family ties and friendships forged, such relationships were severed as these two units were ordered back to England. Despite many of the men using this opportunity to take their discharge and settle in Australia or New Zealand, they, like the military settlers, returned as individuals or small groups. As a result, there was little public acclaim and fanfare to welcome either these former imperial soldiers or the military settlers back – a far cry from the spectacle and public turnouts frequently attending their departure from Australia at the beginning of their war service in New Zealand.

Certainly, the place of the 12th and 40th was taken by new detachments from other regiments such as the 50th, 14th, and finally the 18th, but these were fresh faces, and although their ranks were still filled with veterans of the New Zealand or other wars, their stay in Australia was short-lived. The traditions, experiences, and memory of their involvement were not afforded time to be fully incorporated into colonial society as had been the experience of their imperial predecessors. By early 1870, as regimental entities, they had departed Australian shores – though again, many soldiers from these latter regiments took their discharges during 1866 through to early 1870. Former 'redcoats' were to be a common feature throughout colonial Australia and New Zealand, and their legacy and involvement in the social and economic fabric of their respective colonies should not be underestimated.

There are, however, exceptions to this pattern, one of which is clearly evident in the return of Major-General Pratt and his staff to the colony of Victoria in 1861 aboard HMCS *Victoria* after the termination of the Taranaki War. Victorian society hailed 'their' general, and the officers and crew of the *Victoria*, as heroes and victors, and they were fêted accordingly. The role and service of this Victorian warship in the Taranaki War has been remembered at times, but rarely in the context of the broader Australian involvement in the New Zealand wars. And although an important component, the service of the *Victoria* is but one of many elements of Australian involvement, which in sum provide an effective picture of the scale and importance of the complex support New Zealand actually received. Other earlier exceptions, too, can be viewed through the ongoing garrison stays in Australia of regiments such as the 99th and 96th in the late 1840s into the 1850s. These units did start to commemorate their service and losses in the wars of 1845–46, and events such as Ruapekepeka Day were celebrated, and the memorial raised by the 99th in Hobart is an enduring legacy of the first wars – but again, the departure of these regiments to other postings saw the traditions and memories depart or fade, despite the fact that many veterans of these units discharged and remained in Australasia as settlers.

Memory, or the lack of memory, plays a significant part in downplaying Australian involvement in New Zealand's wars. The colonial and imperial troops who departed Australian shores for the wars across the Tasman generally did not return, or at least did not return en masse or as units to Australia, and this rapidly led to the passing of memory of their service. Australia's involvement in New Zealand is in fact unique when compared with those later generations who went to the Sudan (1885), South Africa (1899–1902), and World Wars I and II. The men and women involved in these later conflicts returned home and received

British Army officer graves following the end of conflict in the Bay of Islands, from the *Illustrated London News*, 16 January 1847.

British military cemetery at Tauranga, in the Bay of Plenty, following the disastrous assault on Gate Pa, from the *Illustrated London News*, 30 July 1864.

public thanks and acknowledgement for their services and sacrifices. In the case of the New Zealand wars, the Australian departures, actions and casualties never received fanfare on return, and so were quickly lost to Australia's collective memory. While in New Zealand itself, the scale of Australian manpower and other support has been largely ignored or passed over as irrelevant.

The tyranny of distance has also played a role in the manner of mourning for dead in the New Zealand wars. The Australian colonial- or imperial-derived casualties were often forgotten, burial sites lost, and few, if any, visited by family or friends from home. Therefore, in the Australian context, no tradition of public memory emerged in relation to those lost in these wars, despite the actual number of casualties involved. The development of separate Australian and New Zealand national identities, especially post-1915, entrenched this historical myopia. In Australia the creation and evolution of the Australian War Memorial, and its emphasis on triumphalism and sacrifice, and perpetration of the World War I mythology of Anzac, has not permitted any effective place for the history or memory of Australia's frontier conflicts, nor Australians' involvement across the Tasman. Australia's costly experience during World War I led to the rise of a fervent martial nationalism, wherein blood sacrifice has helped define the nation's people and identity. Australia today still has a plethora of war memorials in most suburbs, towns and cities, with many still retaining some of the thousands of war prize weapons that were distributed throughout its urban and rural municipalities. In placing considerable emphasis on the 'Anzac tradition', little room is left to reflect on earlier military involvements, and even less so on frontier conflict and warfare.

But on this notion of Anzac as viewed today in Australia, the New Zealand component is often ignored or forgotten. Similarly, contemporary Australian and New Zealand military forces rarely serve together operationally, though the term Anzac is often liberally bandied about in connection with news or discussions about Australia's overseas military or peacekeeping operations. But it was in the New Zealand wars that a true sense of a united war effort and participation by colonists and imperial representatives on both sides of the Tasman marked the real beginnings of a tradition that became more formally recognised in later conflicts.

Brothers in arms

As emphasised from the beginning, this history has not been an attempt to detail in any specificity the military campaigns and events of New Zealand's wars. The investigation has been designed to explore and confirm the nature and extent of the Australian involvement as defining elements in the overall story of these struggles. New Zealand was Australia's first external war involvement, during which its colonies proved to be highly capable logistical staging points for the imperial and colonial might that was marshalled against the Maori throughout these conflicts. Apart from providing this base for planning military operations and ensuring re-supply, the Australian colonies were also the place from which New Zealand quickly sourced imperial troops as well as colonial recruits for its grand military settler schemes. The Australian contribution to personnel for the

LOVING GREETINGS TO
DEAR MOTHER.

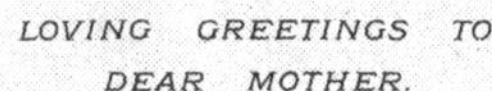

Now many miles between us lie
How clearly I can see
The thoughts and wishes of your heart,
Born of your love for me:

I did not think how strong it was
Till duty called me here,
Nor weighed as carefully my love
For you when you were near;

Your love, a searchlight! shows me how
You wish the absent one
The best of Courage, Hope and Health,
That Duty be "Well Done."

So may it be! and, when we greet
At meeting-time in store,
Our kisses then will be more sweet
Than any given before.

George's last message to his Mother.

In Affectionate Remembrance of our dear Son and Brother, T. GEORGE CLARK, who died of wounds in France, September 7, 1916.
Aged 22 Years and 8 Months.

Memorial card for Australian soldier Corporal T.G. Clark 12th (and later 52nd) Battalion. Clark was wounded in action at the landings at Gallipoli in April 1915, then later was severely wounded in France and died of wounds in September 1916. This Anzac soldier's great grandfather was a sergeant-major who had fought at Waterloo, and his grandfather had served 18½ years in the British Army before taking his discharge after service in the New Zealand wars. (*Author's Research Collection*).

Imperial Commissariat alone is one (largely ignored) element essential to the scale and operations undertaken during 1863–64. The Australian colonies truly played an enormous role throughout all the operations against the Maori, and without their input the course of these wars would have been more prolonged and their outcomes most likely very different.

As part of this complex story, there occurred considerable debate in the Australian colonies over the nature of the wars raging on the other side of the Tasman, including expressions of concern for soldier and settler families, and even the plight or future of the Maori people. But what this discussion shows above all is the existence of an Australian home front running parallel to the military front in New Zealand – an Australian home front, until now, largely ignored in writings on the New Zealand wars. The present investigation has endeavoured to convey an appreciation of the diverse array of Australian involvement throughout these struggles, and in turn direct attention to the true origins of an Australian–New Zealand military history tradition. Despite all that continues to be written about the nature and experience of Anzac – that shared Australian–New Zealand war experience said to have been forged on the bloody shores of Gallipoli in 1915 – it seems that little recognition is accorded the earlier period wherein the origins of this unity or common ground were actually defined. And more importantly, the New Zealand wars in turn not only provide a point of true genesis where Australia and New Zealand meet militarily, but have significant social and economic ramifications. These conjoined beginnings helped shape the progress and development of the two societies which emerged on either side of the Tasman by the early twentieth century. The experience of World War I and its aftermath can in fact be said to have capitalised on the foundations laid down the previous century. The New Zealand wars – that period in which Australia and New Zealand as '*blood brothers*' joined in shared military struggles – should not be viewed in New Zealand isolation, but more broadly by having an Australian component that must be reincorporated into the way the histories of both nations are perceived.

APPENDIX A

Conditions for Military Settler Service for the Province of Taranaki, Gazetted on 6 July 1863

Colonial Secretary's Office,
Auckland, 6th July, 1863

HIS Excellency the Governor has been pleased to direct the publication, for general information, of the following Conditions upon which land situated between Omata and Tataraimaka, in the Province of Taranaki, will be granted to settlers.

Alfred Domett

NEW ZEALAND

CONDITIONS upon which land situate between Omata and Tataraimaka, in the Province of Taranaki, will be granted to settlers:-

1. Settlements will be surveyed and marked out at the expense of the Government.
2. Each settlement will comprise not less than 100 town allotments and 100 farm sections.
3. A stockade on the most eligible site in each settlement will be erected at the expense of the Government.
4. A town will be laid out around or as near as conveniently may be to the stockade in one acre allotments.
5. Farms will be laid out around, or as near as conveniently may be to the town, in sections of 50 acres each.
6. Every settler under these conditions will be entitled to one town allotment and one farm section.
7. Priority of choice will be determined by lot.
8. No man above the age of 45 years will be accepted, and every applicant will be subject to an examination by an officer appointed by the Governor, and must produce such certificates of good health, character, and general fitness for the service, as such officer shall require.

9. Each accepted applicant will be provided, at the expense of the Government, with a steerage passage to New Plymouth. Before embarkation, he will be required to sign a declaration and agreement to the effect that he understands and will be bound by and fulfil these conditions.
10. On arrival at New Plymouth, he will be enrolled and required to serve in the Taranaki Militia. He will be entitled to pay and rations accordingly until he is authorised by the Government to take possession of his land, when he will be relieved of 'actual service'.
11. After taking possession he will be entitled to receive rations, free of cost for twelve months, upon the same scale as supplied to Her Majesty's troops; he will be allowed to retain possession, as a militiaman, of his arms and accoutrements, and he will be supplied with ammunition for use according to militia regulations.
12. No settler after taking possession will be permitted during the first three years after his arrival at New Plymouth to absent himself from his settlement for more than one calendar month in any one year without leave of the Governor first obtained.
13. During such three years he will be liable to be trained and exercised as other Militia men; and whenever a portion only of the Taranaki Militia shall be called out for actual service, each settler will be deemed to be a Volunteer Militiaman, and will be required to serve as such. During such service he will be entitled to the same pay, rations and allowance as other Militiamen.
14. On the expiration of three years from the day of his arrival at New Plymouth each settler, having fulfilled the conditions, but not otherwise, will be entitled to a Crown Grant of the Town allotment and farm section allotted to him; and will thenceforth be subject only to the same Militia services as other colonists.
15. Any settler desiring to leave his settlement will be permitted to do so on providing a substitute approved of by the Government. Such substitute will be subject to the same liabilities and entitled to the same privileges as the settler whose place he takes.
16. In case of the death of any settler before he shall become entitled to his Crown Grant, the land allotted to him will be at the disposal of the Government for the location of another settler under these conditions or for any other purpose, but the value of any improvements made thereon by the deceased settler will be determined by valuation, and the amount paid by the Government to such person (if any) as the deceased settler shall have appointed by writing to receive the same.

FORM OF DECLARATION AND AGREEMENT

I do hereby declare that I fully understand the 'conditions' hereunto annexed, and I do engage and agree to be bound thereby, and punctually on my part to fulfil all the terms thereof.

APPENDIX B

Conditions for Military Settler Service for the Waikato District of the Province of Auckland, Gazetted on 5 August 1863

VOLUNTEER MILITIA SETTLERS

Colonial Secretary's Office,
Auckland, 3rd August, 1863

His Excellency the Governor has been pleased to direct the publication, for general information, of the following Conditions upon which land situated in the Waikato District, will be granted to Volunteer Militiamen in the Province of Auckland.

Alfred Domett

NEW ZEALAND

CONDITIONS upon which land in the Waikato Country, in the Province of Auckland, will be granted to volunteer militiamen willing to perform the after-mentioned military services:-

1. No man above the age of 40 years will be accepted, and every applicant will be subject to an examination by an officer appointed by the Governor, and must produce such certificates of good character, health, and general fitness for the service, as such officer shall require.
2. Each accepted applicant will be required to sign a declaration and agreement to the effect that he understands and will be bound by and fulfil these conditions.
3. He will be enrolled and required to serve in the Militia in the Province of Auckland, and will be entitled to pay, rations, and allowances accordingly, until he is authorised by the Government to take possession of his land, when he will be relieved from 'actual service'.
4. Settlements will be surveyed and marked out at the expense of the Government.
5. Each settlement will comprise not less than 100 allotments and 100 farm sections.

6. A stockade on the most eligible site in each settlement will be erected at the expense of the Government.
7. A town will be laid out around or as near as conveniently may be to the stockade, in one acre allotments.
8. Farms will be laid out around or as near as conveniently may be to the town. The size of the farm sections allotted to each will be according to his rank in the Militia:

For a Field Officer	400 acres
For a Captain	300 acres
For a Surgeon	250 acres
For a Subaltern	200 acres
For a Sergeant	80 acres
For a Corporal	60 acres
For a Private	50 acres

9. Every settler under these conditions, who upon being relieved from actual service, receives a certificate of good conduct, will be entitled to one town allotment and one farm section.
10. Priority of choice for each rank will be determined by lot.
11. After taking possession he will be entitled to receive rations, free of cost for twelve months, upon the same scale as supplied to Her Majesty's troops; he will be allowed to retain possession, as a militiaman, of his arms and accoutrements, and he will be supplied with ammunition for use according to militia regulations.
12. No settler after taking possession will be permitted during the first three years after his enrolment under these conditions to absent himself from his settlement for more than one calendar month in any one year, without the leave of the Governor first obtained.
13. During such three years he will be liable to be trained and exercised as other Militiamen; and whenever a portion only of the Militia shall be called out for actual service, each settler will be deemed to be a Volunteer Militiaman, and will be required to serve as such within the Province. During such service he will be entitled to the same pay, rations and allowances as other Militiamen.
14. On the expiration of three years from his enrolment each settler, having fulfilled the conditions, but not otherwise, will be entitled to a Crown Grant of the Town allotment and farm section to him; and will thenceforth be subject only to the same Militia service as other colonists.
15. Any settler will be permitted to dispose of his land to any person approved of by the Government; and such person undertaking to be subject to the same liabilities will be entitled to the same privileges as the settler whose place he takes.
16. In case of the death of any settler before he shall have become entitled to his Crown Grant, the land to which he is entitled will be granted to his wife or children, or to such other person as he shall by writing appoint, or it may be taken by the Government for the location of another settler under these conditions, or for any other purpose;

but the value thereof in such latter case will be determined by valuation, and the amount paid by the Government to the settler's widow, or children, or other person appointed as aforesaid.

FORM OF DECLARATION AND AGREEMENT

I do hereby declare that I fully understand the 'Conditions' hereunto annexed, and I do engage and agree to be bound thereby, and punctually on my part to fulfil all the terms thereof.

The pay of the militia and volunteers serving in the Province of Auckland (apart from rations and other allowances provided), was also set out for general information in the *New Zealand Gazette* on 5 August 1863:

Captains	11s. 7d. per diem
Lieutenants	6s. 6d. per diem
Ensigns	5s. 3d. per diem
Sergeants	3s. 6d. per diem
Corporals	3s. per diem
Privates	2s. 6d. per diem

APPENDIX C

Conditions for Military Settler Service for the Land Situated in the Northern Island of New Zealand, Gazetted on 12 September 1863

SETTLERS GENERALLY

Colonial Secretary's Office,
Auckland, 3rd August, 1863

His Excellency the Governor has been pleased to direct the publication, for general information, of the following Conditions upon which land situated in the Northern Island of New Zealand, will be granted to settlers willing to perform the after mentioned Military services.

Alfred Domett

NEW ZEALAND

CONDITIONS upon which land in the Northern Island, will be granted to settlers willing to perform the after mentioned Military services:-

1. No man above the age of 40 years will be accepted, and every applicant will be subject to an examination by an officer appointed by the Governor, and must produce such certificates of good character, health, and general fitness for the service, as such officer shall require.
2. Each accepted applicant, if not already in the Northern Island, will be provided with a free passage to a port to be designated, by an agent of the Governor. Before embarkation, he will be required to sign a declaration and agreement to the effect that he understands and will be bound by and fulfil these conditions.
3. On arrival the men will be enrolled in the Militia for services in the Northern Island of the Colony, and formed into companies; constituted as nearly as may be as follows:-

1 Captain
1 Subaltern
5 Sergeants
5 Corporals
100 Privates.

4. Each man according to his rank will be entitled to pay, rations, and allowances, until he is authorised by the Government to take possession of his land, when he will be relieved from 'Actual service'.
5. Settlements will be surveyed and marked out at the expense of the Government, in such localities in the Northern Island as the Government may select for that purpose.
6. Each settlement will comprise not less than 100 town allotments, and 100 farm sections.
7. A stockade on the most eligible site in each settlement will be erected at the expense of the Government.
8. A town will be laid out around, or as near as conveniently may be to the stockade in one acre allotments.
9. Farms will be laid out around, or as near as conveniently may be to the town. The size of the farm section allotted to each will be according to his rank in the Militia.

For a Field Officer	400 acres
For a Captain	300 acres
For a Surgeon	250 acres
For a Subaltern	200 acres
For a Sergeant	80 acres
For a Corporal	60 acres
For a Private	50 acres

10. Every settler under these conditions, who upon being relieved from actual service receives a certificate of good conduct, will be entitled to one town allotment and one farm section.
11. Priority of choice for each rank will be determined by lot.
12. After taking possession he will be entitled to receive rations, free of cost for twelve months, upon the same scale as supplied to Her Majesty's troops; he will be allowed to retain possession, as a militiaman, of his arms and accoutrements, and he will be supplied with ammunition for use according to militia regulations.
13. No settler after taking possession will be permitted during the first three years after his enrolment in the Militia to absent himself from his settlement for more than one calendar month in any one year without the leave of the Governor first obtained.
14. During such three years he will be liable to be trained and exercised as other militiamen; and whenever a portion only of the Militia shall be called out for actual service, each settler will be deemed to be a Volunteer Militiaman, and will

be required to serve as such anywhere that may be required in the Northern Island of the Colony. During such service he will be entitled to the same pay, rations and allowances as other Militiamen.

15. On the expiration of three years from his enrolment, each settler, having fulfilled the conditions, but not otherwise, will be entitled to a Crown Grant of the town allotment and farm section allotted to him; and will thenceforth be subject only to the same Militia services as other colonists.
16. Any settler will be permitted to dispose of his land to any person approved of by the Government; and such person undertaking to be subject to the same liabilities will be entitled to the same privileges as the settler whose place he takes.
17. In case of the death of any settler, before he shall have become entitled to his Crown Grant, the land to which he is entitled will be granted to his wife or children, or to such other persons as he shall by writing appoint; or it may be taken for the location of another settler under these conditions, or for any other purpose, but the value thereof in such latter case will be determined by valuation, and the amount paid by the Government to the settler's widow or children, or other person appointed as aforesaid.

FORM OF DECLARATION AND AGREEMENT

I do hereby declare that I fully understand the 'Conditions' hereunto annexed, and I do engage and agree to be bound thereby, and punctually on my part to fulfil all the terms thereof.

NOTE.– The pay of the Militia and Volunteers serving in New Zealand is as follows:

Captains	11s. 7d. per diem
Lieutenants	6s. 6d. per diem
Ensigns	5s. 3d. per diem
Sergeants	3s. 6d. per diem
Corporals	3s. per diem
Privates	2s. 6d. per diem

– With Rations and other Allowances.

APPENDIX D

Australian-enlisted (or -derived) Taranaki or Waikato Military Settler Casualties, 1863–69

This cannot be viewed as a concise list of Australian-derived military settler casualties, because of difficulties identifying the origins of many New Zealand colonial troops. Further individuals in this category are likely to still come to light.[1]

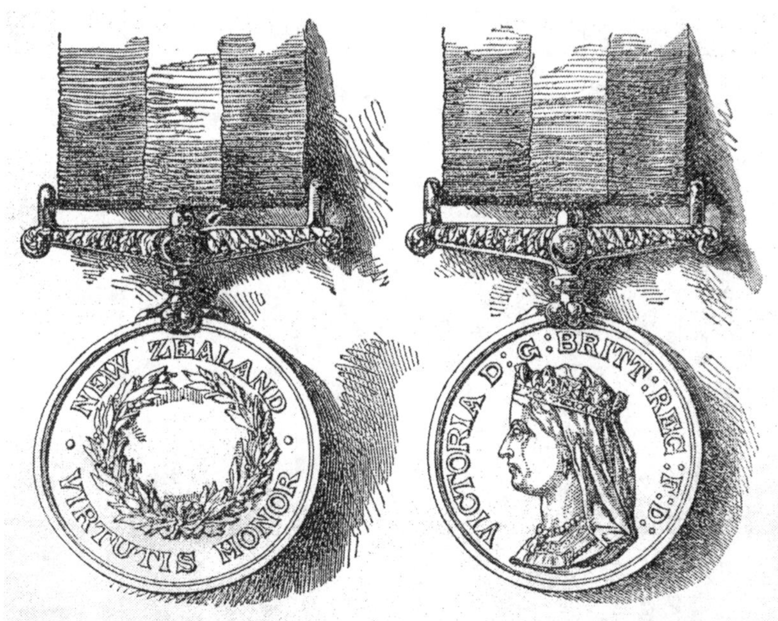

The war medal instituted in 1869 for service in the New Zealand wars, from the *Illustrated London News*, 15 January 1870.

Name & Enlistment Details	Service & Other Details	Date & Cause of Casualty
1. John Spencer Perceval. Lieutenant (& former 55th Regiment officer). Enlisted in Bendigo, Victoria in August 1863. Departed Melbourne with Lieutenant Dunn in command of military settler contingent per *Caduseus* (8 September) and arrived Auckland, 25 September 1863.[2]	No. 9 Company, 1st Waikato Regiment. (Perceval's name is incorrectly listed on the memorial erected by the officers and men of the 1st Waikato Regiment in memory of their comrades 'who fell fighting the rebel natives at Mauku', located in the churchyard of St John's Anglican Church, Drury. William Fraser of the Victorian Contingent reported that a tablet had been ordered in Melbourne 'to be erected to the memory of the first members of the force who have died in the war').[3]	Killed in action, 23 October 1863, Wheeler's Farm on Titi Hill, near Mauku Stockade. Buried 26 October in the burial ground of the Drury Anglican Church, South Auckland.
2. Michael Power. Corporal. No enlistment details recorded, but believed enlisted in 1st Waikato Regiment, Bendigo, Victoria, August 1863.[4]	No. 9 Company, 1st Waikato Regiment. ('Corporal Power . . . who was fighting near Lieutenant Perceval, had bayoneted a Maori, and while thus situated he observed another coming upon him with a tomahawk, and instantly released his bayonet and shot the man, but had in the meantime received a ball himself, which, within a few minutes . . . resulted in his death.')[5]	Killed in action, 23 October 1863, Wheeler's Farm on Titi Hill, near Mauku Stockade. Buried 26 October in the burial ground of the Drury Anglican Church, South Auckland.
3. William Beswick. Private. (Also as 'Beysick', 'Besick', & 'Beyssick'.) No enlistment details recorded, but believed enlisted in 1st Waikato Regiment in Bendigo, Victoria, August 1863.[6]	No. 9 Company, 1st Waikato Regiment.	Killed in action, 23 October 1863, Wheeler's Farm on Titi Hill, near Mauku Stockade. Buried 26 October in the burial ground of the Drury Anglican Church, South Auckland.

Name & Enlistment Details	Service & Other Details	Date & Cause of Casualty
4. William Williamson. Private. No enlistment details recorded, but believed enlisted in 1st Waikato Regiment, Bendigo, Victoria, August 1863. One source confirms Williamson arrived from Melbourne per *Caduseus*. The *Caduseus* departed Melbourne, 8 September 1863, with Lieutenants Dunn and Perceval in command. Because Williamson, Perceval, Power and Beysick were all serving in the same company, presumably they all arrived together as part of the contingent aboard *Caduseus*.[7]	No. 9 Company, 1st Waikato Regiment.	Killed in action, 23 October 1863, Wheeler's Farm on Titi Hill, near Mauku Stockade. Buried 26 October in the burial ground of the Drury Anglican Church, South Auckland. Robert Williamson of Carlton, Victoria, later claimed Private Williamson's New Zealand War Medal.
5. Thomas Heritage. Private. 'He was about thirty-five years of age, and arrived in Auckland by the Star of India, from Melbourne. I understand he has a wife residing in Castlemaine.'[8]	No. 7 Company, 1st Waikato Regiment.	Died 4 November 1863 after a period 'in the hospital belonging to the Waikato volunteers' from bronchitis 'brought on by exposure and by sleeping in a damp tent'.
6. Alexander McHale. Private & as Trooper. (Also as 'Edward McHale'.) 1st Waikato Regiment & Colonial Defence Force. Originally enlisted in 1st Waikato Regiment, September 1863, Melbourne, Victoria and departed per *Star of India*.[9]	1st Waikato Regiment (to January 1864), before transferring to No. 2 Troop, Auckland Colonial Defence Force (cavalry).	Killed in action, Rangiaowhia, 21 February 1864.

Name & Enlistment Details	Service & Other Details	Date & Cause of Casualty
7. William Bush. Private. Enlisted Taranaki Military Settlers, [January 1864?]. (No other details.)[10]	'Melbourne Contingent', Taranaki Military Settlers.	Died in hospital, 31 March 1864.
8. John Banks. Corporal. (Also as 'H. Banks'.) Enlisted Taranaki Military Settlers, 20 January 1864, Victoria.[11]	No. 9 Company, 'Melbourne Contingent', Taranaki Military Settlers.	Killed in action (gunshot wound through abdomen and body decapitated), Te Ahuahu, 6 April 1864. Buried New Plymouth. In the ambush of the detachment of the 57th Regiment and Taranaki Military Settlers commanded by Captain Lloyd, 57th Regiment, at Te Ahuahu on 6 April, there were four confirmed wounded 'Melbourne Contingent' Taranaki Military Settlers listed amongst the casualties: Colour-Sergeant George Bentley, 'gunshot wound in arm, bone fractured, severe', No. 12 Company (Regt. No. 407, Sgt. 'George Bartley', enlisted 18 January 1864, 'Creswicks Creek', Victoria, and departed per *Gresham*); Corporal Robert Stokes, 'gunshot wound right shoulder, slight', No. 12 Company (Regt. No. 66, enlisted 18 January 1864, Ballarat, Victoria, and departed per *Brilliant*); Private Francis Thomas Tomlins, 'gunshot wound upper part thigh, severe', No. 12 Company (Regt. No. 898, & roll records '12th May 1864. On Furlough to Melbourne', presumably returning to Victoria on account of wound); Private Edward Whatmore, 'gunshot wound calf of leg, slight', No. 12 Company (Regt. No. 901, enlisted 21 January 1864, Ballarat, Victoria, and departed per *Brilliant*); and Private James M'Kenna, 'gunshot wound through left side (ball since extracted), dangerous', No. 7 Company (Regt. No. 371, 'James McKenna', though reported as being one of the Victorians was actually 'Otago Contingent', enlisted 31 December 1863, Canterbury).

Name & Enlistment Details	Service & Other Details	Date & Cause of Casualty
9. John Gallagher. Private. Enlisted Taranaki Military Settlers, January 1864, Victoria.[12]	No. 9 Company, 'Melbourne Contingent', Taranaki Military Settlers.	Killed in action, Te Ahuahu, 6 April 1864. Initially listed as missing, but his mutilated remains were later found. His body was decapitated and suffered other mutilations indicating ritual cannibalism. Buried New Plymouth.
10. Charles Hartley. Private. (Also as 'H. Hartley'.) Enlisted Taranaki Military Settlers, January 1864, Victoria, aged 22. Trade or calling: labourer.[13]	No. 9 Company, 'Melbourne Contingent', Taranaki Military Settlers.	Killed in action (gunshot wound through pelvis and body decapitated), Te Ahuahu, 6 April 1864. Buried New Plymouth.
11. James Neagle. Private. (Also as 'Neagles'.) Enlisted Taranaki Military Settlers, [January?] 1864. (No other details.)[14]	'Melbourne Contingent', Taranaki Military Settlers.	Killed in action (gunshot wound through abdomen and three through head), Te Ahuahu, 6 April 1864. Buried New Plymouth.
12. John Silas Brown. Private. Regt. No. 121, 2nd Waikato Regiment. Enlisted 21 August 1863, Sydney, NSW. Trade or calling: policeman.[15]	2nd Waikato Regiment.	Died 24 April 1864, Te Awamutu (cause not stated).
13. William Knee. Private. Enlisted Taranaki Military Settlers, [January?] 1864. (No other details.)[16]	'Melbourne Contingent', Taranaki Military Settlers.	Died in 'Hospital A.P.' [Auckland Province], 5 June 1864.
14. Walter Vernon Herford. Major. Adelaide solicitor & former captain in Kent Rifles (an Adelaide volunteer unit). Departed for New Zealand on own initiative in (October?) 1863.[17]	3rd Waikato Regiment, & Imperial Commissariat Transport Corps.	Died at Otahuhu, 28 June 1864, from wounds sustained on 2 April at Orakau. Buried at the Otahuhu Anglican Church. Herford's widow, Annie, and two daughters, of Adelaide, South Australia, later claimed his New Zealand War Medal, and received a military pension from the New Zealand government.

Name & Enlistment Details	Service & Other Details	Date & Cause of Casualty
15. William Simpson. Private. (Possibly refers to Regt. No. 853, 'William Simpson'. Enlisted in the 2nd Waikato Regiment on 11 September 1863, Sydney, NSW. Trade or calling: seaman.)[18]	3rd Waikato Regiment.	Accidental death, late June 1864: 'On the beach at Small's Point, the mangled body of a young man was found . . . It was recognized as that of William Simpson, a private in the 3rd Waikato Militia. It is supposed the deceased must have met with his death the previous night whilst wandering about . . . in a state of liquor, and that he must have fallen over the cliff.'[19]
16. Augustus Frederick Smith. Captain (and former imperial officer, 99th Regiment officer, & later captain in Hobart Town Volunteer Artillery).	Though not confirmed as a military settler officer appointment, Smith departed Hobart with the 3rd contingent of Tasmanian military settler volunteers per *Reliance*, 17 December 1863. He left 'with a view to obtaining active military employment, [and] is about to be entrusted with . . . command of artillery . . . the result of a professional examination . . . that his qualifications . . . entitle him to this important mark of confidence'.[20]	It was reported in July 1864 that Captain A.F. Smith had recently died 'from inflammation of the brain, in one of the military camps in the neighbourhood of Auckland, New Zealand'.[21]
17. James Black. Ensign. (Presumably refers to Regt. No. 58, Sergeant 'James Blake'. Enlisted 22 January 1864, Melbourne, Victoria, and departed per *Gresham*. Trade or calling: compositor.)[22]	No. 2 Company, 'Melbourne Contingent', Taranaki Military Settlers.	The death of a 'long resident in Geelong, appears in the *Taranaki Herald* . . . [30 July 1864] . . . James Black . . . [Ensign, No. 2 Company], Military Settlers, died after only twenty four hours illness . . . from inflammation of the stomach. The deceased officer was buried with military honours . . . yesterday afternoon.'[23]
18. Edward Land. Private. Regt. No. 216, 4th Waikato Regiment. Enlisted 3 February 1864, Sydney, NSW, and departed per *Kate*. Trade or calling: labourer.[24]	4th Waikato Regiment.	Died 'in the ranks', 3 October 1864 (cause not stated).

Name & Enlistment Details	Service & Other Details	Date & Cause of Casualty
19. Nicholas Courtney. Private. Regt. No. 534, 2nd Waikato Regiment. Enlisted 10 October 1863, Sydney, NSW. Trade or calling: soldier.[25]	2nd Waikato Regiment.	Died 'in the ranks' aged 37 years, 13 October 1864 (cause not stated).
20. Thomas Hull. Private. Regt. No. 558, 2nd Waikato Regiment. Enlisted on 10 October 1863, Sydney, NSW. Trade or calling: iron worker.[26]	2nd Waikato Regiment.	Died 'in the ranks' aged 19 years, 10 January 1865 (cause not stated).
21. John Main. Private. Regt. No. 88, 3rd Waikato Regiment. Enlisted 21 August 1863, Melbourne, Victoria. (Born 'Murray Basin'.)[27]	3rd Waikato Regiment.	Drowned at Ngaruawahia, aged 23, 12 March 1865.
22. Arthur Mateer. Private. (Also as 'Mateeo'.) Regt. No. 137, 4th Waikato Regiment. Enlisted 18 January 1864, Melbourne, Victoria, and departed per *Swiftsure*. Trade or calling: butcher.[28]	4th Waikato Regiment.	Died 17 March 1865, Onehunga Military Hospital, aged 27 (cause not stated).
23. James Bourke. Private. (Also as 'Burke'.) Regt. No. 6, 4th Waikato Regiment. Enlisted 18 January 1864, Melbourne, Victoria, and departed per *Swiftsure*. Trade or calling: labourer.[29]	4th Waikato Regiment.	Died 20 May 1865, aged 29 (cause not stated). 'Widow – Mary Craig Bourke.'

Name & Enlistment Details	Service & Other Details	Date & Cause of Casualty
24. Harry Mathews. Private. (Also as 'Henry Matthews'.) Regt. No. 757, 1st Waikato Regiment. Enlisted 1 September 1863, Melbourne, Victoria. Trade or calling: labourer.[30]	1st Waikato Regiment. ('He was one of the Melbourne Volunteers' known to James Bodell, another 'Melbourne Volunteer' in the 1st Waikato Regiment.)	Blown up and killed, 6 September 1865, while trying to extract powder out of unexploded 110-lb Armstrong artillery shell found near Gate Pa. Buried in the military cemetery, Tauranga.
25. Patrick Parsons. Private. Regt. No. 781, Taranaki Military Settlers. Enlisted 26 January 1864, Melbourne, Victoria, aged 35, and departed per *Gresham*. Trade or calling: labourer.[31]	No. 8 Company, 'Melbourne Contingent', Taranaki Military Settlers.	Killed in action, Te Tarata, Opotiki, 4 (also as 5) October 1865, while serving as part of the East Coast Expeditionary Force which included Nos. 8 & 10 Companies, Taranaki Military Settlers. Nos. 8 & 10 Companies, Taranaki Military Settlers, and the Patea Rangers, were involved on the East Coast of the North Island as part of the East Coast Expeditionary Force 1865–66. This included engagements at Te Tarata, Opotiki, 4 October 1865, and Marumaru (Omaruhakeke), Upper Wairoa (Hawke's Bay), 25 December 1865.[32]
26. Charles Ratsey. Private. (Also as 'Ratsay'.) Regt. No. 786, Taranaki Military Settlers. Enlisted 23 January 1864, Melbourne, Victoria, aged 26, and departed per *Gresham*. Trade or calling: sailmaker.[33]	No. 8 Company, 'Melbourne Contingent', Taranaki Military Settlers.	Killed in action, Te Tarata, Opotiki, 4 (also as 5) October 1865, while serving as part of the East Coast Expeditionary Force which included Nos. 8 & 10 Companies, Taranaki Military Settlers.
27. Patrick Swan. Private. Regt. No. 412, 3rd Waikato Regiment. Enlisted 6 October 1863, Hobart Town, Tasmania. Trade or calling: groom.[34]	3rd Waikato Regiment.	Drowned 25 October 1865, 'river not stated', Auckland Province.

Name & Enlistment Details	Service & Other Details	Date & Cause of Casualty
28. John Jones. Private. Believed to be Charles John Jones, Regt. No. 444, Taranaki Military Settlers. Enrolled 18 January 1864, Melbourne, Victoria, aged 34, and departed per *Gresham*. Trade or calling: plumber, painter and glazer.[35]	'Melbourne Contingent', Taranaki Military Settlers.	Killed in action, Marumaru (Omaruhakeke), inland Wairoa, Hawke's Bay, 25 December 1865, while serving as part of the East Coast Expeditionary Force which included Nos. 8 & 10 Companies, Taranaki Military Settlers.
29. Patrick Walsh. Private. Regt. No. 707, 3rd Waikato Regiment. Enlisted 24 October 1864, Hobart Town, Tasmania. Trade or calling: labourer.[36]	3rd Waikato Regiment.	Died 'in ranks' aged 37, no date recorded (cause not stated).
30. Thomas Harris. Private. Regt. No. 508, 1st Waikato Regiment. Enlisted 1 September 1863, Melbourne, Victoria. Trade or calling: miner.[37]	3rd Waikato Regiment.	Died aged 31 years in Auckland Lunatic Asylum (no date or cause specified).
31. Henry Gilmore. Private. (Also as 'Gilmour'.) Regt. No. 267, 4th Waikato Regiment. Enlisted 15 January 1864, Melbourne, Victoria, and departed per *Thomas Fletcher*. Trade or calling: draper.[38]	4th Waikato Regiment.	Drowned 2 June 1866, Upper Waikato, Auckland Province.
32. Denis Spain. Private. Regt. No. 700, Taranaki Military Settlers. Enlisted 21 January 1864, Melbourne, Victoria, aged 20, and departed per *Gresham*. Trade or calling: coachman.[39]	No. 8 Company, 'Melbourne Contingent', Taranaki Military Settlers.	Accidentally killed in action during the attack on the village of Pokaikai, Patea District, 2 August 1866.[40] His mother, Maria Spain of Fitzroy, Victoria, claimed his New Zealand War Medal, and received a military pension of £20 per annum from the New Zealand government.

Name & Enlistment Details	Service & Other Details	Date & Cause of Casualty
33. Alfred J. Campbell. Private. 1st Waikato Regiment. Cannot ascertain with certainty whether this individual was an Australian enlistee, but is presumed to be one of the Australian enlistments in the 1st Waikato Regiment.[41]	1st Waikato Regiment. (At the time of his death, Campbell was a military settler resident of the Tauranga District.)	Murdered on or about 7 January 1867. Inquest held at Te Papa, 24 August 1867, determined that skeletal remains found 'in the bush' were that of military settler A.J. Campbell, and that he was murdered by Maori 'on or about the road from Waimapu to Orope', Tauranga.[42]
34. William Stevenson. Private. (Also as 'Stephenson'.) Regt. No. 989, 1st Waikato Regiment. Enlisted 2 September 1863, Melbourne, Victoria, and departed per *Caduseus*. Trade or calling: draper.[43]	1st Waikato Regiment.	Killed in action, 23 January 1867, Te Irihanga (Tauranga Bush Campaign). Buried 24 January, military cemetery, Tauranga.[44]
35. Denis Augustus Ward. Private. Regt. No. 123, 1st Waikato Regiment. Enlisted 25 August 1863, Melbourne, Victoria, and arrived per *Star of India*.[45]	1st Waikato Regiment.	Killed in action, 23 January 1867, Te Irihanga (Tauranga Bush Campaign). Buried 24 January, military cemetery, Tauranga.[46] 'Much sympathy is felt for the widow of Ward, who has left a family of four children. Ward was out on duty as a volunteer when shot. He was a man belonging to Captain Fraser's company in the 1st Waikato Regiment; but when his company got their fifty acres they went off pay, and he, being a married man with a family, could have declined falling in as a first-class militiamen: he went out as a volunteer.'

Name & Enlistment Details	Service & Other Details	Date & Cause of Casualty
36. Henry Jeffs. Private. (Also as 'Volunteer, Late 1st W. Reg.', when killed.) Regt. No. 589, 1st Waikato Regiment. Enlisted 1 September 1863, Melbourne, Victoria, aged 19.[47]	No. 8 Company, 1st Waikato Regiment.	Killed in action, 15 February 1867, Whakamarama (Tauranga Bush Campaign). Buried in military cemetery, Tauranga. J.S. Jeffs of Geelong, Victoria, made a claim for Private Jeffs' New Zealand War Medal.
37. Richard Fennessy. Constable. No. 3 Division, Armed Constabulary.	Formerly Regt. No. 632 'Melbourne Contingent', Taranaki Military Settlers. Enrolled 19 January 1864, Melbourne, Victoria, and departed per *Gresham*.	Killed in action, Te Ngutu o te Manu, 7 September 1868.
38. John O'Connor. Constable. No. 2 Division, Armed Constabulary. (Born 1844, Hobart, Tasmania.)	Formerly Regt. No. 780, 'Melbourne Contingent', Taranaki Military Settlers. Enrolled 19 January 1864, Melbourne, Victoria, and departed per *Gresham*.	Killed in action, Te Ngutu o te Manu, 7 September 1868.
39. Richard Walsh. Constable. Nos. 5 & 6 Divisions, Armed Constabulary.	Formerly Regt. No. 609, 2nd Waikato Regiment. Enrolled 10 October 1863, Sydney, NSW, and departed per *Kate*. Trade or calling: policeman.	Killed in action, Te Ngutu o te Manu, 7 September 1868.
40. William Kennealy. Private. (Also as 'Kenneally' and 'Kenealy'.) Patea Rifle Volunteers. (Born: Burke St East, Melbourne, Victoria.)[48]	Formerly Regt. No. 858, 'Melbourne Contingent', No. 9 Company, Taranaki Military Settlers. Enrolled 23 January 1864, Melbourne, Victoria, aged 20, and departed per *Brilliant*. Trade or calling: horse breaker.	Killed in action, Moturoa, 7 November 1868.
41. Charles Newman Stockfish. Corporal. Patea Rifle Volunteers.[49]	Formerly Regt. No. 694, 'Melbourne Contingent', No. 10 Company, Taranaki Military Settlers. Enrolled 21 January 1864, Melbourne, Victoria, aged 39, and departed per *Gresham*. Trade or calling: accountant.	Killed in action, Moturoa, 7 November 1868.

Name & Enlistment Details	Service & Other Details	Date & Cause of Casualty
42. Charles Eastwood. Constable. No. 6 Division, Armed Constabulary.	Formerly Regt. No. 135, 1st Waikato Regiment. Enrolled 11 September 1863, Melbourne, Victoria, and departed per *Star of India*.	Died of wounds, Moturoa, 7 November 1868.
43. Edwin M. Kerwin. Sergeant. (Also as 'Edward Kerwan'.) No. 6 Division, Armed Constabulary.	Formerly Regt. No. 38, 1st Waikato Regiment. Enrolled 1 September 1863, Melbourne, Victoria, and departed per *Golden Age*.	Killed in action, Moturoa, 7 November 1868.
44. William James Lees. Constable. No. 6 Division, Armed Constabulary.	Formerly Regt. No. 656, 1st Waikato Regiment. Enrolled 7 September 1863, Melbourne, Victoria, and departed per *Caduseus*.	Killed in action, Moturoa, 7 November 1868.
45. Joseph Evans Savage. Constable. No. 2 Division, Armed Constabulary.	Formerly Regt. No. 198, 2nd Waikato Regiment. Enrolled 21 August 1863, Sydney, NSW, and departed per *Kate*. Trade or calling: barber.	Killed in action, Moturoa, 7 November 1868.
46. Duncan Michie Brown. Sub-Inspector. (Also as 'David Michie Brown'.) No. 7 Division (had previously served in Nos. 4 & 5 Divisions), Armed Constabulary. He served in this newly raised force from the time of appointment as sub-inspector on 25 October 1867, until his death in action in January 1869.[50]	Believed to be 'Ensign Brown' (and later Lieutenant, 2nd Waikato Regiment) who departed with James Holt (later Captain, 2nd Waikato Regiment) in command of contingent of NSW military settler volunteers, which departed Sydney per *Kate* on 10 October 1863.[51] Brown served in the 2nd and later 4th Waikato Regiments (October 1863–1865+); was appointed Captain on 4 February 1865; and then settled on 300 acres of land on the Ohaupo Road near Hamilton, which he was entitled to as a consequence of his military settler service. He later sold his military settler land grant to a Mr Hammond from Australia.[52]	Killed in action, Ngatapa, January 1869.

Name & Enlistment Details	Service & Other Details	Date & Cause of Casualty
47. John McEwen. Constable. (Also as McEwan.) No. 1 Division, Armed Constabulary.	Formerly Regt. No. 105, No. 8 Company, 1st Waikato Regiment. Enrolled 28 August 1863, Melbourne, Victoria, and departed per *Star of India*.	Killed in action, Ngatapa, 3 January 1869.
48. Bamber Gascoigne. Lieutenant. Taranaki Military Settlers. Enlisted in January 1864, Melbourne, Victoria. Arrived at New Plymouth per *Brilliant*, 17 February 1864, while his wife Annie and eldest child arrived in August 1864.[53]	'Melbourne Contingent', Taranaki Military Settlers.	Former Taranaki Military Settler officer (aged 40) and family comprising wife Annie (27) and their three children, Laura (5), Cecil John (3), and Louisa Annie (3 months), were all killed in White Cliffs (Pukearuhe) Massacre, Taranaki District, 13 February 1869.
49. John Milne. Private. Regt. No. 564, Taranaki Military Settlers. Enlisted 21 January 1864, Castlemaine, Victoria, aged 35, and departed per *Gresham*. Trade or calling: ploughman.[54]	'Melbourne Contingent', Taranaki Military Settlers.	Former Taranaki Military Settler killed in White Cliffs (Pukearuhe) Massacre, Taranaki District, 13 February 1869.
50. Edward Richards. Private. Regt. No. 578, Taranaki Military Settlers. Enlisted 19 January 1864, Melbourne, Victoria, aged 40, and departed per *Gresham*. Trade or calling: gardener.[55]	'Melbourne Contingent', Taranaki Military Settlers.	Former Taranaki Military Settler killed in White Cliffs (Pukearuhe) Massacre, Taranaki District, 13 February 1869.
51. Connell Boyle. Constable. No. 2 Division, Armed Constabulary.	Formerly Regt. No. 179, 4th Company, 4th Waikato Regiment. Enrolled 3 February 1864, Sydney, NSW, and departed per *Kate*.	Killed in action in 'ambuscade' at Karaka, 18 February 1869.

Name & Enlistment Details	Service & Other Details	Date & Cause of Casualty
52. Robert Davis. Constable. No. 1 Division, Armed Constabulary. Enrolled in Armed Constabulary, 8 December 1868, in Melbourne, Victoria, and departed per *Alhambra*.	Formerly Regt. No. 47, 3rd Waikato Regiment. Enrolled 16 September 1863, Melbourne, Victoria.	Died of wounds, Ruatahuna (Orangikawa pa), 8 May 1869.
53. Donald McDonald. Trooper. Bay of Plenty Volunteer Cavalry.[56]	Formerly Regt. No. 367, 3rd Waikato Regiment. Enlisted 6 October 1863, Launceston, Tasmania. Trade or calling: groom.	Killed in action, (variously given as 6 or 7) June 1869, in ambush 'Between Fort Galatea and Runanga', on the Kaingaroa Plains. Trooper McDonald's New Zealand War Medal was claimed by his widow, Elizabeth, on behalf of their infant son.

APPENDIX E

Melbourne Published Enlistment Advertisement for the New Zealand Armed Constabulary, 5 December 1868

NEW ZEALAND ARMED CONSTABULARY

Office – Meagher's Hotel, corner of Lonsdale and Swanston streets.

200 unmarried MEN, of good character, under 40 years of age, and of sound health, are REQUIRED, for the above force, to serve for three years, subject to discharge at the option of the Government. Any men discharged within 12 months with good conduct certificate, to receive a bonus of £15. When on service in the field they will be subject to the Mutiny Act and Articles of War. They will serve generally under the provisions of the Armed Constabulary Act, 1867, and the regulations made under its authority. They will be entitled, when used as a Military force, to the benefits of the Military Pensions Act – pay, 5s. a day without rations, or 3s. 6d. a day when rations are supplied. The Armed Constabulary Act and Regulations, with an extract from the Military Pensions Act, are herewith published for general information.

I propose enrolling men for the above service on Tuesday, the 8th instant, between the hours of 10 a.m. and 4 p.m., and all men enrolled on that day will embark for New Zealand on the 9th instant.

Men desirous of joining the force will call at this office on the 5th and 7th instant, between the above-named hours, with testimonials as to character, and for medical inspection.

In the event of the required number not being obtained on the 8th instant, a subsequent day for enrolling will be advertised.

W.G. STACK, Captain
Agent for the New Zealand Government
Melbourne, Dec. 4, 1868

APPENDIX F

Australian-enlisted (or -derived) Armed Constabulary Casualties, 1868–69

This list of fourteen Australian-derived Armed Constabulary casualties has been compiled from various contemporary government records and other source materials.[57]

Name	Served in	Enlistment Details (& prior service)	Details of Casualty
Richard Fennessy. Constable.	No. 3 Division, A.C.	Formerly 'Melbourne Contingent', Taranaki Military Settlers, Regt. No. 632. Enrolled 19 January 1864, Melbourne, Victoria, and departed per *Gresham*.	Killed in action, Te Ngutu o te Manu, 7 September 1868.
John O'Connor. Constable. (Born 1844, Hobart, Tasmania.)	No. 2 Division, A.C.	Formerly 'Melbourne Contingent', Taranaki Military Settlers, Regt. No. 780. Enrolled 19 January 1864, Melbourne, Victoria, and departed per *Gresham*.	Killed in action, Te Ngutu o te Manu, 7 September 1868.
Richard Walsh. Constable.	Nos. 5 & 6 Divisions, A.C.	Formerly Regt. No. 609, 2nd Waikato Regiment. Enrolled 10 October 1863, Sydney, NSW, and departed per *Kate*. Trade or calling: policeman.	Killed in action, Te Ngutu o te Manu, 7 September 1868.
Charles Eastwood. Constable.	No. 6 Division, A.C.	Formerly Regt. No. 135, 1st Waikato Regiment. Enrolled 11 September 1863, Melbourne, Victoria, and departed per *Star of India*.	Died of wounds, Moturoa, 7 November 1868.
Edwin M. Kerwin. Sergeant. (Also as 'Edward Kerwan'.)	No. 6 Division, A.C.	Formerly Regt. No. 38, 1st Waikato Regiment. Enrolled 1 September 1863, Melbourne, Victoria, and departed per *Golden Age*.	Killed in action, Moturoa, 7 November 1868.
William James Lees. Constable.	No. 6 Division, A.C.	Formerly Regt. No. 656, 1st Waikato Regiment. Enrolled 7 September 1863, Melbourne, Victoria, and departed per *Caduseus*.	Killed in action, Moturoa, 7 November 1868.

APPENDIX F

Name	Served in	Enlistment Details (& prior service)	Details of Casualty
Joseph Evans Savage. Constable.	No. 2 Division, A.C.	Formerly Regt. No. 198, 2nd Waikato Regiment. Enrolled 21 August 1863, Sydney, NSW, and departed per *Kate*. Trade or calling: barber.	Killed in action, Moturoa, 7 November 1868.
Duncan Michie Brown. Sub-Inspector. (Also as 'David Michie Brown'.)	Nos. 4, 5 & 7 Divisions, A.C.	Believed to be the 'Ensign Brown' (and later Lieutenant, 2nd Waikato Regiment, commission dated 20 October 1863) who departed with James Holt in command of contingent of NSW military settler volunteers from Sydney aboard *Kate*, 10 October 1863. Brown served in 2nd & 4th Waikato Regiments, was appointed Captain in 1865, before undertaking service in the newly raised Armed Constabulary 1867–69.	Killed in action, Ngatapa, January 1869.
John McEwen. Constable. (Also as 'McEwan'.)	No. 1 Division, A.C.	Formerly Regt. No. 105, No. 8 Company, 1st Waikato Regiment. Enrolled 28 August 1863, Melbourne, Victoria, and departed per *Star of India*.	Killed in action, Ngatapa, 3 January 1869.
James Banks. Constable.	No. 2 Division, A.C.	Melbourne, Victoria, on 8 December 1868. Departed for Wellington per *Alhambra*, 9 December 1868.	Killed in action, Karaka, 18 February 1869.
Connell Boyle. Constable.	No. 2 Division, A.C.	Formerly Regt. No. 179, 4th Company, 4th Waikato Regiment. Enrolled 3 February 1864, Sydney, NSW.	Killed in action, Karaka, 18 February 1869.
George Richard Horspool. Lance-Corporal. (Also as 'Horspoll'.)	No. 2 Division, A.C.	Melbourne, Victoria, 8 December 1868. Departed for Wellington per *Alhambra*, 9 December 1868. (Had previously served in the Taranaki Volunteers 1864–1866.)	Killed in action, Karaka, 18 February 1869.
Charles Watt. Corporal.	No. 2 Division, A.C.	Melbourne, Victoria, 11 December 1868. Departed for Wellington per *Otago*, 12 December 1868.	Died of wounds, Otauto, 13 March 1869.
Robert Davis. Constable.	No. 1 Division, A.C.	Melbourne, Victoria, 8 December 1868. Departed for Wellington per *Alhambra*, 9 December 1868. (Formerly Regt. No. 47, 3rd Waikato Regiment, enrolled 16 September 1863, Melbourne, Victoria.)	Died of wounds, Ruatahuna (Orangikawa pa), 8 May 1869 (also as 7 May).

BIBLIOGRAPHY

ARCHIVAL SOURCES

Archives Office of New South Wales:

NG/8: Governor of New South Wales Registers of Despatches Received from the Lieutenant Governors of the Other Australian Colonies and the Governor of New Zealand 1851–1856, 1859–1865.

NG/10: Despatches and Enclosures from the Governor of New Zealand 1853–1862.

NG/26: Copies of letters to officials and Private Persons 1855–1890.

NG/29: Copies of Despatches to the Governors or Lieutenant Governors of Other Australian Colonies and New Zealand, the Governor of India, and various Officials and Private Individuals 1849–1862.

Archives Office of Tasmania:

CON 16/3: Controller-General of Male Convicts: Indent of Convicts Arriving in Van Diemen's Land 1845–1849 Per Various Ships: pp. 312–15.

CON 37/3/765–769 & CON 37/7/2205: Conduct Registers of Male Convicts Arriving on Non-Convict Ships or Locally Convicted c. 1840–1893.

Correspondence Files: Maoris; & Maori Wars.

CSD 1/36/328. Colonial Secretary's Office: Correspondence File: 328.

CSD 4/44/596. Colonial Secretary: Correspondence File: 596.

CSD 4/45/636. Colonial Secretary: Correspondence File: 636.

CSD 4/85/411. Colonial Secretary: Correspondence File: 411.

CSD 4/86 & 87/412. Colonial Secretary: Correspondence File: 412.

CSO 8/101: Colonial Secretary's Office: pp. 81–110.

GO 1/51: Governor's Office: Despatch dated 24 April 1845: pp. 218–26.

GO 19/1: Despatches Received from the Governors of Other Colonies & States: Letter from Province of Otago, New Zealand, Superintendents Office, Dunedin, 29 June 1863, to Col. Thomas Gore Browne, C.B., Governor of Tasmania.

GO 47: Governor's Office: Governor's Inward Correspondence on Military Matters, 1861–1870.

NS 21/26/2. Press Cuttings (illustrated) of Tasmanian Interest (esp. Tasmanian history) c. 1840–1935.

NS 776/1. Material Relating to Maoris Transported to Van Diemen's Land, 1846.

Australian Joint Copying Project:

Copy of the Proceedings of the Court Martial, dated 13 October 1846, Enclosure in, C.J. La Trobe, letter to Earl Grey No. 117, Van Diemen's Land, 30 November 1846, CO280/197.

Australian War Memorial:

AWM27 100/6: Photographic Reproductions of Correspondence Relating to the Service of Victorians in the Maori War of 1863–64.

Document Control Centre: Records of Early Wars in New Zealand: 417/008/002.

Document Control Centre: Sheat, A.J. (N.Z.). Historical Records Donation: 417/093/004.

BIBLIOGRAPHY

New South Wales Printed Despatches Presented to both Houses of Parliament: Military Assistance to New Zealand (Despatch No. 58, 27 June 1860); Military Assistance to New Zealand (Despatch No. 82, 13 Oct. 1860); & Respecting Artillery Force Serving in the Colony (Despatches No. 48, 16 April 1860, No. 69, 22 June 1860 & No. 89, 13 Oct. 1860): V355.309944 N532d.

New Zealand Medal: Private H. McAvernon, 40th Regiment of Foot: REL/08526.

New Zealand War: Copy of a Despatch from His Excellency Sir T. Gore Browne, conveying the Thanks of the New Zealand Government for the Services rendered by H.M.C.S., . . .; also copy of His Excellency Sir Henry Barkly's Reply [Ordered Printed, 23 April 1861]: V355.03293 B884n.

Norman Bartlett: ' "Their Promised Land Australians and the Maori Wars 1840–1870": A Study of Australia's Involvement in the Maori Wars, also an Examination of British Colonial Policies during the 19th Century': MSS1048.

Original Letters, of W. Shaw [Bandsman 40th Regiment of Foot] War in New Zealand, 1860: 3DRL/3398A.

Steam Sloop 'Victoria.': Correspondence Relative to the Detention of the Steam Sloop Victoria, on Service in New Zealand [Ordered Printed, 26 June 1860]: F355.03293 S799.

Tasmania Parliamentary Printed Papers: Despatches from Secretary of State: Despatch of Troops to New Zealand (No. 17, 29 June 1864); Despatch of Troops to New Zealand (No. 18, 29 June 1864); & Return of Troops from New Zealand (No. 25, 31 July 1866): V354.946008 T741.

Catholic Church Archives (Brisbane, Queensland):

'Rockhampton News: Death of Rev. Father F.M. Bucas', *The Catholic Advocate*, 30 October 1930, p. 41.

Mitchell Library:

Under The Flag; Reminiscences of the Maori Land (Waikato) War by a Forest Ranger [William Race, c. 1895]: CY POS 127.

National Archives of New Zealand (Wellington Office):

AD 1 1887/2951: Stevens, Campbell. Private, No. 10 Company, 3rd Waikato Regiment.

AD 1 01/4595: Gregory, George.

AD 31/8: Army Department, Taranaki Military Settlers Nominal and Descriptive Roll Book, 1863–69.

AD 32/2639: Dent, Mark. Sergeant, Volunteer Artillery Company and 4th Waikato Regiment.

AD 32/4126: Sire, Francis. Private, No. 8 Company, 'Melbourne Contingent' Taranaki Military Settlers.

AD 36/3: No. 536, Mark Dent, Sergeant Volunteer Artillery Company.

AD 76/2: Nominal and Descriptive Roll. 2nd Waikato Militia Regiment: Reg. No. 608: Vowles, George.

AD 76/3: Nominal and Descriptive Roll. 3rd Waikato Militia Regiment: Reg. No. 1352: Stevens, Campbell.

Armed Constabulary Lists: P8/19: Record of Agreement to take Oath of [signatures of 16 men] in A.C. made at Melbourne, 29 December 1868 – 5 January 1869.

Armed Constabulary Lists: P8/21: Men enrolled at Melbourne by Capt. Stack, Descriptive Roll, draft, full return, dates of Attestation 1868–1869.

Armed Constabulary Lists: P8/21 A: 12 December 1868, Capt. Stack, Melbourne, to Under Secretary Defence, Wellington. Reports shipment of 41 men for A.C. on board s.s. 'Otago' for Wellington.

Armed Constabulary Lists: P8/21 B: 18 December 1868, Capt. Stack, Melbourne, to Under Secretary Defence, Wellington. Forwards Descriptive Return of 30 Men embarked per 'Rangitoto' for Wellington.

Armed Constabulary Lists: P8/21 C: 9 December 1868, Capt. Stack, Melbourne, to Under Secretary Defence, Wellington. Enclosed Nominal Roll of 99 Men per 'Alhambra'.

Armed Constabulary Lists: P8/21 E: Nominal Return of Men [per signed Agreements lists dated 11 Dec. 1868, 18 & 19 Dec. 1868, 24 Dec. 1868 & undated] enrolled at Melbourne and arrived at Wellington per 'Otago', 'Rangitoto', 'Gothenburg', and 'Omeo'.

National Library of Australia:

[George S.] Whitmore's Campaigns in New Zealand [1868–1869]: MS4064.

Letter Dated Auckland, 23 Nov. 1868, to Edward Deas-Thomson, of Sydney, NSW, from [son] Edward R. Deas-Thomson, discussing Mining Field & Prospects & The Maori War: MS3590.

National Museum of Australia:

Letter by Stephen White, dated Auckland, New Zealand, 31 June 1862: Hill Collection: 1986.85.4.

Public Record Office (London):

WO12/9789–9810 Regimental Muster Books and Pay Lists.
WO97/1065 Soldiers' Documents.

Queensland State Archives:

COL/A6: Colonial Secretary's Office: In-Letter 1361, 31 July 1860.
COL/A9: Colonial Secretary's Office: In-Letter 2340, 3 December 1860.
COL/A44: Colonial Secretary's Office: In-Letters 2003, 2 September 1863 & 2153, 31 August 1863.
COL/A51: Colonial Secretary's Office: In-Letter 510, 13 January 1864.
COL/A105: Colonial Secretary's Office: In-Letter 1269, 2 April 1868.
COL/A109: Colonial Secretary's Office: In-Letter 2456, 27 July 1868.
COL/P2: Letterbook of Extra-Colonial Letters, 1864–1869.
COL/Q2: Letterbook of Letters to other Departments, 1862–1864: 63/754 (p. 629), 17 September 1863.
COL/Q3: Letterbook of Letters to other Departments, 1864–1865: 64/45 (p. 19), 16 January 1864.
EDU/V1: Card Index to Registers of Male Teachers, 1860–1903: 'Vowles, George', pp. 87–88 & 92.
GOV/1: Governor's Office: Despatches from the Secretary of State for the Colonies: Vol. 1: 1859–1860.
GOV/2: Governor's Office: Despatches from the Secretary of State for the Colonies: Vol. 2: 1861.
GOV/8: Governor's Office: Despatches from the Secretary of State for the Colonies: Vol. 8: 1867.
GOV/22: Governor's Office: Letterbook of Despatches to the Secretary of State for the Colonies: 1859–1861: Vol. 1.
GOV/23: Governor's Office: Letterbook of Despatches to the Secretary of State for the Colonies: 1861–1863: Vol. 2.
GOV/A1: Governor's Office: In-Letters on Official Subjects: Vol. 1: 1859–1865.
GOV/G1: Governor's Office: Letterbook of Governor's Official Letters to Various Persons: Vol. 1: 1859–1871.

State Records of South Australia:

Chief Secretary's Office: GRG 24, Series 51, Special List Nos. 44–187.

AUSTRALIAN AND NEW ZEALAND PARLIAMENTARY OR OTHER OFFICIAL SOURCES

Appendix to the Journals of the House of Representatives of New Zealand: Volume I: 1869, Wellington: George Didsbury, Government Printer.
Appendix to the Journals of the House of Representatives of New Zealand: Vol. I: Legislative, Political, and Native: 1870, Wellington: George Didsbury, Government Printer.
Appendix to the Journals of the House of Representatives of New Zealand: Vol. III: D.–Miscellaneous: 1870, Wellington: George Didsbury, Government Printer.
Appendix to the Journals of the House of Representatives of New Zealand: Vol. II: 1871, Wellington: George Didsbury, Government Printer.
Appendix to the Journals of the House of Representatives of New Zealand: Vol. III: 1872, Wellington: George Didsbury, Government Printer.
Appendix to the Journals of the House of Representatives of New Zealand: Vol. I: 1888, Wellington.
Journals of the House of Representatives of New Zealand: 1861–1869, Auckland: 1861–1864; Wellington: 1865–1869.
New South Wales Government Gazette/Supplement to the New South Wales Government Gazette, 1846 & 1860–1870.
New Zealand: Parliamentary Debates: 1861 to 1863, Wellington: G. Didsbury, Government Printer, 1886.

Proceedings of the Parliament of South Australia: 1866–7 (Vols. 1 & 2), Adelaide: W.C. Cox, Government Printer.

Queensland Government Gazette, 1860–1868.

'Report from the Joint Select Committee on the Defence of the Colony, together with the Proceedings of the Committee and Minutes of Evidence', *Queensland Votes and Proceedings: 1866*, Brisbane: W.C. Belbridge, Government Printer (1866), pp. 1679–1710.

The New Zealand Army List [1863].

The New Zealand Army List: 30 November 1864.

The New Zealand Army List: Corrected to 29th February, 1872.

The New Zealand Gazette, 1863–1874 & 1877.

Victoria Government Gazette/Supplement to the Victoria Government Gazette, 1859–1869.

Votes and Proceedings of the Legislative Council: 1858–59, 1859–60 & 1861–62, Melbourne: John Ferres, Government Printer.

NEWSPAPERS

British and New Zealand Newspapers

The Illustrated London Times: 1845–1847 & 1860–1870.

The Southern Cross: 8 & 15 July 1843.

The Wellington Independent: 14 October 1846.

Australian Newspapers

New South Wales:

The Illustrated Sydney News, June 1864 – December 1869.

The Morning Chronicle/The Sydney Chronicle: March 1845 – March 1846 & November–December 1846.

The Sydney Mail: 1865–1866.

The Sydney Herald/The Sydney Morning Herald: April 1831 – August 1831; July–September & November 1834; October 1836; July–August 1843; May–August & September 1844; January 1845 – December 1846; March–August 1847; January 1860 – December 1867; November 1868 – March 1869; 18 March 1885; & 20 March 1908.

The Weekly Register: 1845.

Queensland:

Queensland Daily Guardian: August–October 1863 & January–March 1864.

The Darling Downs Gazette: 15 May 1897.

The Gympie Times: And Mary River Mining Gazette: October 1868 – December 1872.

The Moreton Bay Courier (becomes *The Courier* in May 1861; & *The Brisbane Courier* in April 1864): January 1860 – October 1862; June 1863 – June & October 1864; August 1868 – March 1869; and 8 & 11 December 1916.

The Queenslander: 16 December 1916 & 29 November 1928.

The Warwick Examiner and Times: 15 & 19 May 1897.

Toowoomba Chronicle: 15 May 1897.

Van Diemen's Land/Tasmania

Colonial Times and Tasmanian Advertiser: 1846 & 1848.

Launceston Examiner: 1860, 1863–1864 & 17 August 1869.

The Britannia and Trades' Advocate (becomes *The Tasmanian Colonist* in July 1851): 1846, 1848 & 1852.

The Cornwall Chronicle: 1 February 1840, 30 March 1844 & 15 November 1845.

The Hobart Town Advertiser: April 1860 & September–October 1863.

The Hobart Town Courier (and Van Diemen's Land Gazette/Government Gazette): 19 February 1841, June–

December 1843 & 1844–1848.
The Hobart Town Daily Mercury/The Mercury: January 1860 – June 1861, June 1863 – June 1864 and 11 & 13 March 1913.
The Observer: 1845–1846.

Victoria:

Melbourne Punch: June 1861 – December 1869.
The Age: July 1860, October 1862 – March 1863 & 20 March 1908.
The Argus: August 1859 – December 1867, October 1868 – February 1869, 30 August 1879, 15 March 1880 & 20 March 1908.
The Australian News: For Home Readers/The Illustrated Australian News: January 1865 – October 1870.
The Illustrated Melbourne Post: 1862–1865.
The Victorian: August 1863 – February 1864.

South Australia:

The Adelaide Observer: April 1866
The South Australian Register: April–October 1845, April 1860 – April 1861 & April 1863 – November 1864.

Western Australia:

Perth Gazette and Independent Journal of Politics and News (later becomes *Perth Gazette and West Australian Times*): 1864 & August 1868 – June 1869.
West Australian Times: January–September 1864.

PUBLISHED SOURCES AND ARTICLES

Alexander, J.E., *Bush Fighting: Illustrated by Remarkable Actions and Incidents of: The Maori War in New Zealand*, London: Sampson Low, Marston, Low and Searle, 1873.

Anderson, D., 'Sir George Bowen and the Problem of Queensland's Defence, 1859–1868', *Queensland Heritage*, Vol. 2, No. 3 (1970), pp. 32–38.

A Pakeha Maori, *Old New Zealand: A Tale of the Good Old Times, together with a History of the War in the North of New Zealand against the Chief Heke in the year 1845 as told by an Old Chief of the Ngapuhi Tribe, also Maori Traditions*, Reprint, Eighth Impression, Auckland: Whitcombe and Tombs Ltd, 1964.

Austin, M., 'The Strength and Disposition of the Army in Australia 1840–1850', *The Royal Australian Historical Society Journal*, Vol. 61, Part 2 (1975), pp. 91–119.

——, *The Army in Australia 1840–50: Prelude to the Golden Years*, Canberra, ACT: Australian Government Publishing Service, 1979.

——, 'Her Majesty's Colonial Sloop *Victoria*', *Sabretache*, Vol. 22, No. 3 (1981), pp. 26–29.

Australian Council of National Trusts, *Historic Public Buildings of Australia: Historic Buildings of Australia: Volume Two*, Melbourne: Cassell Australia Ltd, 1971.

Bach, J., *The Australia Station: A History of the Royal Navy in the South West Pacific, 1821–1913*, Kensington, NSW: New South Wales University Press, 1986.

Ballara, A., 'The Pursuit of Mana? A Re-evaluation of the Process of Land Alienation by the Maori, 1840–1890', *The Journal of the Polynesian Society*, Vol. 91, No. 4 (1982), pp. 519–41.

——, *Taua: 'Musket Wars', 'Land Wars' or Tikanga? Warfare in Maori Society in the Early Nineteenth Century*, Auckland: Penguin Books, 2003.

Barthorp, M., *The Northamptonshire Regiment: (The 48th/58th Regiment of Foot)*, London: Leo Cooper Ltd, 1974.

——, *To Face the Daring Maoris: Soldiers' Impressions of the First Maori War 1845–47*, London: Hodder and Stoughton, 1979.

Bartlett, N., *Australia at Arms*, Canberra, ACT: Australian War Memorial, 1955.

——, 'Australia and the Maori Wars', *Canberra Historical Journal*, New Series No. 5 (1980), pp. 1–6.

BIBLIOGRAPHY

Barton, L.L., *Australians in the Waikato War: 1863–1864*, North Sydney, NSW: Library of Australian History, 1979.

——, 'Australians in the Waikato War: Additions & Corrections', *Despatch*, Vol. 14, No. 4 (1983), p. 80.

Bastock, J., *Ships on the Australia Station*, Frenchs Forest, NSW: Child & Associates Publishing, 1988.

Belich, J., *The New Zealand Wars: and the Victorian Interpretation of Racial Conflict*, Reprint, Auckland: Penguin Books, 1988.

——, *'I Shall Not Die': Titokowaru's War New Zealand, 1868–9*, Wellington: Allen & Unwin New Zealand Limited in association with the Port Nicholson Press, 1989.

——, *Making Peoples: A History of the New Zealanders: From Polynesian Settlement to the End of the Nineteenth Century*, Auckland: Penguin Books, 1996.

Bell, L., *Colonial Constructs: European Images of Maori 1840–1914*, Carlton, Victoria: Melbourne University Press, 1992.

Bilcliffe, J., *Well Done The 68th: The Durhams in the Crimea and New Zealand 1854–1866*, Wiltshire: Picton Publishing (Chippenham) Ltd, 1995.

Binney, J., *Redemption Songs: A Life of Te Kooti Arikirangi Te Turuki*, Auckland: Auckland University Press, 1995.

Blair, D., *Cyclopaedia of Australasia; or, Dictionary of Facts, Events, Dates, Persons, and Places: Connected with the Discovery, Exploration, and Progress of the British Dominions in the South, From the Earliest Dawn of Discovery in the Southern Ocean to the Year 1881*, Melbourne: Fergusson and Moore, Printers and Publishers, 1881.

Blake, N., 'The Royal New Zealand Fencibles', *Auckland–Waikato Historical Society*, No. 32 (1978), pp. 17–21.

Bohan, E., *Climates of War: New Zealand in Conflict 1859–69*, Christchurch: Hazard Press, 2005.

Borrie, W.D., 'Immigration to New Zealand, 1854–1880: The Struggle of the Remote Islands of the Antipodes', *Royal Australian Historical Society Journal and Proceedings*, Vol. 30, Part 5 (1944), pp. 299–325.

Broeze, F., 'Maritime History in Australia', *Australian Historical Association Bulletin*, Nos. 64–65 (1990), pp. 43–53.

Bryant, S.A., 'Birth of Hamilton in 1864: Pioneers reminiscences and life in early days: by Sarah Ann Bryant, written in 1939', *Auckland–Waikato Historical Journal*, No. 30 (1977), pp. 9–10.

Buick, T.L., *New Zealand's First War, or the Rebellion of Hone Heke*, Wellington: W.A.G. Skinner, Government Printer, 1926.

Bull, J.W., *Early Experiences of Life in South Australia, and an Extended Colonial History*, Adelaide: E.S. Wigg & Son, 1884.

Burge, L., *The New South Wales Military Volunteer Land Grants*, Kensington, NSW: The Clarendon Press, 1976.

Burgess, P., *Warco: Australian Reporters at War*, Richmond, Victoria: William Heinemann Australia, 1986.

Burke's Peerage: Genealogical and Heraldic History of the Baronetage and Knightage: Privy Council & Order of Precedence, 99th edition, London: Burke's Peerage Limited, 1949.

Burroughs, P., 'Imperial Defence and the Victorian Army', *The Journal of Imperial and Commonwealth History*, Vol. 15, No. 1 (1986), pp. 55–72.

Butt, E.A., 'Romantic History of the Waikato', *The Journal of the Auckland Historical Society*, No. 4 (1964), pp. 2–5.

Campbell, R.D., *Captain Cadell and the Waikato Flotilla*, Wellington: Maritime Publications, 1985.

Candy, P.C. & Laurent, J., *Pioneering Culture: Mechanics' Institutes and Schools of Arts in Australia*, Adelaide: Auslib Press, 1994.

Cannon, M., *Who Killed The Koories?*, Port Melbourne, Victoria: William Heinemann Australia, 1990.

Carey, Lieutenant-Colonel, *Narrative of the Late War in New Zealand*, London: Richard Bentley, 1863.

Chaloner, H., 'The Historic River Steamer "Pioneer" ', *The Journal of the Auckland Historical Society*, Vol. 2, No. 1 (1963), pp. 13–15.

Cherrett, O.J., *Without Fear Or Favour: 150 Years Policing Auckland 1840–1990*, The New Zealand Police & L. Patrick Hunter, 1989.

Clark, R., *New Zealand Medal: H.M.C.S. Victoria*, Canberra: ACT Branch of the Military Historical Society of Australia, 1971.

Coates, I., *On Record: Being the Reminiscences of Isaac Coates: 1840–1932*, Hamilton: Paul's Book Arcade, 1962.

Cole, D., ' "The Crimson Thread of Kinship": Ethnic Ideas in Australia, 1870–1914', *Historical Studies*, Vol. 56, No. 14 (1971), pp. 511–25.

Coulthard-Clark, C., *The Diggers: Makers of the Australian Military Tradition*, Carlton, Victoria: Melbourne University Press, 1993.

Cowan, J., *The New Zealand Wars: A History of the Maori Campaigns and the Pioneering Period: Vol. I: (1845–1864)*, Wellington: W.A.G. Skinner, Government Printer, 1922.

——, *The New Zealand Wars: A History of the Maori Campaigns and the Pioneering Period: Vol. II: The Hauhau Wars, 1864–1872*, Wellington: W.A.G. Skinner, Government Printer, 1923.

Cresswell, J.C.M., *The Bay of Plenty Volunteer Cavalry*, Paradise Point, Queensland: PCS Publications, 1991.

Crosby, R., *Gilbert Mair: Te Kooti's Nemesis*, Auckland: Reed Books, 2004.

Crosby, R.D., *The Musket Wars: A History of Inter-iwi Conflict 1806–45*, Auckland: Reed Books, 1999.

Curr, E.M., *The Australian Race: Its Origins, Languages, Customs, Place of Landing in Australia, and the Routes by which it spread itself over that Continent: Volume III.*, Melbourne: John Ferres, Government Printer, 1887.

Daley, C., 'The Early Defences of Melbourne', *The Victorian Historical Magazine*, Vol. 22, No. 1 (1947), pp. 10–22.

Dalton, B.J., 'A New Look at the Maori Wars of the Sixties', *Historical Studies Australia and New Zealand*, Vol. 12, No. 46 (1966), pp. 230–47.

——, *War and Politics in New Zealand: 1855–1870*, Sydney: Sydney University Press, 1967.

Davis, D.F., 'Australia's First Warship, HM Victorian Ship Victoria', *Naval Historical Review*, Vol. 13, No. 4 (1992), pp. 26–27.

Denoon, D., 'The Isolation of Australian History', *Historical Studies*, Vol. 22, No. 87 (1986), pp. 252–60.

De Winton, Major, *Soldiering Fifty Years Ago: Australia in 'The Forties'*, London: European Mail Ltd, 1898.

Duhig, J., *Crowded Years*, Sydney: Angus & Robertson, 1947.

Eadie, Forbes, *Troopships Engaged in the Maori Wars . . . 1840–1865, South African War . . . 1899–1902, The Great War . . . 1914–1918*, Auckland Historical Centennial Research Committee, [1940?].

Elder, Bruce, *Blood on the Wattle: Massacres and maltreatment of Aboriginal Australians since 1788*, Expanded edition, Sydney: New Holland Publishers (Australia) Pty Ltd, 2000.

Evans, R., Saunders, K. & Cronin, K., *Race Relations in Colonial Queensland: A History of Exclusion, Exploitation and Extermination*, St Lucia: University of Queensland Press, 1988.

Evans, Wilson P., *Deeds Not Words*, Melbourne: The Hawthorn Press, 1971.

Featon, J., *The Waikato War: 1863–4*, Auckland: J.D. Wickham, Free Lance General Printing Office, 1879.

Forster, A., *South Australia: Its Progress and Prosperity*, London: Sampson Low, Son, & Marston, 1866.

Fox, W., *The War in New Zealand*, London: Smith, Elder & Co., 1866.

Foxton, J.F.G., 'The Evolution and Development of an Australian Naval Policy', *The Commonwealth Military Journal* (1911), pp. 654–70.

Franklin, J., 'Inspector William James: One of New Zealand's Most Significant Policing Pioneers', *The Journal of the Orders and Medals Research Society*, Vol. 46, No. 4 (2007), pp. 233–37.

Fyler, A.E., *The History of the 50th or (The Queen's Own) Regiment: From the earliest date to the year 1881*, London: Chapman and Hall, 1895.

'General Orders', *United Service Journal*, Part I (1829), p. 512.

Gibbney, H.J. & Smith, A.G. (eds), *A Biographical Register 1788–1939: Notes from the Name Index of the Australian Dictionary of Biography: Vol. II*, Canberra: Australian Dictionary of Biography, Australian National University, 1987.

Gibson, T., *The Wiltshire Regiment: (The 62nd and 99th Regiments of Foot)*, London: Leo Cooper Ltd, 1969.

——, *The Maori Wars: The British Army in New Zealand 1840–1872*, London: Leo Cooper, 1974.

Glen, F., *For Glory and a Farm: The Story of Australia's Involvement in the New Zealand Wars of 1860–66*, 2nd edition, Whakatane: Whakatane & District Historical Society, 1985.

——, 'Howard Willoughby: Australian War Correspondent to the NZ Land War 1863', *The Volunteers: The Journal of the New Zealand Military Historical Society*, Vol. 18, No. 3 (1993), [no page numbers].

——, 'Australians in NZ Wars', *The Volunteers: The Journal of the New Zealand Military Historical Society*, Vol. 24, No. 1 (1998), pp. 26–32.

Greig, A.W., 'The First Australian Warship', *The Victorian Historical Magazine*, Vol. 9, No. 4 (1923), pp. 97–114.

Gordon, H., *An Eyewitness History of Australia*, Adelaide: Rigby Limited, 1976.

Gorst, J.E., 'Our New Zealand Conquests', in D. Masson (ed.), *Macmillan's Magazine*, Vol. 12 (1865), pp. 168–75.

Greville, P.J., *The 5½ inch Coehorn Mortar and its Use in New Zealand: 1845–1864*, Keswick, South Australia: P.J. Greville, 1979.

Gudgeon, T.W., *The Defenders of New Zealand: Being a Short Biography of Colonists who Distinguished Themselves in Upholding Her Majesty's Supremacy in these Islands*, Auckland: H. Brett, 1887.

Gurney, R., *History of the Northamptonshire Regiment: 1742–1934*, Aldershot: Gale & Polden, 1935.

Haigh, J.B., 'The 80th Foot in New Zealand', *The Bulletin of the Military Historical Society*, Vol. 26 (1976), pp. 79–83.

——, 'A Relic of the First Maori War in the Wanganui Area', *The Bulletin of the Military Historical Society*, Vol. 54, No. 214 (2003), pp. 90–92.

Harries-Jenkins, G., *The Army in Victorian Society*, Great Britain: Routledge & Kegan Paul Ltd, 1977.

Harpur, C., *Poems*, Melbourne: George Robertson, 1883.

Haythornthwaite, P.J., *The Colonial Wars Source Book*, London: Arms and Armour Press, 1995.

Headlam, J., *The History of the Royal Artillery: From the Indian Mutiny to the Great War: Volume III – Campaigns. (1860–1914)*, Woolwich: Royal Artillery Institution, 1940.

Hendy-Pooley, G., 'Defenders and Defences of Australia', *The Australian Historical Society: Journal and Proceedings*, Part 6 (1902–3), pp. 109–14.

——, 'Defenders and Defences of Australia, with Military Reminiscences', *The Australian Historical Society: Journal and Proceedings*, Part 7 (1903), pp. 130–40.

Higgins, M., ' "Deservedly respected": A first look at the 11th Regiment in Australia', *Journal of the Australian War Memorial*, No. 6 (1985), pp. 3–12.

Hill, R.S., *Policing the Colonial Frontier: The Theory and Practice of Coercive Social and Racial Control in New Zealand, 1767–1867: Parts One & Two*, The History of Policing in New Zealand, Volume One, Wellington: Historical Publications Branch, Department of Internal Affairs, 1986.

——, *The Colonial Frontier Tamed: New Zealand Policing in Transition 1867–1886*, The History of Policing in New Zealand, Volume Two, Historical Branch, Department of Internal Affairs, GP Books, 1989.

Historical Records of Australia: Series I. Governors' Despatches To and From England: Volume XVII. 1833 – June, 1835, Sydney: The Library Committee of the Commonwealth Parliament, 1923.

Historical Records of Australia: Series 1. Governors' Despatches To and From England: Volume XX. February, 1839 – September, 1840, Sydney: The Library Committee of the Commonwealth Parliament, 1924.

Historical Records of Australia: Series 1. Governors' Despatches To and From England: Volume XXIII. July, 1843 – September, 1844, Sydney: The Library Committee of the Commonwealth Parliament, 1925.

Historical Records of Australia: Series 1. Governors' Despatches To and From England: Volume XXIV. October, 1844 – March, 1846, Sydney: The Library Committee of the Commonwealth Parliament, 1925.

Historical Records of Australia: Series 1. Governors' Despatches To and From England: Volume XXV. April, 1846 – September, 1847, Sydney: The Library Committee of the Commonwealth Parliament, 1925.

Hoare, B., *Figures of Fancy: A Volume of New Poems: The Maori, The Ambush, and Occasional Pieces*, Adelaide: John Howell, 1869.

Hocken, T.M., *The Early History of New Zealand*, Wellington: John Mackay, Government Printer, 1914.

Hodder, E., *The History of South Australia: From Its Foundation to the Year of Its Jubilee: With a Chronology Summary of all the Principal Events of Interest up to Date: Vol. I*, London: Sampson Low, Marston & Company, 1893.

Hodder, M.D.W., 'Publicising the Sources: Australians in the Waikato War', *Archifacts*, No. 14 (1980), pp. 319–25.

Holt, E., *The Strangest War: The Story of the Maori Wars 1860–1872*, London: Putnam & Company Ltd, 1962.

Hopkins [now Hopkins-Weise], J.E., *Selected New Zealand War Medal Rolls of Entitlements, Rejections, and Applications Granted up to 1900*, Brisbane: J.E. Hopkins, 1997.

——, *Further Selected New Zealand War Medal Rolls of Applications Granted up to 1900: Volume 2*, Brisbane: J.E. Hopkins, 1998.

——, ' "Fighting Those Who Came Against Their Country": Maori Political Transportees to Van Diemen's Land

1846–48', *Tasmanian Historical Research Association: Papers and Proceedings*, Vol. 44, No. 1 (1997), pp. 49–67; also republished in: *The Volunteers: The Journal of the New Zealand Military Historical Society*, Vol. 24, No. 3 (1999), pp. 100–17.

Hopkins-Weise, J., 'A History of the Colonial Defence Force (Cavalry): and the Australian Context', *The Volunteers: The Journal of the New Zealand Military Historical Society*, Vol. 26, No. 1 (2000), pp. 5–25; also republished in an edited version as: 'New Zealand's Colonial Defence Force (Cavalry) and its Australian Context, 1863–66', *Sabretache: The Journal and Proceedings of the Military Historical Society of Australia*, Vol. 43, No. 3 (2002), pp. 23–39.

——, 'The Armed Constabulary of New Zealand: and the Australian Context', *The Volunteers: The Journal of the New Zealand Military Historical Society*, Vol. 27, No. 1 (2001), pp. 5–42; also republished in an edited version as: 'New Zealand's Armed Constabulary and its Australian Context, 1867–72', *Sabretache: The Journal and Proceedings of the Military Historical Society of Australia*, Vol. 43, No. 4 (2002), pp. 19–38.

——, 'A Brief History of the Bay of Plenty Cavalry Volunteers, Tauranga Cavalry Volunteers, and the Opotiki Rangers Volunteers', *The Volunteers: The Journal of the New Zealand Military Historical Society*, Vol. 28, No. 1 (2002), pp. 66–70.

——, 'Queensland and the New Zealand Wars of the 1860s', *Journal of the Royal Historical Society of Queensland*, Vol. 18, No. 5 (2003), pp. 209–31.

——, 'Van Diemen's Land and the New Zealand Wars of the 1840s', *Tasmanian Historical Research Association Papers and Proceedings*, Vol. 50, No. 1 (2003), pp. 38–55.

——, 'Tasmania and the New Zealand Wars of the 1860s', *Tasmanian Historical Research Association Papers and Proceedings*, Vol. 50, No. 3 (2003), pp. 176–201; also republished in: *The Volunteers: The Journal of the New Zealand Military Historical Society*, Vol. 29, No. 3 (2004), pp. 67–96.

——, 'The Australian-New Zealand prelude, 1834–45', *The Volunteers: The Journal of the New Zealand Military Historical Society*, Vol. 30, No. 1 (2004), pp. 38–53.

——, 'Australian involvement in the New Zealand Wars, 1845–46', *The Volunteers: The Journal of the New Zealand Military Historical Society*, Vol. 30, No. 2 (2004), pp. 33–52.

——, 'Australian involvement in the New Zealand Wars, 1846–47 (Part 3)', *The Volunteers: The Journal of the New Zealand Military Historical Society*, Vol. 30, No. 3 (2005), pp. 36–51.

——, 'Australia and the Taranaki War: Responses to the Conflict 1860–61', *The Volunteers: The Journal of the New Zealand Military Historical Society*, Vol. 31, No. 3 (2006), pp. 160–75.

——, 'Australia and the Taranaki War — 2: Logistical, commissariat and manpower support, 1860–61', *The Volunteers: The Journal of the New Zealand Military Historical Society*, Vol. 32, No. 1 (2006), pp. 27–49.

——, 'Australia and the Taranaki War — 3: Humanitarianism, 1860–61', *The Volunteers: The Journal of the New Zealand Military Historical Society*, Vol. 32, No. 2 (2006), pp. 102–19.

——, 'Australia's Logistical and Commissariat Support in the New Zealand Wars, 1863–66', *Sabretache: The Journal and Proceedings of the Military Historical Society of Australia*, Vol. 47, No. 4 (2006), pp. 5–24.

——, 'Australia and the New Zealand Crisis of 1868–69', *The Volunteers: The Journal of the New Zealand Military Historical Society*, Vol. 33, No. 1 (2007), pp. 30–55.

——, 'Australia's Military Horse Trade during the New Zealand Wars of the 1860s', *Sabretache: The Journal and Proceedings of the Military Historical Society of Australia*, Vol. 48, No. 3 (2007), pp. 5–12.

——, 'The New Zealand Crisis of 1868–69: Part 2: Australia and the New Zealand Armed Constabulary', *The Volunteers: The Journal of the New Zealand Military Historical Society*, Vol. 33, No. 2 (2007), pp. 104–25.

Howard, G., *Portrait of the Royal New Zealand Navy: A Fiftieth Anniversary Celebration.* Wellington: Grantham House, 1991.

Hughes, H. & L., *Discharged in New Zealand: Soldiers of the Imperial Foot Regiments who took their Discharge in New Zealand: 1840–1870*, Auckland: The New Zealand Society of Genealogists, 1988.

Inglis, K.S., *Sacred Places: War Memorials in the Australian Landscape*, Carlton South, Victoria: Melbourne University Press, 1998.

Jenks, E., *A History of the Australasian Colonies: (From Their Foundations to the Year 1893)*, Reprint, Cambridge: Cambridge University Press, 1896.

Johnson, D., *New Zealand's Maritime Heritage*, Auckland: William Collins Publishers, in association with David

Bateman Ltd, 1987.

Johnson, D.H., *Volunteers at Heart: The Queensland Defence Forces 1860–1901*, St Lucia: University of Queensland Press, 1975.

Jones, C., *Australian Colonial Navies*, Canberra: Australian War Memorial, 1986.

Jones, J.P., *A History of the South Staffordshire Regiment: (1705–1923.)*, Wolverhampton: Whitehead Brothers Ltd, 1923.

Jose, A.W. & Carter, H.J. (eds), *The Australian Encyclopaedia: Vol. II: M to Z*, Sydney: Angus & Robertson Limited, 1926.

King, H., 'Some Aspects of Police Administration in New South Wales, 1825–1851', *Royal Australian Historical Society Journal and Proceedings*, Vol. 42, Part 5 (1956), pp. 205–30.

——, 'Problems of Police Administration in New South Wales, 1825–1851', *Royal Australian Historical Society Journal and Proceedings*, Vol. 44, Part 2 (1958), pp. 49–70.

Knox, B.A., 'Colonial Influence on Imperial Policy, 1858–1866: Victoria and the Colonial Naval Defence Act, 1865', *Historical Studies Australia and New Zealand*, Vol. 11, No. 41 (1963), pp. 61–79.

Laffin, J., *Anzacs at War: The Story of Australian and New Zealand Battles*, London: Abelard-Schuman, 1965.

Lambourn, A., *Major Thomas Bunbury: Envoy Extraordinary: New Zealand's Soldier-Treatymaker*, Waikanae: Heritage Press, 1995.

Laracy, H., 'Australia and New Zealand: Two Parts of the One Story', *Australia 1888*, Bulletin No. 4 (1980), pp. 52–54.

Lawn, C.A., 'Surveyor's Big Role in N.Z. History', *The Journal of the Auckland Historical Society*, Issue No. 8 (1966), pp. 16–25.

Levinge, R.G.A., *Historical Records of the Forty-Third Regiment, Monmouthshire Light Infantry, with a Roll of the Officers and their Services from the period of embodiment to the close of 1867*, London: W. Clowes & Sons, 1868.

Lockwood, R., 'Racism and Militarism', *Australian Left Review* (1968), pp. 53–61.

Lyons, J.K., 'The Monument to the 99th Regiment of Foot (The Wiltshire Regiment) at Anglesea Barracks, Hobart (Tas.)', *Sabretache*, Vol. 11, No. 3 (1970), pp. 68–71.

McCaskill, M., 'The Tasman Connection: Aspects of Australian–New Zealand Relations', *Australian Geographical Studies*, Vol. 20 (1982), pp. 3–23.

McDonnell, T., *An Explanation of the Principal Causes which led to the Present War on the West Coast of New Zealand; in Defence of the Action Taken by Lieut.-Col. Thos. McDonnell, whilst Commanding the Patea Field Force, with a Suggestion as to Future Operations*, Wanganui: Walter Taylor, Times Office, 1869.

MacFarlane, I. & Smith, N., *Victoria: and Australia's First War*, Victoria: Mostly Unsung Military History Research and Publications, 2005.

McGibbon, I. (ed.) (with the assistance of Goldstone, Paul), *The Oxford Companion to New Zealand Military History*, Auckland: Oxford University Press, 2000.

McInnes, I. & Gregson, J.B., *The Army Long Service and Good Conduct Medal 1830–1848*, Lancashire: Jade Publishing Limited, 1995.

McIntyre, W.D. & Gardner, W.J. (eds), *Speeches and Documents in New Zealand History*, Oxford: Oxford University Press, 1971.

McKillop, H.F., *Reminiscences of Twelve Months' Service in New Zealand: As a Midshipman, During the Late Disturbances in that Colony*, London: Richard Bentley, 1849.

McNicoll, A., 'Defence: Australian Navy', *The Australian Encyclopaedia: Volume 2: Charleville to Fergusson*, 3rd edition, Sydney: The Grolier Society of Australia (1977), pp. 220–30.

McNicoll, R., *The Royal Australian Engineers: 1835 to 1902: The Colonial Engineers*, Canberra: Corps Committee of the Royal Australian Engineers, 1977.

Maguire, J., *Prologue: A History of the Catholic Church as seen from Townsville 1863–1983*, Toowoomba: Church Archivist's Society, 1990.

Mair, G., *The Story of Gate Pa: April 29th, 1864*, Tauranga: Bay of Plenty Times Office, 1926.

Manning, R.J., 'Pierre Marie Bucas', *Footprints*, Vol. 1, No. 11 (1973), pp. 23–24.

——,(ed.), *St. Patrick's Christian Brothers College Mackay: The First 50 Years: Golden Jubilee 1929–1979*,

Mackay: Golden Jubilee Celebrations Committee, 1979.

Marsh, S., 'The Last Despatches: Armed Constabulary Field Operations Mounted Against Te Kooti: February–May 1872', *The Volunteers: The Journal of the New Zealand Military Historical Society*, Vol. 27, No. 3 (2002), pp. 141–67.

Marshall, W.B., *A Personal Narrative of Two Visits to New Zealand, in His Majesty's Ship Alligator, A.D. 1834*, London: James Nisbet and Co., 1836.

Melton, J., *Ships' Deserters 1852–1900: including Stragglers, Strays and Absentees from H.M. Ships*, North Sydney: Library of Australian History, 1986.

Mennell, P., *The Dictionary of Australasian Biography: Comprising Notices of Eminent Colonists: From the Inauguration of Responsible Government down to the Present Time: [1855–1892]*, London: Hutchinson & Co., 1892.

Millar, T.B., *Australia in Peace and War: External Relations 1788–1977*, Canberra: Australian National University Press, 1978.

Miller, E.M., *Australian Literature: From Its Beginnings to 1935: Volumes I & II*, Sydney: Sydney University Press, 1940.

Miller, E.M. & Macartney, F.T., *Australian Literature: A Bibliography to 1938: Extended to 1950*, Revised edition, Sydney: Angus & Robertson, 1956.

Moore, C., ' "Restraining Their Savage Propensities" The South Kennedy and North Leichhardt Districts in the 1860s and 1870s', in: Henry Reynolds (ed.), *Race Relations in North Queensland*, New edition, Queensland: Department of History & Politics, James Cook University (1993), pp. 83–114.

——, *New Guinea: Crossing Boundaries and History*, Honolulu: University of Hawai'i Press, 2003.

Moorhead, E.W., 'Excursion to the Victoria Barracks St. Kilda Road', *The Victorian Historical Magazine*, Vol. 26, No. 1 (1954), pp. 14–24.

Moran, P.F., *History of the Catholic Church in Australasia [Volume 1]*, Sydney: The Oceanic Publishing Company, [1894].

Morley, G.L., 'Our Married People', *The United Service Magazine*, Vol. 9 (1894), pp. 66–72.

Morris, N. (ed.), *The Journal of William Morgan: Pioneer Settler and Maori War Correspondent*, Auckland: Libraries Department, Auckland City Council, 1963.

Mudie, I., *Riverboats*, Adelaide: Rigby Limited, 1961.

Murrie-Jones, M., 'Royal New Zealand Fencible Corps Uniforms, Arms & Accoutrements 1847–1858', *The Volunteers: The Journal of the New Zealand Military Historical Society*, Vol. 28, No. 1 (2002), pp. 6–36.

Nairn, B., Serle, G. & Ward, R., *Australian Dictionary of Biography: Volume 4: 1851–1890: D–J*, Reprint, Carlton, Victoria: Melbourne University Press. 1979.

——, *Australian Dictionary of Biography:. Volume 5: 1851–1890: K–Q*, Carlton, Victoria: Melbourne University Press, 1974.

Nicholls, B., *The Colonial Volunteers: The Defence Forces of the Australian Colonies 1836–1901*, North Sydney: Allen & Unwin Australia, 1988.

Nicholson, J., *The Incomparable Captain Cadell*, Crows Nest: A Sue Hines Book, 2004.

Normington-Rawling, J., *Charles Harpur, An Australian*, Sydney: Angus & Robertson, 1962.

Norris, H.C.M., *Armed Settlers: The Story of the Founding of Hamilton, New Zealand, 1864–1874*, Hamilton: Paul's Book Arcade, 1956.

Odgers, G., *Diggers: The Australian Army, Navy and Air Force in Eleven Wars: From 1860 to 5 June 1944*, Sydney: Lansdowne Publishing Pty Ltd, 1994.

O'Donnell, H., *Historical Records of the 14th Regiment, now the Prince of Wales's Own (West Yorkshire Regiment): From its formation, in 1685, to 1892*, Devonport: A.H. Swiss, [1893?].

Oliver, W.H. & Williams, B.R. (eds), *The Oxford History of New Zealand*, Wellington: Oxford University Press, 1981.

Oliver, W.H., *A People's History: Illustrated Biographies from The Dictionary of New Zealand Biography, Volume One, 1769–1869*, Wellington: Bridget Williams Books & the Department of Internal Affairs, 1992.

Orchiston, D.W., 'Preserved Human Heads of the New Zealand Maoris', *The Journal of the Polynesian Society*, Vol. 76, No. 3 (1967), pp. 297–329.

Pearl, C., *Brilliant Dan Deniehy: A Forgotten Genius*, Melbourne: Thomas Nelson (Australia) Ltd, 1972.

Pearse, H.W., *History of the 31st Foot Huntingdonshire Regt. [&] 70th Foot Surrey Regt. Subsequently 1st & 2nd Battalions The East Surrey Regiment: Vol. 1. 1702–1914*, London: Spottiswoode, Ballantyne & Co. Ltd, 1916.

Perkins, E., *The Poetical Works of Charles Harpur*, Sydney: Angus & Robertson, 1984.

Preston, A. & Major, John, *Send a Gunboat!: A Study of the Gunboat and its Role in British Policy, 1854–1904*, London: Longmans, Green & Co. Ltd, 1967.

Penn, W.J., *Taranaki Rifle Volunteers: A Corps with a History*, New Plymouth: Thomas Avery, 1909.

Pugh's Queensland Almanac, Directory, and Law Calender: 1869, Brisbane: Theophilus P. Pugh.

Pugh's Almanac, and Queensland Directory, Law Calender, Coast Guide, Gazetteer, and 'Men Of The Time,' for 1886, Brisbane: Gordon & Gotch, 1886.

Ranfurly, The Earl of, *Roll of Honour, 1840 to 1902: Defenders of the Empire Resident in New Zealand*, Wellington: The New Zealand Times Company, 1902.

Reynolds, H., *With The White People: The crucial role of Aborigines in the exploration and development of Australia*, Ringwood, Victoria: Penguin Books Australia Ltd, 1990.

——, *Fate of a Free People: A Radical Re-Examination of the Tasmanian Wars*, Ringwood, Victoria: Penguin Books, 1995.

Richards, J., *The Secret War: A True History of Queensland's Native Police*, St Lucia: University of Queensland Press, 2008.

Rorke, J., *Policing Two Peoples: A History of Police in the Bay of Plenty 1867–1992*, Jinty Rorke & the New Zealand Police, 1993.

Rose, J.H., Newton, A.P., Benians, E.A., & Hight, J., *The Cambridge History of the British Empire: Volume 7: Part II: New Zealand*, London: Cambridge University Press, 1933.

Ross, J.O'C., *The White Ensign in Early New Zealand*, Wellington: A.H. & A.W. Reed, 1967.

Ruhen, O., *Port of Melbourne 1835–1976*, North Melbourne, Victoria: Cassell Australia, 1976.

Rusden, G.W., *History of New Zealand: Volume II*, 2nd edition, Melbourne: Melville, Mullen & Slade, 1895.

Salmon, H.W., 'The Armed Constabulary in the Waikato', *Journal of the Auckland–Waikato Historical Societies*, No. 22 (1973), pp. 32–36.

Saunders, M., 'Australia's First Expeditionary Force: The New South Wales Contingent to the Sudan', *Sabretache*, Vol. 24, No. 3 (1983), pp. 12–16.

——, 'Peace Dissent in the Australian Colonies: 1788–1900', *Journal of the Royal Australian Historical Society*, Vol. 74, Part 3 (1988), pp. 179–200.

Scholefield, G.H. (ed.), *A Dictionary of New Zealand Biography: Volumes I & II*, Wellington: Department of Internal Affairs, 1940.

Selfe, N., 'Annual Address to the Engineering Section', *Journal and Proceedings of the Royal Society of New South Wales*, Vol. 34 (1900), pp. I–XLVIII.

Serle, G. & Ward, R., *Australian Dictionary of Biography, Volume 6: 1851–1890: R–Z*, Carlton, Victoria: Melbourne University Press, 1976.

Serle, P., *Dictionary of Australian Biography: Volume II*, Sydney: Angus & Robertson, 1949.

Sexton, R., *The Deserters: A Complete Record of Military and Naval Deserters in Australia and New Zealand 1800–65*, Revised & enlarged edition, Magill, South Australia: Australasian Maritime Historical Society, 1985.

Shaw, A.G.L. & Clark, C.M.H. (eds), *Australian Dictionary of Biography: Volume 1: 1788–1850: A–H*, Carlton, Victoria: Melbourne University Press, 1966.

Short History of the '58th' Regiment, 1755 The Rutlandshire Regt., 1782 2nd Battalion The Northhamptonshire Regiment, 1881, Lahore: Printed by the 'Fiftyeighth Press', 1922.

Sinclair, K., *The Origins of the Maori Wars*, Wellington: New Zealand University Press, 1961.

——, 'II.— The Past and Future of Australia–New Zealand Relations', *Australian Outlook*, Vol. 22, No. 1 (1968), pp. 29–38.

——, (ed.), *A Soldier's View of Empire: The Reminiscences of James Bodell, 1831–92*, London: The Bodley Head Ltd, 1982.

——, (ed.), *Tasman Relations: New Zealand and Australia, 1788–1988*, Auckland: Auckland University Press, 1987.

——, (ed.), *The Oxford Illustrated History of New Zealand*, Auckland: Oxford University Press, 1990.

'Sir Peter Nicol Russell: A Great Engineer. The Story of His Life and Work', *The Australasian Engineer*, Vol. 41, No. 303 (1941), pp. 10–11 & 33.

Skelley, A.R., *The Victorian Army at Home: The Recruitment and Terms and Conditions of the British Regular, 1859–1899*, London: Croom Helm Ltd, 1977.

Smythies, R.H.R., *Historical Records of the 40th (2nd Somersetshire) Regiment, now 1st Battalion The Prince of Wales's Volunteers (South Lancashire Regiment): From its Formation, in 1717, to 1893*, Devonport: A.H. Swiss, 1894.

Spring, F.W.M., *The Bombay Artillery: Lists of Officers who have served in The Regiment of Bombay Artillery*, London: William Clowes & Sons, Limited, 1902.

Stanley, P., 'Heritage of Strangers: The Australian Army's British Legacy', *Australian Defence Force Journal*, No. 87 (1991), pp. 21–26.

Stoney, H.B., *A Residence in Tasmania: with a Descriptive Tour through the Island from Macquarie Harbour to Circular Head*, London: Smith, Elder & Co., 1856.

Stowers, R., *Forest Rangers: A History of the Forest Rangers during the New Zealand Wars*. Hamilton: Richard Stowers, 1996.

——, *The New Zealand Medal To Colonials: Detailed medal rolls of officers and men in colonial units who received the New Zealand Medal for service in the New Zealand Wars 1845–1872*, Hamilton: Richard Stowers, 1998.

Swainson, W., *New Zealand and the War*, London: Smith, Elder & Co, 1862.

Tattersall, J., *Maoris on Maria Island: Punishment by Exile*, Napier: Hawke's Bay Art Gallery and Museum, 1973.

Taylor, N.M. (ed.), *Journal of Ensign Best: 1837–1843*, Wellington: R.E. Owen, Government Printer, 1966.

The Cyclopedia of Tasmania: (Illustrated). Volume 1, Hobart: Maitland Krone, 1900.

The Cyclopedia of New Zealand: Volume 2.— Auckland Provincial District, Christchurch: The Cyclopedia Company, Ltd, 1902.

The Dictionary of New Zealand Biography: Volume One: 1769–1869, Wellington: Jointly Published by Allen & Unwin & the Department of Internal Affairs, 1990.

Thomason, W., *Marching to the Waikato 1863: An Outline of the Waikato War with a Nominal Roll of the Volunteers from Bendigo & District*. [No details].

Thomason, W.E., *Marching on: The Bendigo Regiments and Companies 1858–1988*, Bendigo, Victoria: Bendigo Militaria Museum, [1989?].

Thomson, A.S., *The Story of New Zealand: Past and Present — Savage and Civilized: Volume 2*, London: John Murray, 1859.

Urlich, D.U., 'The Introduction and Diffusion of Firearms in New Zealand 1800–1840', *The Journal of the Polynesian Society*, Vol. 79, No. 4 (1970), pp. 399–410.

Vale, W.L., *History of the South Staffordshire Regiment*, Aldershot, Great Britain: Gale & Polden, 1969.

Vane, W.L., *The Durham Light Infantry: The United Red and White Rose*, London: Gale & Polden, 1914.

Vennell, C.W., 'Early Experiments with Pensioner Soldiers', *Auckland–Waikato Historical Journal*, No. 32 (1978), pp. 15–17.

——, 'Early Waikato River Trade', *Auckland-Waikato Historical Journal*, No. 39 (1981), pp. 5 & 10–13.

Vowles, G., *Sunbeams in Queensland*, Brisbane: Rogers & Harley, 1870.

Walker, R.J., 'The Genesis of Maori Activism', *The Journal of the Polynesian Society*, Vol. 93, No. 3 (1984), pp. 267–81.

Ward, G.F., *Victorian Land Forces: 1853–1883*, Croydon, Victoria: G.F. Ward, 1989.

Wards, I., *The Shadow of the Land: A Study of British Policy and Racial Conflict in New Zealand 1832–1852*, Wellington: Historical Publications Branch, Department of Internal Affairs, 1968.

Warre, H.J. (ed.), *Historical Records of the Fifty-Seventh, or, West Middlesex Regiment of Foot, compiled from official and private sources, from the date if its formation in 1755, to the present time, 1878*, London: W. Mitchell & Co., 1878.

Waterson, D.B., *A Biographical Register of the Queensland Parliament 1860–1929*, Canberra: Australian National University Press, 1972.

Webb, E.A.H., *History of the 12th (The Suffolk) Regiment 1685–1913*, London: Spottiswoode & Co., 1914.

Wells, B., *The History of Taranaki: A Standard Work on the History of the Province*, New Plymouth: Edmondson & Avery, Taranaki News Office, 1878.

Whitmore, M., 'A Waikato Tour: Australia and the New Zealand Wars, 1863–64', *Wartime: Official Magazine of the Australian War Memorial*, No. 7 (1999), pp. 44–50.

Wilkinson, J.D., *Early New Zealand Steamers: Volume 1: The Pioneering Years (1840–1861)*, Wellington: Maritime Historical Publications, 1966.

Woollright, H.H., *History of the Fifty-Seventh (West Middlesex) Regiment of Foot, 1775–1881, compiled from Official and Other Sources*, London: Richard Bentley and Son, 1895.

Wylly, H.C., *History of the Manchester Regiment (Late the 63rd and 96th Foot): Vol. I 1758–1883*, London: Forster Groom & Co. Ltd, 1923.

Yarwood, A.T., *Walers: Australian Horses Abroad*, Carlton, Victoria: Melbourne University Press, 1989.

Young, J.M.R., 'Australia's Pacific Frontier', *Historical Studies Australia and New Zealand*, Vol. 12, No. 47 (1966), pp. 373–88.

Young, R., Curnow, H. & King, M., *G.F. von Tempsky: Artist and Adventurer*, Martinborough: Alister Taylor Publishers, 1981.

Zwillenberg, H., 'British Assistance and the Influence of Military Thought', *Sabretache*, Vol. 21, No. 4 (1980), pp. 8–18.

——, 'South Australia's Army'. *Sabretache*, Part 4, Vol. 23, No. 1 (1982), pp. 23–27.

Zwillenberg, H.J., 'The Background to South Australia's Defence Policy', *Sabretache*, Vol. 21, No. 1 (1980), pp. 22–40.

OTHER SOURCES

Belich, J. *The New Zealand Wars* (Documentary Series: Parts 1–5), Television One & Landmark Productions Ltd, 1998.

Interviews by author with Dorothea Cheshire, granddaughter of the New Zealand war veteran and war medal recipient Jacob Cheshire, 3rd Waikato Regiment, in Brisbane, Queensland, December 1995 & June–July 1998.

Genealogical history on Henry Strode Henri, New Zealand war veteran (1st & 2nd Waikato Regiments), and the history of the Henri family, courtesy of Ben Henri of Ascot, Brisbane, Queensland, to this author, October 1995, including: Robin Barker, 'The Henri Letters: Part One' (29 November 1993) & 'The Henri Letters: Part Two' (17 August 1995).

Genealogical history on George Gregory, New Zealand war veteran (serving on Government steamer *Sturt* 1866–68), and history of the Gregory family of Narrabri, New South Wales, courtesy of Stan Hannaford (great-grandson of Nanango, Queensland) to this author, December 1997, September 1998 & March 1999.

'Let's Talk About Anglesea Barracks', Pamphlet, Launceston: Tasmanian Visitor Corporation Ltd.

Macfarlan, E.D., 'Military Pensioners in Auckland: A Reappraisal of the Royal New Zealand Fencibles', MA thesis, University of Auckland, 1981.

Millar, T.B., 'The History of the Defence Forces of the Port Phillip District and Colony of Victoria 1836–1900', MA thesis, University of Melbourne, September 1957.

Page, I.W., 'Relations Between New Zealand and the Australian Colonies, 1850–1870', MA thesis, University of Otago, New Zealand, December 1956.

Zwillenberg, H.J., 'Citizens and Soldiers: The Defence of South Australia 1836–1901', MA thesis, University of Adelaide, 1970.

ENDNOTES

INTRODUCTION

1 Refer to one recent overview of the available literature dealing with the New Zealand wars, in: E. Bohan, *Climates of War* (Christchurch, NZ: Hazard Press, 2005), p. 10.
2 D. Cole, ' "The Crimson Thread of Kinship": Ethnic Ideas in Australia, 1870–1914', *Historical Studies*, Vol. 56, No. 14, (1971), p. 516.
3 H. Reynolds, *Fate of a Free People* (Ringwood: Penguin Books, 1995), p. 209.
4 J. Laffin, *Anzacs at War* (London: Abelard-Schuman, 1965), pp. 15–16.
5 C. Moore, *New Guinea* (Honolulu: University of Hawai'i Press, 2003), pp. 154–78.
6 Histories exploring aspects of this shared history include: J. Belich, *Making Peoples* (Auckland: Penguin Books, 1996), pp. 128–29, 131–32, 134, 313–14, 316 & 325; K. Sinclair, 'II.- The Past and Future of Australia–New Zealand Relations', *Australian Outlook*, Vol. 22, No. 1 (April 1968), pp. 29–30; T.B. Millar, *Australia in Peace and War* (Canberra: Australian National University Press, 1978), pp. 56 & 317; H. Laracy, 'Australia and New Zealand: Two Parts of the One Story', *Australia 1888*, Bulletin No. 4 (May 1980), pp. 52–53; M. McCaskill, 'The Tasman Connection: Aspects of Australian–New Zealand Relations', *Australian Geographical Studies*, Vol. 20 (1982), pp. 4 & 6–8; K. Sinclair (ed.), *Tasman Relations* (Auckland: Auckland University Press, 1987), pp. 7–9; D. Denoon, 'The Isolation of Australian History', *Historical Studies*, Vol. 22, No. 87 (Oct. 1986), pp. 252, 254–55, 257–68 & 260; & F. Broeze, 'Maritime History in Australia', *Australian Historical Association Bulletin*, Nos. 64–65 (Oct.–Dec. 1990), pp. 43, 46, 49 & 50.
7 *Sydney Morning Herald*, 15 August 1863, p. 6.
8 F. Glen, 'Australians in NZ Wars', *The Volunteers*, Vol. 24, No. 1 (July 1998), p. 29.
9 *Argus*, 22 January 1864, p. 6.
10 M. Saunders, 'Australia's First Expeditionary Force: The New South Wales Contingent to the Sudan', *Sabretache*, Vol. 24, No. 3 (July–Sept. 1983), p. 13.
11 Glen (1998), *op. cit.*, p. 29; & 'Military Law', in Ian McGibbon (ed.), *The Oxford Companion to New Zealand Military History* (Auckland: Oxford University Press, 2000), p. 323.
12 A.S. Thomson, *The Story of New Zealand . . . Volume 2* (London: John Murray, 1859), pp. 166–67; M. Murrie-Jones, 'Royal New Zealand Fencible Corps Uniforms, Arms & Accoutrements 1847–1858', *The Volunteers*, Vol. 28, No. 1 (July 2002), pp. 6–7; C.W. Vennell, 'Early Experiments with Pensioner Soldiers', *Auckland-Waikato Historical Journal*, No. 32 (April 1978), pp. 15–17; N. Blake, 'The Royal New Zealand Fencibles', *Auckland–Waikato Historical Journal*, No. 32 (April 1978), pp. 17–21; & E.D. Macfarlan, 'Military Pensioners in Auckland: A Reappraisal of the Royal New Zealand Fencibles', MA thesis, University of Auckland, 1981, p. i of Abstract.
13 F. Glen, *For Glory and a Farm* (Whakatane: Whakatane & District Historical Society, 1985). Also refer to: Glen (1998), *op. cit.*, pp. 26–32; *idem.*, 'Howard Willoughby: Australian War Correspondent to the NZ Land War 1863', *The Volunteers*, Vol. 18, No. 3 (Feb. 1993), [no page numbers]; & most recently, *idem.*, 'Australian involvement in New Zealand Wars', in McGibbon, *op. cit.*, pp. 384–86.
14 N. Bartlett, 'Australia and the Maori Wars', *CHJ*, New Series, No. 5 (March 1980), pp. 1–6; *idem*, ' "Their Promised Land Australians and the Maori Wars 1840–1870": . . .': MSS1048, *AWM*; & *idem*, 'War along the Waikato', *Australia at Arms* (Canberra: Australian War Memorial, 1955), pp. 5–20.

ENDNOTES

15 L.L. Barton, *Australians in the Waikato War* (North Sydney: Library of Australian History, 1979); & also refer to: *idem*, 'Australians in the Waikato War: Additions & Corrections', *Despatch*, Vol. 14, No. 4 (Oct. 1983), p. 80.

16 Refer to: T.W. Gudgeon, *The Defenders of New Zealand* (Auckland: H. Brett, 1887); J. Cowan, *The New Zealand Wars: . . . Vol. I: (1845–1864)* (Wellington: W.A.G. Skinner, Government Printer, 1922); & J. Cowan, *The New Zealand Wars: . . . Vol. II: The Hauhau Wars, 1864–1872* (Wellington: W.A.G. Skinner, Government Printer, 1923).

17 Recent Australian offerings in this populist format include: G. Odgers, 'Taranaki and Waikato', in *Diggers: . . . From 1860 to 5 June 1944* (Sydney: Lansdowne Publishing Pty Ltd, 1994), pp. 10–17; & M. Whitmore, 'A Waikato Tour: Australia and the New Zealand Wars, 1863–64', *Wartime*, No. 7 (Spring 1999), pp. 44–50.

18 B.J. Dalton, 'A New Look at the Maori Wars of the Sixties', *Historical Studies Australia and New Zealand*, Vol. 12, No. 46 (April 1966), pp. 230–47.

19 *Ibid.*, pp. 246–47.

20 J. Belich, *The New Zealand Wars* (Auckland: Penguin Books, 1988); & also refer to: *idem, 'I Shall Not Die': Titokowaru's War New Zealand, 1868–9* (Wellington: Allen & Unwin NZ Ltd in association with the Port Nicholson Press, 1989); *idem, op. cit.* (1996); & *The New Zealand Wars* [Documentary Series: Parts 1–5] (Television One & Landmark Productions Ltd, 1998).

21 Cole, *op. cit.*, p. 511.

22 For contemporary definitions of 'Australasia' and 'British Australasia', refer to: D. Blair, *Cyclopaedia of Australasia* (Melbourne: Fergusson and Moore, 1881), p. 17; & E. Jenks, *A History of the Australasian Colonies* (London: Cambridge University Press, 1896), p. 166.

23 W.D. Borrie, 'Immigration to New Zealand, 1854–1880', *Royal Australian Historical Society*, Vol. 30, Part 5 (1944), pp. 308–9.

24 G. Harries-Jenkins, *The Army in Victorian Society* (Great Britain: Routledge & Kegan Paul Ltd, 1977), p. 178.

25 P. Burroughs, 'Imperial Defence and the Victorian Army', *Journal of Imperial and Commonwealth History*, Vol. 15, No. 1 (Oct. 1986), p. 58.

26 One example, Hugh McAvernon, enlisted in the 40th in Melbourne in 1857, and saw active service in New Zealand during 1860–65. REL/08526: NZ War Medal: Private H. McAvernon, 40th Regiment of Foot, *AWM*.

27 'A 5: Defences of the Colony: . . . Ordered by the Council to be Printed, 9th February, 1860', *Votes and Proceedings of the Legislative Council: 1859–60* (Melbourne: John Ferres, Government Printer), p. 11; & *Argus*, 8 October 1859, p. 5.

28 R. Sexton, *The Deserters* (Magill: Australasian Maritime Historical Society, 1985), pp. 56, 64 & 67–70; & H. & L. Hughes, *Discharged in New Zealand* (Auckland: The New Zealand Society of Genealogists, 1988), pp. 13, 24 & 26–31.

29 *Argus*, 27 June 1866, p. 1.

30 J. Bach, *The Australia Station* (Kensington: NSW University Press, 1986), p. 3. For additional information on the history and vessels of the Australia Station, refer to: J. Bastock, *Ships on the Australia Station* (Frenchs Forest, NSW: Child & Associates Publishing, 1988).

31 *Ibid.*, p. 17.

32 *Ibid.*, p. 71; & also refer to: *Ibid.*, pp. 17–18 & 69–81.

33 J. Melton, *Ships' Deserters 1852–1900* (North Sydney: Library of Australian History, 1986), pp. 168, 177, 182, 199, 204, 206, 209, 227, 231, 236, 245, 287, 289–90, 303 & 306; & Sexton, *op. cit.*, pp. 85, 89 & 92.

34 Some of the few sources to make any mention of Taranaki settler relief or British soldier family relief are: Glen (1985), *op. cit.*, pp. 4 & 31; & E.W. Moorhead, 'Excursion to the Victoria Barracks St Kilda Road', *Victorian Historical Magazine*, Vol. 26, No. 1 (Sept. 1954), p. 17.

35 A.R. Skelley, *The Victorian Army at Home* (London: Croom Helm Ltd, 1977), p. 216.

36 P.C. Candy & J. Laurent, *Pioneering Culture* (Adelaide: Auslib Press, 1994), p. 9 (and also refer to pp. 1–2).

37 Examples of press on the human cost of the Civil War include: 'The Cost of War', *Courier*, 11 June 1863;

'The Horrors of War', *Courier*, 29 October 1863; & 'The Cost of the American War', *Courier*, 4 March 1864.

38 *Mercury*, 25 June 1864; *Argus*, 21 June, p. 4 & 27 June 1864, p. 3, 12 September, p. 7 & 23 September 1865, pp. 4–5; & *Sydney Morning Herald*, 22 June, p. 2, 24 June, p. 4, 21 July, p. 6, 25 July, p. 5 & 12 August 1864, p. 8 and 28 November 1865, p. 6. Also refer to: *NZG*, No. 20, 21 May 1864, pp. 231–36; 'A.-No. 6: Despatches from the Right Hon. The Secretary of State for the Colonies to the Governor of NZ', *JHRNZ: 1865* (Wellington), pp. 21–22 of A.-No. 6; & K. Sinclair, *The Origins of the Maori Wars* (Wellington: NZ University Press, 1961), pp. 21–24.

39 J.M.R. Young, 'Australia's Pacific Frontier', *Historical Studies Australia and New Zealand*, Vol. 12, No. 47 (Oct. 1966), p. 374.

40 W.B. Marshall, *A Personal Narrative of Two Visits to New Zealand, in His Majesty's Ship Alligator, A.D. 1834* (London: James Nisbet and Co., 1836), pp. 304–5.

41 D.U. Urlich, 'The Introduction and Diffusion of Firearms in New Zealand 1800–1840', *Journal of the Polynesian Society*, Vol. 79, No. 4 (Dec. 1970), pp. 399–410; & Belich (1996), *op. cit.*, p. 157 (and also refer to pp. 156–64). For expansive treatment of this period known as the 'Musket Wars', see: A. Ballara, *Taua* (Auckland, NZ: Penguin Books, 2003); & R.D. Crosby, *The Musket Wars* (Auckland, NZ: Reed Books, 1999).

42 Belich (1996), *op. cit.*, p. 165; & *idem* (1988), pp. 20, 21–22 & 24–25.

43 H.F. McKillop, *Reminiscences of Twelve Months' Service in New Zealand* (London: Richard Bentley, 1849), pp. 161–62.

44 *Sydney Herald*, 18 April, 25 April, 2 May, 9 May, 16 May, 23 May & 30 May 1831.

45 *Ibid.*, 1 August 1831.

46 D.W. Orchiston, 'Preserved Human Heads of the New Zealand Maoris', *Journal of the Polynesian Society*, Vol. 76, No. 3 (Sept. 1967), p. 297.

47 *Sydney Herald*, 25 April 1831 (and for other details on aspects of this trade, refer to 2 May 1831); & also refer to: I. Wards, *The Shadow of the Land* (Wellington: Historical Publications Branch, Department of Internal Affairs, 1968), p. 6.

48 T.M. Hocken, *The Early History of New Zealand* (Wellington: John Mackay, Government Printer, 1914), pp. 26–27; & Orchiston, *op. cit.*, p. 297.

49 C. Orange, 'The Maori People and the British Crown (1769–1840)', in K. Sinclair (ed.), *The Oxford Illustrated History of New Zealand* (Auckland: Oxford University Press, 1990), p. 26.

50 Cowan (1922), *op. cit.*, pp. 10–11.

51 T.L. Buick, *New Zealand's First War* (Wellington: W.A.G. Skinner, Government Printer, 1926), pp. 167 & 258; & Belich (1988), *op. cit.*, p. 292.

52 Belich (1988), *op. cit.*, pp. 21–22; & also refer to: Cowan (1922), *op. cit.*, p. 7.

53 Belich (1996), *op. cit.*, p. 134.

54 *Ibid.*

55 *Sydney Herald*, 18 August 1834.

56 *Ibid.*

57 *Ibid.*, 21 August 1834.

58 *HRA: Series I. Governors' Despatches To and From England: Volume XVII. 1833 – June, 1835* (Sydney: The Library Committee of the Commonwealth Parliament, 1923), Despatch dated 23 September 1834, pp. 544–45.

59 *Sydney Herald*, 28 August 1834; & also refer to: *Ibid.*, 25 August 1834.

60 *Sydney Herald*, 1 September & 4 September 1834; Marshall, *op. cit.*, pp. 149–50; & *HRA: Series I. Governors' Despatches To and From England: Volume XVII. 1833 – June, 1835*, *op. cit.*, p. 545.

61 *Sydney Herald*, 4 September 1834.

62 Marshall, *op. cit.*, pp. 342–43.

63 *Ibid.*, pp. 202–3.

64 *Ibid.*, p. 301.

65 *Sydney Herald*, 13 November 1834.

66 *Ibid.*, 17 November 1834.

67 *Hobart Town Courier*, 12 December 1834.

68 R.S. Hill, *Policing the Colonial Frontier: . . . Part One* (Wellington: Historical Publications Branch, Department of Internal Affairs, 1986), p. 67.

69 *HRA: Series I. Governors' Despatches To and From England: Volume XVII. 1833 – June, 1835, op. cit.*, Despatch dated 6 December 1834, pp. 596–97.

70 *HRA: Series 1. Governors' Despatches To and From England: Volume XX. February, 1839 – September, 1840* (Sydney: The Library of the Commonwealth Parliament, 1924), pp. 493–94; & Buick, *op. cit.*, pp. 4, 8 & 13–14.

71 For history of the 80th in Australia and New Zealand during 1836–44, refer to: J.P. Jones, *A History of the South Staffordshire Regiment* (Wolverhampton: Whitehead Brothers Ltd, 1923), pp. 54–55; W.L. Vale, *History of the South Staffordshire Regiment* (Aldershot, Great Britain: Gale & Polden, 1969), pp. 110–12; & J.B. Haigh, 'The 80th Foot in New Zealand', *Bulletin of the Military Historical Society*, Vol. 26 (1976), pp. 79–83.

72 *HRA: Series 1. Governors' Despatches To and From England: Volume XX. February, 1839 – September, 1840, op. cit.*, p. 592; Cowan (1922), *op. cit.*, p. 431; Buick, *op. cit.*, p. 16; Wards, *op. cit.*, pp. 44–46; Haigh, *op. cit.*, pp. 79–80; & M. Austin, *The Army in Australia 1840–50* (Canberra: Australian Government Publishing Service, 1979), pp. 95 & 141.

73 Austin, *op. cit.*, p. 104; Buick, *op. cit.*, pp. 17–18; N.M. Taylor (ed.), *Journal of Ensign Best* (Wellington, NZ: R.E. Owen, Government Printer, 1966), pp. 374–75 & 378–400; Wards, *op. cit.*, pp. 64–68; Haigh, *op. cit.*, pp. 80–81; Hughes, *op. cit.*, p. 118; & A. Lambourn, *Major Thomas Bunbury* (Waikanae: Heritage Press, 1995), pp. 141–60.

74 M.P.K. Sorrenson, 'Maori and Pakeha', in W.H. Oliver & B.R. Williams (eds), *The Oxford History of New Zealand* (Wellington, NZ: Oxford University Press, 1981), pp. 168–69; & A. Ballara, 'The Pursuit of Mana? A Re-evaluation of the Process of Land Alienation by the Maori, 1840–1890', *Journal of the Polynesian Society*, Vol. 91, No. 4 (Dec. 1982), p. 527.

75 Sorrenson, *op. cit.*, p. 169.

76 *Cornwall Chronicle, and Commercial and Agricultural Register*, 1 February 1840, p. 2.

77 *Hobart Town Courier and Van Diemen's Land Gazette*, 19 February 1841, p. 2.

78 *Britannia and Trades' Advocate*, 2 July 1846.

79 J. Belich, 'The Governors and the Maori (1840–1872)', in K. Sinclair (ed.), *The Oxford Illustrated History of New Zealand* (Auckland: Oxford University Press, 1990), p. 83.

80 R.J. Walker, 'The Genesis of Maori Activism', *Journal of the Polynesian Society*, Vol. 93, No. 3 (Sept. 1984), p. 269.

81 *Sydney Morning Herald*, 7 July 1843.

82 *Ibid.*, 13 July 1843. Also refer to Van Diemen's Land coverage in: *Hobart Town Courier and Van Diemen's Land Gazette*, 28 July 1843; & for examples of New Zealand press reportage, refer to: 'Serious Affray with the Natives' & the 'Weiroa Massacre', *Southern Cross*, 8 & 15 July 1843.

83 *Sydney Morning Herald*, 18 July 1843.

84 *HRA: Series 1. Governors' Despatches To and From England: Volume XXIII. July, 1843 – September, 1844* (Sydney: The Library Committee of the Commonwealth Parliament, 1925), p. 72.

85 *Sydney Morning Herald*, 1 & 2 August 1843; & CSO 8/101: Colonial Secretary's Office: William Fox, Agent for the NZ Co. at Nelson, to the Governor of Van Diemen's Land, dated 27 September 1843, pp. 87–90, *AOT*.

86 Wards, *op. cit.*, pp. 82–83; Austin, *op. cit.*, p. 104; & Haigh, *op. cit.*, p. 81.

87 CSO 8/101: Memorial from Nelson, to the Governor of Van Diemen's Land, dated 27 September 1843, pp. 83–86, *AOT*.

88 CSO 8/101: Colonial Secretary's Office, to the Brigade Major, Van Diemen's Land, dated 14 October 1843, pp. 91–92, *AOT*.

89 Wards, *op. cit.*, p. 79.

90 CSO 8/101: Colonial Secretary's Office, to the Brigade Major, Van Diemen's Land, dated 14 October 1843, pp. 91–92, *AOT*.

91 CSO 8/101: Captain Nicholson, 99th Regiment, Commanding Detachment to NZ per the *Emerald Isle*,

to the Military Secretary to His Excellency, the Commander of the Forces, dated Sydney, 9 November 1843, pp. 95–100, *AOT.*

92 *Hobart Town Courier and Van Diemen's Land Gazette*, 15 December 1843.

93 *Cornwall Chronicle*, 30 March 1844; H.C. Wylly, *History of the Manchester Regiment . . . Vol. I* (London: Forster Groom & Co. Ltd, 1923), pp. 219–20; Jones, *op. cit.*, p. 55; Buick, *op. cit.*, pp. 20–21; Haigh, *op. cit.*, pp. 81–82; & Hughes, *op. cit.*, pp. 117–18.

94 Wards, *op. cit.*, p. 90.

95 Austin, *op. cit.*, p. 105.

96 Belich (1988), *op. cit.*, p. 33.

97 Buick, *op. cit.*, pp. 23, 25, 31 & 33; Wards, *op. cit.*, pp. 95–97 & 100; Belich (1988), *op. cit.*, pp. 29–36; & Belich (1990), *op. cit.*, pp. 85–86.

98 Wards, *op. cit.*, pp. 104–5; & also refer to: Hocken, *op. cit.*, pp. 78–79; Cowan (1922), *op. cit.*, pp. 17–18; Buick, *op. cit.*, pp. 39, 40 & 42–43; & M. Barthorp, *To Face the Daring Maoris* (London: Hodder and Stoughton, 1979), pp. 47–48.

99 *Sydney Morning Herald*, 3 August 1844; & also refer to: *HRA: Series 1. Governors' Despatches To and From England: Volume XXIII. July, 1843 – September, 1844*, *op. cit.*, p. 713; & *HRA: Series 1. Governors' Despatches To and From England: Volume XXIV. October, 1844 – March, 1846* (Sydney: The Library Committee of the Commonwealth Parliament, 1925), p. 254. For Van Diemen's Land press coverage of these events, refer to: *Hobart Town Courier and Van Diemen's Land Gazette*, 23 & 30 August 1844.

100 *Sydney Morning Herald*, 5 & 6 August 1844.

101 *Ibid.*, 16 & 17 September 1844; *HRA: Series 1. Governors' Despatches To and From England: Volume XXIII. July, 1843 – September, 1844*, *op. cit.*, p. 790; & Wards, *op. cit.*, pp. 105–8.

102 *Sydney Morning Herald*, 12 February 1845.

103 *Ibid.*, 12 February 1845.

104 *HRA: Series 1. Governors' Despatches To and From England: Volume XXIV. October, 1844 – March, 1846*, *op. cit.*, pp. 254–55; & Wards, *op. cit.*, pp. 112–15. Also refer to: Hocken, *op. cit.*, pp. 81–83; Cowan (1922), *op. cit.*, pp. 18–20; Buick, *op. cit.*, pp. 47–50; & Barthorp, *op. cit.*, pp. 49–50.

105 *Sydney Morning Herald*, 15 February 1845; & also refer to: Wards, *op. cit.*, p. 114.

106 *HRA: Series 1. Governors' Despatches To and From England: Volume XXIV. October, 1844 – March, 1846*, *op. cit.*, pp. 288 & 313–15. Tenders were also called on 4 March 1845 for supplying stores for HMS *North Star* prior to this vessel's departure for New Zealand. *Sydney Morning Herald*, 4 & 5 March 1845.

107 Wards, *op. cit.*, pp. 114–15.

108 *Weekly Register*, 22 February 1845, p. 87; & *South Australian Register*, 12 April 1845.

109 *Sydney Morning Herald*, 31 March 1845. For other press coverage of the growing disturbances in the northern and southern districts of the North Island, refer to: *Sydney Morning Herald*, 5, 6, 13 & 28 February and 22 & 29 March 1845; *Weekly Register*, 8 February, p. 66, 15 February, p. 77 & 29 March 1845, pp. 147 & 155; & *Morning Chronicle*, 22 March & 2 April 1845.

110 *Sydney Morning Herald*, 4 March 1845.

111 *Sydney Morning Herald*, 8, 10, 11, 12 & 13 March 1845.

CHAPTER ONE

1 *Sydney Morning Herald*, 4 April 1845; & *Weekly Register*, 5 April 1845, pp. 158 & 166.

2 *Morning Chronicle*, 5 April 1845; & also refer to: *Sydney Morning Herald*, 4 April 1845; *South Australian Register*, 30 April 1845; & *Hobart Town Courier and Van Diemen's Land Gazette*, 24 April 1845.

3 T.L. Buick, *New Zealand's First War* (Wellington: W.A.G. Skinner, Government Printer, 1926), pp. 88–89.

4 *Morning Chronicle*, 30 April 1845.

5 *Sydney Morning Herald*, 5 April 1845; & *Morning Chronicle*, 5 April 1845.

6 *Supplement to the Sydney Morning Herald*, Monday, 5 April 1845 [*sic* date error here, should be 7 April]; 'New Zealand.—Public Meeting', *Morning Chronicle*, 9 April 1845; & *Weekly Register*, 12 April 1845, p. 170.

7 *Sydney Morning Herald*, 8 April 1845.

8 *Ibid.*, 8 April 1845; *Morning Chronicle*, 9 April 1845; & *Weekly Register*, 12 April 1845, p. 170.
9 *Sydney Morning Herald*, 8 April 1845.
10 *Ibid.*
11 *Ibid.*, 22 April 1845. 'Philo Tangata Maori' or 'Philo-Maori' continued to express such viewpoints; refer to: *Morning Chronicle*, 3 May, 21 June and 13 & 27 August 1845.
12 *Sydney Morning Herald*, 2 August 1845; & also refer to: *Observer*, 25 & 29 July 1845.
13 *Sydney Morning Herald*, 26 June 1846.
14 I. Wards, *The Shadow of the Land* (Wellington: Historical Publications Branch, Department of Internal Affairs, 1968), p. 125.
15 Wilmot received FitzRoy's despatch (dated 20 March) in Hobart on Saturday 19 April 1845. GO 1/51: Governor's Office: Attached Letter to Despatch dated 24 April 1845, pp. 218 & 224–26, *AOT*. Also refer to: Wards, *op. cit.*, p. 125.
16 *Sydney Morning Herald*, 7, 8, 9, 10, 11, 12 & 15 April 1845; *Morning Chronicle*, 9 April 1845; *Weekly Register*, 12 April 1845, p. 179; Wards, *op. cit.*, p. 131; J.B. Haigh, 'The 80th Foot in New Zealand', *Bulletin of the Military Historical Society*, Vol. 26 (1976), endnote 5, p. 83; & M. Barthorp, *To Face the Daring Maoris* (London: Hodder and Stoughton, 1979), p. 81.
17 *Weekly Register*, 22 February, p. 87 & 3 May 1845, p. 213; *South Australian Register*, 12 April 1845; & Wards, *op. cit.*, p. 131.
18 GO 1/51: Despatch dated 24 April 1845, pp. 218–23, *AOT*; & also refer to: *Sydney Morning Herald*, 6 May 1845; & Barthorp, *op. cit.*, p. 87.
19 Wards, *op. cit.*, p. 152; Buick, *op. cit.*, pp. 153, 156–57, 161, 250–51 & 263; & Barthorp, *op. cit.*, p. 87.
20 AD 32/2639: Dent, Mark. Sergeant, Volunteer Artillery Company & 4th Waikato Regiment; & AD 36/3: NZ War Medal Register: No. 536, Mark Dent, Sergeant Volunteer Artillery Company, *NANZ*; 'G.-No. 1a: Further Papers Relative to the Issue of the NZ War Medal', *AJHRNZ: Vol. II: 1871* (Wellington), p. 3 of G.-No. 1a; *NZG*, No. 55, 12 October 1871, p. 550; L.L. Barton, *Australians in the Waikato War* (North Sydney: Library of Australian History, 1979), p. 82; & R. Stowers, *The New Zealand Medal To Colonials* (Hamilton: Richard Stowers, 1998), p. 82.
21 *Weekly Register*, 3 May 1845, p. 213; & also in: *South Australian Register*, 7 May 1845.
22 *Sydney Morning Herald*, 9 & 15 April 1845.
23 *HRA: Series 1. Governors' Despatches To and From England: Volume XXIV. October, 1844 – March, 1846* (Sydney: The Library Committee of the Commonwealth Parliament, 1925), pp. 313–15 & 316–17.
24 *HRA: Series 1. Governors' Despatches To and From England: Volume XXIV. October, 1844 – March, 1846*, *op. cit.*, p. 351; & Wards, *op. cit.*, pp. 147–48.
25 *Sydney Morning Herald*, 5, 6, 7, 12, 13, 14, 15, 17 & 19 May 1845; & *Weekly Register*, 17 May, p. 231 & 24 May 1845, p. 251; Wards, *op. cit.*, pp. 147–48; & T.M. Hocken, *The Early History of New Zealand* (Wellington: John Mackay, Government Printer, 1914), pp. 98–99.
26 *Sydney Morning Herald*, 19 May 1845; & also refer to: *Morning Chronicle*, 21 May 1845.
27 *HRA: Series 1. Governors' Despatches To and From England: Volume XXIV. October, 1844 – March, 1846*, *op. cit.*, p. 351.
28 *Sydney Chronicle*, 25 November 1846.
29 *Tasmanian Colonist*, 20 May 1852; & also refer to: P.J. Haythornthwaite, *The Colonial Wars Source Book* (London: Arms and Armour Press, 1995), pp. 146–47.
30 *Sydney Morning Herald*, 12 April 1845.
31 *Ibid.*
32 *Ibid.*, 11 April 1845.
33 *Ibid.*, 12, 14 & 15 April 1845.
34 *Ibid.*, 5 September 1845.
35 *South Australian Register*, 19 July 1845.
36 *Ibid.*, 9 & 12 April 1845.
37 *Ibid.*, 7 May 1845.
38 *Ibid.*, 19 July 1845.
39 *Sydney Morning Herald*, 5 April 1845.

40 *Ibid.*, 12 April 1845.
41 *Hobart Town Courier*, 24 April 1845; & also refer to: *Sydney Morning Herald*, 6 May 1845; & *South Australian Register*, 14 May 1845.
42 *Observer*, 19 August 1845.
43 *Sydney Morning Herald*, 14 April 1845.
44 *Morning Chronicle*, 19 April 1845; & also refer to: 'The Germans at Nelson, New Zealand', *South Australian Register*, 25 June 1845.
45 *South Australian Register*, 14 June & 24 September 1845.
46 *Sydney Morning Herald*, 9 April 1845.
47 *Ibid.*, 10 September 1845; & also refer to similar concerns in 1847 in: *Hobart Town Courier and Gazette*, 15 December 1847.
48 *Sydney Morning Herald*, 8 April 1845; & also refer to: *Supplement to the Sydney Morning Herald*, 5 April 1845; & *Morning Chronicle*, 9 April 1845.
49 *South Australian Register*, 10 May 1845.
50 Wards, *op. cit.*, p. 196.
51 *Ibid.*, p. 97.
52 *Ibid.*, p. 98.
53 T. Gibson, *The Maori Wars* (London: Leo Cooper, 1974), p. 58; Hocken, *op. cit.*, p. 112; & Buick, *op. cit.*, pp. 228–29.
54 CSD 1/36/328. Colonial Secretary's Office: Correspondence File: 328, *AOT*; & *NSWGG*, No. 8, 27 January 1846, pp. 114–15. Also refer to: *Sydney Morning Herald*, 12 January 1846; Wards, *op. cit.*, pp. 196–97; & Buick, *op. cit.*, pp. 228–29.
55 CSD 1/36/328. Correspondence File: 328, *AOT*.
56 *NSWGG*, No. 8, 27 January 1846, pp. 114–15; & *NSWGG*, No. 14, 17 February 1846, p. 227.
57 *Sydney Morning Herald*, 10 October 1845.
58 *Ibid.*, 13 October 1845.
59 *Ibid.*, 13, 15, 16 & 17 October and 6 December 1845; & *HRA: Series 1. Governors' Despatches To and From England: Volume XXIV. October, 1844 – March, 1846*, *op. cit.*, pp. 635–37.
60 *Sydney Morning Herald*, 13 & 14 May and 3 June 1847.
61 Wards, *op. cit.*, pp. 168–69; & *South Australian Register*, 26 July & 24 September 1845.
62 *South Australian Register*, 15 & 18 October 1845.
63 *Ibid.*, 15 October 1845.
64 *Ibid.*, 25 October 1845.
65 *Ibid.*, 29 October 1845.
66 *Ibid.*, 14 & 18 June 1845.
67 *Ibid.*, 2 July 1845. For other information on Angas, refer to: L. Bell, *Colonial Constructs* (Victoria: Melbourne University Press, 1992), pp. 9–11, 13–14, 16–17 & 25.
68 *South Australian Register*, 21 June 1845.
69 *Ibid.*, 21 June 1845.
70 *Ibid.*, 2 & 5 July and 18 October 1845; *Sydney Morning Herald*, 9, 21, 22, 28, 29 & 30 July, 2, 7, 8, 16 & 20 August and 6 October 1845; *Weekly Register*, 26 July, p. 41 & 2 August 1845, p. 53; & *Morning Chronicle*, 30 July & 2 August 1845.
71 *Sydney Morning Herald*, 29 October, 1 November & 18 November 1845; M. Austin, 'The Strength and Disposition of the Army in Australia 1840–1850', *Royal Australian Historical Society*, Vol. 61, Part 2 (June 1975), pp. 92–93; M. Austin, *The Army in Australia 1840–50* (Canberra, ACT: Australian Government Publishing Service, 1979), pp. 21–23; & M. Higgins, ' "Deservedly respected": A first look at the 11th Regiment in Australia', *Journal of the Australian War Memorial*, No. 6 (April 1985), p. 3.
72 *Sydney Morning Herald*, 13 June 1845; & *Weekly Register*, 14 June 1845, p. 287.
73 *Sydney Morning Herald*, 13 June 1845.
74 *Ibid.*, 13 June 1845.
75 HMS *North Star* also carried Captain Egerton, the replacement captain for HMS *Hazard*. *Ibid.*, 2, 3, 17 & 18 July 1845.

76 *Ibid.*, 14 June 1845.
77 *Ibid.*, 30 July 1845.
78 *Ibid.*, 8 September 1845.
79 *Ibid.*, 13 & 15 August 1845; & *Weekly Register*, 16 August 1845, pp. 82–83.
80 *Sydney Morning Herald*, 1 September 1845.
81 *HRA: Series 1. Governors' Despatches To and From England: Volume XXIV. October, 1844 – March, 1846*, *op. cit.*, pp. 431–32.
82 J. Headlam, *The History of the Royal Artillery: ... Volume III – Campaigns. (1860–1914)* (Woolwich: Royal Artillery Institution, 1940), p. 172.
83 *Ibid.*
84 F.W.M. Spring, *The Bombay Artillery: Lists of Officers who have served in The Regiment of Bombay Artillery* (London: William Clowes & Sons Ltd, 1902), p. 89; & H.J. Gibbney & A.G. Smith (eds), *A Biographical Register 1788–1939: ... Vol. II* (Canberra: Australian Dictionary of Biography, Australian National University, 1987), p. 77.
85 Mann's other NSW civil service included appointment as first Chief Commissioner for Railways in 1855, and later becoming the founding captain of the colony's Volunteer Engineer Corps in December 1870. *NSWGG*, No. 322, 30 December 1870, p. 2897; R. McNicoll, *The Royal Australian Engineers: ... The Colonial Engineers* (Canberra: Corps Committee of the Royal Australian Engineers, 1977), pp. 10, 16 & 67; & P.J. Greville, *The 5½ inch Coehorn Mortar and its Use in New Zealand* (Keswick, South Australia: P.J. Greville, 1979), p. 8.
86 G. Hendy-Pooley, 'Defenders and Defences of Australia, with Military Reminiscences', *The Australian Historical Society: Journal and Proceedings*, Part 7 (1903), p. 136.
87 *Sydney Morning Herald*, 9 September 1845; & also refer to similar, but more detailed, account in: *South Australian Register*, 11 October 1845.
88 Greville, *op. cit.*, pp. 1, 17 & Annex C Enclosure 7; Buick, *op. cit.*, pp. 214–15, 235 & 251–52; Wards, *op. cit.*, pp. 199–201; & A Pakeha Maori [Frederick Maning], *Old New Zealand* (Auckland: Whitcombe and Tombs Ltd, 1964), pp. 278–79.
89 *Sydney Morning Herald*, 16 August 1845.
90 *Ibid.*, 28 August and 10, 17 & 20 September 1845.
91 *Ibid.*, 20, 22 & 23 September 1845; *Morning Chronicle*, 20 September 1845; *HRA: Series 1. Governors' Despatches To and From England: Volume XXIV. October, 1844 – March, 1846*, *op. cit.*, pp. 559–60; & Wards, *op. cit.*, pp. 186–87.
92 Sims was buried in Toowoomba, Queensland. *Darling Downs Gazette*, 15 May 1897; & also refer to: *Warwick Examiner*, 15 & 19 May 1897; & *Toowoomba Chronicle*, 15 May 1897.
93 *Sydney Morning Herald*, 29 September 1845; & *Weekly Register*, 4 October 1845, p. 166.
94 *Sydney Morning Herald*, 11 June 1846.
95 Hendy-Pooley (1903), *op. cit.*, p. 136.
96 Millington had a lengthy and excellent service record, and was accordingly recommended for the Long Service and Good Medal (with gratuity) in late 1846, which he received in 1851, after it was sent to him care of the Commissariat Officer in Sydney. WO12/9789–9810 & WO97/1065, *PRO*; & I. McInnes & J.B. Gregson, *The Army Long Service and Good Conduct Medal 1830–1848* (Lancashire: Jade Publishing, 1995), p. 262.
97 The *Regia* departed Sydney on 18 October. *Sydney Morning Herald*, 17 & 20 October 1845; *Morning Chronicle*, 18 October 1845; *Weekly Register*, 25 October 1845, p. 203; Wards, *op. cit.*, p. 187; & Buick, *op. cit.*, p. 213.
98 The *Waterlily* arrived at Norfolk Island with the 11th Regiment contingent on 5 January, and then departed for New Zealand with the 58th detachment on 8 January 1846. *Sydney Morning Herald*, 29 October, 13 & 14 November 1845 and 30 January 1846. Also refer to: Wards, *op. cit.*, pp. 362-363; & Buick, *op. cit.*, p. 238.
99 *Sydney Morning Herald*, 18 November 1845.
100 This detachment comprised two officers, twenty-nine other ranks, and eight artillery pieces. *Sydney Morning Herald*, 16 & 18 December 1845 and 13 January 1846; *Morning Chronicle*, 13 December 1845 & 13 January

1846; & *Weekly Register*, 13 December 1845, p. 281.

101 *Sydney Morning Herald*, 8, 9 & 13 January 1846; *Morning Chronicle*, 10 & 14 January 1846; & *HRA: Series 1. Governors' Despatches To and From England: Volume XXIV. October, 1844 – March, 1846, op. cit.*, pp. 706–7.

102 G. Hendy-Pooley, 'Defenders and Defences of Australia', *The Australian Historical Society: Journal and Proceedings*, Part 6 (1902–3), p. 113.

103 *Sydney Morning Herald*, 10 & 12 January 1846.

104 *Ibid.*, 10 & 14 January 1846.

105 *Ibid.*, 14 & 16 February 1846.

106 *Britannia and Trades' Advocate*, 18 June 1846; & J. Belich, *The New Zealand Wars* (Auckland: Penguin Books, 1988), p. 73.

107 Wards, *op. cit.*, p. 272.

108 *HRA: Series 1. Governors' Despatches To and From England: Volume XXV. April, 1846 – September, 1847* (Sydney: The Library Committee of the Commonwealth Parliament, 1925), p. 116.

109 *Sydney Morning Herald*, 8, 9 & 10 July 1846; & Wards, *op. cit.*, pp. 279–80.

110 *Sydney Morning Herald*, 11 & 20 June and 17 & 18 July 1846.

111 HMS *Driver* was the first steam-driven warship to visit Australian or New Zealand waters. J. Bastock, *Ships on the Australia Station* (Frenchs Forest, NSW: Child & Associates Publishing, 1988), p. 18.

112 *Sydney Morning Herald*, 10, 13, 20, 21 & 26 January and 19 March 1846.

113 *Ibid.*, 23 March and 15 & 26 September 1846.

114 *Ibid.*, 23 February, 19 & 24 March, 6, 12, 13 & 27 May, 17 June, 20 July, 28 & 31 August, 18 & 25 September, 2, 23 & 28 October and 17 December 1846; *Observer*, 17 March 1846; *Britannia and Trades' Advocate*, 18 June, 9 July, 30 July, 24 September & 1 October 1846; & *Hobart Town Courier and Van Diemen's Land Gazette*, 14 October 1846 & 16 January 1847.

115 Belich, *op. cit.*, p. 74; & also refer to: *Britannia and Trades' Advocate*, 1 October & 19 November 1846; H.F. McKillop, *Reminiscences of Twelve Months' Service in New Zealand* (London: Richard Bentley, 1849), pp. 197–205; & A.S. Thomson, *The Story of New Zealand: ...: Volume 2* (London: John Murray, 1859), pp. 133–35 & 162–64.

116 *Sydney Morning Herald*, 1 & 18 September, 23 October, 25 November and 5 & 7 December 1846.

117 Wards, *op. cit.*, p. 73.

118 Wards, *op. cit.*, pp. 282 & 293; & McKillop, *op. cit.*, pp. 210–11.

119 Wards, *op. cit.*, p. 285; McKillop, *op. cit.*, p. 239; & J. Tattersall, *Maoris on Maria Island* (Napier: Hawke's Bay Art Gallery and Museum, 1973), p. 4.

120 Wards, *op. cit.*, p. 293.

121 *Ibid.*, pp. 293–94; & Tattersall, *op. cit.*, p. 6.

122 Thomson, *op. cit.*, pp. 138–40; Wards, *op. cit.*, p. 294; & Tattersall, *op. cit.*, pp. 6–7.

123 Thomson, *op. cit.*, p. 140.

124 Wards, *op. cit.*, p. 294.

125 *Wellington Independent*, 14 October 1846; Wards, *op. cit.*, pp. 294–95; & Tattersall, *op. cit.*, pp. 7–9.

126 Wards, *op. cit.*, p. 295.

127 Copy of the Proceedings of the Court Martial, dated 13 October 1846, Enclosure in: C.J. La Trobe, letter to Earl Grey No. 117, Van Diemen's Land, 30 November 1846, CO280/197, *Australian Joint Copying Project*; Correspondence File: Maoris & NS 776/1 Material Relating to Maoris Transported to Van Diemen's Land 1846, *AOT*; & Tattersall, *op. cit.*, pp. 25–30.

128 Wards, *op. cit.*, pp. 281 & 295; Tattersall, *op. cit.*, pp. 10–11; & R. Wilkie, 'Hohepa Te Umuroa: ?–1847: Te Ati Haunui-a-Paparangi Youth, Political Prisoner', in W.H. Oliver (ed.), *A People's History: ... Volume One, 1769–1869* (Wellington: Bridget Williams Books & the Department of Internal Affairs, 1992), p. 245.

129 *Hobart Town Courier and Government Gazette*, 7 November 1846, p. 3.

130 *Ibid.*

131 *Ibid.*, 9 December 1846, p. 4.

132 *Colonial Times and Tasmanian*, 13 November 1846, p. 4.

133 *Ibid.*, 24 November 1846, p. 3.

134 CON 37/3/765–769: Conduct Registers of Male Convicts Arriving on Non-Convict Ships or Locally Convicted c. 1840–1893; & CON 16/3: Controller-General of Convicts: Indent of Convicts Arriving in Van Diemen's Land 28 May 1845 – 16 Jan. 1849 per Various Ships: pp. 312–15, *AOT*; & also refer to: *Wellington Independent*, 14 October 1846; McKillop, *op. cit.*, p. 191; & Wards, *op. cit.*, pp. 248–49.

135 *Hobart Town Courier and Government Gazette*, 25 November 1846, p. 2.

136 *Ibid.*

137 For detailed analysis of the events associated with these Maori political transportees, refer to this author's article: ' "Fighting Those Who Came Against Their Country": Maori Political Transportees to Van Diemen's Land 1846–48', *Tasmanian Historical Research Association: Papers and Proceedings*, Vol. 44, No. 1 (March 1997), pp. 49–67.

138 *Sydney Morning Herald*, 15, 17 & 21 October 1846.

139 *Ibid.*, 2 November 1846.

140 *Ibid.*, 3 & 7 November 1846.

141 R. Gurney, *History of the Northamptonshire Regiment* (Aldershot: Gale & Polden, 1935), p. 207; & H. & L. Hughes, *Discharged in New Zealand* (Auckland: The NZ Society of Genealogists, 1988), p. 43.

142 *Sydney Morning Herald*, 30 March 1847.

143 *Ibid.*, 2 April 1847.

144 *Ibid.*, 16 April 1847; & also refer to: *Ibid.*, 'Our Military Reductions' (editorial), 14 April 1847.

145 *HRA: Series 1. Governors' Despatches To and From England: Volume XXV. April, 1846 – September, 1847*, *op. cit.*, pp. 263–64.

146 *Ibid.*, p. 532 (and also refer to array of correspondence on this subject: pp. 279–80 & 531–35).

147 *Sydney Morning Herald*, 24 May & 21 June 1847.

148 *Ibid.*, 23, 26, 28, 29 & 30 June and 1 & 2 July 1847.

149 H. King, 'Some Aspects of Police Administration in New South Wales, 1825–1851', *Royal Australian Historical Society*, Vol. 42, Part 5 (1956), p. 226.

150 H. King, 'Problems of Police Administration in New South Wales, 1825–1851', *Royal Australian Historical Society*, Vol. 44, Part 2 (1958), p. 64.

151 For an example in relation to Bathurst, refer to: *Sydney Morning Herald*, 11 May 1847.

152 *Ibid.*, 27 May (account of the debate in the NSW Legislative Council on the colony's 'Protective Force') & 28 May 1847 ('The Debate on the Withdrawal of Troops').

153 *Ibid.*, 17 June 1847 ('New Zealand' (editorial)).

154 *Ibid.*, 17 June 1847 ('New Zealand Extracts: Wanganui and Manawatu').

155 *Ibid.*, 18 June 1847.

156 Wards, *op. cit.*, p. 333.

157 *Ibid.*, pp. 333–34.

158 *Sydney Morning Herald*, 25 June 1847; & also refer to: *Britannia and Trades' Advocate*, 17 & 24 June, 8 July and 15 September 1847.

159 *Sydney Morning Herald*, 13 July 1847.

160 J. Cowan, *The New Zealand Wars: . . . Vol. I: (1845–1864)* (Wellington: W.A.G. Skinner, Government Printer, 1922), pp. 137–39; Wards, *op. cit.*, pp. 342–44; Belich, *op. cit.*, p. 74; & J.B. Haigh, 'A Relic of the First Maori War in the Wanganui Area', *Bulletin of the Military Historical Society*, Vol. 54, No. 214 (2003), pp. 90–92.

161 *Sydney Morning Herald*, 9 August 1847; & Wards, *op. cit.*, pp. 344–45.

162 Histories dealing with the service of these respective regiments during 1846–47 include: T. Gibson, *The Wiltshire Regiment* (London: Leo Cooper Ltd, 1969), pp. 68–69; & H.C. Wylly, *History of the Manchester Regiment . . .: Vol. I* (London: Forster Groom & Co. Ltd, 1923), p. 222.

163 Gurney, *op. cit.*, p. 209. Also refer to: *Short History of the '58th' Regiment* (Lahore: Printed by the 'Fiftyeighth Press', 1922), pp. 25–29 & 32; & M. Barthorp, *The Northamptonshire Regiment* (London: Leo Cooper Ltd, 1974), p. 45.

164 Hughes, *op. cit.*, pp. 5 & 67.

165 E.M. Miller, *Australian Literature: . . . Volume I* (NSW: Sydney University Press, 1940), pp. 254–55; E.M.

Miller & F.T. Macartney, *Australian Literature: . . . Extended to 1950* (Sydney: Angus & Robertson, 1956), pp. 213–14; & B. Nairn, G. Serle & R. Ward, *ADB: Volume 4: 1851–1890: D–J* (Victoria: Melbourne University Press, 1972), p. 327.

166 J. Normington-Rawling, *Charles Harpur, An Australian* (Sydney: Angus & Robertson, 1962), p. 109.

167 *Weekly Register*, 13 September 1845, p. 126.

168 Normington-Rawling, *op. cit.*, p. 109.

169 *Ibid.*

170 *Weekly Register*, 26 July 1845, p. 41.

171 A.G.L. Shaw & C.M.H. Clark (eds), *ADB: Volume 1: 1788–1850: A–H* (Victoria: Melbourne University Press, 1966), pp. 514–15; Miller (*Vol. I*, 1940), *op. cit.*, pp. 25–26 & 231; & Miller & Macartney, *op. cit.*, p. 218.

172 C. Harpur, *Poems* (Melbourne: George Robertson, 1883), 'John Heki', p. 244. Another version of 'John Heki' is found in: E. Perkins, *The Poetical Works of Charles Harpur* (Sydney: Angus & Robertson, 1984), p. 420.

173 Normington-Rawling, *op. cit.*, p. 115.

174 *Britannia and Trades' Advocate*, 31 August, 14, 21 & 28 September, 3 October and 2 November 1848.

175 *Ibid.*, 1 April 1847.

176 *Tasmanian Colonist*, 15 January 1852.

177 H.B. Stoney, *A Residence in Tasmania* (London: Smith, Elder & Co., 1856), p. 257; & also refer to: Appendix E: 'Military Settlers', pp. 301–3.

178 'Let's Talk About Anglesea Barracks' Pamphlet (Launceston: Tasmanian Visitor Corporation Ltd); Australian Council of National Trusts, *Historic Public Buildings of Australia: . . . Volume Two* (Melbourne: Cassell Australia Ltd, 1971), pp. 12 & 19; & K.S. Inglis, *Sacred Places* (Victoria: Melbourne University Press, 1998), p. 15.

179 Gibson, *op. cit.*, p. 69; & Wylly, *op. cit.*, pp. 224–25. Also refer to: NS 21/26/2: Press Cuttings (Illustrated) of Tasmanian Interest (esp. Tas. history) c. 1840–1935: p. 139, *AOT*; & J.K. Lyons, 'The Monument to the 99th Regiment of Foot (The Wiltshire Regiment) at Anglesea Barracks, Hobart (Tas.)', *Sabretache*, Vol. 11, No. 3 (Jan. 1970), pp. 68 & 70.

CHAPTER TWO

1 W.D. McIntyre & W.J. Gardner (eds), *Speeches and Documents in New Zealand History* (Oxford: Oxford University Press, 1971), pp. 459–60.

2 *Sydney Morning Herald*, 26 July 1860, p. 4.

3 NG/29: Copies of Despatches to the Governors or Lieutenant Governors of Other Australian Colonies and NZ, the Governor of India, and various Officials and Private Individuals: Despatch dated 17 Sept. 1855, p. 54, *AONSW*.

4 *Sydney Morning Herald*, 6 April 1860, pp. 3–4 & 5.

5 *Ibid.*, 23 April 1860, p. 2; & *Argus*, 20 April 1860, p. 5.

6 *Supplement to the NSWGG*, No. 86, 8 May 1860, pp. 883–84.

7 *Ibid.*, No. 187, 17 October 1862, pp. 2019–20; & *Sydney Morning Herald*, 25 September 1863, pp. 3–4 & 5. New South Wales's 1862 Act was also published for general information in New Zealand; refer to: *NZG*, No. 2, 23 January 1863, pp. 18–19.

8 CSD 1/36/328. Colonial Secretary's Office: Correspondence File: 328, *AOT*. Tasmania's 1860 Proclamation was also published in New Zealand; refer to: *NZG*, No. 24, 28 July 1860, p. 131.

9 CSD 1/36/328, *AOT*; *Hobart Town Daily Mercury*, 2 May 1860; & *Launceston Examiner*, 19 April, p. 2 & 1 May 1860, p. 2. Other Tasmanian government correspondence reveals the interaction between the Australasian colonies on this issue into late 1860; refer to: CSD 1/36/328, *AOT*.

10 *Argus*, 16 April 1860, p. 5.

11 *Supplement to VGG*, No. 48, 17 April 1860, p. 707; & *Argus*, 18 April 1860, p. 5.

12 *VGG*, No. 87, 17 July 1860, p. 1305; & *Argus*, 18 July 1860, p. 5.

13 *Age*, 21 July 1860, p. 5. The press also informed its readers of problems with the enforcement of New Zealand's own 1860 Arms Act; refer to: *Argus*, 1 April 1861, p. 6; & *Sydney Morning Herald*, 4 July 1861, p. 5.

14 *South Australian Register*, 21 April 1860.

15 *NZG*, No. 24, 28 July 1860, pp. 131–32.

16 *Moreton Bay Courier*, 14 April 1860.

17 COL/A6: Colonial Secretary's Office: In: Letter 1361, dated 31 July 1860, *QSA*.

18 An attached letter by Deputy Commissioner J. Hamilton to the acting collector of customs at Lyttelton detailed this vessel's transgressions. *Ibid.*

19 GOV/G1: Letterbook of Governor's Official Letters to Various Persons: Vol. 1: Despatch No. 37, dated Brisbane, 20 Sept. 1860, pp. 52–53, *QSA*; GOV/A1: In-Letters on Official Subjects: Vol. 1: Letter dated 29 Oct. 1860, pp. 187–88, *QSA*; & COL/A9: Colonial Secretary's Office: In: Letter 2340, dated 3 Dec. 1860, *QSA*.

20 GOV/23: Governor's Letterbook of Despatches to the Secretary of State for the Colonies: Vol. 2: Despatch No. 14, dated 5 April 1862, p. 169, *QSA*.

21 A.W Jose & H.J. Carter (eds), 'Military Defence', *The Australian Encyclopaedia: Vol. II: M to Z* (Sydney: Angus & Robertson Limited, 1926), pp. 84–85; & L. Burge, *The New South Wales Military Volunteer Land Grants* (Kensington: The Clarendon Press, 1976), pp. 1–3.

22 *Sydney Morning Herald*, 9 April 1860, p. 8.

23 *Ibid.*, 17 July 1860, p. 2.

24 *Ibid.*, 'The Maori War', 13 July, p. 2, 'Arming the People', 17 July, p. 2 & 'An Australian Guard' & 'Military Organisation of the Colonies', 19 July 1860, p. 2.

25 *Argus*, 17 August 1860, p. 5; *Sydney Morning Herald*, 18 August 1860, p. 7; & *Mercury*, 22 August 1860.

26 *Sydney Morning Herald*, 16 October 1860, p. 5.

27 NG/26: Copies of letters to officials and Private Persons: Despatch dated Sydney, 24 November 1860, pp. 578–79, *AONSW*.

28 Jose & Carter, *op. cit.*, pp. 84–85; & Burge, *op. cit.*, p. 3.

29 *Sydney Morning Herald*, 21 January 1861, p. 4.

30 *South Australian Register*, 17 May 1860; & also refer to: 15 & 22 May 1860.

31 For press coverage of events associated with the 1st military contingent to Lambing Flats (Feb.–June 1861), refer to: *Sydney Morning Herald*, 22 February, p. 5, 23 February, pp. 4 & 6, 25 February, p. 4, 26 February, p. 5, 2 March, p. 5, 4 March, p. 5, 5 March, p. 5, 9 March, p. 6, 12 March, p. 3, 5 June, p. 5 & 8 June 1861, pp. 3 & 5.

32 For press coverage of events associated with the 2nd military contingent to Lambing Flats (July–Sept. 1861), refer to: *Sydney Morning Herald*, 18 July, p. 4, 19 July, pp. 4 & 5, 22 July, p.5, 23 July, p. 5, 24 July, p. 4, 26 July, p. 4, 30 July, p. 8, 31 July, p. 5, 2 August, p. 5, 27 August, p. 4 & 20 September 1861, p. 5.

33 C. Daley, 'The Early Defences of Melbourne', *Victorian Historical Magazine*, Vol. 22, No. 1 (June 1947), p. 14; R. McNicoll, *The Royal Australian Engineers* (Canberra: Corps Committee of the Royal Australian Engineers, 1977), p. 47; & G.F. Ward, *Victorian Land Forces* (Croydon: G.F. Ward, 1989), pp. 18–20 & 22.

34 *Argus*, 18 July, pp. 6 & 7 and 19 July 1860, pp. 4 & 6; & *Age*, 18 July 1860, p. 7.

35 *Argus*, 6 November 1860, p. 4.

36 *Age*, 16 July 1860, p. 6.

37 *Argus*, 11 October 1860, p. 5.

38 *Ibid.*, 17 April 1860, p. 5.

39 *Ibid.*, 13 July 1860, p. 5.

40 *Ibid.*, 16 July 1860, p. 7.

41 For indications of the numbers and sentiments contained in these New Zealand volunteer letters, refer to: *Argus*, 20 July, p. 3, 21 July, p. 5, 18 August, p. 5, 22 August, p. 5, 24 August, p. 5, 27 August, p. 5 & 28 August 1860, p. 6.

42 *Ibid.*, 29 August 1860, p. 5. Also refer to: *Ibid.*, 30 August, p. 5, 31 August, p. 5 & 1 September 1860, p. 5; & *South Australian Register*, 3 September 1860.

43 T.B. Millar, 'The History of the Defence Forces of the Port Phillip District and Colony of Victoria 1836–1900', MA thesis, University of Melbourne (September 1957), pp. 86–87.

44 *Argus*, 31 July, p. 5 & 1 August 1861, p. 5 and 26 June 1863, p. 5; *Sydney Morning Herald*, 1 August 1861,

p. 4; Millar, *op. cit.*, pp. 86–87; & B. Nicholls, *The Colonial Volunteers* (North Sydney: Allen & Unwin Australia, 1988), p. 34.

45 GOV/22: Letterbook of Despatches to the Secretary of State for the Colonies: Vol. 1: Despatch No. 30 (Military), dated Brisbane, Qld, 4 April 1860, p. 166, *QSA*. Also refer to: *Moreton Bay Courier*, 7 February 1860.

46 GOV/A1: Letter 60/107, 17 April 1860, pp. 43–45, *QSA*.

47 GOV/A1: Letter 60/218, 4 July 1860, pp. 63–64, *QSA*.

48 *QGG*, No. 48, 25 August 1860, p. 274; & *Moreton Bay Courier*, 1, 8 & 15 September 1860.

49 *Sydney Morning Herald*, 10 January 1861, pp. 4 & 5; *Moreton Bay Courier*, 15 January 1861; & E.A.H. Webb, *History of the 12th (The Suffolk) Regiment 1685–1913* (London: Spottiswoode & Co., 1914), p. 281.

50 Chief Secretary's Office: GRG 24, Series 51, Special List No. 44, *SRSA*.

51 R.H.R. Smythies, *Historical Records of the 40th (2nd Somersetshire) Regiment* (Devonport: A.H. Swiss, 1894), footnote on p. 390; & other information on Nelson (as well as Capt. Blyth) referred to in: H. Zwillenberg, 'South Australia's Army: Part Four', *Sabretache*, Vol. 23, No. 1 (Jan.–March 1982), p. 24; & H.J. Zwillenberg, 'Citizens and Soldiers: The Defence of South Australia 1836–1901', MA thesis, University of Adelaide, 1970, p. 202.

52 Chief Secretary's Office: GRG 24, Series 51, Special List Nos. 45 & 46, *SRSA*; *South Australian Register*, 18, 24 & 25 April and 9 & 10 August 1860; & Smythies, *op. cit.*, pp. 521–22 (and for information on Nelson arriving in Taranaki, see pp. 361–62).

53 *South Australian Register*, 1 December 1860; & also refer to: 1 October & 21 November 1860 and 4 February 1861.

54 *Ibid.*, 16 April 1860; & also refer to a letter in reply by 'F.A.R.' on 17 April 1860.

55 *Ibid.*, 17 April 1860. The sentiments of 'Marksman' saw a stinging letter of reply that questioned whether the author was even English for his stance and disdain for the regular soldier's duty. *Ibid.*, 19 April 1860.

56 *Ibid.*, 12 July 1860.

57 *Ibid.*, 14 July 1860.

58 *Ibid.*, 19, 20 & 27 July 1860; & *Argus*, 27 July 1860, p. 5.

59 *South Australian Register*, 20 July 1860.

60 For the government's reply to Biggs, refer to: *Ibid.*, 26 July 1860.

61 *Ibid.*, 24 July 1860.

62 *Ibid.*

63 No doubt a reference to the Taranaki Rifle Volunteers established during 1858–59, who saw active service during 1860–61, and again in 1863–66. W.J. Penn, *Taranaki Rifle Volunteers: A Corps with a History* (New Plymouth: Thomas Avery, 1909).

64 *Moreton Bay Courier*, 15 March 1860.

65 M. Saunders, 'Peace Dissent in the Australian Colonies: 1788–1900', *Royal Australian Historical Society*, Vol. 74, Part 3 (Dec. 1988), pp. 179–80.

66 *Mercury*, 23 July 1860.

67 Saunders, *op. cit.*, p. 186.

68 *Sydney Morning Herald*, 9 October 1860, p. 3; & also refer to follow-on letter: 'The War Spirit in the Colonies Justifiable on Other Grounds Besides Scriptural' by J.H. Hewitt, *ibid.*, 22 October 1860, p. 2.

69 *Argus*, 5 June 1860, p. 5.

70 For an 1863 example of this, refer to: *Mercury*, 24 November 1863.

71 For examples of press news on this military build-up from England, refer to: *Argus*, 14 January, p. 5, 19 January, p. 7 & 15 April 1861, p. 5; & *Sydney Morning Herald*, 16 July 1861, p. 8.

72 H.J. Warre (ed.), *Historical Records of the Fifty-Seventh, or, West Middlesex Regiment of Foot* (London: W. Mitchell & Co., 1878), pp. 155–59; H. O'Donnell, *Historical Records of the 14th Regiment* (Devonport: A.H. Swiss, [1893?]), pp. 185–86; H.H. Woollright, *History of the Fifty-Seventh (West Middlesex) Regiment of Foot* (London: Richard Bentley and Son, 1895), pp. 300–3; & H.W. Pearse, *History of the 31st Foot Huntingdonshire Regt. [&] 70th Foot Surrey Regt.* (London: Spottiswoode, Ballantyne & Co. Ltd, 1916), p. 320.

73 NG/8: Governor of NSW Registers of Despatches Received from the Lieutenant Governors of the Other

Australian Colonies & the Governor of NZ: Despatch dated 21 March 1860, p. 25 of reel; & NG/10: Despatches and Enclosures from the Governor of NZ: Despatch dated 21 March 1860, pp. 47–59 of reel, *AONSW.*

74 Gore Browne described Hall as 'a Resident Magistrate and has just resigned his seat in the House of Representatives'. NG/10: Despatch dated 21 March 1860, pp. 49–50 of reel, *AONSW.*

75 NG/10: Despatch dated 26 March 1860, pp. 58–59 of reel; & NG/8: Despatch dated 26 March 1860, p. 25 of reel, *AONSW.*

76 *Sydney Morning Herald*, 10 April, p. 4 & 11 April 1860, p. 4.

77 NG/10: Despatch dated 27 April 1860, pp. 60–62, *AONSW.* Accompanying Browne's letter was a memo from Frederick Whitaker (dated 27 April 1860, p. 61), advising the governor to seek 500 Enfield rifles from Australia.

78 NG/10: Despatch dated 4 April 1860, pp. 63–64, *AONSW.*

79 NG/29: Despatch dated Sydney, 3 May 1860, p. 90, *AONSW.*

80 NG/8: Despatch dated 28 May 1860, p. 26 of reel, *AONSW.*

81 NG/10: Despatch dated 6 July 1860, pp. 66–79, *AONSW.*

82 NG/8: Despatch dated 3 November 1860, p. 28 of reel, *AONSW.*

83 'B-No. 5: Return of the Amount Expended out of the War Loan of £150,000, From 1st October, 1860, To 12th June, 1861', *JHRNZ: 1861* (Auckland, NZ), p. 3 of B-No. 5.

84 *Sydney Morning Herald*, 29 December 1860, p. 5; & also refer to: *Ibid.*, 1 January 1861, p. 5.

85 *Ibid.*, 15 November 1861, pp. 4 & 5; & also refer to: *Ibid.*, 6 December 1861, pp. 3 & 4.

86 *Argus*, 7 April, p. 4, 18 April, p. 4 & 20 April 1860, p. 4.

87 *South Australian Register*, 12 May 1860.

88 Chief Secretary's Office: GRG 24, Series 51, Special List No. 48, *SRSA*; *South Australian Register*, 14 July 1860; & *Sydney Morning Herald*, 25 July 1860, p. 5.

89 *South Australian Register*, 24 August 1860.

90 Chief Secretary's Office: GRG 24, Series 51, Special List No. 60, *SRSA.*

91 *Ibid.*, Special List No. 62, *SRSA.*

92 *South Australian Register*, 24 August 1860; & *Sydney Morning Herald*, 17 September 1860, p. 5.

93 Also refer to: H. Zwillenberg, 'British Assistance and the Influence of Military Thought', *Sabretache*, Vol. 21, No. 4 (1980), p. 9.

94 *South Australian Register*, 27 November, 13 December & 26 December 1860 and 16 February 1861.

95 *Argus*, 14 January 1861, p. 5 & 19 January 1861, p. 7; *Mercury*, 28 January 1861; & J. Headlam, *The History of the Royal Artillery: ... Volume III – Campaigns. (1860–1914)* (Woolwich: Royal Artillery Institution, 1940), pp. 167–68.

96 *Sydney Morning Herald*, 9 March 1861, pp. 5 & 6.

97 *Ibid.*, 8 March 1861, p. 4. This activity was conducted by a Mr Burt, though the actual selection and purchase was carried out by a Mr M'Kenzie. Also refer to: *Ibid.*, 7 March, p. 6 & 9 March 1861, p. 5.

98 *Ibid.*, 8 July 1861, p. 4; & *Argus*, 10 July 1861, p. 5.

99 *Ibid.*, 8 July 1861, p. 4.

100 NG/10: Despatch dated 21 March 1860, *AONSW.*

101 NG/8: Despatch dated 21 March 1860, p. 25 of reel, *AONSW*; & NG/29: Despatch dated Sydney, 9 April 1860, p. 89, *AONSW.*

102 *Sydney Morning Herald*, 13 March 1860, p. 9.

103 *Ibid.*, 6 April 1860, p. 5.

104 *Ibid.*, 7 April, p. 4, 9 April, p. 4 & 10 April 1860, p. 4.

105 J. Bastock, *Ships on the Australia Station* (Frenchs Forest, NSW: Child & Associates Publishing, 1988), pp. 27–30 & 33.

106 *Ibid.*, 14 April, p. 9, 8 May, p. 5 & 21 December 1860, p. 8; & *Argus*, 7 May 1860, p. 5.

107 *Sydney Morning Herald*, 9 April, p. 5, 10 April, p. 4, 11 April, p. 4 & 23 April 1860, p. 4; & also refer to: *Argus*, 11 April, p. 5 & 16 April 1860, p. 5; & J.D. Wilkinson, *Early New Zealand Steamers* (Wellington: Maritime Historical Publications, 1966), p. 208.

108 NSW Despatches Presented to both Houses of Parliament: Respecting Artillery Force Serving in the Colony:

Despatch No. 48, dated 16 April 1860: V355.309944 N532d, *AWM.*

109 NSW Despatch No. 69, dated 22 June 1860: V355.309944 N532d, *AWM.*

110 NSW Despatch No. 89, 13 October 1860: V355.309944 N532d, *AWM.* Also refer to press item 'Colonial Military Expenditure', *Sydney Morning Herald*, 18 June 1861, p. 8.

111 NG/26: Despatch dated 20 June 1860, p. 538, *AONSW.*

112 NG/26: Despatch dated 11 July 1860, pp. 541–42, *AONSW.*

113 *Ibid.*, pp. 543–44.

114 *Sydney Morning Herald*, 12 July 1860, p. 4; & NG/26: Addendum to Despatch dated 11 July 1860, p. 544, *AONSW.*

115 *Sydney Morning Herald*, 14 July, p. 4 & 16 July 1860, p. 4.

116 *Ibid.*, 18 July 1860, p. 4.

117 *Ibid.*, 30 July 1860, p. 4.

118 *Ibid.*, 16 July 1860, p. 4; & also refer to: *Ibid.*, 13 July 1860, p. 4.

119 NG/10: Despatch dated 30 July 1860, pp. 80–82; & NG/8: Despatch dated 30 July 1860, p. 27 of reel, *AONSW.* Also refer to: NSW Despatches Presented to both Houses of Parliament: Military Assistance to NZ: Despatch No. 58, dated 27 June 1860; & Military Assistance to NZ: Despatch No. 82, dated 13 October 1860: V355.309944 N532d, *AWM*; & *Sydney Morning Herald*, 27 September, p. 4, 28 September, p. 2 & 3 October 1860, p. 8.

120 *Argus*, 7 April 1860, p. 5; & also refer to: *Ibid.*, p. 4 & 9 April 1860, p. 4; & *Sydney Morning Herald*, 13 April 1860, p. 4.

121 *Argus*, 10 April, p. 4 & 14 April 1860, p. 5; & *Sydney Morning Herald*, 11 April, p. 4 & 16 April 1860, p. 7.

122 *Argus*, 18 April 1860, p. 4; & *Sydney Morning Herald*, 18 April 1860, p. 4. Also refer to: *Argus*, 16 April, p. 4 & 17 April 1860, pp. 4 & 5; & *Sydney Morning Herald*, 23 April 1860, pp. 4 & 5. Another account of this departure stated it comprised 227 officers and men. *Sydney Morning Herald*, 23 April 1860, p. 5; & also refer to: Smythies, *op. cit.*, p. 361.

123 For other information on the service and crew of this vessel, including those who served ashore as part of the Naval Brigade, refer to: A.W. Greig, 'The First Australian Warship', *Victorian Historical Magazine*, Vol. 9, No. 4 (Sept. 1923), pp. 97–114; W.P. Evans, *Deeds Not Words* (Melbourne: The Hawthorn Press, 1971); R. Clark, *New Zealand Medal: H.M.C.S. Victoria* (Canberra: ACT Branch of the Military Historical Society of Australia, 1971); O. Ruhen, *Port of Melbourne 1835–1976* (North Melbourne: Cassell Australia, 1976); M. Austin, 'Her Majesty's Colonial Sloop *Victoria*', *Sabretache*, Vol. 22, No. 3 (July–Sept. 1981), pp. 26–29; D.F. Davis, 'Australia's First Warship, HM Victorian Ship Victoria', *Naval Historical Review*, Vol. 13, No. 4 (Dec. 1992), pp. 26–27; & I. MacFarlane & N. Smith, *Victoria: and Australia's First War* (Victoria: Mostly Unsung Military History Research and Publications, 2005).

124 *Argus*, 19 April 1860, p. 4.

125 *Ibid.*, 7 April 1860, p. 4.

126 For information on Norman, refer to: Evans, *op. cit.*, pp. 9–16, 59 & 149; & C. Jones, *Australian Colonial Navies* (Canberra: Australian War Memorial, 1986), pp. 15–16, 19–20, 22–24, 33 & 166.

127 *Argus*, 18 April 1860, p. 4.

128 'A 10: H.M.S.S. "Victoria"', *Votes and Proceedings of the Legislative Council: 1861–62* (Melbourne: John Ferres, Government Printer), p. 191. Reimbursement to the Victorian government for these expenses would in turn drag on into 1863. *Argus*, 10 April, pp. 4 & 6 and 11 April 1861, p. 6; 14 May, p. 6 & 21 May 1862, p. 5; & 4 September 1863, p. 6.

129 *Ibid.*, 20 April 1860, p. 4.

130 Steam Sloop 'Victoria': Correspondence Relative to the Detention of the Steam Sloop *Victoria*, on Service in NZ [Ordered Printed, 26 June 1860]: F355.03293 S799, *AWM*; & 'A 13: Correspondence Relative to the Detention of the S.S. "Victoria" in NZ', *Votes and Proceedings of the Legislative Council: 1859–60* (Melbourne: John Ferres, Government Printer), p. 359.

131 *Argus*, 22 August 1860, p. 6.

132 Lieutenant-Colonel Carey, *Narrative of the Late War in New Zealand* (London: Richard Bentley, 1863), p. 20.

133 *Argus*, 13 July, p. 5, 31 July, p. 5 & 7 August 1860, p. 6; *Sydney Morning Herald*, 8 August 1860, p. 5;

& B. Wells, *The History of Taranaki* (New Plymouth: Edmondson & Avery, 'Taranaki News' Office, 1878), pp. 209, 210, 215, 217–19 & 226.

134 *Sydney Morning Herald*, 8 September 1860, p. 8; & *Argus*, 12 September 1860, p. 7. Also refer to: J.O'C. Ross, *The White Ensign in Early New Zealand* (Wellington: A.H. & A.W. Reed, 1967), p. 63; F. Glen, *For Glory and a Farm* (Whakatane: Whakatane & District Historical Society, 1985), Appendix 8: Table 2, p. 125; F. Glen, 'Australian involvement in New Zealand Wars', in I. McGibbon (ed.), *The Oxford Companion to New Zealand Military History* (Auckland, NZ: Oxford University Press, 2000), pp. 383–86; & Davis, *op. cit.*, p. 27.

135 *Sydney Morning Herald*, 12 January, p. 6, 14 January, p. 8 & 21 January 1861, pp. 6–7; *Supplement to the Argus*, 16 January 1861, p. 1; *Argus*, 25 January 1861, p. 6; & Greig, *op. cit.*, p. 104.

136 J. Belich, *The New Zealand Wars* (Auckland: Penguin Books, 1988), p. 108; & for Pratt's despatch to Governor Gore Browne regarding Matarikoriko, refer to: 'E-No. 1a: Further Papers Relative to the Native Insurrection', *JHRNZ: 1861* (Auckland), pp. 8–10 of E-No. 1a.

137 *Argus*, 28 February 1861, pp. 4 & 6.

138 *Ibid.*, 17 May 1860, pp. 4 & 6.

139 GOV/1: Despatches from the Secretary of State for the Colonies: Vol. 1: Circular Despatch dated 10 August 1860, *QSA*; GOV/2: Despatches from the Secretary of State for the Colonies: Vol. 2: Duplicate Queensland Circular, 26 January 1861 (pp. 29–31), *QSA*; J.F.G. Foxton, 'The Evolution and Development of an Australian Naval Policy', *Commonwealth Military Journal* (Nov. 1911), pp. 654–55; Millar, *op. cit.*, pp. 53–55; B.A. Knox, 'Colonial Influence on Imperial Policy, 1858–1866: Victoria and the Colonial Naval Defence Act, 1865', *Historical Studies Australia and New Zealand*, Vol. 11, No. 41 (Nov. 1963), pp. 61, 62 & 65; & A. McNicoll, 'Defence: Australian Navy', in *The Australian Encyclopaedia: Volume 2* (Sydney: The Grolier Society of Australia, 1977), p. 221.

140 *Argus*, 14 July 1860, p. 4.

141 *Ibid.*, p. 6.

142 *Votes and Proceedings of the Legislative Council: 1859–60* (Melbourne: John Ferres, Government Printer), p. 151; *Argus*, 18 July 1860, p. 7; & *Age*, 18 July 1860, p. 7.

143 *Argus*, 16 July 1860, p. 5.

144 *Ibid.*, pp. 5 & 6.

145 *Ibid.*, 18 July 1860, p. 5; & *Age*, 18 July 1860, p. 5.

146 *Ibid.*

147 *Argus*, 19 July 1860, p. 5.

148 *Age*, 19 July 1860, p. 5. Numbers of troops involved extracted from account in: *Argus*, 19 July 1860, p. 5. For other coverage of this departure, refer to: *Argus*, 19 July 1860, pp. 4 & 5; & *Sydney Morning Herald*, 23 July 1860, p. 5; and an account of the voyage, arrival and reception of this contingent in Taranaki found in: *Argus*, 7 August 1860, p. 5.

149 *Argus*, 18 July 1860, p. 4.

150 *Ibid.*; 23 July 1860, p. 4.

151 *Ibid.*, 23 July 1860, p. 4.

152 *Sydney Morning Herald*, 25 July 1860, p. 4; & also refer to: *Argus*, 25 July 1860, p. 5.

153 *Argus*, 25 July 1860, p. 5; & also refer to: *Ibid.*, p. 4. Other coverage of the departure of the *Victoria* and General Pratt found in: *Supplement to the Argus*, 25 July 1860, p. 2; & *Sydney Morning Herald*, 25 July, p. 4, 27 July, p. 4 & 31 July 1860, p. 8.

154 *Argus*, 25 July 1860, p. 5.

155 For press information on Pasley's Victorian and New Zealand service, refer to: *Argus*, 25 July, p. 5, 4 August, p. 6, 22 November, p. 5 and 14 December 1860, p. 4, 24 January 1861, p. 5 & 11 December 1863, p. 5; & *Sydney Morning Herald*, 6 March 1861, p. 3. For other sources refer to: *VGG*: No. 2, 7 January 1859, p. 11, No. 9, 17 January 1860, p. 109, No. 17, 3 February 1860, p. 239 & No. 63, 18 May 1860, p. 953; P. Mennell, *The Dictionary of Australasian Biography* (London: Hutchinson & Co., 1892), pp. 365–66; B. Nairn, G. Serle & R. Ward, *ADB. Volume 5: 1851–1890: K–Q* (Carlton: Melbourne University Press, 1974), pp. 409–11; & C. Coulthard-Clark, *The Diggers* (Carlton: Melbourne University Press, 1993), pp. 46–48.

156 *Argus*, 5 August 1862, p. 4; & R. McNicoll, *op. cit.*, p. 52.

157 *Hobart Town Daily Mercury*, 17 & 20 April 1860; & *Launceston Examiner*, 17 April 1860, p. 3.

158 *Hobart Town Daily Mercury*, 23 & 24 April 1860; *Launceston Examiner*, 26 April 1860, p. 3; & also refer to: Smythies, *op. cit.*, pp. 361–62.

159 *Hobart Town Mercury*, 24 April & 14 May 1860; & *Launceston Examiner*, 24 April, p. 2 & 2 June 1860, p. 2.

160 *Launceston Examiner*, 19 May 1860, p. 3.

161 *Mercury*, 17 July 1860; & also reported in: *Moreton Bay Courier*, 9 August 1860; *Sydney Morning Herald*, 31 July 1860, p. 8; & *Argus*, 23 July 1860, p. 5.

162 GO 47: Governor's Inward Correspondence on Military Matters: Letter from Major General Pratt, to the Governor of Tasmania, dated Head Quarters, Melbourne, 12 February 1862, *AOT.*

163 *Hobart Town Daily Mercury*, 24 April 1860.

164 *Ibid.*, 28 April 1860.

165 *Ibid.*

166 *Mercury*, 17 July 1860.

CHAPTER THREE

1 *The Cyclopedia of Tasmania … Volume I* (Hobart: Maitland Krone, 1900), p. 208; *Sydney Morning Herald*, 18 March 1885, p. 6; & *Votes and Proceedings of the Legislative Council: 1858–59*, pp. 1–2 of B 1: Indian Relief Fund (pp. 397–98).

2 J. Bach, *The Australia Station* (Kensington: New South Wales University Press, 1986), pp. 76, 80 & 159.

3 *Mercury*, 21 October 1863 & 4 June 1864; *Launceston Examiner*, 7 June 1864, p. 5; *Argus*, 9 May 1864, p. 5; & *Sydney Morning Herald*, 26 January, p. 4 & 8 March 1864, p. 5.

4 'General Orders', *United Service Journal*, Part I (1829), p. 512. For other information dealing with marriage, wives and children of soldiers in the British Army, refer to: G.L. Morley, 'Our Married People', *United Service Magazine*, Vol. 9 (May–Sept. 1894), pp. 66–72; I. Wards, *The Shadow of the Land* (Wellington: Historical Publications Branch, Department of Internal Affairs, 1968), pp. 377–78; H. King, 'Some Aspects of Police Administration in New South Wales, 1825–1851', *Royal Australian Historical Society*, Vol. 42, Part 5 (1956), p. 225; A.R. Skelley, *The Victorian Army at Home* (London: Croom Helm Ltd, 1977), pp. 30–31; & M. Barthorp, *To Face the Daring Maoris* (London: Hodder and Stoughton, 1979), pp. 27–28.

5 R.H.R. Smythies, *Historical Records of the 40th (2nd Somersetshire) Regiment* (Devonport: A.H. Swiss, 1894), pp. 331–60 & 395–96; & E.A.H. Webb, *History of the 12th (The Suffolk) Regiment 1685–1913* (London: Spottiswoode & Co., 1914), pp. 268–96.

6 W. Swainson, *New Zealand and the War* (London: Smith, Elder & Co., 1862), pp. 169–70.

7 'E-No. 1: Section II: Despatches from Governor Sir G. Grey, K.C.B.: Enclosure 5 in No. 4: Estimate of Losses of Settlers at Taranaki from the Late War', *JHRNZ: 1862* (Auckland, NZ), pp. 10–11 of E-No. 1 (Sec. II).

8 'D.-No. 8: Papers Relative to a Grant of £1,000 by the Legislature of the Colony of Victoria, in Aid of the Taranaki Relief Fund', *JHRNZ: 1861* (Auckland, NZ).

9 *Argus*, 24 January, p. 5 & 8 February 1861, p. 4. In August 1861 the New Zealand government passed a resolution thanking Victoria for this liberal monetary grant. *JHRNZ: 1861* (Auckland, NZ), pp. 149–50; & *Votes and Proceedings of the Legislative Council: 1861–62* (Melbourne: John Ferres, Government Printer), p. 21; & also refer to: *Argus*, 23 October 1861, pp. 4 & 6.

10 *NZPD: 1861 to 1863* (Wellington: G. Didsbury, Government Printer, 1886), p. 324.

11 *Argus*, 16 July 1867, p. 7.

12 *Ibid.*, 27 August 1860, p. 5.

13 *Ibid.*, 6 September, p. 4 & 8 September 1860, pp. 4 & 5.

14 *Ibid.*, 13 September, p. 5, 22 September, p. 5, 25 September, p. 5, 27 September, p. 5, 29 September, p. 4, 5 October, pp. 4 & 5, 6 October, p. 4, 12 October, p. 5, 23 October, p. 5 & 3 November 1860, p. 4; & 19 January, p. 5 & 20 June 1861, p. 5; & *Supplement to the Argus*, 12 October 1860, p. 1.

15 *Argus*, 6 October 1860, p. 4.

16 *Argus*, 3 November 1860, p. 4.

17 *Sydney Morning Herald*, 3 September, pp. 4 & 8 and 16 November 1860, p. 3.

18 *Ibid.*, 11 September, p. 5, 12 September, p. 5, 18 September, p. 5 & 21 September 1860, p. 5; & *Argus*, 17 September 1860, p. 6.

19 *Sydney Morning Herald*, 22 September, p. 4 & 1 October 1860, p. 4.
20 *Ibid.*, 2 October 1860, p. 4 (and for detailed coverage refer to pp. 4–5); & 6 October 1860, p. 4.
21 *Ibid.*, 6 October 1860, p. 4; & also refer to: *Argus*, 2 October, p. 5 & 3 October 1860, p. 5.
22 *Sydney Morning Herald*, 13 October, p. 7, 28 November, p. 6, 1 December, p. 8 & 15 December 1860, p. 5.
23 *Ibid.*, 16 January, p. 5 & 12 April 1861, p. 6.
24 *Hobart Town Daily Mercury/Mercury*, 30 May & 27 October 1860.
25 'Soldiers' Wives and their Children' by 'Inquirer', *Sydney Morning Herald*, 23 July 1860, p. 8; & also refer to: letters to editor by 'Homo' & 'Vox Humana', 27 July, p. 5 & 28 July 1860, p. 5.
26 *Moreton Bay Courier*, 31 July 1860.
27 *Sydney Morning Herald*, 26 July 1860, p. 4.
28 *Ibid.*
29 *Ibid.*, 28 July 1860, p. 8.
30 *Ibid.*, 4 August 1860, p. 4.
31 *Ibid.*, 25 August 1860, p. 6 & 21 September 1860, p. 5.
32 *Ibid.*, 22 November 1860, p. 5.
33 *Ibid.*, 26 April, p. 2, 16 June, p. 7 & 20 August 1860, p. 2.
34 *Ibid.*
35 Original Letters, of W. Shaw [Bandsman, 40th Regiment] War in NZ, 1860: 3DRL/3398A, *AWM.*
36 *Argus*, 9 August, p. 7, 18 September, p. 5, 27 October, p. 5 & 26 November 1860, p. 5; & *South Australian Register*, 26 November 1860.
37 *Argus*, 26 November 1860, p. 5.
38 *Ibid.*, 19 April 1861, p. 7.
39 *Ibid.*, 16 July 1860, p. 7.
40 *Ibid.*, 20 July 1860, p. 5.
41 *Ibid.*, 1 August 1860, pp. 4 & 6; & also refer to: *Ibid.*, 25 July, p. 4, 26 July, pp. 5 & 6, 27 July, p. 6 & 31 July 1860, p. 5.
42 *Ibid.*, 19 July, p. 5, 28 July, p. 4 & 1 August 1860, p. 4.
43 *Ibid.*, 28 July, p. 4, 3 August, p. 5, 4 August, pp. 4 & 5, 8 August, p. 5, 30 August, p. 5 & 1 September 1860, p. 5.
44 *Ibid.*, 18 August 1860, p. 4.
45 *Ibid.*, 3 October 1860, p. 5.
46 *Ibid.*, 3 October, p. 5, 26 October, p. 5 & 2 November 1860, p. 5.
47 *Ibid.*, 13 November 1860, p. 5.
48 *Argus*, 16 November, p. 5, 28 November, p. 5, 1 December, p. 4, 4 December, p. 4, 6 December, p. 5 & 7 December 1860, p. 5 and 15 January, p. 5 & 24 January 1861, p. 5; *Sydney Morning Herald*, 12 December 1860, p. 3; & also refer to: E.W. Moorhead, 'Excursion to the Victoria Barracks St Kilda Road', *Victorian Historical Magazine*, Vol. 26, No. 1 (Sept. 1954), p. 17.
49 *Argus*, 15 January 1861, p. 5.
50 *Ibid.*, 20 March 1861, p. 4.
51 *Ibid.*, 23 April 1861, p. 5.
52 *Ibid.*, 23 May 1861, p. 5.
53 *Ibid.*, 30 July 1862, p. 5.
54 For examples of this coverage, refer to: *Hobart Town Daily Mercury/Mercury*, 30 May, 14, 21 & 24 September and 27 October 1860 & 18 February 1861; & *Launceston Examiner*, 15 September, p. 2, 27 September, p. 2 & 6 October 1860, p. 2.
55 *Mercury*, 20 July 1860.
56 *Ibid.*, 23 July 1860.
57 Tasmanian press also republished letters from British troops in Taranaki which were found in other papers such as the *Argus*; refer to: *Mercury*, 1 & 29 November and 4 December 1860; & *Launceston Examiner*, 4 December 1860, p. 2.
58 *Mercury*, 5 March 1861.
59 Examples here include: *South Australian Register*, 3 & 27 August (soldier family relief) and 26 September

& 1 October 1860 (Taranaki settler relief); & *Moreton Bay Courier*, 12 June (Taranaki settler relief) and 31 July 1860 (soldier family relief).

60 *South Australian Register*, 5 September 1860.

61 *Sydney Morning Herald*, 20 September 1860, p. 2. The *South Australian Register* reported this same information later on 26 September, but appears to be referring to events that occurred in Victoria, rather than South Australia, though this is not entirely clear. *South Australian Register*, 26 September 1860.

62 *Argus*, 12 April 1861, pp. 4 & 5; & also refer to: *Ibid.*, 11 April 1861, pp. 4 & 5.

63 *Ibid.*, 12 April, pp. 4, 5 & 6, 17 April, p. 6, 18 April, p. 6, 19 April, p. 6, 23 April, p. 4, 24 April, pp. 4 & 6 and 25 April 1861, p. 5.

64 *Ibid.*, 15 April, p. 4 & 19 April 1861, p. 5.

65 *Ibid.*, 19 April 1861, p. 5.

66 *Ibid.*, 19 April, p. 5, 23 April, p. 4 & 24 April 1861, p. 5.

67 NZ War: Copy of a Despatch from His Excellency Sir T. Gore Browne, conveying the Thanks of the NZ Government for the Services rendered by H.M.C.S. *Victoria*, . . .; also copy of His Excellency Sir Henry Barkly's Reply [Ordered Printed, 23 April 1861]: V355.03293 B884n, *AWM*; & also refer to: *Argus*, 4 May 1861, p. 7.

68 T.B. Millar, 'The History of the Defence Forces of the Port Phillip District and Colony of Victoria 1836–1900', MA thesis, University of Melbourne (September 1957), p. 40.

69 *Sydney Morning Herald*, 16 July, p. 4 & 17 July 1861, p. 5.

70 *Ibid.*, 17 October 1861, pp. 2 & 5; *Argus*, 17 October 1861, p. 5; & NG/8: Governor of NSW Registers of Despatches Received from the Lieutenant Governors of the Other Australian Colonies & the Governor of NZ: Despatch No. 717, 1 October 1861, p. 29 of reel, *AONSW*.

71 NG/29: Copies of Despatches to the Governors or Lieutenant Governors of Other Australian Colonies and NZ, the Governor of India, and various Officials and Private Individuals: Despatch dated Sydney, 12 March 1862, *AONSW*.

72 NG/10: Despatches and Enclosures from the Governor of NZ: Despatch dated 15 April 1862, p. 83 of reel; & NG/8: Despatch dated 15 April 1862, p. 29 of reel, *AONSW*.

CHAPTER FOUR

1 Letter by Stephen White, dated Auckland, NZ, 31 June 1862: Hill Collection: 1986.85.4, *National Museum of Australia*; & also refer to: J. Belich, *The New Zealand Wars* (Auckland: Penguin Books, 1988).

2 *NZG*, No. 29, 15 July 1863, pp. 277–78.

3 B.J. Dalton, 'A New Look at the Maori Wars of the Sixties', *Historical Studies Australia and New Zealand*, Vol. 12, No. 46 (April 1966), p. 238; & also refer to: Belich, *op. cit.*, p. 133.

4 *NZPD: 1861 to 1863* (Wellington: G. Didsbury, Government Printer, 1886), pp. 733–34, 738 & 754; & also refer to: G.W. Rusden, *History of New Zealand: Volume II* (Melbourne: Melville, Mullen & Slade, 1895), p. 245.

5 Research by Glen has previously indicated sizes of the Australian-recruited elements for each of the five main regiments of military settlers. He also emphasises that it is almost impossible to gain exact figures for all Australian enlistments. F. Glen, *For Glory and a Farm* (Whakatane: Whakatane & District Historical Society, 1985), p. 109.

6 AD 31/8: Army Department, Taranaki Military Settlers Nominal and Descriptive Roll Book, 1863–69, *NANZ*.

7 *Argus*, 26 January, p. 4 & 2 February 1864, p. 4; Document Control Centre: Records of Early Wars in NZ: 417/008/002, *AWM*; AD 31/8: Nominal & Descriptive Roll of the 'Melbourne Contingent', p. 67, *NANZ*; & AD 32/4126: Sire, Francis. Private, No. 8 Company, 'Melbourne Contingent' of Taranaki Military Settlers, *NANZ*.

8 T. McDonnell, *An Explanation of the Principal Causes which led to the Present War on the West Coast of New Zealand* (Wanganui: Walter Taylor, Times Office, 1869), pp. 9–11.

9 AD 32/4126: Sire, Francis. Private, No. 8 Company, 'Melbourne Contingent' of Taranaki Military Settlers, *NANZ*; *NZG*, No. 46, 25 May 1877, p. 577; & J.E. Hopkins, *Further Selected New Zealand War Medal Rolls of Applications Granted up to 1900* (Brisbane: J.E. Hopkins, 1998), p. 45.

10 J.E. Hopkins-Weise, 'A History of the Colonial Defence Force (Cavalry): and the Australian Context', *The Volunteers*, Vol. 26, No. 1 (July 2000), pp. 5–25; & also refer to: Hopkins (1998), *op. cit.*, p. 49.

11 South Australian Register, 28 September 1863.

12 *Ibid.*, 29 December 1863.

13 *Ibid.*, 19 July 1864.

14 *Ibid.*, 21 April, 18 August, 4 October & 5 December 1860.

15 Document Control Centre: Records of Early Wars in NZ: 417/008/002, *AWM*.

16 For such press coverage refer to: *South Australian Register*, 19, 21, 24, 25, 26, 27 & 31 August and 1, 2, 8 & 24 September 1863.

17 *South Australian Register*, 29 December 1863; & also refer to: *Ibid.*, 15 September 1864.

18 *Ibid.*, 29 December 1863.

19 *Ibid.*, 23 January 1864; *NZG*, No. 55, 27 October 1863, p. 460; *NZAL 1863*, p. 3; & T.W. Gudgeon, *The Defenders of New Zealand* (Auckland: H. Brett, 1887), p. 84.

20 *South Australian Register*, 1 November 1864; & Document Control Centre: Records of Early Wars in NZ: 417/008/002, *AWM*.

21 William Race enlisted in the 1st Waikato Regiment at Melbourne, Victoria, on 1 September 1863, and later served in No. 2 Company, Forest Rangers during December 1863 to May 1864. L.L. Barton, *Australians in the Waikato War* (North Sydney: Library of Australian History, 1979), p. 64; & R. Stowers, *Forest Rangers* (Hamilton: Richard Stowers, 1996), p. 245.

22 CY POS 127: Under The Flag; Reminiscences of the Maori Land (Waikato) War by a Forest Ranger [William Race, c. 1895], pp. 176–77 of reel, *Mitchell Library*; & also refer to: Gudgeon, *op. cit.*, p. 84.

23 *NZG*, No. 12, 9 April 1864, pp. 155 & 157; *South Australian Register*, 4 May, 16, 19 & 23 July 1864; & *Illustrated Sydney News*, 16 July 1864, p. 6.

24 *South Australian Register*, 1 November 1864; Document Control Centre: Records of Early Wars in NZ: 417/008/002, *AWM*; R. Stowers, *The New Zealand Medal To Colonials* (Hamilton: Richard Stowers, 1998), p. 101; 'D.-No. 19. Return of Pensions and Allowances: Paid by the Colonial Government', *JHRNZ: 1868*, p. 4 of D.-No. 19; & 'B.-18: Pensions Paid By The Colony (List of): Return showing Names of Persons drawing Pensions, &c.', *AJHRNZ: Vol. I: 1888* (Wellington), p. 4 of B.-18.

25 H.W. Pearse, *History of the 31st Foot Huntingdonshire Regt. [&] 70th Foot Surrey Regt.* (London: Spottiswoode, Ballantyne & Co. Ltd, 1916), pp. 321–34 (reference to Captain D.M. Fraser, p. 324).

26 Fraser was appointed ensign in 1846, lieutenant in 1849, and captain in 1858. He served with the 80th Regiment during the Burmese War (1852–53), then the 'Indian Mutiny' (1858), before active service in New Zealand. *Sydney Morning Herald*, 16 December 1864, p. 4.

27 *Ibid.*, 7 December 1863, p. 4. For other information on Phelps, refer to: *Ibid.*, 5 December, p. 7 & 21 December 1863, pp. 11–12; *Argus*, 8 December 1863, p. 5; J. Featon, *The Waikato War* (Auckland: J.D. Wickham, Free Lance General Printing Office, 1879), pp. 26 & 60–64; H. O'Donnell, *Historical Records of the 14th Regiment* (Devonport: A.H. Swiss, [1893?]), pp. 191–93.

28 M. Barthorp, *To Face the Daring Maoris* (London: Hodder and Stoughton, 1979), p. 62; & J. Bach, *The Australia Station* (Kensington: New South Wales University Press, 1986), p. 5.

29 AD 31/8: Nominal & Descriptive Roll of the 'Otago Contingent', pp. 2, 3, 6, 15, 16, 17, 23, 26 & 30, *NANZ*.

30 AD 1 1887/2951: Stevens, Campbell. Private, No. 10 Company, 3rd Waikato Regiment; AD 76/3 (repro 14): Nominal and Descriptive Roll. 3rd Waikato Militia Regiment: Reg. No. 1352: Stevens, Campbell, *NANZ*; J.E. Hopkins, *Selected New Zealand War Medal Rolls of Entitlements, Rejections, and Applications Granted up to 1900* (Brisbane: J.E. Hopkins, 1997), p. 84; & Barton (1979), *op. cit.*, p. 79.

31 Glen (1985), *op. cit.*, p. 109; Barton (1979), *op. cit.*, p. 52; L.L. Barton, 'Australians in the Waikato War: Additions & Corrections', *Despatch*, Vol. 14, No. 4 (Oct. 1983), p. 80; & M.D.W. Hodder, 'Publicising The Sources: Australians in the Waikato War', *Archifacts*, No. 14 (June 1980), pp. 319–25.

32 *Sydney Morning Herald*, 3 February 1864, p. 5; & *Argus*, 8 February 1864, p. 5.

33 *NZG*, No. 17, 9 May 1864, p. 206 (and for full correspondence refer to pp. 203–10); & G. Mair, *The Story of Gate Pa* (Tauranga: Bay of Plenty Times Office, 1926), pp. 11–19 & 29–35.

34 *Sydney Morning Herald*, 8 July, p. 4, 9 July, p. 4 & 18 July 1864, p. 2.

35 Chief Secretary's Office: GRG 24, Series 51, Special List No. 124, *SRSA*.

36 Chief Secretary's Office: GRG 24, Series 51, Special List No. 125, *SRSA*.

37 *South Australian Register*, 'Charitable People' by 'Industrious' & 'The Soldiers' Families' by 'Another Lady', 5 October; 'Soldiers' Bazaar' by 'A Private Soldier', 6 October; 'The Soldiers' Families' by 'Reliable', 21 October; & 'Soldiers' Families' by 'A Labouring Man', 24 October 1863.

38 *Ibid.*, 10 November 1863; & repeated for 'English Summary', 26 November 1863.

39 *Ibid.*, 3 October 1863.

40 *Ibid.*, 3, 8 & 12 October 1863.

41 *Ibid.*, 13 October 1863.

42 *Ibid.*, 15 October 1863.

43 *Ibid.*, 26 October 1863.

44 *Ibid.*, 29 & 30 October 1863.

45 *Ibid.*, 31 October 1863.

46 *Ibid.*, 7, 18, 20, 21, 23, 24 November and 4 & 8 December 1863.

47 *Ibid.*, 17 & 28 December 1863 and 5, 15, 26, 27 & 29 January and 2 February 1864.

48 *Ibid.*, 8, 22, 26 & 29 March and 5 April 1864.

49 *Ibid.*, 3 May 1864.

50 *Ibid.*, 3 May, 9 June, 5 July & 2 August 1864.

51 *Ibid.*, 8 & 13 September and 4 October 1864.

52 *Mercury*, 28 August 1863. To maintain public focus on this relief effort the advertisement for this bazaar was carried in the press from 29 September until 6 October. *Mercury*, 29 & 30 September, 1, 2, 3, 5 & 6 October 1863.

53 *Ibid.*, 7, 8, 9 & 23 October 1863.

54 *Ibid.*, 10 October 1863.

55 *Ibid.*, 5 April 1864.

56 *Ibid.*

57 *Ibid.*

58 *Ibid.*, 6 April 1864.

59 *Ibid.*, 8 April 1864.

60 *NZG*, No. 50, 24 September 1863, p. 428.

61 *Sydney Morning Herald*, 10 October, p. 1 & 13 October 1863, p. 1.

62 *NZPD: 1861 to 1863* (Wellington: G. Didsbury, Government Printer, 1886), p. 821.

63 *Mercury*, 26 December 1863.

64 *Ibid.*, 28 December 1863.

65 Tasmanian press also provided coverage of the similar experiences being faced by the wives and families of military settlers in other colonies, including efforts to organise transportation for such families, as well as their situation and accommodation once in New Zealand. Refer to: *Ibid.*, 11 & 23 January and 24 March 1864; & *Launceston Examiner*, 23 February, p. 2, 28 June, p. 3 & 14 July 1864, pp. 3 & 5.

66 *Mercury*, 1 January 1864.

67 *Ibid.*, 26 February 1864; & also refer to: 17, 21, 22 & 27 February 1864.

68 *Ibid.*, 15 April 1864.

69 *Ibid.* Several days later the *Mercury* followed up with further details on the 'Wives and Children of the Auckland Volunteers'. *Ibid.*, 18 April 1864.

70 *Launceston Examiner*, 31 December 1864, p. 3.

71 CSD 4/45/636. Colonial Secretary: Correspondence File: 636, *AOT*.

72 *Argus*, 16 December 1863, p. 7.

73 *Launceston Examiner*, 23 February 1864, p. 2.

74 Attached details to letter to Victorian Chief Secretary, from James Boyd, M.D., Honorary Secretary of the Bendigo Benevolent Asylum, dated Sandhurst, 4 June 1864, AWM27 100/6: Photographic Reproductions of Correspondence Relating to the Service of Victorians in the Maori War of 1863–64, *AWM*.

75 Letter to the Victorian Chief Secretary, from James Boyd, M.D., Honorary Secretary of the Bendigo Benevolent Asylum, dated Sandhurst, 4 June 1864, AWM27 100/6, *AWM*.

ENDNOTES

76 *Argus*, 11 July, p. 5, 16 July, p. 5, 18 July, p. 4, 20 August, p. 4 & 26 August 1864, p. 4.

77 The following month these restrictions were amended so as not to apply to 'Friendly Natives', but only to those districts where the Maori were 'in arms against Her Majesty's Government'; and later in 1865, additional items were added to the list of restricted imports. *NZG*: No. 36, 6 August 1863, p. 307, No. 42, 21 August 1863, p. 354 & No. 18, 31 May 1865, p. 157.

78 For examples refer to: *South Australian Register*, 17 June 1863; *Sydney Morning Herald*, 21 August 1863, p. 16, 2 April, p. 8 & 12 May 1864, p. 4; *Mercury*, 28 August 1863; & *Argus*, 22 April 1864, p. 5.

79 Also refer to: 'D.-No. 16: Papers relative to the Supply of Ammunition to Rebel Natives', *JHRNZ: 1865* (Wellington); see especially pp. 3–4 of D.-No. 16.

80 *Argus*, 14 December 1863, p. 4; & *South Australian Register*, 26 December 1863, p. 6.

81 *Sydney Morning Herald*, 20 February, p. 13 & 26 May 1864, p. 5; *Launceston Examiner*, 3 March 1864, p. 5; & *South Australian Register*, 6 June 1864.

82 *Sydney Morning Herald*, 27 June 1863, p. 7.

83 *Launceston Examiner*, 17 October 1863, p. 5.

84 *Argus*, 22 January 1864, p. 6.

85 *Courier*, 29 June 1863; & also refer to: *Mercury*, 2 July 1863.

86 NG/26: Copies of letters to officials and Private Persons: Despatch dated 10 July 1863, pp. 105–6, *AONSW*.

87 NG/26: 2 Despatches dated 12 December 1863, pp. 129–30, *AONSW*.

88 *South Australian Register*, 28 August 1863; & *VGG*, No. 96, 18 September 1863, p. 2063.

89 *Supplement to the NSWGG*, No. 187, 17 October 1862, pp. 2019–20; *NZG*, No. 2, 23 January 1863, pp. 18–19; & *Supplement to the NSWGG*, No. 81, 2 May 1865, pp. 961–62.

90 *Sydney Morning Herald*, 17 July 1863, p. 3.

91 *VGG*, No. 79, 4 August 1863, pp. 1695–96.

92 *Argus*, 3 August 1863, p. 5; & also refer to: *Ibid.*, 4 August 1863, p. 3.

93 Major De Winton, *Soldiering Fifty Years Ago* (London: European Mail Ltd, 1898), p. 69.

94 *Argus*, 20 March 1908, p. 4; & also refer to detailed obituary, *Sydney Morning Herald*, 20 March 1908, p. 7.

95 P. Mennell, *The Dictionary of Australasian Biography* (London: Hutchinson & Co., 1892), pp. 512–13; P. Serle, *Dictionary of Australian Biography: Volume II* (Sydney: Angus & Robertson, 1949), p. 490; G. Serle & R. Ward, *ADB: Volume 6: 1851–1890: R–Z* (Carlton: Melbourne University Press, 1976), p. 409; H. Gordon, *An Eyewitness History of Australia* (Adelaide: Rigby Limited, 1976), pp. 82–84; Glen (1985), *op. cit.*, pp. 39–43; P. Burgess, *Warco* (Richmond: William Heinemann Australia, 1986), pp. 13–14; & F. Glen, 'Howard Willoughby: Australian War Correspondent to the NZ Land War 1863', *The Volunteers*, Vol. 18, No. 3 (Feb. 1993), [no page numbers].

96 *Argus*, 7 November 1863, pp. 4–5.

97 *Ibid.*, 7 December 1863, pp. 4 & 5.

98 Glen (1985), *op. cit.*, p. 40.

99 For Willoughby's detailed war reports (apart from those cited elsewhere here) refer to: *Argus*, 12 December, pp. 5–6 & 28 December 1863, pp. 5–6 and 6 January, p. 5, 13 January, p. 6, 16 January, p. 5, 22 January, p. 6, 26 January, p. 5, 9 February, p. 5, 29 February, p. 6 & 28 March 1864, p. 6; & *Supplement to the Argus*, 13 February, pp. 1–2 & 16 March 1864, pp. 1–2.

100 *Argus*, 4 April 1864, p. 5 (and continues on to p. 6).

101 *Ibid.*, 4 April 1864, p. 6.

102 *Sydney Morning Herald*, 5 September 1864, p. 5.

103 The first report appears to be: 'The War In New Zealand. Urgent Demand For More Soldiers.... [From Our Own Correspondent.]', *Ibid.*, 12 September 1863, p. 7; & other reports during 1863–64 include: 21 November, p. 13 & 8 December 1863, p. 5 and 21 March, p. 9, 5 April, p. 5, 10 May, p. 5, 23 May, p. 5, 17 June, p. 5, 20 June, p. 5, 21 June, pp. 10–11, 29 September, p. 5, 10 October, p. 5, 26 October, p. 5, 3 November, p. 5, 9 November, p. 5, 9 December, p. 5 & 21 December 1864, p. 9.

104 Glen (1985), *op. cit.*, p. 27.

105 *Sydney Morning Herald*, 12 September 1863, p. 7 (and republished, 21 September 1863, p. 7).

106 *Argus*, 29 February 1864, p. 6.

107 Editorial entitled 'Maoriland "Civilised" ', *Victorian*, 23 January 1864, pp. 577–78; & also refer to: B. Nairn, G. Serle & R. Ward, *ADB: Volume 4: 1851–1890: D–J* (Carlton: Melbourne University Press, 1972), pp. 44–45; & C. Pearl, *Brilliant Dan Deniehy* (Melbourne: Thomas Nelson Ltd, 1972), pp. 105 & 110.

108 'The Maori War', *Victorian*, 12 December 1863, p. 506.

109 For Hoare's explanation, refer to: 'First Preface To The Maori' in B. Hoare, *Figures of Fancy* (Adelaide: John Howell, 1869).

110 *War Things That Matter* (Melbourne: E.W. Cole, 1918).

111 *Ibid.*, refer to 'Canto First.: II.', p. 6; & for full text of poem 'The Maori: A Tale', see pp. 5–40. E.M. Miller, *Australian Literature: . . . Volumes I & II* (Sydney: Sydney University Press, 1940), pp. 246 & 382 (Vol. I) & p. 869 (Vol. II).

CHAPTER FIVE

1 *NZPD: 1861 to 1863* (Wellington: G. Didsbury, Government Printer, 1886), pp. 759–60.

2 For example, refer to: *Sydney Morning Herald*, 24 July 1863, p. 5.

3 Refer to this author's articles: 'A History of the Colonial Defence Force (Cavalry): and the Australian Context', *The Volunteers*, Vol. 26, No. 1 (July 2000), pp. 5–25; or 'New Zealand's Colonial Defence Force (Cavalry) and its Australian Context, 1863–66', *Sabretache*, Vol. 43, No. 3 (Sept. 2002), pp. 23–39.

4 *NZPD: 1861 to 1863, op. cit.*

5 For an example of this, refer to: 'Commercial' news, *Launceston Examiner*, 1 September 1863, p. 4.

6 *Ibid.*, 19 December 1863, p. 4.

7 *Ibid.*, 19 March 1864, p. 4.

8 'A.-No.6: Further Papers Relating to the Military Defence of NZ: Memorandum on Measures of Defence in Northern Island', *JHRNZ: 1863* (Auckland), p. 1 of A.-No.6; & also refer to: F. Glen, *For Glory and a Farm* (Whakatane: Whakatane & District Historical Society, 1985), p. 38.

9 W. Fox, *The War in New Zealand* (London: Smith, Elder and Co., 1866), p. 13.

10 *Sydney Morning Herald*, 28 January, p. 8 & 4 March 1864, p. 5.

11 *Ibid.*, 12 September 1863, p. 9.

12 *Argus*, 15 January 1864, p. 7; & also refer to: Glen, *op. cit.*, p. 38.

13 Glen, *op. cit.*, p. 28.

14 *Mercury*, 1, 2 & 4 June 1863.

15 *Ibid.*, 10, 15 & 16 June 1863; & *South Australian Register*, 25 June 1863.

16 CSD 4/85/411. Colonial Secretary: Correspondence File: 411, *AOT*; & *The Mercury*, 5 & 6 August 1863.

17 E. Hodder, *The History of South Australia: . . . Vol. 1* (London: Sampson Low, Marston & Co., 1893), pp. 356–57; D. Anderson, 'Sir George Bowen and the Problems of Queensland's Defence 1859–1868', *Queensland Heritage*, Vol. 2, No. 3 (Nov. 1970), p. 32; H.J. Zwillenberg, 'The Background to South Australia's Defence Policy', *Sabretache*, Vol. 21, No. 1 (1980), p. 28; & A. Preston & J. Major, *Send a Gunboat!* (London: Longmans, Green & Co. Ltd, 1967), pp. 82–83.

18 GO 19/1: Letter from Province of Otago, Superintendents Office, Dunedin, 29 June 1863, to Col. Thomas Gore Browne, C.B., Governor of Tasmania, *AOT.*

19 *Ibid.*

20 *Mercury*, 2, 4 & 6 February 1864.

21 *Ibid.*, 21 March 1864; & also refer to: J. Featon, *The Waikato War* (Auckland: J.D. Wickham, Free Lance General Printing Office, 1879), p. 68.

22 *Launceston Examiner*, 9 April 1864, p. 5.

23 *Mercury*, 26 & 30 April 1864.

24 NG/26: Copies of letters to officials & Private Persons: Despatch dated Sydney, 9 July 1863, pp. 104–5; & also refer to: Despatch dated Sydney, 30 June 1863, p. 103, *AONSW.*

25 *Sydney Morning Herald*, 14 August 1863, p. 6.

26 NG/26: Despatch dated Sydney, 18 August 1863, p. 110, *AONSW.*

27 *Sydney Morning Herald*, 17 August 1863, p. 4.

28 *Ibid.*, 20 August 1863, pp. 4 & 5.

29 *Ibid.*, 25 September 1863, p. 4.

30 *Ibid.*, 26 September 1863, p. 6.

31 NG/26: Despatch dated Sydney, 16 September 1863, p. 114; & Despatch dated Sydney, 21 September 1863, p. 116, *AONSW.*

32 *Sydney Morning Herald*, 22 September, pp. 4 & 5, 23 September, p. 4 & 26 September 1863, p. 9.

33 *Ibid.*, 22 September 1863, p. 4; *Argus*, 26 September 1863, p. 7; & *Courier*, 22 & 23 September 1863.

34 *Sydney Morning Herald*, 21 November 1863, p. 13; & J.E. Alexander, *Bush Fighting* (London: Sampson Low, Marston, Low and Searle, 1873), p. 92.

35 *Argus*, 24 July 1863, p. 6; *Mercury*, 17 & 28 July and 21 September 1863; *Launceston Examiner*, 21 July 1863, p. 4; & *Sydney Morning Herald*, 28 August, p. 5 & 11 September 1863, p. 4.

36 The *Herald* also provided extensive details of the construction, dimensions and propulsion of this gunboat. *Sydney Morning Herald*, 15 September, p. 4 & 21 September 1863, p. 3; & also refer to: *Argus*, 22 September 1863, p. 6; & *Mercury*, 28 September 1863.

37 Glen, *op. cit.*, pp. 27–28.

38 *Sydney Morning Herald*, 24 August, p. 8, 25 August, p. 8, 18 September, p. 1, 19 September, p. 1 & 21 September 1863, p. 1.

39 *Sydney Morning Herald*, 14 October 1863, p. 4; & also refer to: H. Chaloner, 'The Historic River Steamer "Pioneer" ', *Journal of the Auckland Historical Society*, Vol. 2, No. 1 (Oct. 1963), p. 14.

40 *Sydney Morning Herald*, 16 November 1863, p. 4; *Mercury*, 30 November 1863; & *Launceston Examiner*, 3 December 1863, p. 4.

41 *Sydney Morning Herald*, 22 September, pp. 4 & 5, 23 September, p. 4, 26 September, p. 9 & 14 October 1863, p. 4; *Argus*, 26 September 1863, p. 7; *Mercury*, 22 October 1863; & Chaloner, *op. cit.*, p. 14.

42 *Sydney Morning Herald*, 21 November 1863, p. 13; & also refer to: *NZG*, No. 58, 7 November 1863, pp. 486–87; J.E. Gorst, 'Our New Zealand Conquests', *Macmillan's Magazine*, Vol. 12 (May 1865 – Oct. 1865), p. 169; & Alexander, *op. cit.*, pp. 91–92.

43 Featon, *op. cit.*, p. 55; Chaloner, *op. cit.*, p. 15; & R.D. Campbell, *Captain Cadell and the Waikato Flotilla* (Wellington: Maritime Publications, 1985), p. 26.

44 *Sydney Morning Herald*, 6 October 1863, p. 4; J. Cowan, *The New Zealand Wars:... Vol. I: (1845–1864)* (Wellington: W.A.G. Skinner, Government Printer, 1922), p. 303; Glen, *op. cit.*, p. 28; & G. Howard, *Portrait of the Royal New Zealand Navy* (Wellington: Grantham House, 1991), p. 7.

45 *Sydney Morning Herald*, 6 October 1863, p. 5; & *Mercury*, 21 October 1863.

46 N. Selfe, 'Annual Address to the Engineering Section', *Journal and Proceedings of the Royal Society of New South Wales*, Vol. 34 (1900), pp. xxiii–xxiv & xxvii–xxviii; & also refer to: 'Sir Peter Nicol Russell: A Great Engineer. The Story of His Life and Work', *Australasian Engineer*, Vol. 41, No. 303 (7 Aug. 1941), p. 10.

47 *Sydney Morning Herald*, 15 December, p. 4 & 16 December 1863, p. 5 and 8 January 1864, p. 5; & *Argus*, 2 January, p. 6 & 13 January 1864, p. 5.

48 *Sydney Morning Herald*, 22 January 1864, p. 8.

49 *Ibid.*, 18 January 1864, p. 4; & *Argus*, 8 February 1864, p. 4.

50 *Sydney Morning Herald*, 12 February, p. 5 & 17 February 1864, p. 4; Featon, *op. cit.*, pp. 75–76; J. O'C. Ross, *The White Ensign in Early New Zealand* (Wellington: A.H. & A.W. Reed, 1967), p. 89; & J. Belich, *The New Zealand Wars* (Auckland: Penguin Books, 1988), p. 161.

51 *Sydney Morning Herald*, 11 April 1864, p. 5.

52 Campbell, *op. cit.*, p. 26.

53 *Sydney Morning Herald*, 13 February, p. 7, 15 February, p. 4 & 10 March 1864, p. 5; S.A. Bryant, 'Birth of Hamilton in 1864: Pioneers reminiscences and life in early days: by Sarah Ann Bryant, written in 1939', *Auckland-Waikato Historical Journal*, No. 30 (April 1977), pp. 9–10; E.A. Butt, 'Romantic History of the Waikato', *Journal of the Auckland Historical Society*, No. 4 (April 1964), p. 5; Ross, *op. cit.*, p. 89; & Campbell, *op. cit.*, p. 26.

54 *Argus*, 22 August 1863, pp. 4 & 5.

55 *Ibid.*, 26 August 1863, p. 5; & also refer to: *Ibid.*, pp. 4 & 6.

56 *Ibid.*, 28 August 1863, p. 4.

57 *Ibid.*, 9 November 1863, p. 4, & 7 December 1863, p. 5.

58 'B.-No.2a: Papers Respecting The One Million Loan', *JHRNZ: 1864* (Auckland).

59 *South Australian Register*, 30 November 1863.
60 *Ibid.*, 13 January 1864.
61 *Proceedings of the Parliament of South Australia: 1866–7: Volume 1* (Adelaide: W.C. Cox, Government Printer, 1867), pp. 2, 3 & 5; & *Proceedings of the Parliament of South Australia: 1866–7: Volume 2* (Adelaide: W.C. Cox, Government Printer, 1867), 'No. 34. Receipt and Disposition of Small Arms'.
62 *South Australian Register*, 12, 16 & 17 June and 30 July 1863.
63 *Sydney Morning Herald*, 29 March 1864, p. 5; & also refer to: *Ibid.*, 30 March 1864, p. 5.
64 *South Australian Register*, 6 April 1864; & also refer to: *Mercury*, 5 April 1864.
65 Campbell, *op. cit.*, pp. 11, 14–16, 26 & 27.
66 *South Australian Register*, 23 February, 15, 16 & 17 March, 5, 18 & 19 May and 16 June 1864; *Mercury*, 2 April 1864; & *Launceston Examiner*, 26 May 1864, p. 4.
67 *Sydney Morning Herald*, 12 January 1865, p. 5; & *Argus*, 12 January 1865, p. 5. For press coverage of this vessel's vital role on the Whanganui River and surrounding west coast region, refer to: *Sydney Morning Herald*, 28 February, p. 3 & 9 March 1865, p. 8; & *Sydney Mail*, 11 March 1865, p. 11.
68 *NZG*, No. 13, 25 April 1865, p. 124.
69 Campbell, *op. cit.*, pp. 10–11, 16, 25 & 26; & I. Mudie, *Riverboats* (Adelaide: Rigby Ltd, 1961), pp. 48, 50 & 66.
70 P. Mennell, *The Dictionary of Australasian Biography* (London: Hutchinson & Co., 1892), pp. 75–76. For other information on Cadell, refer to: *Argus*, 31 October 1862, p. 7, 30 August 1879, p. 9 & 15 March 1880, p. 7; J.W. Bull, *Early Experiences of Life in South Australia* (Adelaide: E.S. Wigg & Son, 1884), p. 318; Mudie, *op. cit.*, pp. 36–45, 46–54, 55–61 & 66; & J Nicholson, *The Incomparable Captain Cadell* (Crows Nest, NSW: A Sue Hines Book, 2004).
71 *South Australian Register*, 26 June & 12 August 1863; Campbell, *op. cit.*, pp. 9 & 25; & Mudie, *op. cit.*, pp. 54 & 56.
72 *Argus*, 15 January 1864, p. 4; *South Australian Register*, 16 March 1864; & Campbell, *op. cit.*, p. 10.
73 Campbell, *op. cit.*, pp. 10 & 16.
74 Alexander, *op. cit.*, pp. 56–57; Cowan, *op. cit.*, pp. 300–3; Ross, *op. cit.*, pp. 85–90; C.W. Vennell, 'Early Waikato River Trade', *Auckland–Waikato Historical Journal*, No. 39 (Sept. 1981), p. 11; D. Johnson, *New Zealand's Maritime Heritage* (Auckland: William Collins Publishers, 1987), pp. 96–98; & Howard, *op. cit.*, pp. 6–8 & 135.
75 'E.-No.2: Papers Relative to Native Policy, including the following subjects:- . . . Military Settlements', *JHRNZ: 1864* (Auckland), p. 64 of E.-No.2; & also refer to correspondence on pp. 64–66.
76 *Supplement to the Adelaide Observer*, 28 April 1866, p. 4; & also refer to: Campbell, *op. cit.*, p. 17.
77 Genealogical history on George Gregory, New Zealand war veteran (serving on government steamer *Sturt* 1866–68) & history of the Gregory family of Narrabri, NSW, courtesy of Stan Hannaford (great-grandson of Nanango, Queensland) to this author during 1997–99; & AD 1 01/4595 (War Medal application file): Gregory, George, *NANZ*.
78 *Sydney Morning Herald*, 8 December 1864, p. 8.
79 *Ibid.*, 31 January, p. 2 & 2 February 1865, p. 6.
80 *Ibid.*, 20 August 1863, p. 5.
81 *Ibid.*, 21 August 1863, p. 4.
82 *Hobart Town Daily Mercury/Mercury*, 11, 18 & 23 April 1860; & *Launceston Examiner*, 12 April, p. 2, 14 April, p. 2 & 5 May 1860, p. 2.
83 *Argus*, 28 August, p. 8 & 29 August 1863, p. 8.
84 *Ibid.*, 3 November, p. 4, 6 November, p. 5, 7 November, pp. 4–5 & 9 November 1863, p. 4; & *Sydney Morning Herald*, 5 December 1863, p. 6.
85 *Argus*, 28 December, p. 4 & 30 December 1863, p. 4.
86 *Ibid.*, 10 December, pp. 2 & 3 and 12 December 1864, p. 5.
87 *South Australian Register*, 26 December 1863.
88 *Sydney Morning Herald*, 19 December 1863, p. 6 & 19 February 1864, p. 4; & *South Australian Register*, 21, 22, 23, 24 & 26 December 1863 and 6 January 1864.
89 *Sydney Morning Herald*, 10 September 1864, pp. 4 & 7; *Launceston Examiner*, 8 October 1864, p. 5.

ENDNOTES

90 *Argus*, 3 November, p. 5 (and also refer to:*Ibid.*, p. 4) & 7 November 1864, p. 4; & *Launceston Examiner*, 8 November 1864, p. 3.

91 *Sydney Morning Herald*, 1 August, p. 5, 8 August, p. 3 & 9 August 1864, p. 4.

92 *Ibid.*, 19 December 1864, p. 2.

93 *Ibid.*, 25 December 1865, p. 8; & *Argus*, 8 January, p. 5, 17 January, p. 5 & 9 February 1866, p. 5.

94 *Sydney Morning Herald*, 12 March, p. 6 & 16 March 1866, p. 8.

95 *Mercury*, 26 March 1864.

96 Cheshire later became Postmaster at Inglewood, and died in 1898. L.L. Barton, *Australians in the Waikato War* (North Sydney: Library of Australian History, 1979), p. 71; & Interview and information gathered by this author from Dorothea Cheshire, granddaughter of the New Zealand war veteran & medal recipient Jacob Cheshire, 3rd Waikato Regiment, Brisbane, December 1995 & June–July 1998.

97 Also as Henri/Henry De Leon & Henry Strode Henri. Robin Barker, 'The Henri Letters: Part One' (29 November 1993) & 'The Henri Letters: Part Two' (17 August 1995). This genealogical history on Henry Strode Henri & the history of the Henri Family, courtesy of Ben Henri, of Ascot, Brisbane to this author in October 1995; & also refer to: Barton, *op. cit.*, pp. 68 & 92.

98 Henry Strode Henri (also as Henriques DeLeon & Henri/Henry De Leon) became a Professor of Languages, and died in South Brisbane, Queensland in 1925. Barker, *op. cit.*; & 'G.-No. 1: Papers Relative To The Issue Of The NZ War Medal: Enclosure 4 in No. 3: List No. 9', *AJHRNZ: Vol. II: 1871*, pp. 18–19 of G.-No. 1; & also in: *NZG*, No. 31, 31 May 1871, pp. 254–55.

99 Refer to this author's articles: 'A History of the Colonial Defence Force (Cavalry): and the Australian Context', *The Volunteers*, Vol. 26, No. 1 (July 2000), pp. 5–25; & 'New Zealand's Colonial Defence Force (Cavalry) and its Australian Context, 1863–66', *Sabretache*, Vol. 43, No. 3 (Sept. 2002), pp. 23–39.

100 Glen, *op. cit.*, p. 39; & Barton, *op. cit.*, p. 25.

101 'G.-No. 1: Papers Relative To The Issue Of The NZ War Medal: Enclosure 4 in No. 3: List of Officers and Men of the Local Forces, and Civilians, in NZ, who were employed in the Imperial Transport Corps, and paid from Imperial funds, entitled to the NZ Medal', *AJHRNZ: Vol. II: 1871*, pp. 11–20 of G.-No. 1; & also in: *NZG*, No. 31, 31 May 1871, pp. 247–56.

102 N. Morris (ed.), *The Journal of William Morgan* (Auckland: Libraries Department, Auckland City Council, 1963); for references to 'Mokes' refer to pp. 129, 135 & 138.

103 Yarwood in his expansive study of Australia's horse trade with India only makes a very brief reference to a horse trade with New Zealand. A.T. Yarwood, *Walers* (Carlton: Melbourne University Press, 1989), pp. 16 & 207 (Chapter 2, note 3). Also refer to: J. Hopkins-Weise, 'Australia's Military Horse Trade during the New Zealand Wars of the 1860s', *Sabretache*, Vol. 48, No. 3 (Sept. 2007), pp. 5–12.

104 *Sydney Morning Herald*, 21 August 1863, p. 9; & also refer to: *Ibid.*, 15 August 1863, p. 6.

105 Glen, *op. cit.*, p. 24.

106 *Sydney Morning Herald*, 15 August 1863, p. 6.

107 *Ibid.*, 20 August 1863, p. 1.

108 *Ibid.*, 24 August 1863, p. 1. For the continuation of advertisements for 'Troop Horses' & 'Cavalry Horses for New Zealand' in Sydney, refer to: *Ibid.*, 25 August, p. 1, 26 August, p. 1 & 27 August 1863, p. 1; & *South Australian Register*, 9 September 1863.

109 *Sydney Morning Herald*, 24 August, p. 8 & 25 August 1863, p. 8.

110 *Ibid.*, 16 September 1863, p. 5; & also refer to: *Ibid.*, 6 October 1863, p. 4.

111 Morris, *op. cit.*, p. 108.

112 *Sydney Morning Herald*, 6 October 1863, pp. 4 & 5; & also refer to: Glen, *op. cit.*, p. 24.

113 *Sydney Morning Herald*, 24 December 1863, p. 4.

114 *Argus*, 15 January 1864, p. 7 & 30 January 1864, p. 7; *Sydney Morning Herald*, 1 February 1864, p. 2; & *Mercury*, 22 February 1864.

115 *Mercury*, 22 February 1864.

116 *Ibid.*, 30 January 1864.

117 *Sydney Morning Herald*, 13 February 1864, p. 12. These advertisements for horses for the Colonial Defence Force continued in *Sydney Morning Herald*, on: 15 February, p. 8, 18 February, p. 2, 19 February, p. 6, 22 February, p. 2, 4 March, p. 6, 7 March, p. 6 & 14 March 1864, p. 6.

118 *Ibid.*, 23 May 1864, p. 3.
119 *South Australian Register*, 2 July 1863.
120 *Mercury*, 22 July 1863, p. 7.
121 *Sydney Morning Herald*, 17 September 1863, p. 4; & also refer to: *Argus*, 18 September 1863, p. 5.
122 *Sydney Morning Herald*, 10 December 1863, p. 4.
123 *Mercury*, 10 December 1863.
124 *Launceston Examiner*, 16 August 1864, p. 2.
125 *Sydney Morning Herald*, 4 October 1864, p. 4.
126 *Ibid.*, 3 November, p. 6, 8 November, p. 2 & 8 December 1864, p. 8; & Fox, *op. cit.*, p. 13.
127 *Sydney Morning Herald*, 11 January, p. 4, 18 January, p. 4, 13 February, p. 7, 18 February, p. 5, 8 March, p. 5, 6 July, p. 3 & 10 October 1864, p. 4.
128 *Ibid.*, 9 March 1864, p. 5; & also referred to in: *Mercury*, 24 March 1864.
129 *Sydney Morning Herald*, 3 October 1865, p. 4.
130 I.W. Page, 'Relations Between NZ and the Australian Colonies, 1850–1870', MA thesis, University of Otago, NZ (Dec. 1956), p. 81.
131 *Ibid.*, p. 90.
132 J. Belich, *Making Peoples* (Auckland: Penguin Books, 1996), p. 357.
133 *Ibid.*
134 Page, *op. cit.*, pp. 90–91.
135 *South Australian Register*, 15 June 1864.
136 *Sydney Morning Herald*, 13 January 1865, p. 4; & this editorial republished: *Ibid.*, 20 January 1865, p. 6.
137 *Ibid.*, 13 January, p. 6, 19 January, p. 6 & 20 January 1865, p. 2.
138 *Launceston Examiner*, 3 September 1863, p. 3; & also refer to: G.H. Scholefield (ed.), *A Dictionary of New Zealand Biography: Volume II: M–Addenda* (Wellington: Department of Internal Affairs, 1940), p. 232.
139 *Sydney Morning Herald*, 17 February 1864, p. 8.
140 *Ibid.*, 10 March, p. 5 & 19 March 1864, p. 5.
141 *Ibid.*, 31 August, p. 6, 1 September, p. 6, 3 September, p. 2, 5 September, p. 6, 7 September, p. 6 & 14 September 1864, p. 6. At this same time the provincial government of Canterbury was also advertising for tenders for the construction of railway works.
142 *Ibid.*, 21 November 1864, p. 8; & *Illustrated Sydney News*, 15 October 1864, p. 7.
143 *Sydney Morning Herald*, 28 June 1864, p. 1.
144 C.A. Lawn, 'Surveyor's Big Role in N.Z. History', *Journal of the Auckland Historical Society*, No. 8 (April 1966), p. 16.
145 *Argus*, 19 March 1864, p. 5; & *The Launceston Examiner*, 24 March 1864, p. 3.
146 *Argus*, 10 August, p. 5, 29 September, p. 5 & 3 October 1864, p. 5; & editorial in: *Sydney Morning Herald*, 3 October 1864, p. 4.
147 *Sydney Morning Herald*, 15 May 1866, p. 8.

CHAPTER SIX

1 R.G.A. Levinge, *Historical Records of the Forty-Third Regiment* (London: W. Clowes & Sons, 1868), pp. 280–81; A.E. Fyler, *The History of the 50th or (The Queen's Own) Regiment* (London: Chapman and Hall, 1895), p. 270; W.L. Vane, *The Durham Light Infantry* (London: Gale & Polden, 1914), pp. 95–96; H. & L. Hughes, *Discharged in New Zealand* (Auckland: The NZ Society of Genealogists, 1988), pp. 32, 34 & 105; & J. Bilcliffe, *Well Done The 68th* (Wiltshire: Picton Publishing Ltd, 1995), pp. 123–24 & 131–32.
2 *Sydney Morning Herald*, 19 June, p. 4, 26 June, p. 4 & 27 June 1863, p. 6; & *Argus*, 27 June 1863, p. 5.
3 NG/26: Copies of letters to officials and Private Persons: Letter dated Sydney, 30 June 1863, p. 103, *AONSW*; & also refer to: NG/26: Letter dated Sydney, 9 July 1863, pp. 104–5, *AONSW*.
4 *Sydney Morning Herald*, 15 August 1863, p. 6; & NG/26: Governor John Young to Colonel Hamilton, dated Sydney, 17 August 1863; Governor Young to Brigadier-General Chute, dated Sydney, 18 August 1863; Governor Young to Governor George Grey, dated Sydney, 18 August 1863; & Governor Young to Commodore Sir William Wiseman, dated Sydney, 21 September 1863: pp. 109–10 & 116, *AONSW*.
5 *Sydney Morning Herald*, 15 August 1863, p. 6; & republished: *Ibid.*, 21 August 1863, p. 6.

ENDNOTES

6 *Ibid.*, 15 August 1863, p. 6.
7 *Ibid.*, 19 August 1863, pp. 4 & 5.
8 *Ibid.*, 1 September 1863, p. 3.
9 NG/26: Letter dated Sydney, 18 August 1863, p. 110, *AONSW.*
10 *Sydney Morning Herald*, 18 August, p. 4, 19 August, p. 4, 20 August, pp. 4 & 5 and 12 September 1863, p. 7.
11 NG/26: Letter dated Sydney, 20 August 1863, pp. 110–11, *AONSW.*
12 *Sydney Morning Herald*, 12 September 1863, pp. 5 & 6; & also refer to: *Courier*, 14 September 1863, p. 2.
13 *Ibid.*, 14 September 1863, p. 4.
14 HMS *Curacoa* arrived in Sydney (from Portsmouth) on 13 September. *Ibid.*, 14 September 1863, p. 4; & also refer to: NG/26: Letter dated Sydney, 16 September 1863, p. 114, *AONSW.*
15 *Sydney Morning Herald*, 16 September 1863, p. 5; & NG/26: Letter dated Sydney, 18 September 1863, p. 115, *AONSW.*
16 *Sydney Morning Herald*, 21 September, p. 4 & 22 September 1863, pp. 1, 4 & 5.
17 NG/26: Letter dated Sydney, 16 September 1863, p. 114, *AONSW.*
18 *Sydney Morning Herald*, 19 September 1863, p. 4.
19 *Ibid.*, 18 September, p. 5, 21 September, p. 13, 22 September, p. 5 & 23 September 1863, p. 4; & also refer to: N. Bartlett, 'Australia and the Maori Wars', *Canberra Historical Journal*, New Series No. 5 (March 1980), p. 4.
20 *Sydney Morning Herald*, 23 September p. 4 & 14 October 1863, p. 8; & also refer to: F. Eadie, *Troopships Engaged in the Maori Wars . . . 1840–1865* (NZ: Auckland Historical Centennial Research Committee, [1940?]), p. 2.
21 *Sydney Morning Herald*, 25 September 1863, p. 4.
22 NG/26: Letter dated Sydney, 19 September 1863, pp. 115–16, *AONSW.*
23 During November despatches were received from both the Home government and Governor Grey thanking NSW for its provision of military aid, and both letters were subsequently tabled in Parliament. *Sydney Morning Herald*, 28 November, p. 5 & 30 November 1863, p. 4.
24 NG/26: Letter dated Sydney, 13 January 1864, p. 132, *AONSW.*
25 NG/26: Letter dated Sydney, 20 January 1864, p. 134, *AONSW.*
26 *Sydney Morning Herald*, 20 November 1863, p. 5.
27 *Ibid.*, 8 December 1863, p. 3.
28 *Ibid.*
29 *Ibid.*, 15 December 1863, p. 5.
30 *Argus*, 21 May, p. 5 & 28 May 1863, p. 5.
31 *Sydney Morning Herald*, 21 August 1863, p. 12.
32 *Ibid.*, 31 August, p. 4, 14 September, p. 4, 21 September, p. 4, 22 September, pp. 4 & 5, 23 September, p. 4 & 26 September 1863, p. 9.
33 *Ibid.*, 14 September 1863, p. 4 & 6 November 1863, p. 4; *Argus*, 17 October, p. 4 & 19 October 1863, p. 4; *Courier*, 14 November 1863; & J. Bach, *The Australia Station* (Kensington: New South Wales University Press, 1986), p. 76 & Appendix Four.
34 Bach, *op. cit.*, p. 77; G. Howard, *Portrait of the Royal New Zealand Navy* (Wellington: Grantham House, 1991), pp. 8 & 135; & E. Holt, *The Strangest War* (London: Putnam & Co. Ltd, 1962), pp. 195–96.
35 J.E. Alexander, *Bush Fighting* (London: Sampson Low, Marston, Low and Searle, 1873), pp. 56–57.
36 *Argus*, 25 May 1864, p. 5; & also refer to: G. Mair, *The Story of Gate Pa* (Tauranga: Bay of Plenty Times Office, 1926), pp. 11–19 & 29–35.
37 *Argus*, 23 May 1863, p. 5.
38 *Ibid.*, p. 6.
39 *Ibid.*, 28 August 1863, p. 4.
40 *Ibid.*, 3 September 1863, p. 6.
41 *Ibid.*, 28 August, p. 8, 29 August, p. 8 & 2 September 1863, p. 4.
42 *Ibid.*, 3 September 1863, p. 7.
43 *Ibid.*, 4 September 1863, p. 7.

44 *Ibid.*, 5 September 1863, p. 5.

45 *Ibid.*, 4 September, p. 4 & 5 September 1863, p. 4; & also refer to: R.H.R. Smythies, *Historical Records of the 40th (2nd Somersetshire) Regiment* (Devonport: A.H. Swiss, 1894), p. 396.

46 *Argus*, 5 September 1863, p. 5. This 40th contingent arrived in Auckland on 21 (also cited as 19) September 1863. Smythies, *op. cit.*, p. 396; & Eadie, *op. cit.*, p. 5.

47 *South Australian Register*, 23 June 1863.

48 *Ibid.*, 15 August 1863.

49 *Argus*, 4 March 1863, p. 5.

50 *South Australian Register*, 3 September 1863.

51 *Ibid.*, 4 September 1863.

52 Chief Secretary's Office: GRG 24, Series 51, Special List No. 122: Circular Despatch 63/42 (dated 23 August 1863); & Report dated 4 September 1863, *SRSA*; *South Australian Register*, 5 September & 9 September 1863; & Smythies, *op. cit.*, p. 396.

53 *South Australian Register*, 5 September 1863.

54 *Ibid.*, 9 September 1863. For other press coverage of this decision for the 'Removal Of Troops', refer to: *Ibid.*, 8, 16 & 18 September 1863; *Sydney Morning Herald*, 5 September, p. 5, 10 September, pp. 5 & 7 and 30 September 1863, p. 4; & *Argus*, 17 September 1863, p. 5.

55 GRG 24, Series 51, Special List Nos. 123 & 126, *SRSA*.

56 The 40th soldiers themselves also paid tribute to Neville Blyth, MP, as indicated in the *Register* during October. *South Australian Register*, 6, 7, 9 & 26 October 1863.

57 *Ibid.*, 21 September 1863.

58 *Ibid.*, 24 & 25 September 1863.

59 'Tribute to the Soldiers of the Fortieth' by 'M.G.J.', *Ibid.*, 30 September 1863.

60 *Ibid.*, 3 October 1863.

61 *Ibid.*, 7 October & 10 October 1863.

62 *Ibid.*, 23 September & 6 October 1863.

63 *Ibid.*, 12, 13 & 26 October 1863. Also refer to: E. Hodder, *The History of South Australia: ... Vol. I* (London: Sampson Low, Marston & Co., 1893), p. 357; Eadie, *op. cit.*, p. 4; & H.J. Zwillenberg, 'Citizens and Soldiers: The Defence of South Australia 1836–1901', MA thesis, University of Adelaide, 1970, Appendix B on p. 6 & pp. 40, 43–44 & 56.

64 *South Australian Register*, 12 October 1863; & 'Departure Of The Military For New Zealand', repeated: *Ibid.*, 26 October 1863.

65 This press coverage of the activities of South Australia's former 40th garrison also included the service of Major F.S. Blyth. *Ibid.*, 25 & 27 April, 24 June & 25 November 1863 and 20 January 1864. For other information on Blyth, refer to: Smythies, *op. cit.*, pp. 521–22; & H. Zwillenberg, 'South Australia's Army: Part Four', *Sabretache*, Vol. 23, No. 1 (Jan.–March 1982), p. 24.

66 *South Australian Register*, 7 December 1863; & also refer to later casualty amendments or updates: *Ibid.*, 8 & 30 December 1863 and 19 July 1864.

67 *Argus*, 1 March 1864, p. 5; *South Australian Register*, 5 March 1864; & also refer to: J. Cowan, *The New Zealand Wars: ... Vol. I: (1845–1864)* (Wellington: W.A.G. Skinner, Government Printer, 1922), pp. 337–40.

68 *South Australian Register*, 29 March 1864.

69 *Ibid.*, 19 April 1864.

70 *Ibid.*

71 *Ibid.*, 26 December 1863.

72 A. Forster, *South Australia* (London: Sampson Low, Son, and Marston, 1866), pp. 142–43; Chief Secretary's Office: GRG 24, Series 51, Special List Nos. 136 (dated Melbourne, 12 Sept. 1866); 137 (dated Auckland, 2 Oct. 1866); 138 (dated Adelaide, 8 Oct. 1866); 139 (dated Melbourne, 15 Oct. 1866); 140 (dated Auckland, 15 Oct. 1866); & 141 (dated Adelaide, 6 Nov. 1866), *SRSA*. Also refer to: H. O'Donnell, *Historical Records of the 14th Regiment* (Devonport: A.H. Swiss, [1893?]), pp. 199 & 202–3.

73 *Sydney Morning Herald*, 22 July 1862, p. 4; & *Courier*, 24 July 1862. Also refer to: *QGG*, Vol. III, No. 48, 21 June 1862, p. 290; Vol. III, No. 52, 28 June 1862, p. 305; Vol. III, No. 55, 5 July 1862, p. 323; Vol. III,

No. 68, 19 July 1862, p. 378; Vol. III, No. 84, 13 September 1862, p. 515; & Vol. III, No. 86, 27 September 1862, p. 535.

74 For example, refer to: GOV/A1: Governor's Office: In-Letters on Official Subjects. Vol. 1: Letter 62/50, 13 February 1862, pp. 315–17, *QSA*.

75 GOV/A1: Letter 62/83, 10 March 1862, pp. 329–30, *QSA*. Also refer to: GOV/A1: Letter 62/106, 26 March 1862, p. 335, *QSA*; D. Anderson, 'Sir George Bowen and the Problem of Queensland's Defence, 1859–1868', *Queensland Heritage*, Vol. 2, No. 3 (Nov. 1970), p. 33; & D.H. Johnson, *Volunteers at Heart* (St Lucia: University of Queensland Press, 1975), pp. 51–53.

76 *Courier*, 1 September 1863; & also refer to: *Ibid.*, 5 September 1863.

77 GOV/G1: Governor's Office: Letterbook of Governor's Official Letters to Various Persons: Vol. 1: Despatch No. 9, dated Brisbane, 8 September 1863, pp. 125–27, *QSA*. Also refer to: GOV/G1: Despatch No. 10, dated Brisbane, 8 September 1863, pp. 127–29; & GOV/23: Governor's Office: Letterbook of Despatches to the Secretary of State for the Colonies: Vol. 2: Despatch No. 70 (Military), dated Brisbane, 14 December 1863, pp. 511–17, *QSA*.

78 GOV/A1: Letter 63/235, dated 3 October 1863, pp. 528–29; & also refer to: Letter 63/234, dated 3 October 1863, pp. 530–31, *QSA*.

79 *Courier*, 11 September 1863; & GOV/G1: Despatch No. 9, dated Brisbane, 8 September 1863, pp. 125–27, *QSA*.

80 *Brisbane Courier*, 11 October, p. 2, 13 October, p. 6, 15 October, p. 2, 16 October, p. 2 & 17 October 1866, p. 2; & GO 47: Governor's Inward Correspondence on Military Matters: Copy of Brigade Order No. 446, dated Head Quarters, Melbourne, 27 September 1866, *AOT*.

81 *Sydney Morning Herald*, 23 October, p. 4, 24 October, p. 4, 31 October, p. 4 & 1 November 1866, p. 4.

82 *Ibid.*, 18 October 1866, p. 4; & also refer to: *Ibid.*, 20 October 1866, p. 8.

83 E.A.H. Webb, *History of the 12th (The Suffolk) Regiment 1685–1913* (London: Spottiswoode & Co., 1914), pp. 281 & 296–98; K. Sinclair (ed.), *A Soldier's View of Empire* (London: The Bodley Head Ltd, 1982), pp. 164–66; J. Cowan, *The New Zealand Wars: ... Vol. II: The Hauhau Wars, 1864–1872* (Wellington: W.A.G. Skinner, Government Printer, 1923), pp. 148–54; & J. Rorke, *Policing Two Peoples* (Jinty Rorke & the NZ Police, 1993), pp. 1–2.

84 *Mercury*, 1 August 1863 (& also refer to: questions asked in the House of Assembly on 31 July: 'Despatch of the Military to New Zealand'); & *Launceston Examiner*, 1 August, p. 5 & 4 August 1863, p. 2.

85 GO 47: Letter from Major Eagar, Commanding Troops, to Governor Gore Browne, dated Hobart Town, 31 July 1863, *AOT*; & *Mercury*, 1 August 1863.

86 *Launceston Examiner* (news from the *New Zealander*, 17 August), 8 September 1863, p. 5; & also refer to: Tasmania Parliamentary Printed Papers: Despatches from Secretary of State: Despatch of Troops to NZ. (No. 17, 29 June 1864): V354.946008 T741, *AWM*.

87 CSD 4/44/596. Colonial Secretary: Gore Browne Period. Correspondence File: 596: Letter from Asst. Adj. Office, to the Colonial Secretary, dated 3 August 1863; Letter from the Colonial Secretary's Office, to the Officer Commanding the Troops, dated 5 August 1863; & Memorandum from The Sheriff, to the Colonial Secretary's Office, dated 7 August 1863, *AOT*.

88 CSD 4/44/596. Letter from the Asst. Adj. Office, to the Colonial Secretary, dated 8 August 1863, *AOT*.

89 *Ibid.*; & CSD 4/44/596. Letter from the Colonial Secretary's Office, to the Officer Commanding The Troops, dated 11 August 1863, *AOT*.

90 *Mercury*, 3 August 1863.

91 *Ibid.*, 4 August & 13 August 1863.

92 *Ibid.*, 4, 6, 10, 11 & 12 August 1863.

93 *Ibid.*, 13 August 1863.

94 *Ibid.*, 14 August 1863; & also refer to: Smythies, *op. cit.*, p. 396.

95 *Mercury*, 14 August 1863; & also refer to: 22 August 1863; & *Launceston Examiner*, 22 August 1863, p. 2.

96 *Mercury*, 16 September & 23 October 1863; J. Featon, *The Waikato War: 1863–4* (Auckland: J.D. Wickham, Free Lance General Printing Office, 1879), p. 44; *The Cyclopedia of Tasmania ... Volume I* (Hobart: Maitland Krone, 1900), p. 22; & Eadie, *op. cit.*, p. 3.

97 *Mercury*, 23 October 1863.

98 *Ibid.*, 14 October 1863; *Hobart Town Advertiser*, 14 October 1863; & *Launceston Examiner*, 15 October 1863, p. 5.

99 *Ibid.*, 2 January 1864.

100 Chesney held the local rank of lieutenant-colonel whilst commanding the troops in Tasmania, and commanding the Southern District of Tasmania's Volunteers. He departed for New Zealand in February, but returned to Hobart in July 1864. CSD 4/86 & 87/412. Colonial Secretary: Correspondence File: 412, *AOT*; & *Mercury*, 17, 18, 22 & 26 February 1864.

101 GO 47: Copy of Brigade Order No. 466, dated Head Quarters, Melbourne, 27 September 1866, enclosed with Letter No. 93/66, *AOT*; & *Sydney Morning Herald*, 24 October, p. 4 & 31 October 1866, p. 4; & also refer to: Webb, *op. cit.*, p. 297.

102 CSD 4/44/596, *AOT*; & Tasmania Parliamentary Printed Papers: Despatches from Secretary of State: Return of Troops from NZ. (No. 25, 31 July 1866): V354.946008 T741, *AWM*.

103 CSD 4/44/596: Letter from the Colonial Secretary, to Colonel T. Browne, dated 20 September 1866, *AOT*.

104 GO 47: Letter from Major General Chute, to Colonel T.G. Browne, Government House, Hobart Town, dated Head Quarters, Auckland, 15 October 1866, *AOT*; & O'Donnell, *op. cit.*, p. 199.

CHAPTER SEVEN

1 J. Cowan, *The New Zealand Wars: . . . Vol. I: (1845–1864)* (Wellington: W.A.G. Skinner, Government Printer, 1922), p. 236; J.H. Rose, et al., *The Cambridge History of the British Empire: Volume 7: Part II: New Zealand* (London: Cambridge University Press, 1933), p. 141; H.C.M. Norris, *Armed Settlers* (Hamilton: Paul's Book Arcade, 1956), pp. 16 & 19–25; L.L. Barton, *Australians in the Waikato War* (North Sydney: Library of Australian History, 1979), pp. 15–16; N. Bartlett, 'Australia and the Maori Wars', *Canberra Historical Journal*, New Series No. 5 (March 1980), pp. 3–5; & F. Glen, *For Glory and a Farm* (Whakatane: Whakatane & District Historical Society, 1985), pp. 13–20.

2 'A.-No. 8: Papers relative to the Formation of Military Settlements in the Northern Island of NZ: Enclosure 1. to No. 1. Memorandum For His Excellency', *JHRNZ: 1863* (Auckland), p. 2 of A.-No. 8.

3 *JHRNZ: 1863* (Auckland), p. 4.

4 *NZPD: 1861 to 1863* (Wellington: G. Didsbury, Government Printer, 1886), p. 941.

5 *NZG*, No. 27, 6 July 1863, p. 265. For Taranaki service conditions gazetted on 6 July 1863, refer to Appendix A.

6 *Argus*, 25 May, p. 5, 26 May, pp. 5–6, 30 May, p. 6, 25 July, p. 5, 27 July, p. 7 & 16 September 1863, p. 4; *Mercury*, 6 June and 8 & 16 September 1863; & *Launceston Examiner*, 11 June, p. 5, 28 July, p. 3 & 8 September 1863, p. 3. The Australian press had earlier followed the proposal to introduce Germans as military settlers. *Launceston Examiner*, 25 April 1863, p. 3.

7 *Launceston Examiner*, 10 September 1863, p. 2.

8 'A.-No. 8: Papers Relative to the Formation of Military Settlements in the Northern Island of NZ', *JHRNZ: 1863* (Auckland), pp. 10–12 of A.-No. 8.

9 *Ibid.*, p. 13 of A.-No. 8.

10 *NZG*, No. 35, 5 August 1863, pp. 303–6; & also found in: 'A.-No. 8: Papers Relative to the Formation of Military Settlements in the Northern Island of NZ: Enclosure 2 to No. 1.', *op. cit.*, pp. 4–7 of A.-No. 8. For Waikato service conditions gazetted on 5 August 1863, refer to Appendix B. The 'Waikato country' conditions were later cancelled on 27 June 1865. *NZG*, No. 23, 11 July 1865, p. 216.

11 'A.-No. 8: Papers Relative to the Formation of Military Settlements in the Northern Island of NZ: No. 17.', *op. cit.*, p. 13 of A.-No. 8.

12 *Ibid.*, pp. 14–15 of A.-No. 8.

13 *NZG*, No. 46, 12 September 1863, pp. 378–79; & also in: 'A.-No. 8: Papers Relative to the Formation of Military Settlements in the Northern Island of NZ: No. 20.', *op. cit.*, pp. 15–16 of A.-No. 8. For Northern Island service conditions gazetted on 12 September 1863, refer to Appendix C.

14 'A.-No. 8: Papers Relative to the Formation of Military Settlements in the Northern Island of NZ: No. 21.', *op. cit.*, p. 16 of A.-No. 8.

15 *Mercury*, 17 February 1864.

16 G.H. Scholefield (ed.), *A Dictionary of New Zealand Biography: Volume II: M–Addenda* (Wellington: Department of Internal Affairs, 1940), p. 170.

17 J.P. Jones, *A History of the South Staffordshire Regiment* (Wolverhampton: Whitehead Brothers Ltd, 1923), pp. 54 & 434; & J.B. Haigh, 'The 80th Foot in New Zealand', *Bulletin of the Military Historical Society*, Vol. 26 (1976), pp. 82 & 83.

18 *Second Supplement to the VGG*, No. 119, 27 July 1859, p. 1575; *Supplement to the VGG*, No. 63, 18 May 1860, p. 953; *VGG*, No. 9, 17 January 1860, p. 109, No. 60, 16 May 1862, p. 831, No. 3, 12 January 1864, p. 63, No. 39, 15 April 1864, p. 873, No. 76, 29 July 1864, p. 1619, No. 46, 5 May 1865, p. 1014 & No. 83, 7 July 1865, p. 1483; *Argus*, 1 March, p. 5 & 15 March 1862, p. 5 and 16 July, p. 5 & 18 July 1863, p. 5; *Illustrated Melbourne Post*, 22 March 1862, p. 19; Scholefield (*Volume II*, 1940), *op. cit.*, p. 170; & G.F. Ward, *Victorian Land Forces* (Croydon: G.F. Ward, 1989), pp. 18–19 & 24.

19 *NZG*, No. 28, 11 July 1863, p. 271.

20 *Argus*, 21 July 1863, p. 5; & also in: *South Australian Register*, 1 August 1863.

21 *NZAL 1863*, p. 2; & *NZAL 1864*, p. 3.

22 Glen, *op. cit.*, p. 93.

23 *Sydney Morning Herald*, 15 August 1863, p. 6.

24 *Ibid.*

25 *Ibid.*, 15 August, p. 1, 17 August, p. 1, 18 August, p. 1, 19 August, p. 2, 20 August, p. 8, 24 August, p. 1, 25 August, p. 1, 26 August, p. 1 & 27 August 1863, p. 1.

26 *Ibid.*, 19 August 1863, p. 4.

27 *NZAL 1863*, pp. 1 & 2; *NZAL 1864*, p. 1; & *The Cyclopedia of New Zealand: Volume 2.– Auckland Provincial District* (Christchurch: The Cyclopedia Co. Ltd, 1902), pp. 430–31.

28 *Sydney Morning Herald*, 20 August, p. 5 & 22 August 1863, p. 6.

29 *Ibid.*, 21 August 1863, p. 4.

30 *Ibid.*, pp. 4 & 16.

31 *Ibid.*, 31 August 1863, p. 5

32 *Ibid.*, 18 August 1863, p. 8.

33 *Ibid.*, 22 August 1863, p. 7.

34 *Ibid.*, 27 August 1863, p. 5.

35 *Ibid.*, 27 August, p. 5; & also refer to: *Ibid.*, 25 August 1863, p. 4.

36 *Ibid.*, 27 August 1863, p. 5.

37 *Ibid.*, 28 August 1863, p. 5.

38 Coulter was appointed ensign on 3 September 1863, then lieutenant on 13 September 1864, and served in the 2nd Waikato Regiment. *NZAL 1863*, p. 3; *NZAL 1864*, p. 5; & Glen, *op. cit.*, pp. 25–26.

39 *Sydney Morning Herald*, 27 August, p. 5, 28 August, p. 5 & 21 September 1863, p. 4.

40 *Ibid.*, 2 September 1863, p. 5.

41 *Ibid.*, 21 September 1863, p. 2.

42 *Ibid.*, 28 September 1863, p. 5.

43 *Ibid.*, 28 August, p. 1, 29 August, p. 2, 31 August, p. 2, 1 September, p. 2, 2 September, p. 2, 3 September, p. 6, 4 September, p. 6, 5 September, p. 9, 7 September, p. 8, 9 September, p. 1, 10 September, p. 6 & 12 September 1863, p. 9.

44 *Ibid.*, 12 September, pp. 6 & 7 and 14 September 1863, p. 4; & *South Australian Register*, 28 September 1863.

45 *Sydney Morning Herald*, 15 August 1863, p. 6; & also refer to: *NZAL 1863*, p. 1.

46 Advertisements detailing conditions of military settler service for land in the Waikato country were placed in *Sydney Morning Herald* from 14 to 22 September, refer to: *Ibid.*, 14 September, p. 6, 15 September, p. 8, 16 September, p. 6, 17 September, p. 2, 18 September, p. 6, 21 September, p. 12 & 22 September 1863, p. 2.

47 *Ibid.*, 15 September, p. 4, 16 September, p. 5 & 6 October 1863, p. 4; & also refer to: F. Eadie, *Troopships Engaged in the Maori Wars . . . 1840–1865* (NZ: Auckland Historical Centennial Research Committee, [1940?]), p. 2; & 417/008/002: Document Control Centre: Records of Early Wars in NZ, *AWM.*

48 *Sydney Morning Herald*, 19 September 1863, p. 4.

49 *Ibid.*, 26 September 1863, p. 6.

50 *Ibid.*, 6 October 1863, p. 4.

51 Holt was appointed captain on 20 October 1863, and served in the 2nd Waikato Regiment. *NZAL 1863*, p. 3; *NZAL 1864*, p. 5; *NZG*, No. 55, 27 October 1863, p. 460; & *Sydney Morning Herald*, 7 October 1863, p. 5.

52 D.M. Brown was appointed lieutenant on 20 October 1863, and served initially in the 2nd Waikato Regiment. *NZAL 1863*, p. 3; *NZAL 1864*, p. 5; & *NZG*, No. 55, 27 October 1863, p. 460. Also refer to Appendices D & F.

53 *Sydney Morning Herald*, 7 October 1863, p. 5.

54 *Ibid.*, 12 October 1863, p. 5; & also refer to: *Ibid.*, 10 October, p. 6, 12 October, p. 4 & 17 October 1863, p. 5.

55 *Ibid.*, 3 December 1863, p. 5.

56 Barton, *op. cit.*, p. 69.

57 *Sydney Morning Herald*, 31 October 1864, p. 2.

58 *Argus*, 15 August 1863, p. 5.

59 *Ibid.*, p. 8.

60 *Ibid.*, 17 August, p. 8, 18 August, p. 8, 19 August, p. 8, 20 August, p. 8 & 21 August 1863, p. 8.

61 *Ibid.*, 22 August 1863, pp. 4 & 5.

62 *Ibid.*, 20 August 1863, p. 5.

63 *Ibid.*, 24 August 1863, p. 4.

64 *Ibid.*, 22 August, p. 6, 24 August, p. 5, 26 August, p. 5, 27 August, p. 5, 28 August, p. 4, 1 September, p. 5, 3 September, p. 5, 4 September, p. 5, 14 September, p. 5 & 22 September 1863, p. 7; & *Victorian*, 22 August, p. 316 & 29 August 1863, p. 332.

65 *Argus*, 17 August, p. 8, 18 August, p. 8, 19 August, p. 8, 20 August, p. 8 & 21 August 1863, p. 8.

66 *Ibid.*, 22 August, p. 8, 24 August, p. 8, 25 August, p. 8, 26 August, p. 8, 28 August, p. 8, 29 August, p. 3, 31 August, p. 8 & 1 September 1863, p. 8.

67 *Ibid.*, 24 August 1863, p. 5; & also refer to: *Ibid.*, 25 August 1863, p. 4.

68 *Ibid.*, 26 August 1863, p. 5 (& also refer to: *Ibid.*, pp. 4 & 6 for more detailed coverage of parliamentary discussions on 'The New Zealand War').

69 *Ibid.*, 26 August 1863, p. 4.

70 *Ibid.*, 27 August 1863, p. 6; & also refer to: *Victorian*, 29 August 1863, p. 328.

71 *Argus*, 29 August 1863, p. 6.

72 *Victorian*, 5 September 1863, p. 343.

73 *Argus*, 3 September 1863, p. 7.

74 *Ibid.*, 17 August 1863, p. 5.

75 *Victorian*, 22 August 1863, p. 318.

76 *Argus*, 24 August 1863, p. 5.

77 Fraser (also as Frazer) was appointed lieutenant in September 1863, captain in November 1863, served in 1st Waikato Regiment (1863–67), was still serving in the NZ Militia in 1872. *NZG*, No. 55, 27 October 1863, p. 460 & No. 58, 7 November 1863, p. 487; *NZAL 1863*, p. 2; *NZAL 1864*, p. 4; *NZAL 1872*, p. 4; & Ward, *op. cit.*, p. 54.

78 *Argus*, 25 August 1863, p. 5.

79 *Ibid.*, 12 September 1863, p. 7.

80 *Argus*, 28 August, p. 7 & 29 August 1863, p. 6; & for information on Wallace, refer to: Ward, *op. cit.*, pp. 24 & 87–89.

81 *Argus*, 26 August 1863, p. 4.

82 *Ibid.*, 27 August 1863, p. 4.

83 *Ibid.*, 28 August 1863, p. 6.

84 *Ibid.*, 31 August, pp. 4 & 8 and 1 September 1863, pp. 4 & 8.

85 H.G. Smith was appointed captain in August 1863 and served in 1st Waikato Regiment and Imperial Commissariat Transport Corps. W.A. Smith was appointed lieutenant in September 1863, captain in February 1865, and served in 1st Waikato Regiment. Lomax was appointed lieutenant in September 1863 and served in 1st Waikato Regiment until February 1865 when his commission was cancelled; and Nunnington was appointed lieutenant in September 1863 and served in 1st Waikato Regiment briefly, but resigned his

commission in December 1863. *Argus*, 29 August, p. 5 & 31 August 1863, p. 5 and 6 January 1864, p. 5; *NZG*, No. 50, 24 September 1863, pp. 427–28, No. 4, 6 February 1865, p. 27 & No. 15, 4 May 1865, p. 138; *Index to the NZG For 1863*, p. XIII; *NZAL 1863*, p. 2; *NZAL 1864*, p. 4; J. Featon, *The Waikato War* (Auckland: J.D. Wickham, Free Lance General Printing Office, 1879), p. 69; Ward, *op. cit.*, pp. 83, 107 & 118; & R. Stowers, *The New Zealand Medal To Colonials* (Hamilton: Richard Stowers, 1998), p. 91.

86 *Argus*, 1 September 1863, p. 5.

87 *Ibid.*

88 *Ibid.*

89 *Ibid.*, 2 September 1863, p. 4. One member of this first Victorian contingent was James Bodell. His recollections provide an account of the recruiting in Melbourne, including the voyage aboard the *Star of India*. K. Sinclair (ed.), *A Soldier's View of Empire* (London: The Bodley Head Ltd, 1982), and especially refer to pp. 125–27, 132–33, 138–39, 147 & 161–67; & also refer to: Barton, *op. cit.*, pp. 56 & 91; & *The Dictionary of New Zealand Biography: Volume One: 1769–1869* (Wellington: Jointly Published by Allen & Unwin and the Department of Internal Affairs, 1990), pp. 31–32.

90 *Victorian*, 5 September 1863, p. 338.

91 *Argus*, 2 September, pp. 3, 4 & 5, 3 September, p. 3, 4 September, p. 8, 5 September, p. 3 & 7 September 1863, p. 8.

92 Skene was appointed captain in August 1863 and served in 1st and 2nd Waikato Regiments and Imperial Commissariat Transport Corps. *NZG*, No. 55, 27 October 1863, p. 460; *NZAL 1863*, p. 2; *NZAL 1864*, p. 4; Barton, *op. cit.*, p. 94; & Stowers, *op. cit.*, p. 97.

93 *Argus*, 4 September 1863, p. 7.

94 *Ibid.*, 7 September 1863, p. 6; Ward, *op. cit.*, pp. 97 & 140; W.E. Thomason, *Marching on* (Bendigo: Bendigo Militaria Museum, [1989?]), pp. 4, 6, 10, 13 & 91; & W. Thomason, *Marching to the Waikato 1863*, [no details or date], pp. 10, 13, 14 & 32.

95 *Argus*, 5 September 1863, p. 5.

96 *Ibid.*

97 Dunn (also as Dunne) was appointed lieutenant in September 1863 and served in 1st Waikato Regiment. Perceval was appointed lieutenant in September 1863 and served in 1st Waikato Regiment. (For more detailed information on Perceval, refer to Appendix D.) Wallace, son of Major Robert Wallace, was appointed lieutenant in September 1863 and served in the 1st Waikato Regiment until resigning his commission in April 1864. *Argus*, 8 September 1863, p. 7; *NZG*, No. 51, 30 September 1863, p. 434 & No. 13, 16 April 1864, p. 166; *NZAL 1863*, p. 2; & *NZAL 1864*, p. 4.

98 Refer to Appendix D.

99 *Argus*, 8 September 1863, p. 7.

100 *Ibid.*, p. 5.

101 The complement aboard *Caduceus* varies in available sources, but appears to comprise Lieutenants Dunn, Perceval and Wallace, and 387 other rank Victorian volunteers. *Ibid.*, 9 September 1863, pp. 4 & 5; & *Victorian*, 12 September 1863, p. 355.

102 Believed to be George Popplewell Walker, who was appointed lieutenant in September 1863, captain in May 1865, and served in 1st Waikato Regiment (1863–67). *NZG*, No. 55, 27 October 1863, p. 460 & No. 19, 7 June 1865, p. 174; *NZAL 1863*, p. 2; *NZAL 1864*, p. 4; & Stowers, *op. cit.*, pp. 91–92.

103 *Argus*, 14 September, p. 8, 15 September, p. 8 & 16 September 1863, p. 8.

104 *Ibid.*, 15 September 1863, p. 5.

105 *Ibid.*, 18 September 1863, p. 5.

106 *Ibid.*, 21 September, p. 4 & 24 September 1863, p. 4.

107 *Ibid.*, 21 September 1863, p. 5.

108 *Ibid.*, 20 October 1863, p. 6 (and originally published in the *Mount Alexander Mail* on 19 October).

109 *Ibid.*

110 Moore enlisted in Melbourne in September 1863 and initially served in the 1st Waikato Regiment. Barton, *op. cit.*, p. 53.

111 *Argus*, 21 June 1864, p. 6 (and originally published in the *Ballarat Star*).

112 *Ibid.*

113 For press coverage of the recruiting in other Australian colonies, refer to: *Courier*, 15, 18, 20, 22 & 27 August, 1, 7, 8 & 14 September and 6 November 1863; & *Queensland Daily Guardian*, 18, 20, 22, 26, 27, 28 & 31 August, 5, 7, 15, 16, 18 & 21 September and 7 & 12 October 1863.

114 Captain Pitt is confirmed as the officer initiating the recruiting efforts in Brisbane, refer to editorial: *Courier*, 8 September 1863.

115 *Ibid.*, 19 August 1863.

116 *Ibid.*, 22 August 1863.

117 *Queensland Daily Guardian*, 18 August 1863, p. 3; & also refer to: *Courier*, 22 August 1863.

118 *Queensland Daily Guardian*, 20 August 1863, p. 2; & *The Courier*, 20 August 1863.

119 *Courier*, 24 August 1863.

120 *Ibid.*, 26 August 1863. The military settler advertisements were published thereafter in: *Ibid.*, 27 August 1863; & *Queensland Daily Guardian*, 27 August, p. 4 & 28 August 1863, p. 4.

121 *Courier*, 26 August 1863.

122 *Ibid.*, 29 August 1863.

123 *Ibid.*, 28 & 31 August 1863; & also refer to: *Ibid.*, 10 September 1863.

124 *Queensland Daily Guardian*, 3 September 1863, p. 2.

125 *Courier*, 8 September 1863.

126 *Ibid.*

127 *Ibid.*, 8 & 9 September 1863; & *Queensland Daily Guardian*, 8 September 1863, p. 2.

128 COL/A44: Colonial Secretary's Office: In-Letter 2003, 2 September 1863; & COL/Q2: Letterbook of Letters to other Departments: 63/754 (p. 629), 17 September 1863, *QSA*.

129 *Sydney Morning Herald*, 29 September 1860, p. 6, 18 July, p. 4 & 27 August 1861, p. 4 and 28 July 1862, p. 5.

130 *Ibid.*, 31 July 1862, p. 8. Pitt later accompanied Governor Bowen to New Zealand following Bowen's appointment to take up that colony's governorship in January 1868, and where he continued to serve as Bowen's private secretary and aide-de-camp.

131 Pitt was also prominent in the Queensland Rifle Association and Queensland Turf Club. *Courier*, 28 & 31 July, 1, 2, 4, 7, 8 & 23 August and 1 September 1862, 3 & 25 June and 4 August 1863 and 17 & 18 February 1864; *Queensland Daily Guardian*, 4 August 1863 and 13 & 19 January 1864. Also refer to: *QGG*, Vol. III, No. 69, 26 July 1862, p. 381; Vol. III, No. 72, 2 August 1862, p. 393; Vol. III, No. 80, 30 August 1862, pp. 455–57; & Vol. VII, No. 97, 18 August 1866, p. 781.

132 COL/A51: Colonial Secretary's Office: In-Letter 510, dated 13 January 1864; & COL/Q3: Letterbook of Letters to other Departments: Letter 64/45 (p. 19), dated 16 January 1864, *QSA*; *Queensland Daily Guardian*, 20 January 1864, p. 2; & *Sydney Morning Herald*, 22 January 1864, p. 4.

133 'Report from the Joint Select Committee on the Defence of the Colony, together with the Proceedings of the Committee and Minutes of Evidence', *Queensland Votes and Proceedings: 1866* (Brisbane: W.C. Belbridge, Government Printer, 1866), pp. 1700–3.

134 *Queensland Daily Guardian*, 9 September 1863, p. 2.

135 *Ibid.*, 10 September 1863, p. 2. The *Courier* reported these volunteers had been mustered in the barrack yard before being marched down Queen Street, and that a total of 50 men embarked. *Courier*, 10 September 1863.

136 *Courier*, 10 September 1863.

137 This temporary 'field commission' was given to Reilly to command the Brisbane volunteers on their journey. Presumed to be Eugene Reilly, a sergeant in the 2nd Waikato Regiment, who also volunteered for service in the Imperial Commissariat Transport Corps. *Courier*, 18 September 1863; 'G.-No. 1: Papers Relative to the Issue of the NZ War Medal: No. 3: Enclosure 4 in No. 3: List No. 4', *AJHRNZ: Vol. II: 1871*, pp. 14–15 of G.-No. 1; Barton, *op. cit.*, p. 94; & Stowers, *op. cit.*, p. 97.

138 *Courier*, 11 September 1863; *Queensland Daily Guardian*, 11 September 1863, p. 2; & *Sydney Morning Herald*, 11 September 1863.

139 *Queensland Daily Guardian*, 11 September 1863, p. 2; *Courier*, 14 September & 19 September 1863; & *Sydney Morning Herald*, 12 September, p. 7 & 14 September 1863, p. 4.

140 *Courier*, 18 September 1863.

141 *Moreton Bay Courier*, 11 September 1860, and 7 January & 12 October 1863; & *QGG*, Vol. III, No. 1, 4 January 1862, p. 2.

142 *Courier*, 12 October 1863; & also refer to: *Queensland Daily Guardian*, 12 October 1863, p. 2.

143 *NZG*, No. 50, 24 September 1863, pp. 427–28, No. 25, 21 July 1865, p. 226 & No. 31, 31 May 1871, p. 248; *NZAL 1863*, p. 3; *NZAL 1864*, p. 6; & 'G.-No. 1: Papers Relative to the Issue of the NZ War Medal: No. 3: Enclosure 4 in No. 3: List No. 1', *AJHRNZ: Vol. II: 1871*, pp. 11–12 of G.-No. 1.

144 During August–October 1863 the Tasmanian press extensively reported on the arrival, recruiting activities, and success of the New Zealand government officials and military officers who arrived in Sydney and Melbourne. *Launceston Examiner*, 18 August, p. 3, 22 August, p. 5, 27 August, p. 3, 5 September, p. 5, 8 September, p. 3, 24 September, p. 3, 13 October, p. 3, 20 October, p. 3, 22 October, p. 2 and 3 November 1863, p. 3; & *Mercury*, 24, 28 & 29 August and 1, 7, 16, 23 & 25 September 1863.

145 *Mercury*, 28 August 1863. This advertisement was continued up to the departure of the first contingent of volunteers: *Mercury*, 29 & 31 August, 1, 2, 3, 4, 5, 7, 8, 9, 10, 12, 14, 15, 16, 18, 19, 21, 22, 23, 24, 25, 26, 28, 29 & 30 September, and 1, 2, 3, 5 & 6 October 1863; & *Launceston Examiner*, 1 October, p. 2, 3 October, p. 2 & 6 October 1863, p. 2.

146 *Mercury*, 1 & 8 September 1863.

147 *Ibid.*, 1 September 1863.

148 Lt. Prideaux Owen Rickards' name is often spelt incorrectly in the original press sources as 'Richards'. *Launceston Examiner*, 10 September, p. 5 & 26 September 1863, p. 5; *Mercury*, 22 & 26 September 1863; *NZG*, No. 55, 27 October 1863, p. 460; *NZAL 1863*, p. 3; & *NZAL 1864*, p. 6.

149 *Mercury*, 28 September 1863. The *Mercury's* editorial also accompanied an advertisement which informed candidates what documentation they had to produce to be accepted, and other requirements. This was repeated in conjunction with the full conditions of service. *Mercury*, 29 & 30 September and 1, 2, 3 5 & 6 October 1863.

150 *Ibid.*, 30 September 1863.

151 *Ibid.*, 1 October 1863. Thereafter this advertisement was repeated in conjunction with the previous advertisements associated with the military settler recruiting; refer to: *Ibid.*, 2, 3, 5 & 6 October 1863.

152 *Launceston Examiner* reported: 'Of a dozen applicants none were enrolled, two being refused by the doctor, and the other failing to produce a good character.' *Launceston Examiner*, 3 October 1863, p. 5; & also refer to: *Mercury*, 30 September 1863.

153 *Mercury*, 3, 5 & 6 October 1863.

154 *Ibid.*, 6 October 1863.

155 Ashton was appointed lieutenant in October 1863, and served in the 3rd Waikato Regiment. *NZG*, No. 55, 27 October 1863, p. 460; & *NZAL 1863*, p. 3.

156 *Mercury*, 7 October 1863; *Launceston Examiner*, 8 October 1863, p. 5; & also refer to: Correspondence Files: Maori Wars, *AOT*.

157 *Mercury*, 8 October & 30 November 1863; & *Launceston Examiner*, 8 October 1863, p. 4. One of those removed was William M'Neil, a 16-year-old native of the colony. In the Hobart Police Court on 29 October, he was charged by F.R. Lees 'with absenting himself from his service' and pleaded guilty. *Launceston Examiner*, 29 October 1863, p. 3. The Hobart Police Court had also earlier heard the case against George Cook and Alfred Mansfield, after being charged by 'Mr. Smith, the Quarter-Master of the City Guards, with attempting to leave the colony and their corps without paying for their uniform clothing'. *Launceston Examiner*, 10 October, p. 5 & 22 October 1863, p. 2; & *Courier*, 14 November 1863.

158 *Mercury*, 12 October 1863. This advertisement continued until the departure of the second contingent of volunteers: *Mercury*, 13, 14, 15, 16, 17, 19, 20, 21, 22, 23 & 24 October 1863.

159 *Ibid.*, 14 October 1863; & *Launceston Examiner*, 15 October 1863, p. 5.

160 Gregson was appointed lieutenant in October 1863, and served in the 3rd Waikato Regiment. *NZAL 1863*, p. 3; & *NZAL 1864*, p. 7.

161 *Mercury*, 17 October 1863; & associated advertisements continued on 19, 20, 21 & 22 October 1863.

162 *Ibid.*, 23 & 24 October 1863; & *Launceston Examiner*, 27 October 1863, p. 5.

163 *Mercury*, 26 October & 23 November 1863; & *Launceston Examiner*, 27 October, p. 5 & 21 November 1863, p. 3.

164 *Mercury*, 26 October 1863. This 2nd Tasmanian contingent of one officer and 50 other ranks arrived in Auckland on 8 November. *Mercury*, 30 November 1863; & also refer to: *Ibid*., 10 December 1863.

165 Miller was appointed lieutenant in January 1864, and served in the 3rd Waikato Regiment. *NZAL 1864*, p. 7; *NZG*, No. 3, 26 January 1864, p. 22; & *Mercury*, 4 & 5 November 1863. Advertisements associated with raising this 3rd contingent were extensively repeated: *Mercury*, 5, 6, 7, 9, 11, 12, 13, 14, 16, 17, 18, 19, 20, 21, 23, 24, 25, 26, 27, 28 & 30 November and 1, 2, 3, 4, 7, 8, 9, 10, 11, 12, 14, 15 & 16 December 1863; & *Launceston Examiner*, 15 December 1863, p. 5. Chesney directed Miller to seek permission from the governor to enrol further volunteers, and he accordingly received Gore Browne's approval. CSD 4/45/636. Colonial Secretary: Correspondence File: 636: Letter dated Hobart Town, 31 October 1863, *AOT*.

166 *Mercury*, 26, 27 & 31 October and 2 & 3 November 1863; & *Launceston Examiner*, 3 November 1863, p. 4.

167 *Mercury*, 5 November 1863; & also refer to: *Ibid*., editorial on 31 October 1863.

168 *Ibid*., 9 December 1863.

169 *Ibid*., 19 December 1863.

170 On the eve of this departure one last advertisement was issued for the northern areas. Any prospective persons at Launceston, if after successful medical examination, would have all expenses paid by the government including a coach fare to Hobart Town so as to depart with the planned draft. *Ibid*., 10, 11, 12, 14, 15 & 16 December 1863; & *Launceston Examiner*, 15 December 1863, p. 5.

171 Pogue was appointed ensign in February 1864 and served in the 4th Waikato Regiment. In April 1864 it was reported that Captain A.F. Smith was about to be entrusted with command of artillery in New Zealand, but shortly after in July, news arrived that he died from 'inflammation of the brain' in a military camp near Auckland. *Mercury*, 17 & 18 December 1863; *Launceston Examiner*, 19 December, p. 4 & 23 December 1863, p. 4, 7 April, p. 5 & 19 July 1864, p. 5; *NZG*, No. 7, 24 February 1864, p. 83; & *NZAL 1864*, p. 8.

172 The appointed Tasmanian volunteer officers/recruiting officers (i.e. Lieutenants Ashton, Gregson and de Burgh Miller, Ensign Pogue, and Capt. A.F. Smith) who departed with these three contingents generally appear to not be included in the total number of men reported per contingent (except in the case of Lt. Ashton). They are therefore additional to totals in press sources, whereby arriving at the total of 162 officers and men.

173 *Mercury*, 22 December 1863.

174 *Ibid*., 10 October 1863.

175 'Camp Otahuhu, Sunday, 13th Sept.', *Ibid*., 15 October 1863.

176 *Ibid*., 5 January 1864; & also republished in: *Launceston Examiner*, 7 January, p. 5 & 23 January 1864, p. 2.

177 *Launceston Examiner*, 30 April 1864, p. 3 (and originally published in the *Hobart Town Advertiser*).

178 This first-hand Tasmanian report provides an illuminating account of the events at Orakau, including the fatal wounding of Captain Herford, 3rd Waikato Regiment, and the Maori exodus and chase by imperial and colonial forces. *Launceston Examiner*, 10 May 1864, p. 2.

179 For Tasmanian press coverage of news of plans for, subsequent commencement of, and men (and families) obtained during this second recruiting mission, refer to: *Launceston Examiner*, 12 December, p. 3 & 31 December 1863, p. 5 and 12 January, p. 3, 23 January, p. 5, 2 February, p. 2, 9 February, p. 3 & 11 February 1864, p. 2; & *Mercury*, 25 & 27 January, 2, 6 & 9 February and 12 & 19 March 1864.

180 *Mercury*, 20 January 1864.

181 *Ibid*., 2 February 1864.

182 *Ibid*., 1 March 1864.

183 Indications that Pitt would come back were evident regarding his planned return to make arrangements for the conveyance of wives and families of volunteers enlisted in 1863, apart from recommencing recruiting for the 'Waikato Militia'. *Argus*, 16 December 1863, p. 7 & 6 January 1864, p. 5.

184 The *Argus* in error initially cites Keddell as 'Cadell'. Keddell was a former Victorian and then Otago policeman, who in November 1863 was appointed captain in the 4th Waikato Regiment. Lt. C.D. Pitt was the son of Colonel G.D. Pitt. Pitt (junior) served in the 1st Waikato Regiment (1863–67) and later in the Armed Constabulary (1867–74). *Argus*, 15 January 1864, p. 4; & *Illustrated Melbourne Post*, 25 January 1864, p. 13.

185 *Argus*, 15 January, p. 7 & 16 January 1864, p. 7; & also refer to Appendix C.
186 *Argus*, 15 January, pp. 5 & 7 and 18 January 1864, p. 4.
187 *Ibid.*, 18 January 1864, p. 4.
188 *Ibid.*, 20 January 1864, p. 4.
189 *Ibid.*
190 'Military Settlers For New Zealand', by 'Uncle Toby' (dated Jan. 18), *Ibid.*, 20 January 1864, p. 5.
191 'Military Settlers In New Zealand', by 'Caution', *Ibid.*, 21 January 1864, p. 7.
192 'The New Zealand War And Colonization', by 'R.B.' (dated Jan. 20), *Ibid.*
193 Advertisements outlining the full details of service for military settlers for 'Land in the Northern Island of New Zealand', found in: *Ibid.*, 15 January, p. 7, 16 January, p. 7 & 21 January 1864, p. 3.
194 *Ibid.*, 22 January 1864, p. 4.
195 East served as captain in the Prahran and South Yarra Battery of the Victorian Volunteer Artillery (1861–63), and then briefly as captain in the Metropolitan Battery Field Artillery (1863–64). After enlisting for New Zealand, he was appointed captain in January 1864, served in 4th Waikato Regiment, where he was also appointed adjutant in May 1864. *Ibid.*, 22 January 1864, p. 4; *NZG*, No. 8, 3 March 1864, p. 94 & No. 19, 14 May 1864, p. 225; *NZAL 1864*, p. 8; Ward, *op. cit.*, pp. 62 & 70; & Stowers, *op. cit.*, p. 105.
196 Pennefather was appointed lieutenant in January 1864, captain in April 1864, and served in the Taranaki Military Settlers (1864–66). Jackson is presumed to be J.R. Jackson who was appointed lieutenant in 30 January 1864, and served in the Taranaki Military Settlers until his commission was cancelled in late 1864. *NZG*, No. 7, 24 February 1864, p. 83 & No. 16, 6 May 1864, p. 189; *Index to NZG, 1864*, p. vii; *NZAL 1864*, pp. 19–20; & Stowers, *op. cit.*, p. 71.
197 'Colonel Pitt's Military Settlers', by 'HY.M.M.', *Argus*, 23 January 1864, p. 5. In defence of East's decision to enlist for New Zealand, one Victorian volunteer responded to 'HY.M.M.'. Refer to: 'Captain East', by 'A South Yarra Volunteer', *Argus*, 29 January 1864, p. 7.
198 Letter to the editor entitled 'Colonel Pitt And His Settlers', by 'H.M.M.', *Ibid.*, 29 January 1864, p. 7.
199 *Ibid.*, 27 January 1864, pp. 5 & 6.
200 *Ibid.*, p. 6.
201 AWM27 100/6: Photographic Reproductions of Correspondence Relating to the Service of Victorians in the Maori War of 1863–64 (Jan.–Aug. 1864), *AWM*; & also found in: *Argus*, 27 January 1864, p. 6.
202 *Ibid.*
203 *Argus*, 26 January 1864, p. 6.
204 AWM27 100/6, *op. cit.*, *AWM.*
205 *Victorian*, 30 January 1864, p. 590.
206 *Argus*, 22 January, pp. 4 & 8, 23 January, pp. 5 & 7 and 25 January 1864, p. 5.
207 *Ibid.*, 25 January 1864, p. 4.
208 *Ibid.*, 23 January 1864, p. 5.
209 Sisson was incorrectly reported as 'Vesson'; he was appointed lieutenant in January 1864, served in the Taranaki Military Settlers, and in June 1865 was placed on the unattached NZ Militia list. Clarke was appointed lieutenant in January 1864, captain in September 1865, and served in the Taranaki Military Settlers (1864–67). The *Gresham* did not actually sail for Taranaki until 31 January, but this delay may in part be explained by an accident reported to have befallen one volunteer on board. *NZG*, No. 7, 24 February 1864, p. 83, No. 23, 11 July 1865, p. 216 & No. 37, 22 September 1865, p. 284; *NZAL 1864*, p. 20; *Argus*, 23 January, pp. 4 & 5, 26 January, pp. 4 & 5, 27 January, p. 4 & 2 February 1864, p. 4; & Stowers, *op. cit.*, p. 68.
210 Roddy presumably departed instead of Clarke, who departed later aboard the *Brilliant*. Roddy was appointed ensign in January 1864, lieutenant in June 1866, and served in the Taranaki Military Settlers. *NZG*, No. 7, 24 February 1864, p. 83 & No. 39, 29 June 1866, p. 272; *NZAL 1864*, p. 20; *Sydney Morning Herald*, 10 March 1864, p. 5; B. Wells, *The History of Taranaki* (New Plymouth: Edmondson & Avery, Taranaki News Office, 1878), p. 258; & Glen, *op. cit.*, p. 70.
211 Horne was appointed ensign in January 1864, serving initially in 4th Waikato Regiment, then the Imperial Commissariat Transport Corps, and later the 1st Waikato Regiment. The *Thomas Fletcher* did not actually sail for Auckland until 7 February. *NZG*, No. 8, 3 March 1864, p. 94; *NZAL 1864*, p. 8; *Argus*, 23 January, p. 5, 25 January, p. 7, 26 January, p. 6, 27 January, p. 7, 28 January, pp. 4 & 7, 2 February, p. 4, 3 February,

p. 4 & 9 February 1864, p. 4; *Victorian*, 6 February 1864, p. 608; & also refer to news received from the *Sydney Morning Herald*'s 'Own Correspondent' in Auckland: *Sydney Morning Herald*, 10 March 1864, p. 5; & Norris, *op. cit.*, pp. 22 & 57–58.

212 *Argus*, 2 February 1864, p. 4.

213 *Ibid.*, 26 January, p. 4, 2 February, p. 4 & 3 February 1864, p. 4.

214 Stewart was appointed captain in January 1864, though his commission was later cancelled during 1864. One paper reported the *Swiftsure*'s contingent as 586 adults. *NZG*, No. 7, 24 February 1864, p. 82; *Index to NZG, 1864*, p. xi; & *Victorian*, 6 February 1864, p. 608.

215 *Argus*, 8 February 1864, p. 4; & Norris, *op. cit.*, pp. 23 & 24.

216 Kirkby was appointed lieutenant in February 1864, and served in the Taranaki Military Settlers. On the *Brilliant* he was accompanied by his wife and two children. His commission was later cancelled in May 1865. Gascoigne was appointed lieutenant in January 1864, and served in the Taranaki Military Settlers. Gascoigne and all his family were later killed in the White Cliffs Massacre on 13 February 1869 (also refer to Appendix D). Jackson was appointed lieutenant in January 1864, served in the Taranaki Military Settlers, though his commission was cancelled later during 1864. *Argus*, 4 February, p. 4, 8 February, p. 4 & 9 February 1864, p. 4; *Victorian*, 6 February 1864, p. 608; *NZG*, No. 7, 24 February 1864, p. 83 & No. 19, 7 June 1865, p. 175; *Index to NZG, 1864*, p. vii; *NZAL 1864*, p. 20; Wells, *op. cit.*, p. 258; 417/008/002: Document Control Centre: Records of Early Wars in NZ, *AWM*.; & Glen, *op. cit.*, pp. 84 & 124.

217 Colonel Pitt, Captains Fraser, Hunter and Keddell, and Lt. Pitt left Melbourne on 8 February for Sydney en route to Auckland; and Lt. Percival was to follow by the mail steamer. *Victorian*, 13 February 1864, p. 615. An 1878 source refers to the arrival of a group of 40 volunteers at New Plymouth aboard the *Choice* from Melbourne via Lyttelton in the South Island of New Zealand in December 1863. This author has been unable to determine whether these are actual Victorian volunteers, but believe they are more likely to be South Island enlistees. Wells, *op. cit.*, p. 257.

218 *Argus*, 30 March 1864, p. 6 (and originally published in *The Daylesford Mercury* on 29 March).

219 *Ibid.*

220 *South Australian Register*, 19 August 1863. Thereafter this paper continued to follow recruiting commenced in other Australian colonies and especially the enthusiasm for volunteering evident in Victoria during August–September: *South Australian Register*, 21, 24, 25, 26, 27 & 31 August and 1, 2, 3, 8 & 24 September 1863. This also included news of the arrival in New Zealand of the various Australian contingents and their service (including families): *South Australian Register*, 2, 6 & 15 October 1863 and 6 April, 3 & 24 June 1864.

221 *Mercury*, 28 August & 1 September 1863; *Sydney Morning Herald*, 26 August 1863, p. 5; & *Argus*, 26 August 1863, p. 5.

222 Williams entered the Army as an ensign in the 12th Regiment in October 1853, served at the storming of Eureka Stockade in 1854, became lieutenant in 1857, and in 1860 was appointed lieutenant on the volunteer staff of South Australia. In Sydney at the commencement of military settler recruiting in 1863, he was appointed lieutenant in September 1863 and put in command of the 'Sydney volunteers', and served in the 2nd Waikato Regiment (1863–65). He continued to serve in the NZ Militia into the early 1870s, but returned to South Australia, where in July 1877 he was appointed lieutenant on staff of South Australian Military Forces, later captain and staff-adjutant, and then honorary major. P. Mennell, *The Dictionary of Australasian Biography* (London: Hutchinson & Co., 1892), p. 510. Also refer to: *NZAL 1863*, p. 3; *NZAL 1864*, p. 5; & *NZAL 1872*, p. 5.

223 *South Australian Register*, 28 September 1863.

224 *Ibid.*, 'Volunteers For New Zealand', 28 September 1863; 'Adelaideans In New Zealand', 29 December 1863; 'South Australians In New Zealand', 4 May 1864; & 'A South Australian In The New Zealand War', 19 July 1864. Also refer to Appendix D.

225 *South Australian Register*, 7 December 1863; & also refer to: 12 December 1863 & 19 January 1864. For subsequent reportage of events associated with the second recruiting mission in Victoria, refer to: *South Australian Register*, 21, 25 & 27 January 1864.

226 *Ibid.*, 15 January 1864; & advertisement repeated on 16 & 21 January 1864.

227 *Ibid.*, 15 January 1864.

228 *Ibid.*, 21 January 1864; & advertisement repeated on 22 & 23 January 1864.

229 William Magee (also as McGhee) Hunter of the Auckland Rifle Volunteers was appointed captain in the Auckland Militia in July 1863. Here he became involved in the formation and recruitment of military settlers for the 1st Waikato Regiment. With the disbandment of the military settler regiments in 1867, he joined the Armed Constabulary and was killed in action at Moturoa in November 1868. *NZG*, No. 26, 4 July 1863, p. 258 & No. 43, 27 August 1863, p. 361; J. Cowan, *The New Zealand Wars:... Vol. II: The Hauhau Wars, 1864–1872* (Wellington: W.A.G. Skinner, Government Printer, 1923), pp. 253–54; G.H. Scholefield (ed.), *A Dictionary of New Zealand Biography: Volume I: A–L* (Wellington: Department of Internal Affairs, 1940), pp. 421–22; & *The Dictionary of New Zealand Biography: Volume One: 1769–1869, op. cit.*, pp. 207–8.

230 *South Australian Register*, 23 January 1864; (& advertisement repeated on 25 January).

231 *Ibid.*, 25 & 26 January 1864.

232 *Ibid.*, 25 January 1864; (& advertisement repeated on 26 January).

233 For various editorials on the impact of, or concerns related to, this second recruiting mission to South Australia and other Australian colonies, refer to: *Ibid.*, 16, 26 & 28 January 1864.

234 *Ibid.*, 19 January 1864.

235 *Ibid.*, 28 January 1864.

236 *Ibid.*, 26 & 27 January 1864.

237 *Ibid.*, 28 January 1864.

238 *Ibid.*, 30 January & 1 February 1864.

239 *Ibid.*, 1 February 1864.

240 *Ibid.*

241 *Argus*, 2 February 1864, p. 4.

242 *South Australian Register*, 10 May 1864; & also refer to: *Ibid.*, 28 January 1864.

243 *Sydney Morning Herald*, 29 December 1863, p. 5.

244 *Argus*, 14 January 1864, p. 7.

245 *NZG*, No. 31, 22 July 1863, p. 287 & No. 13, 16 April 1864, p. 166; & *NZAL 1864*, p. 8.

246 Norris, *op. cit.*, p. 21.

247 *Ibid.*, p. 24.

248 *Ibid.*, pp. 21–22.

249 *Ibid.*, p. 22.

250 The passenger list for this vessel records '58 in the steerage'. The *Kate* was also carrying '54 packages, H.M. Government', which appears to be a consignment of Commissariat stores. *Sydney Morning Herald*, 3 February, p. 4 & 4 February 1864, p. 4; Eadie, *op. cit.*, p. 3; & 417/008/002:... Records of Early Wars in NZ, *AWM*.

251 Norris, *op. cit.*, p. 22.

252 *Ibid.*, p. 23.

253 The *Phoebe* 'carried some who were attested at about the same time' as these other contingents from Sydney, though no dates or numbers involved are detailed. Similarly, the *Fanny Fisher* is listed carrying fourteen passengers who might be Sydney-enlisted volunteers, though with both these vessels these are not confirmed as military settler contingents. *Ibid.*, pp. 22–24; & 417/008/002:... Records of Early Wars in NZ, *AWM*.

254 *Courier*, 15 February 1864; & also republished 17 February 1864.

255 *Ibid.*, 29 February 1864.

256 *Ibid.*, 8 March 1864.

257 *Ibid.*, 7 March 1864. The criticism by 'Dragoon Guards' appears to be directed at the head of the military in Queensland, Captain Pitt, RA, who had been involved in the military settler recruiting during 1863. Press commentary thereafter appears to initially indicate that Pitt was indeed the person being criticised (see 8 March). But 'Dragoon Guards' himself approached the *Courier* and asked that it be made clear that it was 'not his wish to refer in any way to the gentleman who at present is in command of her Majesty's forces in this colony'. *Ibid.*, 8 & 9 March 1864.

258 *Ibid.*, 7 March 1864.

259 *Ibid.*, 8 & 9 March 1864; *Queensland Daily Guardian*, 9 March 1864, p. 2; & *Sydney Morning Herald*, 12 March 1864, p. 6.

260 A 'Militia General Order' ordered the following corps to be disbanded on 31 October 1867: 1st, 2nd, 3rd, and 4th Regiments of Waikato Militia; 1st and 2nd Companies of Forest Rangers; the 10 Companies of Taranaki Military Settlers; Hawke's Bay Military Settlers; Patea Rangers; Wanganui Rangers; and the Wanganui Yeomanry Cavalry. *NZG*, No. 55, 22 October 1867, p. 405; & also refer to: 'D.-No. 21: Enclosure No. 101: Return of Arms, Ammunition, and Accoutrements issued to Military Settlers during the Years 1865, 1866, 1867, and 1868', *JHRNZ: 1868* (Wellington), p. 37 of D.-No. 21.

261 *NZG*, No. 49, 18 September 1863, p. 414 (and for all correspondence pertaining to this engagement, see pp. 413–17).

262 *Sydney Morning Herald*, 3 October, p. 7, 5 October, p. 8 & 6 October 1863, p. 5; *Argus*, 7 October, p. 7 & 13 October 1863, p. 7; *NZAL 1863*, p. 2; *NZAL 1864*, p. 3; *NZG*, No. 23, 25 June 1864, pp. 277–78 & No. 26, 9 July 1864, pp. 292–96; J.E. Alexander, *Bush Fighting* (London: Sampson Low, Marston, Low and Searle, 1873), pp. 217–24; Featon, *op. cit.*, pp. 95–97; & M. Barthorp, *To Face the Daring Maoris* (London: Hodder and Stoughton, 1979), pp. 20, 73, 95 & 186.

263 Glen, *op. cit.*, pp. 45, 46 & 48; N. Morris (ed.), *The Journal of William Morgan* (Auckland: Libraries Department, Auckland City Council, 1963), pp. 82, 83–84 & 96; Cowan (1922), *op. cit.*, pp. 273–75; Cowan (1923), *op. cit.*, p. 492; & Bartlett, *op. cit.*, pp. 282 & 283.

264 Refer to Appendix D. See in particular the deaths of Lieutenant John Spencer Perceval, Corporal Michael Power and Privates William Beswick & William Williamson — all Victorian enlistees.

265 Refer to Appendix D. See in particular the deaths of Privates William Stevenson, killed in action 23 January 1867, Denis Augustus Ward, killed in action 23 January 1867 & Henry Jeffs, killed in action 15 February 1867. For information on the Tauranga Bush Campaign, refer to: E.A.H. Webb, *History of the 12th (The Suffolk) Regiment 1685–1913* (London: Spottiswoode & Co., 1914), pp. 281 & 296–98; Sinclair, *op. cit.*, pp. 164–66; Cowan (1923), *op. cit.*, pp. 148–54; & J. Rorke, *Policing Two Peoples* (Jinty Rorke & the NZ Police, 1993), pp. 1–2.

266 *Sydney Morning Herald*, 30 March 1864, p. 5; *Argus*, 1 April 1864, p. 5; *NZG*, No. 11, 6 April 1864, pp. 146–49; & 'E.-No. 3: Further Papers Relative to the Native Insurrection', *JHRNZ: 1864*, 'No. 35', 'Enclosure in No. 35', 'Sub-Enclosure 1 in No. 35', 'Sub-Enclosure 2 in No. 35', & 'Sub-Enclosure 3 in No. 35', pp. 47–50. Also refer to: Wells, *op. cit.*, pp. 241–42.

267 *NZG*, No. 13, 16 April 1864, p. 160 (and for full despatch and associated enclosures pertaining to this attack and capture of Kaitake pa, see pp. 160–65); & also refer to: *Sydney Morning Herald*, 11 April 1864, p. 5; & *Argus*, 16 April 1864, p. 7.

268 *NZG*, No. 13, 16 April 1864, p. 165; & also refer to: Cowan (1922), *op. cit.*, pp. 223–24; & Glen, *op. cit.*, pp. 70–71. Captain Corbett's Company of Taranaki Military Settlers sustained one casualty on 25 March 1864: Sergeant James Appleby, 'Otago Contingent', died of wounds. AD 31/8: Army Department, Taranaki Military Settlers Nominal and Descriptive Roll Book, 1863–69: Nominal & Descriptive Roll of the 'Otago Contingent' of Taranaki Military Settlers', p. 1, *NANZ*; & also refer to: *Sydney Morning Herald*, 11 April 1864, p. 5; & *Argus*, 16 April 1864, p. 7.

269 Refer to Appendix D. See in particular the deaths of Corporal John Banks and Privates John Gallagher, Charles Hartley & James Neagle. For other details on the ambush at Te Ahuahu, refer to: *Sydney Morning Herald*, 19 April, p. 5 & 11 May 1864, p. 8; *Argus*, 19 April, p. 5, 22 April, p. 7 & 25 April 1864, p. 6; Wells, *op. cit.*, pp. 242–44; Cowan (1923), *op. cit.*, pp. 15–18 & 492–93; & Glen, *op. cit.*, pp. 72–73.

270 *NZG*, No. 20, 21 May 1864, pp. 237–39.

271 Refer to Appendix D. See in particular the deaths of Private Denis Spain, accidentally killed 2 August 1866, and Lt. Bamber Gascoigne & family, and Privates John Milne & Edward Richards — all killed on 13 February 1869.

272 *NZG*, No. 55, 22 October 1867, p. 405. Also refer to Appendices D & F.

CHAPTER EIGHT

1 *Argus*, 15 October 1868, pp. 4–5.

2 *Sydney Morning Herald*, 4 November 1868, p. 4.

3 *Ibid.*

4 *Ibid.*

ENDNOTES

5 For detailed treatment of the life and impact of Titokowaru, it is recommended readers consult: J. Belich, *'I Shall Not Die': Titokowaru's War, New Zealand, 1868–9* (Wellington, NZ: Allen & Unwin NZ Ltd in association with the Port Nicholson Press, 1989).

6 For expansive treatment of the life and impact of Te Kooti, it is recommended readers consult: J. Binney, *Redemption Songs: A Life of Te Kooti Arikirangi Te Turuki* (Auckland, NZ: Auckland University Press, 1995). For studies detailing the military campaigns against Te Kooti from 1868 into 1872, refer to: S. Marsh, 'The Last Despatches: Armed Constabulary Field Operations Mounted Against Te Kooti: February – May 1872', *The Volunteers*, Vol. 27, No. 3 (March 2002), pp. 141–67; & R. Crosby, *Gilbert Mair: Te Kooti's Nemesis* (Auckland, NZ: Reed Books, 2004).

7 J. Belich, *The New Zealand Wars* (Auckland: Penguin Books, 1988), pp. 252–53.

8 Belich (1989), *op. cit.*, p. 215.

9 *Argus*, 4 December 1868, p. 4.

10 *Ibid.*

11 Press coverage and editorials on the Poverty Bay Massacre (10 November 1868), include: *Argus*, 20 November 1868, p. 4; *Sydney Morning Herald*, 20 November 1868, pp. 4 & 5; *Illustrated Sydney News*, 28 November 1868, p. 94; *Brisbane Courier*, 20 November, p. 2 & 24 November 1868, p. 3; *Gympie Times*, 24 & 26 November 1868; & *Perth Gazette and West Australian Times*, 25 December 1868.

12 MS3590: Letter dated Auckland, 23 Nov. 1868, to Edward Deas-Thomson, of Sydney, NSW, from {son} Edward R. Deas-Thomson, Discussing Mining Field and Prospects and The Maori War, *National Library of Australia.*

13 An example of this practice is evident in a column in the *Argus* entitled 'The War In New Zealand', originally derived from a Bendigo man, following receipt of a letter from a brother at Poverty Bay, dated 2 October. *Argus*, 11 November 1868, p. 7.

14 *Ibid.*, 7 December, p. 5 & 8 December 1868, p. 5.

15 *Sydney Morning Herald*, 4 December 1868, p. 4.

16 *Ibid.*, 4 March 1869, p. 4.

17 *Brisbane Courier*, 6 March 1869, p. 4.

18 *Sydney Morning Herald*, 5 March 1869, p. 4. For other press coverage and editorials on the White Cliffs Massacre, refer to: *Sydney Morning Herald*, 4 March, pp. 3 & 4, 5 March, pp. 4 & 6 and 8 March 1869, p. 5; *Illustrated Sydney News*, 20 March 1869, pp. 154–55; *Brisbane Courier*, 11 March 1869, p. 3; & *Gympie Times*, 18 March 1869.

19 The last known former Australian military settler death was Donald McDonald, a Tasmanian enlistee in the 3rd Waikato Regiment, killed in an ambush in June 1869 while serving in the Bay of Plenty Cavalry Volunteers. J. Hopkins-Weise, 'A Brief History of the Bay of Plenty Cavalry Volunteers, Tauranga Cavalry Volunteers, and the Opotiki Rangers Volunteers', *The Volunteers*, Vol. 28, No. 1 (July 2002), p. 68. Also refer to Appendix D.

20 Gascoigne was appointed lieutenant, Taranaki Militia, on 20 January 1864. He arrived at New Plymouth from Melbourne aboard the *Brilliant* on 17 February 1864, his wife Annie and eldest child arriving in August 1864. *NZG*, No. 7, 24 February 1864, p. 83; & F. Glen, *For Glory and a Farm* (Whakatane: Whakatane & District Historical Society, 1985), p. 84.

21 John Milne, Regt. No. 564, 'Melbourne Contingent', Taranaki Military Settlers. Enlisted: 21 January 1864, Castlemaine (Victoria). Trade or calling: Ploughman; Age at Enlistment: 35; and Ship: *Gresham.* Edward Richards, Regt. No. 578, 'Melbourne Contingent', Taranaki Military Settlers. Enlisted: 19 January 1864, Melbourne (Victoria). Trade or calling: Gardener; Age at Enlistment: 40; and Ship: *Gresham.* AD 31/8: Army Department, Taranaki Military Settlers Nominal & Descriptive Roll Book, 1863–69, Nominal & Descriptive Roll of the 'Melbourne Contingent', pp. 57 & 65, *NANZ.* For press information on Rev. Whiteley, refer to: *Brisbane Courier*, 19 March, p. 2 & 22 March 1869, p. 2.

22 Glen, *op. cit.*, p. 87; & for information on the White Cliffs Massacre, refer to pp. 84–85 & 87. Also refer to Appendix D.

23 *Brisbane Courier*, 9 December 1868, p. 3.

24 *Sydney Morning Herald*, 17 December 1868, p. 5.

25 *Argus*, 29 October 1868, p. 7; & also found in: *Brisbane Courier*, 7 November 1868, p. 3.

26 *Argus*, 30 October 1868, p. 6; & also found in: *Gympie Times*, 15 December 1868.

27 *Argus*, 21 October 1868, p. 5.

28 *Sydney Morning Herald*, 6 January 1869, p. 4.

29 *Launceston Examiner*, 17 August 1869, p. 2.

30 *Illustrated Australian News*, 4 September 1869, p. 170.

31 W.D. McIntyre & W.J. Gardner (eds), *Speeches and Documents in New Zealand History* (Oxford: Oxford University Press, 1971), pp. 460 & 463.

32 *Argus*, 6 February 1867, p. 5.

33 *VGG*, No. 141, 24 December 1867, p. 2413.

34 'A.-No. 4: Reports on the Social And Political State Of The Natives In Various Districts At The Time Of The Arrival of Sir G.F. Bowen', *JHRNZ: 1868* (Wellington), p. 2 of A.-No. 4.

35 COL/A105: Colonial Secretary's Office: In-Letter 1269, dated 2 April 1868, *QSA*. The Queensland colonial secretary, A.H. Palmer, officially responded to the New Zealand government on this matter, dated 15 May 1868. COL/P2: Letterbook of Extra-Colonial Letters: 68/100, Letter dated 15 May 1868, to the Colonial Secretary NZ, p. 536, *QSA*.

36 *VGG*, No. 82, 10 July 1868, pp. 1257–58; & also republished, for example, in: *QGG*, Vol. IX, No. 81, 15 August 1868, p. 950.

37 COL/A109: Colonial Secretary's Office: In-Letter 2456, dated 27 July 1868, *QSA*; COL/P2: 68/177, Letter dated 10 Aug. 1868 to the Chief Secretary Victoria, p. 572, *QSA*; & for the republication of Victoria's proclamation, in: *QGG*, Vol. IX, No. 81, 15 August 1868, p. 950.

38 *Argus*, 20 November 1868, p. 5.

39 *Brisbane Courier*, 24 November 1868, p. 2.

40 *Argus*, 25 November 1868, p. 4.

41 *Ibid.*, 2 December 1868, p. 4; also refer to: *Ibid.*, 11 December 1868, p. 4. The *Argus*'s commentary from 2 December was also reprinted in: *Sydney Morning Herald*, 7 December 1868, p. 5.

42 Belich (1989), *op. cit.*, pp. 219–20.

43 *Brisbane Courier*, 4 December 1868, p. 2.

44 *Argus*, 12 December 1868, p. 5. Also refer to: J. Bach, *The Australia Station* (Kensington: NSW University Press, 1986), Appendix Four: Commodores and their ships, Australia Station 1859 – 1884, & p. 78.

45 *Argus*, 14 December 1868, p. 4.

46 *Ibid.*, 15 December 1868, p. 5.

47 *Ibid.*, 24 December 1868, p. 5.

48 *Sydney Morning Herald*, 21 December 1868, pp. 3 & 5; & *Brisbane Courier*, 26 December 1868, p. 5.

49 'A.-No. 8: Papers relative to Imperial Troops in NZ: . . .: Enclosure in No. 7', *AJHRNZ: Vol. I: 1869* (Wellington: George Didsbury, Government Printer), p. 6 of A.-No. 8.

50 *Argus*, 9 January, p. 4, 11 January, p. 4 & 14 January 1869, p. 5. Chute and Stack arrived in Sydney on 12 January, and thereafter departed for Auckland on 14 January. *Sydney Morning Herald*, 13 January, p. 4 & 15 January 1869, p. 4.

51 'A.-No. 9: Correspondence with the NZ Commissioners relative to the Employment of Imperial Troops: . . .: No. 2', *AJHRNZ: Vol. I. Legislative, Political, and Native: 1870* (Wellington: George Didsbury, Government Printer), pp. 4–5 of A.-No. 9.

52 *Brisbane Courier*, 24 November 1868, p. 3; & an abridged version of this commentary by 'A Sydney Man' published in: *Sydney Morning Herald*, 11 January 1869, p. 5.

53 *Argus*, 21 January 1869, p. 5; & also reported in: *Gympie Times*, 27 February 1869.

54 For sources dealing with the Native Police forces in Australia, refer to: M. Cannon, *Who Killed The Koories?* (Port Melbourne: William Heinemann Australia, 1990); B. Elder, *Blood on the Wattle* (Sydney: New Holland Publishers, 2000); R. Evans, K. Saunders & K. Cronin, *Race Relations in Colonial Queensland* (St Lucia: University of Queensland Press, 1988); H. Reynolds, *With The White People* (Ringwood: Penguin Books, 1990); & most recently, J. Richards, *The Secret War* (St Lucia: University of Queensland Press, 2008).

55 *Gympie Times*, 14 January 1869.

56 *Brisbane Courier*, 2 December 1868, p. 3.

57 An obituary in the *Queenslander* in 1916 recounted the life of this former Queensland MLA as well as

his 1869 offer. Hamilton died in Brisbane on 7 December 1916. *Queenslander*, 16 December 1916, p. 16; & also refer to: *Brisbane Courier*, 8 December, p. 6 & 11 December 1916, p. 11.

58 *Gympie Times*, 12 January 1869.

59 *Ibid.*, 1 May 1869.

60 *Ibid.*

61 For other information on John Hamilton refer to: *Pugh's Almanac . . . for 1886* (Brisbane: Gordon & Gotch, 1886), p. 409; D.B. Waterson, *A Biographical Register of the Queensland Parliament 1860–1929* (Canberra: Australian National University Press, 1972), pp. 77–78; & B. Nairn, G. Serle & R. Ward, *ADB: Volume 4: 1851–1890: D–J* (Carlton: Melbourne University Press, 1979), pp. 330–31.

62 T.W. Gudgeon, *The Defenders of New Zealand* (Auckland: H. Brett, 1887), p. 234.

63 'Coromandel' by 'G.F. Von Tempsky', *Argus*, 17 October 1862, p. 6; & also refer to: *The Dictionary of New Zealand Biography: Volume One: 1769–1869* (Wellington: Jointly Published by Allen & Unwin and the Department of Internal Affairs, 1990), p. 530.

64 Gudgeon, *op. cit.*, pp. 230–34; P. Mennell, *The Dictionary of Australasian Biography* (London: Hutchinson & Co., 1892), p. 484; R. Young, H. Curnow & M. King, *G.F. von Tempsky* (Martinborough: Alister Taylor Publishers, 1981), pp. 65 & 77; & *The Dictionary of New Zealand Biography: Volume One: 1769–1869, op. cit.*, pp. 529–30.

65 'A.-No. 3g: Return of the Killed and Wounded Europeans and Natives', *AJHRNZ: Vol. I: 1869* (Wellington: George Didsbury, Government Printer), p. 3 of A.-No. 3g; 'G.-No. 1: ...: Roll D. Nominal Return of Officers and Men of the Colonial Forces who have been Killed in Action or who have Died of Wounds subsequent to the 11th of July, 1868', *AJHRNZ: Vol. II: 1871* (Wellington: George Didsbury, Government Printer), p. 9 of G.-No. 1; *NZG*, No. 31, 31 May 1871, p. 246; & Belich (1989), *op. cit.*, pp. 114–37.

66 *Brisbane Courier*, 28 September 1868, p. 3. Also refer to: *Brisbane Courier*, 29 September 1868, p. 3; *Gympie Times*, 29 October 1868 & 28 January 1869; & *Argus*, 14 October 1868, p. 5 & 12 January 1869, p. 5.

67 'B.-18: Pensions Paid by the Colony (List Of): Return showing Names of Persons drawing Pensions, &c', *AJHRNZ: Vol. I: 1888* (Wellington), p. 5 of B.-18.

68 *Illustrated Sydney News*, 3 October 1868, p. 54.

69 *Ibid.*, 31 October 1868, p. 67.

70 *Brisbane Courier*, 12 October 1868.

71 *Ibid.*, 9 February 1869, p. 3. Also refer to: *Sydney Morning Herald*, 5 February 1869, p. 5; *Argus*, 30 January 1869; & *Gympie Times*, 13 February 1869.

72 *Argus*, 15 December 1868, p. 5.

73 *Brisbane Courier*, 19 March 1869, p. 2.

74 AD 76/2: Nominal and Descriptive Roll. 2nd Waikato Militia Regiment: Reg. No. 608: Vowles, George, *NANZ*; EDU/V1. Card Index to Registers of Male teachers. 1860–1903. 'Vowles, George', pp. 87–88 & 92, *QSA*; & *Queenslander*, 29 November 1928, p. 22. Also refer to: N. Bartlett: ' "Their Promised Land Australians and the Maori Wars 1840–1870": ...', p. 273: MSS1048, *AWM*; L.L. Barton, *Australians in the Waikato War* (Sydney: Library of Australian History, 1979), p. 71; H.J. Gibbney & A.G. Smith (eds), *A Biographical Register 1788–1939* (Canberra: Australian Dictionary of Biography, Australian National University, 1987), p. 319; E.M. Miller, *Australian Literature ... Volume I* (Sydney: Sydney University Press, 1940), pp. 171 & 247; & E.M. Miller & F.T. Macartney, *Australian Literature ... Extended to 1950* (Sydney: Angus & Robertson, 1956), p. 475.

75 *Queenslander*, 29 November 1928, p. 22.

76 Miller (*Vol. I*, 1940), *op. cit.*, p. 247.

77 Poems by Vowles with a war, peace, or soldier content include: 'The Battle-field' (pp. 36–38); 'The Soldier' (pp. 83–84); 'The Dying Soldier' (pp. 113–15); 'To Peace' (p. 118.); 'War' (p. 119); 'The Battle' (p. 120); & 'Peace' (p. 121). G. Vowles, *Sunbeams in Queensland* (Brisbane: Rogers & Harley, 1870).

78 *Ibid.*, pp. 77–78.

79 GOV/8: Governor's Office: Despatches from the Secretary of State for the Colonies. Vol. 8: Duplicate Qld. No. 25, 24 August 1867, *QSA*.

80 *Pugh's Queensland Almanac ... for 1869* (Brisbane: Theophilus P. Pugh), p. 2.

81 D. Anderson, 'Sir George Bowen and the Problem of Queensland's Defence, 1859–1868', *Queensland*

Heritage, Vol. 2, No. 3 (Nov. 1970), pp. 33–35; & D.H. Johnson, *Volunteers at Heart* (St Lucia: University of Queensland Press, 1975), pp. 23–24 & 52–54.

82 Belich (1989), *op. cit.*, pp. 218–20.

83 'Rockhampton News: Death of Rev. Father F.M. Bucas', *Catholic Advocate*, 30 October 1930, p. 41, *Catholic Church Archives* (Brisbane, Qld); & E.M. Curr, *The Australian Race... Volume III* (Melbourne: John Ferres, Government Printer, 1887), p. 48.

84 One source states he arrived in New Zealand as a deacon in 1864 and was ordained by Bishop Pompallier in 1865. J. Maguire, *Prologue: A History of the Catholic Church as seen from Townsville 1863–1983* (Toowoomba: Church Archivists' Society, 1990), footnote 186, p. 351.

85 R.J. Manning, 'Pierre Marie Bucas', *Footprints*, Vol. 1, No. 11 (July 1973), pp. 23–24; Maguire, *op. cit.*, footnote 186, p. 351; P.F. Moran, *History of the Catholic Church in Australasia [Volume 1]* (Sydney: The Oceanic Publishing Company, [1894]), p. 420; J. Duhig, *Crowded Years* (Sydney: Angus & Robertson, 1947), pp. 47–48; R.J. Manning (ed.), *St Patrick's Christian Brothers College Mackay* (Mackay: Golden Jubilee Celebrations Committee, 1979), p. 4; & C. Moore, '"Restraining Their Savage Propensities" The South Kennedy and North Leichhardt Districts in the 1860s and 1870s', in Henry Reynolds (ed.), *Race Relations in North Queensland* (Queensland: Department of History and Politics, James Cook University, 1993), pp. 84, 89, 104–5 & 112–13.

86 *NZG*, No. 55, 22 October 1867, p. 405; & also refer to: R.S. Hill, *The Colonial Frontier Tamed* (Historical Branch, Department of Internal Affairs, GP Books, 1989), pp. 10–17.

87 J. Rorke, *Policing Two Peoples* (Jinty Rorke & the NZ Police, 1993), pp. 1 & 2; & also refer to: H.W. Salmon, 'The Armed Constabulary in the Waikato', *Journal of the Auckland–Waikato Historical Society*, No. 22 (April 1973), p. 32.

88 Also refer to this author's articles (one of which includes rolls for the five contingents of Melbourne recruits): J.E. Hopkins-Weise, 'The Armed Constabulary of New Zealand: and the Australian Context', *The Volunteers*, Vol. 27, No. 1 (July 2001), pp. 6–42; & 'New Zealand's Armed Constabulary and its Australian Context, 1867–72', *Sabretache*, Vol. 43, No. 4 (Dec. 2002), pp. 19–38.

89 R.S. Hill, *Policing the Colonial Frontier... Part Two* (Wellington: Historical Publications Branch, Department of Internal Affairs, 1986), p. 940.

90 J. Cowan, *The New Zealand Wars ... Vol. II* (Wellington: W.A.G. Skinner, Government Printer, 1923), p. 481; H. King, 'Some Aspects of Police Administration in New South Wales, 1825–1851', *Royal Australian Historical Society*, Vol. 42, Part 5 (1956), pp. 225–26; & H. King, 'Problems of Police Administration in New South Wales, 1825–1851', *Royal Australian Historical Society*, Vol. 44, Part 2 (1958), pp. 61–63.

91 Gudgeon, *op. cit.*, p. 189.

92 *NZAL 1872*, p. 15; G.H. Scholefield (ed.), *A Dictionary of New Zealand Biography: Volume II: M–Addenda* (Wellington: Department of Internal Affairs, 1940), pp. 118–19; & The Earl of Ranfurly, *Roll of Honour, 1840 to 1902* (Wellington: The NZ Times Company, 1902), p. 36.

93 *NZG*, No. 26, 4 July 1863, p. 258; Glen, *op. cit.*, p. 84; & Gudgeon, *op. cit.*, p. 211. For subsequent promotions and service into 1864, refer to: *NZG*, No. 58, 7 November 1863, p. 487; *NZAL 1863*, p. 2; & *NZAL 1864*, p. 4.

94 Pitt was appointed inspector in 1869. *NZG*, No. 17, 25 March 1868, pp. 159–60, No. 22, 17 April 1869, p. 192, No. 25, 13 May 1869, p. 219 & No. 71, 18 December 1869, p. 667; & Glen, *op. cit.*, p. 95.

95 His last appointment was as commandant at Poverty Bay, Wairoa Militia District. *NZG*, No. 15, 12 March 1874, p. 195; *NZAL 1872*, pp. 2 & 15; Glen, *op. cit.*, pp. 84 & 95; Gudgeon, *op. cit.*, pp. 210–11; & also refer to: The Earl of Ranfurly, *op. cit.*, p. 39.

96 *HRA: Series 1. Governor's Despatches To and From England: Volume XX. February, 1839 – September, 1840* (Sydney: The Library Committee of the Commonwealth Parliament, 1924), pp. 493–94; & T.L. Buick, *New Zealand's First War* (Wellington: W.A.G. Skinner, Government Printer, 1926), pp. 13–14.

97 R.S. Hill, *Policing the Colonial Frontier ... Part One* (Wellington: Historical Publications Branch, Department of Internal Affairs, 1986), p. 127.

98 Ian Wards, *The Shadow of the Land* (Wellington: Historical Publications Branch, Department of Internal Affairs, 1968), pp. 41 & 47.

99 King (1956), *op. cit.*, pp. 224–25; & J.P. Jones, *A History of the South Staffordshire Regiment* (Wolverhampton:

Whitehead Brothers Ltd, 1923), p. 55; & also referred to in: W.L. Vale, *History of the South Staffordshire Regiment* (Aldershot: Gale & Polden, 1969), p. 111.

100 For other information on the NSW Mounted Police detachment in New Zealand, refer to: Hill (*Part One*, 1986), *op. cit.*, pp. 237–39.

101 J. Franklin, 'Inspector William James: One of New Zealand's Most Significant Policing Pioneers', *The Journal of the Orders and Medals Research Society*, Vol. 46, No. 4 (Dec. 2007), pp. 233–37.

102 O.J. Cherrett, *Without Fear Or Favour* (NZ: The NZ Police & L. Patrick Hunter, 1989), p. 93; & Franklin, *op. cit.*, p. 234.

103 Hill (1989), *op. cit.*, pp. 13, 24–25, 54 & 308–9.

104 Hill (*Part Two*, 1986), *op. cit.*, p. 555.

105 Keddell was initially appointed captain in the 3rd Waikato Regiment on 28 August 1863, before later service in the 4th Waikato Regiment where he was appointed major on 25 February 1864. *NZAL 1863*, p. 3; *NZAL 1864*, p. 8; & *NZG*, No. 8, 3 March 1864, p. 94.

106 H.C.M. Norris, *Armed Settlers* (Hamilton: Paul's Book Arcade, 1956), pp. 20–21, 27 & 53.

107 *Ibid.*, pp. 126–27.

108 *Ibid.*, pp. 157–58.

109 Some of the few sources which acknowledge this recruiting include: Belich (1989), *op. cit.*, pp. 181 & 255; Belich (1988), *op. cit.*, p. 253; B.J. Dalton, *War and Politics in New Zealand* (Sydney: Sydney University Press, 1967), pp. 268–69; T. Gibson, *The Maori Wars* (London: Leo Cooper, 1974), p. 219; Gudgeon, *op. cit.*, p. 251; Hill (1989), *op. cit.*, p. 25; & E. Holt, *The Strangest War* (London: Putnam & Co. Ltd, 1962), p. 254.

110 *Argus*, 30 November 1868, p. 4.

111 *NZG*, No. 24, 25 June 1863, p. 241; *NZAL 1863*, p. 2; *NZAL 1864*, p. 3; & R. Stowers, *The New Zealand Medal To Colonials* (Hamilton: Richard Stowers, 1998), p. 91.

112 N. Morris (ed.), *The Journal of William Morgan* (Auckland: Libraries Department, Auckland City Council, 1963), pp. 106–7; Gudgeon, *op. cit.*, p. 211; & also refer to: J.E. Hopkins [now Hopkins-Weise], *Selected New Zealand War Medal Rolls of Entitlements, Rejections, and Applications Granted up to 1900* (Brisbane: J.E. Hopkins & the Victoria Barracks Historical Society, Brisbane, 1997), p. 59; & Stowers, *op. cit.*, p. 91.

113 *NZG*, No. 2, 11 January 1868, pp. 17–18.

114 *NZG*, No. 19, 18 March 1871, p. 141; & *NZAL 1872*, p. 15.

115 *Argus*, 2 December, p. 4 & 11 December 1868, p. 4; & also refer to: *Sydney Morning Herald*, 7 December 1868, p. 5.

116 *Ibid.*

117 *Argus*, 5 December 1868, p. 4.

118 *Sydney Morning Herald*, 1 February 1869, p. 5; & also in: *Gympie Times*, 18 February 1869.

119 *Argus*, 16 November 1861, p. 5.

120 For information dealing with the personnel, material and policing methods derived from Victoria, refer to: Hill (1989), *op. cit.*, pp. xi, 40, 42–43, 47–48, 54, 137–38 & 309; Hill (*Part Two*, 1986), *op. cit.*, pp. 536–49 & 554–56; G.H. Scholefield (ed.), *A Dictionary of New Zealand Biography: Volume I: A–L* (Wellington: Department of Internal Affairs, 1940), pp. 90 & 96–97; *The Dictionary of New Zealand Biography: Volume One: 1769–1869*, *op. cit.*, pp. 36-38, 41–42, 393–94, 536–37 & 581–82; & Franklin, *op. cit.*, pp. 233–34.

121 *Argus*, 9 December 1868, p. 5.

122 Hill (1989), *op. cit.*, p. 25.

123 *Argus*, 5 December 1868, p. 5.

124 *Argus Supplement*, 5 December 1868, p. 2. Refer to Appendix E.

125 *Ibid.*

126 *Melbourne Punch*, 10 December 1868, p. 187.

127 *Ibid.*, p. 192.

128 *Argus*, 7 December 1868, p. 3.

129 *Ibid.*

130 *Ibid.*, p. 4.

131 *Ibid.*, 9 December 1868, p. 5.

132 *Ibid.*, 10 December 1868, p. 4.

133 *Ibid.*, p. 5.

134 Armed Constabulary Lists: P8/21 C: 9 December 1868, Capt. Stack, Melbourne, to Under Secretary Defence, Wellington, *NANZ.*

135 Armed Constabulary Lists: P8/19: Record of Agreement to take Oath of in A.C. made at Melbourne, 29 December 1868 – 5 January 1869; & also: P8/21 E: Nominal Return of Men enrolled at Melbourne and arrived at Wellington per 'Otago', 'Rangitoto', 'Gothenburg', and 'Omeo', *NANZ.*

136 *Argus*, 7 January 1869, p. 5.

137 These rolls show that there were at least 33 former military settlers — at least 19 former Waikato military settlers, and 14 Taranaki military settlers; 13 men acknowledged prior service with British, Australian or Indian police forces; while 28 individuals can be confirmed to have had prior service in the British Army (including Artillery cadets); 9 in the Royal Navy (and Naval Brigade); and 4 in the East India Company Army or Navy (including other Indian military forces). Twenty-six men were recorded with prior British Empire volunteer or militia service — and of these, 13 indicated service in Victorian volunteer units, 1 with the NSW volunteers, 1 with the Tasmanian volunteers, and 2 with the South Australian volunteers.

138 P. Stanley, 'Heritage of Strangers: the Australian Army's British Legacy', *Australian Defence Force Journal*, No. 87 (March/April 1991), p. 24.

139 *Argus*, 12 December 1868, p. 5.

140 *Ibid.*, 19 December 1868, p. 4.

141 *Ibid.*, 11 December 1868, p. 4.

142 *Ibid.*, 10 December 1868, p. 4.

143 *Melbourne Punch*, 10 December 1868, p. 191.

144 *Argus*, 12 December 1868, p. 5.

145 *Ibid.*, 14 December 1868, pp. 4 & 5 and 7 January 1869, p. 5. In a report dated 12 December 1868, to the Under Secretary Defence, Wellington, Stack confirmed shipment of 41 men on the *Otago*. Armed Constabulary Lists: P8/21 A: 12 December 1868, Capt. Stack, Melbourne, to Under Secretary Defence, Wellington. Reports shipment of 41 men for A.C. on board s.s. 'Otago' for Wellington, *NANZ.*

146 *Argus*, 16 December 1868, p. 1; & also refer to: *Ibid.*, p. 4.

147 *Ibid.*, 18 December, p. 5 & 21 December 1868, p. 4. In a report dated 18 December 1868, to the Under Secretary Defence, Wellington, Stack confirmed the embarkation of 30 men on the *Rangitoto*. Armed Constabulary Lists: P8/21 B: 18 December 1868, Capt. Stack, Melbourne, to Under Secretary Defence, Wellington. Forwards Descriptive Return of 30 Men embarked per 'Rangitoto' for Wellington, *NANZ.*

148 *Argus*, 21 December 1868, p. 5.

149 *Ibid.*, 23 December 1868, p. 5.

150 *Melbourne Punch*, 24 December 1868, p. 207.

151 *Argus*, 28 December, p. 4 & 31 December 1868, p. 5.

152 *Ibid.*, 31 December 1868, p. 5. Another summary of Stack's recruiting efforts and the response from the Victorian government can be viewed in: *Illustrated Australian News*, 1 January 1869, pp. 1–2 & 3; & also refer to: *Brisbane Courier*, 14 December 1868, p. 3; *Illustrated Sydney News*, 21 January 1869, p. 122; & *Perth Gazette and West Australian Times*, 1 & 22 January 1869.

153 *Argus*, 6 January 1869, pp. 4 & 5.

154 *Argus Supplement*, 4 January 1869, p. 1.

155 *Argus*, 4 January 1869, p. 5; & see also: *Ibid.*, 6 January 1869, p. 5.

156 *Ibid.*, 9 January, p. 4, 11 January, p. 4 & 14 January 1869, p. 5; & *Sydney Morning Herald*, 13 January, p. 4 & 15 January 1869, p. 4.

157 MS4064: (George S.) Whitmore's Campaigns in NZ (1868–1869), *National Library of Australia*; & also refer to: *Argus*, 2 December, p. 4 & 11 December 1868, p. 4; *Sydney Morning Herald*, 7 December 1868, p. 5; & *Perth Gazette and West Australian Times*, 1 January 1869.

158 Refer to Appendix F. Total for overall Armed Constabulary fatal casualties 1868–70, derived from: 'G. -No. 1: Papers Relative to the Issue of the NZ War Medal: Roll D: Nominal Roll of Officers and Men of the Colonial Forces who have been Killed in Action or who have Died of Wounds subsequent to the

11th July, 1868', *AJHRNZ: Vol. II: 1871* (Wellington: George Didsbury, Government Printer, 1871), pp. 8–10 of G.-No. 1; & also found in: *NZG*, No. 31, 31 May 1871, pp. 246–47. Another source provides a figure totalling 74 fatal casualties for this same period; refer to: Gudgeon, *op. cit.*, pp. 34–36 of Addenda.

CONCLUSION

1 R. Lockwood, 'Racism and Militarism', *Australian Left Review* (Dec. 1968), p. 54.
2 *Ibid.*, p. 55.
3 J. Richards, *The Secret War: A True History of Queensland's Native Police* (St Lucia, Qld: University of Queensland Press, 2008), p. 16.
4 This figure is calculated by including Lt. Wilmot, RA, Lt. C.P. O'Connell, 51st Regiment, and the two retired Royal Artillery sergeants from Van Diemen's Land, apart from the various detachments conveyed aboard vessels cited. The 182 troops of the 58th Regiment that departed aboard the *Pestonjee Pomanjee* in July 1847 had already served in New Zealand during 1845–46, and had returned to NSW in late 1846, before the orders received from London for all the 58th to be permanently stationed in New Zealand had arrived.
5 An example of the Royal Navy personnel involved ashore is as part of General Pratt's field force of 1001 officers and men used in the capture of the Matarikoriko pa over 29 and 30 December 1860. Pratt's report to Governor Browne on 31 December stated: 'My force, after being joined by parties from the Waitara Camp and the other positions . . . was all I could muster after leaving the Town and other posts in security, and required some assistance from H.M.S. "Cordelia," and H.M.C.S. "Victoria," . . .'. The Naval Brigade component here amounted to 139 officers and men; HMCS *Victoria*'s contribution being Lt. Woods, Midshipman Horn, and 24 seamen. 'E-No. 1a: Further Papers Relative to the Native Insurrection', *JHRNZ: 1861* (Auckland), pp. 8–9 of E.-No. 1a.
6 This figure includes Major Nelson, 40th Regiment, who volunteered and departed South Australia in April, and Captain Pasley, RE, who volunteered and departed Victoria in July, but does not include General Pratt and his staff.
7 'A.-No. 26a: Return showing the Effectives Of All Ranks In Each Arm Of The Service which were Actually Stationed In The Several Colonies And Garrisons Abroad And In India, *On the 31st day of March in each year, for the last ten years*', *AJHRNZ: 1870: Vol. I. Legislative, Political, and Native* (Wellington: George Didsbury, Government Printer), pp. 4–5 of A.-No. 26a.

APPENDICES

1 Sources consulted include: 'G.-No. 1a: . . . Roll E: Nominal Return of Officers and men of the Colonial Forces who have been Killed in Action or who have Died of Wounds prior to the 11th July, 1868', *AJHRNZ: Vol. II: 1871* (Wellington), p. 7 of G.-No. 1a; also found in: *NZG*, No. 55, 12 October 1871, pp. 553–4. Also refer to: 'G.-No. 1: . . . Roll D: Nominal Return of Officers and Men of the Colonial Forces who have been Killed in Action or who have Died of Wounds subsequent to the 11th of July, 1868 [to 29 April 1870]', *AJHRNZ: Vol. II: 1871* (Wellington), pp. 8–10 of G.-No. 1; also found in: *NZG*, No. 31, 31 May 1871, pp. 246–47.
2 Perceval (born 1833, England) was appointed Lieutenant in the Auckland Militia, 1 September 1863. He was the second son of Spencer Perceval, a long-time Member of the House of Commons, as well as a grandson of Spencer Perceval, First Lord of the Treasury, and Prime Minister in 1809, who was assassinated in the lobby of the House of Commons on 11 May 1812. *Argus*, 5 September, p. 5, 9 September, pp. 4 & 5, 9 November, p. 5 & 13 November 1863, p. 5; & *Sydney Morning Herald*, 12 November 1863, p. 5; *NZG*, No. 51, 30 September 1863, p. 434 & No. 57, 31 October 1863, pp. 474–75; N. Morris (ed.), *The Journal of William Morgan* (Auckland: Libraries Department, Auckland City Council, 1963), pp. 103–6; J. Featon, *The Waikato War* (Christchurch: Capper Press, 1971), p. 57; *Burke's Peerage* (London: Burke's Peerage Limited, 1949), p. 689; & F. Glen, *For Glory and a Farm* (Whakatane: Whakatane & District Historical Society, 1985), pp. 48–52 & 124.
3 *Argus*, 20 November 1863, p. 5; & also refer to: *Launceston Examiner*, 28 November 1863, p. 5. In error, this memorial lists 'Lieutenant William Percival', an officer in the 3rd Waikato Regiment. The other 1st Waikato Regiment names (apart from the four Victorians killed) recorded on this memorial include: 'Lieut. Thomas Norman', 'Corpl. Michael Power', and Privates 'William Beswick', 'M. Gilom', 'William Williamson', 'George Oborn', and 'Farquhar McGilvray'. Document Control Centre: Sheat, A.J. (NZ), Historical Records

Donation: 417/093/004; & Document Control Centre: Records of Early Wars in NZ: 417/008/002, *AWM*. Also refer to: *Argus*, 13 November 1863, p. 5; Morris, *op. cit.*, p. 110; Glen, *op. cit.*, pp. 50–1; & C. Coulthard-Clark, *The Diggers* (Carlton: Melbourne University Press, 1993), p. 2.

4 *NZG*, No. 57, 31 October 1863, pp. 474–75; Morris, *op. cit.*, pp. 103–6; & Glen, *op. cit.*, pp. 48–50 & 124.

5 *Argus*, 18 November 1863, p. 7.

6 *NZG*, No. 57, 31 October 1863, pp. 474–75; Morris, *op. cit.*, pp. 103–6; & Glen, *op. cit.*, pp. 48–50 & 124.

7 'G.-No. 1: Papers Relative to the Issue of the NZ War Medal: No. 2: Roll C', *AJHRNZ: Vol. III: 1872* (Wellington), p. 5 of G.-No.1; *NZG*, No. 57, 31 October 1863, pp. 474–75 & No. 28, 29 May 1872, p. 350; Morris, *op. cit.*, pp.103–6; Glen, *op. cit.*, pp. 48–50 & 124; & R. Stowers, *The New Zealand Medal To Colonials* (Hamilton: Richard Stowers, 1998), p. 92.

8 Morris, *op. cit.*, p. 113.

9 Under The Flag; Reminiscences of the Maori Land (Waikato) War by a Forest Ranger [William Race, c. 1895]: CY POS 127: Mitchell Library: p. 124 of reel; J.E. Hopkins-Weise, 'A History of the Colonial Defence Force (Cavalry): and the Australian Context', *The Volunteers*, Vol. 26, No. 1 (July 2000), pp. 13 & 21; L.L. Barton, *Australians in the Waikato War* (North Sydney: Library of Australian History, 1979), p. 32; & Stowers, *op. cit.*, p. 31.

10 AD 31/8: Army Department, Taranaki Military Settlers Nominal & Descriptive Roll Book, 1863–69: Nominal & Descriptive Roll of the 'Melbourne Contingent' of Taranaki Military Settlers, p. 37, *NANZ*.

11 *Sydney Morning Herald*, 19 April 1864, p. 5; *Argus*, 19 April, p. 5 & 22 April 1864, p. 7; AD 31/8: Nominal & Descriptive Roll of the 'Melbourne Contingent' of Taranaki Military Settlers, p. 34, *NANZ*; & Glen, *op. cit.*, pp. 72–3 & 124.

12 *Sydney Morning Herald*, 19 April, p. 5 & 11 May 1864, p. 8; *Argus*, 19 April, p. 5 & 22 April 1864, p. 7; AD 31/8: . . . 'Melbourne Contingent' Taranaki Military Settlers, p. 46, *NANZ*; & Glen, *op. cit.*, pp. 72–3 & 124.

13 *Sydney Morning Herald*, 19 April 1864, p. 5; *Argus*, 19 April, p. 5 & 22 April 1864, p. 7; AD 31/8: . . . 'Melbourne Contingent' Taranaki Military Settlers, p. 48, *NANZ*; & Glen, *op. cit.*, pp. 72–3 & 124.

14 *Sydney Morning Herald*, 19 April 1864, p. 5; *Argus*, 19 April, p.5 & 22 April 1864, p. 7; AD 31/8: . . . 'Melbourne Contingent' Taranaki Military Settlers, p. 60, *NANZ*; & Glen, *op. cit.*, pp. 72–3 & 124.

15 Barton, *op. cit.*, p. 68; & Glen, *op. cit.*, p. 125.

16 AD 31/8: . . . 'Melbourne Contingent' Taranaki Military Settlers, p. 54, *NANZ*.

17 Under The Flag; Reminiscences of the Maori Land (Waikato) War by a Forest Ranger [William Race, c. 1895]: CY POS 127: Mitchell Library: pp. 176–77 of reel; T.W. Gudgeon, *The Defenders of New Zealand* (Auckland: H. Brett, 1887), p. 84; Glen, *op. cit.*, pp. 56, 58, 60 & 124; & Stowers, *op. cit.*, p. 101.

18 Barton, *op. cit.*, p. 72.

19 *Argus*, 13 July 1864, p. 5.

20 *Launceston Examiner*, 7 April 1864, p. 5.

21 *Ibid.*, 19 July 1864, p. 5.

22 AD 31/8: . . . 'Melbourne Contingent' Taranaki Military Settlers, p. 35, *NANZ*.

23 *Argus*, 26 August 1864, p. 5.

24 Barton, *op. cit.*, p. 83; & Glen, *op. cit.*, p. 125.

25 Barton, *op. cit.*, p. 70; & Glen, *op. cit.*, p. 125.

26 *Ibid.*

27 Barton, *op. cit.*, p. 75; & Glen, *op. cit.*, p. 125.

28 Barton, *op. cit.*, p. 82; & Glen, *op. cit.*, p. 125.

29 Barton, *op. cit.*, p. 80; & Glen, *op. cit.*, p. 125.

30 K. Sinclair (ed.), *A Soldier's View of Empire* (London: The Bodley Head Ltd, 1982), pp. 160–61; & Barton, *op. cit.*, p. 62. Glen cites Henry Matthews, 1st Waikato Regiment, as 'killed at Gate Pa, 6 September aged 27 years', and buried in the military cemetery at Tauranga, though Glen is incorrect in the assumption that this individual died of wounds sustained at the 1864 Gate Pa engagement. Glen, *op. cit.*, pp. 62 & 124.

31 AD 31/8: . . . 'Melbourne Contingent' Taranaki Military Settlers, p. 62, *NANZ*; & Stowers, *op. cit.*, p. 71.

32 For information, refer to: 'A.-No. 5a: Despatches from the Governor of NZ to the Secretary of State: No. 15', *JHRNZ: 1865* (Wellington), pp. 9–10 of A.-No. 5a; *NZG*, No. 44, 18 November 1865, pp. 343–47; 'A.-No. 6: Despatches from Major Fraser, Commanding Forces at Turanganui', *JHRNZ: 1866* (Wellington), No. 5, pp. 6–7 of A.-No. 6; *NZG*, 18 January 1866, pp. 25–26; W. Fox, *The War in New Zealand* (London: Smith, Elder & Co., 1866), pp. 226–227; J. Cowan, *The New Zealand Wars: ... Vol. II: The Hauhau Wars, 1864–1872* (Wellington: W.A.G. Skinner, Government Printer, 1923), pp. 102–112, 125–31, & 494–495; T. Gibson, *The Maori Wars* (London: Leo Cooper, 1974), pp. 163–68 & 184; & Glen, *op. cit.*, p. 82.

33 AD 31/8: ... 'Melbourne Contingent' Taranaki Military Settlers, p. 64, *NANZ*; & Stowers, *op. cit.*, p. 72.

34 'D.-No. 46: Return of the Names of Persons Drowned in NZ from the 1st January, 1840', *AJHRNZ: Vol. III: D.–Miscellaneous: 1870* (Wellington), p. 7 of D.-No. 46; Barton, *op. cit.*, p. 77; & Glen, *op. cit.*, p. 125.

35 AD 31/8: ... 'Melbourne Contingent' Taranaki Military Settlers, p. 52, *NANZ*; & Stowers, *op. cit.*, p. 70.

36 Barton, *op. cit.*, p. 78; & Glen, *op. cit.*, p. 125.

37 Glen, *op. cit.*, p. 125.

38 'D.-No. 46: Return of the Names of Persons Drowned in NZ from the 1st January, 1840', *AJHRNZ: Vol. III: D.–Miscellaneous: 1870* (Wellington), p. 7 of D.-No. 46; Barton, *op. cit.*, p. 84; & Glen, *op. cit.*, p. 125.

39 AD 31/8: ... 'Melbourne Contingent' Taranaki Military Settlers, p. 68, *NANZ*; & Stowers, *op. cit.*, p. 72.

40 The attack on the Maori village of Pokaikai in the Patea District involved Nos. 8 & 10 Companies, Taranaki Military Settlers, Patea and Wanganui Rangers, and Wanganui Cavalry. In early 1868 a commission of inquiry, following allegations of acts of cruelty and wanton outrage alleged carried out during this attack, investigated the events associated with it. For information on these events, refer to: 'A.-No. 3: Report of the Pokaikai Commission', *JHRNZ: 1868* (Wellington); T. McDonnell, *An Explanation of the Principal Causes which led to the Present War on the West Coast of New Zealand* (Wanganui: Walter Taylor, Times Office, 1869); Cowan, *op. cit.*, pp. 139–41 & 521–22; Gibson, *op. cit.*, p. 188; & Glen, *op. cit.*, p. 84.

41 'Alfred J. Campbell' could be: Regt. No. 318, John Campbell, enrolled 19 September 1863, Melbourne; or Regt. No. 319, James Campbell, enrolled 9 September 1863, Melbourne; and noting that there are several other privates with this surname in this regiment. Barton, *op. cit.*, p. 56.

42 *Sydney Morning Herald*, 9 September 1867, p. 3. Also refer to information contained in report dated 7 March 1868, from H.T. Clarke, Civil Commissioner, Tauranga, to the new New Zealand Governor, G.F. Bowen, regarding the affairs at Tauranga, including mention of the death of the military settler named Campbell. 'A.-No. 4: Reports on the Social And Political State Of The Natives In Various Districts At The Time Of The Arrival Of Sir G.F. Bowen', *JHRNZ: 1868* (Wellington), p. 10 of A.-No. 4.

43 Barton, *op. cit.*, pp. 50 & 65; Glen, *op. cit.*, pp. 83–4 & 124; Stowers, *op. cit.*, p. 91; & Bartlett (MSS1048), *op. cit.*, p. 409.

44 'The men under Colonel Harington [late on 23 January] returned by another route – crossing the clearing of Whakamarama. When the advanced guard ... reached the head of the clearing at this place, a heavy fire was opened by the rebels from some growing corn .... Private Stevenson ... was here shot (since dead).' *Sydney Morning Herald*, 9 February 1867, p. 7; & *Argus*, 9 February 1867, p. 5.

45 Barton, *op. cit.*, pp. 50 & 54; Glen, *op. cit.*, pp. 83–4 & 124; & Stowers, *op. cit.*, p. 92.

46 'The men, early in the morning [23 January], under Colonel Harington, of the 1st Waikato Regiment, moved across the Wairoa river, and proceeded on their march to Te Irihanga. The natives, said to be about twenty-five, were ready prepared for them, but they soon fled. A stand was made for a time, and many shots passed from the rebels. Here [P]rivate Ward ... fell mortally wounded. The village, once in the hands of our men, was soon in ashes, and the crops completely destroyed.' *Sydney Morning Herald*, 9 February 1867, p. 7; & *Argus*, 9 February 1867, p. 5.

47 'G.-No. 1: Papers Relative to the Issue of the NZ War Medal: No. 2: Roll C', *AJHRNZ: Vol. III: 1872* (Wellington), p. 5 of G.-No. 1; *NZG*, No. 28, 29 May 1872, p. 350; Barton, *op. cit.*, pp. 60 & 89; Glen, *op. cit.*, pp. 83–4 & 124; & Stowers, *op. cit.*, p. 87.

48 AD 31/8: ... 'Melbourne Contingent' Taranaki Military Settlers, p. 53, *NANZ*; & Stowers, *op. cit.*, p. 64.

49 AD 31/8: ... 'Melbourne Contingent' Taranaki Military Settlers, p. 69, *NANZ*; & Stowers, *op. cit.*, p. 64.

50 *NZG*, No. 17, 25 March 1868, p. 159; Cowan, *op. cit.*, pp. 268–73; J. Belich, *'I Shall Not Die'* (Wellington: Allen & Unwin NZ Limited in association with the Port Nicholson Press, 1989), pp. 102, 123, 143, 181, 229

& 232; & Stowers, *op. cit.*, p. 7.

51 *Sydney Morning Herald*, 10 October, p. 6, 12 October, pp. 4 & 5 and 17 October 1863, p. 5. Duncan Michie Brown was appointed Lieutenant in the 2nd Waikato Regiment, 20 October 1863. *NZAL 1863*, p. 3; *NZAL 1864*, p. 5; & *NZG*, No. 55, 27 October 1863, p. 460.

52 *NZG*, No. 4, 6 February 1865, p. 27; & I. Coates, *On Record* (Hamilton: Paul's Book Arcade, 1962), p. 71.

53 Bamber Gascoigne was appointed Lieutenant in the Taranaki Militia, 20 January 1864. *NZG*, No. 7, 24 February 1864, p. 83; *NZAL 1864*, p. 20; & Glen, *op. cit.*, pp. 84 & 124.

54 AD 31/8:... 'Melbourne Contingent' Taranaki Military Settlers, p. 57, *NANZ*.

55 *Ibid.*, p. 65; & also refer to: Glen, *op. cit.*, pp. 86–7 & 124.

56 Barton, *op. cit.*, p. 76; J.C.M. Cresswell, *The Bay of Plenty Volunteer Cavalry* (Paradise Point: PCS Publications, 1991), refer to chapters 'Introduction', '1869', & 'Roll Of Volunteers' [no pages cited]; & Stowers, *op. cit.*, p. 28.

57 AD 31/8: Army Department, Taranaki Military Settlers Nominal & Descriptive Roll Book, 1863–69, pp. 44 & 61, *NANZ*; Armed Constabulary Lists: P8/21: Men enrolled at Melbourne by Capt. Stack, Descriptive Roll, draft, full return, dates of Attestation 1868–1869, *NANZ*; 'G.-No. 1:...:Roll D: Nominal Roll of Officers and Men of the Colonial Forces who have been Killed in Action or who have Died of Wounds subsequent to the 11th of July, 1868', *AJHRNZ: 1871: Vol. II* (Wellington: George Didsbury, Government Printer), pp. 8–10 of G.-No. 1; *NZG*, No. 31, 31 May 1871, pp. 246–47; T.W. Gudgeon, *The Defenders of New Zealand* (Auckland: H. Brett, 1887), pp. 34–6 of Addenda; I. Coates, *On Record* (Hamilton: Paul's Book Arcade, 1962), p. 71; L.L. Barton, *Australians in the Waikato War* (North Sydney: Library of Australian History, 1979), pp. 53, 54, 61, 69, 71, 83 & 91; J. Belich, *'I Shall Not Die'* (Wellington: Allen & Unwin NZ Limited in association with the Port Nicholson Press, 1989), pp. 232 & 254–55; & R. Stowers, *The New Zealand Medal To Colonials* (Hamilton: Richard Stowers, 1998), pp. 5, 6, 7, 9, 10, 12, 13, 14, 18, 20 & 114.

INDEX

Names of vessels and journals are in *italics*.

N